TOMMY'S PEACE

TOMMY'S PEACE

A Family Diary 1919–33

**THOMAS
CAIRNS LIVINGSTONE**

Edited by Ronnie Scott

**MAINSTREAM
PUBLISHING**

EDINBURGH AND LONDON

Diary extracts and illustrations abridged and selected from
The Diaries of Thomas Cairns Livingstone © The Estate of Thomas Cairns
Livingstone 2010, under licence to Shaun Sewell

Footnotes and historical background text © Ronnie Scott, 2010

First published in Great Britain in 2010 by
MAINSTREAM PUBLISHING COMPANY
(EDINBURGH) LTD
7 Albany Street
Edinburgh EH1 3UG

ISBN 9781845966539

A catalogue record for this book is available
from the British Library

Typeset in Bodoni and Caslon

Printed in Great Britain by
CPI Mackays, Chatham ME5 8TD

In memory of the late Michael Morrison

Contents

About the diaries

The war had finally ended and peace reigned throughout Europe. The enormous task of rebuilding war-torn lands was about to commence. It might have been an ideal time for Thomas Cairns Livingstone to retire his pen and pencils and rest on his laurels, having recorded the most momentous time in modern history.

Thomas, a clerk from Rutherglen, had already dutifully recorded his daily life since 1913 in his red bound Collins diaries, describing the early years of married life and newly acquired status of being a father. However, the domestic musings of the Livingstone family were soon to be affected by events that made even the factor seem tolerable. The dark clouds of war were starting to engulf Europe and Thomas' diary entries were soon to describe the significant events of the First World War and its impact upon him, his family and Glasgow.

But Thomas didn't start his diary merely to record a war that hadn't been started by him or that he could do anything about. Thomas wanted to record the daily happenings of his beloved family and how the Livingstones coped and succeeded in the challenging times of the early twentieth century. As Thomas' father, Joseph, had recorded the achievements of his children growing up in Lurgan and Glasgow, Thomas centred his diary upon his own son, Tommy, who proved to be well worth the ink and paper.

This is a family diary, a diary that records a love of a father and husband who wanted his family to be happy and safe. He penned his feelings of pride as Tommy excelled at school and his words of worry as his wife Agnes' health declined.

The more you read Thomas' entries, the more you understand just how special he was. There were hard and sad times, but Thomas was never down for too long; there was always the next invention or glowing school report to distract him from being worried. Perhaps we should all be a bit more like Thomas in these testing times.

For me, it's been quite a journey and probably the most rewarding excursion I have ever embarked upon. Thomas has allowed me to have an adventure that I would never have thought possible. Fate is a funny thing and I have found that you should let it run its course. I am so proud that Thomas' writing has brought so much pleasure to so many people and relieved that his work wasn't lost.

While the publication of Thomas' diaries has been the highlight of this adventure, it was the people I've met along the way who made it special for me. I would like to thank the late Michael Morrison, Helen Carlyle, Colin Brown and the remarkable Ella Carlyle for their help and friendship. I will be eternally gratefully to Gordon Wise at Curtis Brown for watching the *Antiques Roadshow* back in 2007 and for all his hard work and guidance in getting Thomas in print. Ronnie Scott, who brought Thomas' world so vividly to life and added such carefully researched detail, also deserves my highest praise.

More thanks to Bill Campbell and his team at Mainstream for picking up the mantle and producing such a wonderful book, BBC *Antiques Roadshow*, Carol Clewlow, Shaheeda Sabir, Andrew Hartley at BBC *Inside Out*, Muriel Murphy, Joanna Holloway, Irene O'Brien and of course my partner, Joan Bower, for her non-stop support and love.

None of us are here for ever, but if we make the effort to record our time we will not be forgotten: start that diary today!

Shaun Sewell
Northumberland, June 2010

People and places

Thomas referred to many people and places in his diaries, and often used a place name as shorthand for people. For example, when he said he had visited Greenlodge, he meant the house at 3 Greenlodge Terrace, Greenlodge Street, Bridgeton, where his father and other members of his family lived. The people and places that feature most often in the diaries are detailed here and others are explained in footnotes.

ALEXANDER BAXTER JUNIOR
Senior partner of Paterson, Baxter and Company, which employed Thomas. Son of Alexander Baxter Senior, who died in July 1920. He lived with his family in Kildare, a villa in Milngavie. Thomas was a respected employee, and he and his family were invited to spend July 1925 and June and July 1926 in Kildare, when the Baxters were on holiday.

BRIDGETON
District of Glasgow in the East End of the city. Thomas' father lived there, at 3 Greenlodge Terrace. Thomas often used the local pronunciation, 'Brigton'.

ELLA CARLYLE
Thomas' niece, born in Edinburgh. She trained as a nurse in Glasgow, at Stobhill Hospital, and often visited Thomas and his family.

MARY CARLYLE (NÉE LIVINGSTONE)
Sister of Thomas, born in Balmoral Terrace, Hill Street, Lurgan, County Armagh, in the north of Ireland, on 27 September 1884. Her mother died two weeks after her birth. Mary married Thomas Carlyle on 16 July 1904; he was 34, some 14 years older than her. He was a shirt-cutter; she was a shirt-fitter. None of the family witnessed the marriage, and the couple moved to Edinburgh shortly afterwards. The difference in the couple's ages seems to have sparked a family row, which ended only when Mary returned to visit her dying. father in 1921. Mary and her husband had

four children: Thomas, Helen (or Ella), Jane (or Jean) Weir and
Dorothy.

MR AND MRS CARMICHAEL
Neighbours of Thomas and Agnes at 14 Morgan Street who
became close friends. They had a daughter, Peggy, and a son, Alex,
who played the fiddle. They spent time in the village of Furnace, on
the shore of Loch Fyne, Argyll, and may have been born there.

COATBRIDGE
Home of the Crozier family, relatives of Agnes.

THE COOK FAMILY
Agnes' relatives, who lived at 37 Whitefield Road, Ibrox, Glasgow.

HENRIETTA ('HETTY') COOK
Cousin of Agnes, who married Gordon Mossman in Glasgow on 18
December 1918 at the age of 23 (he was 26). They were married 'by
declaration' in front of witnesses and by warrant issued by the Sheriff
Substitute of Lanarkshire, a form peculiar to Scotland, regulated by
the Marriage (Scotland) Act 1916. Her civil marriage was in contrast
to the religious services preferred by most of her family. Described
on her marriage certificate as an 'engineer's clerkess', living at 11
Leven Street, Glasgow. She was usually known as Hetty.

   She and her husband had a son, Wee Billy, in January 1920, and
a daughter, Etta, in October 1921. At the time, they were living
in Dennistoun, sharing a house with her brother James. She had
a third baby in 1924, called Grace, who died of pneumonia at the
age of one. The Mossmans moved to a new house in King's Park in
February 1929.

JAMES COOK
Cousin of Agnes and brother of Hetty Cook. Shot in the hand
during the First World War and nursed in the Victoria Hospital,
a military hospital in Bellahouston Park, Glasgow. He died in
Stobhill Hospital, in the north of the city, on 22 January 1922. He
had been a witness to the marriage of Hetty Cook and Gordon
Mossman in December 1918, and was described on the certificate
as 'mercantile clerk; sapper, Royal Engineers'.

Mrs Cormack

A family friend who lived in Coatbridge. She had two young daughters.

The Cowie family

Friends of the Livingstones. Old Mrs Cowie was the mother of Young Mrs Cowie, who was the mother of Wee Helen (who died in February 1933).

The Crozier family

Agnes' Aunt Agnes married Robert Chapman Crozier in 1881. They lived in the Blairhill area of Coatbridge, a town to the east of Glasgow. Robert, or 'Uncle Bob', ran a grocery and spirit shop at 142 Bank Street, Coatbridge, before moving into the hotel trade, managing the Royal Hotel in the same town between the end of the First World War and his death, in May 1921. Robert and Agnes had four daughters: Margaret (possibly known as Daisy or Meg), Mary (May), Jeanie (Jean) and Henrietta (Hetty). May died of Spanish flu while on holiday in Rothesay in 1918 at the age of 24.

Donald Ferguson

Married Josephine, Thomas' sister, on 10 June 1898. He died of epilepsy and heart failure on 19 October 1916, at Beracah, Paisley Road, Barrhead (an address connected with the Christian Brethren), although his usual address was 3 Greenlodge Terrace, Bridgeton, Glasgow. On his death certificate, the occupation of his late father Samuel is given as 'shepherd'.

Isabella McArthur Ferguson

Daughter of Donald and Josephine Ferguson. Thomas' niece. Also known as Isa. Born 20 October 1900 at 204 French Street, Bridgeton, Glasgow. She married Jack Archibald in January 1927 and had a baby girl in November the same year.

Jack Ferguson

Son of Donald and Josephine Ferguson. Thomas' nephew.

JOSEPHINE FERGUSON (NÉE LIVINGSTONE)
Sister of Thomas. Born in Silverwood, near Lurgan, County
Armagh, in August 1874. Firstborn of Joseph's children with Mary
Cairns. First worked as a shirt-maker. Married Donald Ferguson in
Glasgow on 10 June 1898 and honeymooned in Belfast. At the time
of their marriage, Donald was living at 175 Gallowgate, Glasgow,
and Josephine at 10 India Street, Rutherglen. Both Josephine and
her husband worked in a grocery shop, possibly the Bridgeton
branch of Cochrane's, a Glasgow chain. They had three children:
Isabella (Isa), Lily and Jack. Donald died of epilepsy and heart
failure on 19 October 1916, and Josephine continued working
in the grocery business. When her employer went bankrupt in
1919, she set up in business as a draper in Parkhead. She died of
tuberculosis in September 1930 at the age of 56 and was buried in
Riddrie Park Cemetery in the north-east of Glasgow.

LILY FLORENCE LIVINGSTONE FERGUSON
Daughter of Donald and Josephine Ferguson. Thomas' niece. Born
4 May 1899 at 204 French Street, Bridgeton, Glasgow. Worked
as a clerkess. Also known as Wee Lily. She married John Martin
in September 1925, had a baby boy in July 1927, another in April
1930, and lived in Partick.

JENNY GALLOWAY
A young woman who worked for a time as a typist in Thomas'
office and became a friend of the family. She lived in Dennistoun.

THE GORDON FAMILY
Relatives of Agnes who lived in Ibrox, Glasgow. The family were
Mr and Mrs Gordon and their children, Nannie and Ella. Nannie
became engaged to Charles Petrie in December 1932. Ella had a
baby boy, Ronnie, in August 1920 and moved to Mount Florida;
she was married in December 1927. Ella had a second baby boy in
February 1933.

GOVANHILL
Residential district to the south of central Glasgow. Thomas and
his family lived at 14 Morgan Street, in the north of the district.
Thomas borrowed books from Govanhill Public Library (which

he often called Calder Street library, from its address). He also patronised Stirling's Public Library, in Miller Street in the city centre (which was close to his office), and other public libraries on the south side of the city. Other amenities included Govanhill Park (known as the 'Wee Park') and the Public Baths in Calder Street (which offered both slipper baths and swimming pools).

GREENLODGE
Thomas' father, Joseph Livingstone, lived at 3 Greenlodge Terrace, Greenlodge Street, Bridgeton, Glasgow. His daughter Josephine and her husband, Donald Ferguson, also lived there with their children, a fairly usual arrangement at the time.

ANDREW HAMILTON
Former office boy in Paterson, Baxter and Company. Married Nellie Pettigrew in July 1915. They lived in Hickman Street, Govanhill, and had a son in 1918. They then moved to Rutherglen. Andrew was wounded during the First World War and was in Stobhill Military Hospital in April 1919 and Erskine Hospital in 1923. He died in September 1923 and was buried in Glasgow Necropolis.

NINIAN (NIN) HENDERSON
Uncle of Agnes. Married to Lizzie (née Campbell). They lived in Montrose Street with their two daughters, Agnes and Susan.

IBROX
Home of the Cook family and the Gordon family, Agnes' relatives.

AGNES SMART LIVINGSTONE (NÉE COOK)
Agnes was born in Braid Street, Glasgow (near St George's Cross), on 10 November 1879 to James and Agnes Cook (née Henderson). Her parents were married on 7 November 1879 (three days before she was born) in the St Rollox district of Glasgow. Her father was a lithographer and Agnes herself was a cardboard-cutter at the time of her marriage to Thomas on 10 June 1910. She died at 1058 Cathcart Road, Govanhill, on 27 February 1950.

Duncan Graham Livingstone

Brother of Thomas, born in Balmoral Terrace, Lurgan, on 2 June 1880. Worked for Anchor Line Cruises and sailed the Glasgow to New York route aboard the TSS (twin-screw steamship) *Columbia* from 1908 to 1910. Served in the Army Service Corps from 1918 to 1919. Lived with his father in Glasgow, then moved to Belfast in October 1920 to start a business as a sign-writer.

Joseph Livingstone

Father of Thomas, born in 1847 in Lurgan, the son of John Livingstone, a teacher of English, and Mary Ann Livingstone (née Hare); she died near Rutherglen in March 1881. Lurgan is 19 miles south-west of Belfast and was a hub of the linen industry. Joseph was married three times: to Sarah Gilpin in 1867 in Seagoe Parish Church (she died in January 1873); to Mary Cairns on 3 October 1873 (she died in October 1884); and to Jane Weir in 1885 (she died in 1909). All of his children were with Mary Cairns, whom he married in Maralin (or Magheralin) in County Down in the north of Ireland. She had previously been married to a Mr McKinlay. Mary died two weeks after the birth of her youngest daughter, Mary Livingstone, in the house of her father, Thomas Cairns, in Lurgan.

Joseph moved to Scotland and worked as a clerk for the Caledonian Railway Company from 1876, and later as a mercantile clerk. He moved to 10 India Street, Rutherglen, in the 1880s, then lived at 3 Greenlodge Terrace, Bridgeton, Glasgow. He was a member of the Ancient Order of Foresters, a friendly society, and the Carnbroe Loyal Orange Lodge, a Loyalist and Unionist fraternity with its origins in the north of Ireland. Carnbroe is a village to the south of Coatbridge. He died from pneumonia on 11 March 1921 and was buried in Rutherglen Cemetery in the same grave as his third wife.

Josephine Livingstone

Daughter of Samuel and Nellie Livingstone. Thomas' niece. Born 28 April 1902 in Glasgow. Also known as Ina. Married Charles Edward Reynolds, a civil engineer, in St Mary's Episcopalian Cathedral, Glasgow, on 25 April 1931. Her marriage certificate shows her address as 105 Mill Street, Rutherglen.

Mary Ann Livingstone (née Hare)
Mother of Joseph and paternal grandmother of Thomas. Died of chronic bronchitis on 7 March 1881 at 3 George Gray Street, Eastfield, Rutherglen.

Nellie Livingstone (née Muir Meikleham)
Married to Samuel, Thomas' brother. Her parents were James Meikleham and Elizabeth Meikleham (née Muir). She died in November 1931.

Samuel John Livingstone
Brother of Joseph and uncle of Thomas. Born in 1856 and worked as a railway clerk and as a coal merchant. His business, Livingstone and Milne, was based at Kelvinbridge, in the West End of Glasgow. He was married to Mary Elizabeth McColl, a draper's assistant, in 1883 by a Church of Scotland minister at their home at 543 Dalmarnock Road, Glasgow.

Samuel John Livingstone
Brother of Thomas, born in Balmoral Terrace, Lurgan, in 1878. Worked as a grocer's assistant, then a grocer's manager, in a branch of Cochrane's. Sam was married to Nellie Muir Meikleham on 28 January 1902 at 217 Broad Street, Mile-End, Glasgow, by a minister of the United Free Church. They lived in Mill Street, Rutherglen, and had two children: Josephine (Ina) in 1902 and Samuel John in 1919. Sam died on 27 September 1919, a week after his son was born. He was buried in Rutherglen Cemetery.

Samuel John Livingstone Junior
Son of Samuel and Nellie Livingstone. Thomas' nephew. Born 19 September 1919. Known as Wee Sammy and later as John.

Thomas Cairns Livingstone
Thomas was born on 4 June 1882 at 10 India Street, Rutherglen, the youngest of the six children of Joseph and Mary Livingstone (née Cairns) and the only one born in Glasgow. Josephine, Lily, Duncan, Samuel and Mary were born in or near Lurgan. Thomas' mother died in 1884, when Thomas was aged two, and he was raised by his father, his older siblings and his step-mother, Jane. The family

moved to 4 French Street, Bridgeton, around 1900. He was schooled in Rutherglen and took extra classes in English and French.

Thomas started work in 1895 and began courting Agnes Smart Cook in 1903. They were engaged on 19 December 1908 and married on 10 June 1910 in Agnes' home at 37 Whitefield Road, Ibrox, by the Reverend John Tainsh of the Tron United Free Church, in Dundas Street, central Glasgow.

Their first home was at 20 Morgan Street in Govanhill, where their son Thomas Cairns Livingstone Junior was born in 1911. They moved to a similar tenement house at 14 Morgan Street in 1913.

Thomas worked as a mercantile clerk in the warehouse of Paterson, Baxter and Company, 170 Ingram Street, Glasgow, a firm of linen and jute merchants, and sailcloth manufacturers. From 1932, he worked as a travelling salesman for the same company.

After the period covered in the diaries, he moved to 1058 Cathcart Road, Govanhill, where he died in 1964 at the age of 81.

THOMAS CAIRNS LIVINGSTONE JUNIOR
Born on 9 August 1911, the only child of Thomas and Agnes Livingstone. Attended Victoria Primary School in Batson Street, Govanhill, then Strathbungo and Pollokshields secondary schools. Matriculated at Glasgow University in October 1929. His university friends included James Geddes (a veterinary student), Kenneth MacPherson, Mr McLennan, John McKendrick, Abraham (or Aby) Bloch, Angus Nicolson and Mr Goldman. After he completed his studies, he taught English Literature at Glasgow University. He took over the rent of the flat at 1058 Cathcart Road after the death of his father in 1964. He retired from teaching in 1976 and moved to live with Ethel Ann Morrison in Morpeth, Northumberland, where he died in 1995. He was cremated in Blyth, in the same county.

MRS MACKENZIE
A near neighbour of Thomas and Agnes. She lived with her children, Willie and Maggie. Maggie married Arthur Fraser and had a baby called Malcolm.

CLAUDE MAXWELL
Friend of Thomas and Agnes. One of his sisters, Miss Maxwell, became Tommy's teacher at Victoria Primary School. During

the First World War, Claude joined the Highland Light Infantry as a private and was commissioned as a second lieutenant in the Durham Light Infantry. He was wounded, but served the full term of the war. He was awarded the Military Cross. Claude lived with his two sisters and brother Herbert in Langside.

GORDON MOSSMAN
Husband of Hetty Cook. He had two sisters.

PATERSON, BAXTER AND COMPANY
Thomas' employer. A firm of linen and jute merchants, and sailcloth manufacturers, founded in 1877. Thomas was employed as a mercantile clerk in the firm's warehouse in 170 Ingram Street, in central Glasgow. The company moved in 1925 to new premises at 6 Frederick Lane (which ran between North Hanover Street and North Frederick Street, opposite the side entrance to Queen Street Station). The firm had other offices in East Parade, Leeds, and Monkwell Street, London, as well as in Cape Town, Johannesburg, Oslo and Copenhagen.

JENNY ROXBURGH
Close friend of Thomas and Agnes. Lived with her sister Kate in Radnor Street, Clydebank. Jenny probably knew Agnes through their early employment in the stationery trade, Jenny as a stationery assistant and Agnes as a cardboard-cutter. Jenny later worked as a nurse in Maryhill, in the north of Glasgow. Jenny died in November 1918 and was buried in the Western Necropolis.

RUGLEN
The local pronunciation of Rutherglen, a burgh to the south-east of Glasgow. The principal industries were coal-mining, heavy engineering, steel-making and chemicals. Thomas and his family moved here when he was 12, and he left the area when he married at the age of 28. Thomas' brother Sam and his family lived at 105 Mill Street. Before Thomas was married, he lived at 200 Main Street. During the years of the diary, this was the home of his Uncle Willie and Aunt Mina.

JOHN WHITE
Married to Lily, Thomas' sister. He was a telegraphist who worked for the Post Office.

LILY FLORENCE WHITE (NÉE LIVINGSTONE)
Sister of Thomas. Born in Hill Street, Lurgan, on 15 May 1878. She worked as a power-loom weaver, and on 9 November 1911 was married in Trinity Church, Anderston, Glasgow, to John White, a telegraphist. At the time, her address was 3 Greenlodge Terrace, Bridgeton, and his was 1054 Argyle Street, both in Glasgow. She died on 28 October 1914, probably of pleurisy, at her father's home at 3 Greenlodge Terrace, although her married residence was 44 Clincarthill Road, Rutherglen. She was buried in Rutherglen Cemetery.

Note: genealogy research by Shaun Sewell

1919

For Thomas and his family, the year was one of adjustment. They had to deal with industrial and social unrest caused by demobilised workers returning to claim their jobs, and the continuing rationing of basic foodstuffs. There was also an influenza pandemic to worry about, and every sniffle and runny nose was a cause for severe concern.

In Britain, the aftermath of war included strikes and other unrest, as the government attempted to get the country back onto a peace economy, but with both the railways and mines nationalised. Soldiers were clamouring for speedy demobilisation, but releasing workers too quickly would have resulted in mass unemployment.

In the wider world, the news was also dominated by the fallout from the Great War. The Paris Peace Conference and the League of Nations were overseeing the dismantling of the Russian, Turkish and Austrian empires, and the distribution of the colonies of the losers to the winners. Reparations against the Central Powers were also pursued. The Allies were still at war, but this time against the Red Army, which was forging a new Soviet Russia. Britain was at war, too, with Irish Republicans, who were determined to establish an independent Irish state.

Overall, though, Thomas has a routine life. He works all day Monday to Friday and Saturday mornings. He comes home for his dinner, the main meal of the day, around half-way through his working day. He has tea after finishing work, and some supper before bed. He travels by tramcar to work, although he sometimes calls it a car, and walks for pleasure.

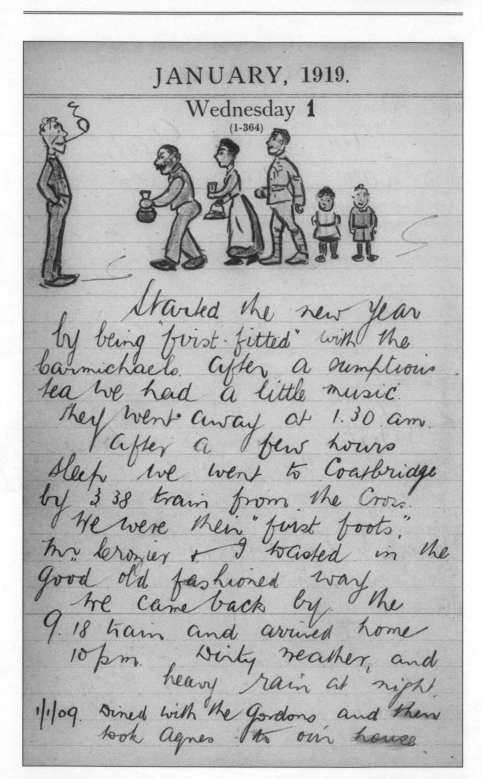

JANUARY, 1919.

Wednesday 1
(1-364)

Started the new year
by being "first-fitted" with the
Carmichaels. After a sumptious
tea we had a little music.
They went away at 1.30 am.
After a few hours
sleep we went to Coatbridge
by 3.38 train from the Cross.
We were their "first foots."
Mr Crozier & I toasted in the
good old fashioned way.
we came back by the
9.18 train and arrived home
10 pm. Dirty weather, and
heavy rain at night.
1/1/09. Dined with the Gordons and then
took Agnes to our house

Wednesday, 1 January

Started the new year by being 'first fitted'[1] with the Carmichaels.
After a sumptuous tea we had a little music. They went away
at 1.30 a.m. After a few hours' sleep, we went to Coatbridge by
3.38 train from the Cross.[2] We were their 'first foots'. Mr Crozier
and I toasted in the good old fashioned way.[3] We came back by
the 9.18 train and arrived home 10 p.m.

Thursday, 2 January

I took a turn into town in the afternoon before dinner. Mrs
Cormack was in when I got back.[4] She invited us out for
Saturday. We went down to Ibrox at night.[5] Mr Gordon in bed
with a cold. We were 'first foot' again. We had some music and
Nannie sung a few things in a tasteful manner.[6]

Friday, 3 January

Resumed my work today at usual hour, and got away at usual hour.
Andrew's wife up in afternoon.[7] She gave Tommy a box of blocks.
Agnes baked a new fashion of cake at night.

Saturday, 4 January

*We attired ourselves in our best,
and at 5 p.m. sallied forth and
visited the Cormacks. Quite a crowd
there. We had some music and Mrs
Cormack sung a score or two of songs.
Agnes sang one song to show how it
should be done.*

Sunday, 5 January

Took a walk by myself in afternoon by Queen's Park and
Shawlands.[8] Another spree on tonight. We had tea in the
Carmichaels. Wee Alex gave us some sounds out of his fiddle. We
left at 10.45 p.m., and had to walk home. As our door is opposite
theirs, no harm was done.

---

1   Traditionally, the first person to visit a house each year brings good fortune.

2   Glasgow Cross Station, operated by the Caledonian Railway.

3   The Crozier family were relatives of Agnes; Thomas is probably referring obliquely to whisky.

4   Mrs Cormack lived in Coatbridge. She was a family friend.

5   The Gordon family, who were close friends of Thomas and Agnes, lived in Ibrox.

6   Nannie Gordon.

7   Nellie Hamilton was the wife of Andrew, a former office boy where Thomas worked.

8   Two districts to the south of Govanhill.

Monday, 6 January

Loaned all our kitchen chairs to the Carmichaels, as they are entertaining on a large scale tonight. Smoked my cigar tonight (Mr Gordon gave it to me). Agnes did a washing and put the clothes-pole up and down a few times round about my neck and ears.[9] I forgive her freely. During the war, Germany lost 202 submarines.[10]

Tuesday, 7 January

Agnes did machine work on some of my undergarments, which were slightly frayed.

Wednesday, 8 January

Got my 'fast-turning-white' locks shorn. Discontent spreading through Army and Navy. Slowness in demobilisation.

Thursday, 9 January

When I got home, Daisy was in.[11] She and Agnes baked some fancy stuff at night. I put Daisy into train at Glasgow Cross at 9.35 p.m. British Naval officers in Germany take over all Zeppelins. Most bloody fighting in Berlin revolution.[12]

Friday, 10 January

Tommy confined to bed with a very bad cold. Agnes baked a currant cake at night. I did a few household duties.

Saturday, 11 January

Tommy got up in the afternoon. At night. Mr and Mrs Gordon and Nannie and Ella here. We had a few songs and instrumental music.

---

9 Agnes has evidently hung the wet washing on the pulley in the kitchen, above her husband.

10 A fact gleaned from the local newspapers.

11 Daisy Crozier.

12 Socialist demonstrations in Berlin escalated into an attempted communist revolution.

Sunday, 12 January

We were expecting Josephine tonight, but she did not oblige.[13] We sat in the room and got melancholy singing hymns.

Monday, 13 January

This is Victory Week in Glasgow.[14] Saw the two big tanks Haig and Beatty meandering around the square, and then I saw the whippet tank Julian's Baby.[15] In the afternoon, I saw a balloon going up from the square. It was a great day. This is all to raise money to 'carry on the peace'. The alarm clock struck work tonight again. The peace conference looks like making a start now.[16]

Tuesday, 14 January

Bought Tommy a kazoo yesterday.[17] An unholy sort of instrument. Went over myself at night to Greenlodge to keep father company, all the folks there being at some religious sort of tea meeting.[18] Father seems to be not so bad now.[19]

Wednesday, 15 January

Agnes spent all day in the washing house.[20] The newspapers now put out bills in the morning after an absence of about two years.[21] British troops in Vienna feeding the starving natives.[22]

---

13 Josephine was Thomas' sister.

14 Victory Week was a UK-wide celebration of winning the First World War, and a fund-raising event.

15 The square was George Square, Glasgow's main civic space; the large tanks were named after Field Marshal Sir Douglas Haig (later Earl Haig), Commander of the British Expeditionary Force in France and Belgium from 1915 to 1918, and Admiral of the Fleet David Beatty. The name Julian's Baby comes from the tank Julian, which toured Britain during 1918 to raise funds for the war effort.

16 The peace conference, which would agree the settlements against the Central Powers, opened on 12 January 1919 in Paris.

17 A kazoo is a simple musical instrument that makes a buzzing noise when blown.

18 Greenlodge Terrace in Bridgeton was Thomas' father's address.

19 Thomas' father Joseph had been operated on for suspected cancer in December 1918.

20 The occupants of each tenement shared a wash house in the back court. It was equipped with a boiler, at least one sink and a wringer.

21 Newspaper bills, attached to billboards, advertise the headlines or special offers in each day's newspapers.

22 Order in Austria had collapsed after its defeat.

Thursday, 16 January

Our respected elder up tonight.[23] He left two tickets admitting us to the Communion on Sunday first.[24] Agnes rubbed a hot iron on a few articles of clothing this evening. During the war, Paris lost by air raids and bombardments: 522 killed and 1,223 injured.[25]

Friday, 17 January

The balloon went up again from the square today. Being a gentleman of leisure, I watched it for a space. Mended Tommy's bed at night. He handles it very carelessly. Agnes baked some toothsome articles. Wrote to Duncan.[26] He is rusticating in Salonica with the ASC (not with my wife).[27]

Saturday, 18 January

Foggy and frosty in Glasgow, but nice and clear at Govanhill (it being in the country). In order to bring a touch of colour to our faded cheeks, we took a walk through Queen's Park and Shawlands in the afternoon. It made Agnes so vigorous that she wiped me out at Cassino in the evening.[28] The great peace conference gets started at last.[29]

Sunday, 19 January

Dirty wet day. I did not go out at all. As Tommy intends resuming school tomorrow, I wrote the usual 'Please excuse Tommy etc'. If he did not bring it, I suppose he would be imprisoned or transported. Prince John (King's youngest son) died yesterday.[30]

Monday, 20 January

Tommy started school again. Agnes went to her doctor tonight and 'passed'.[31] I feel a bit easier now. Glasgow collected £11,313,734

---

23 A church elder, in the Presbyterian tradition, is a lay member of the committee that runs each church.

24 The tickets were issued to members of the church who were in good standing.

25 A fact gleaned from local newspapers.

26 Thomas' brother Duncan was still on active service.

27 The initials stand for both Army Service Corps and Agnes Smart Cook.

28 Cassino is a card game first played in Italy.

29 The Paris Peace Conference would draw up the treaties that officially ended the First World War.

30 Prince John, the youngest son of King George V and Queen Mary, died age 13.

31 Agnes had been under the care of the doctor since December 1918. Thomas did not specify what was ailing her, but Agnes was later diagnosed with rheumatic rheumatism, which we now know as fibromyalgia.

during Victory Week last week. TCL collected last week (from his pay) a shilling or two.[32]

Tuesday, 21 January

Lily and Jack here at night.[33] They couldn't get a car home, so I made them walk.[34] Got home myself at 11.30 p.m. and had to walk. The whippet tank, which has been stuck since Saturday, got started today.

Wednesday, 22 January
Took Tommy out at night to get his hair cut. The Sinn Feiners declare Ireland a republic in Dublin.[35] New Zealand casualties in Great War: 16,456 killed, 41,404 wounded.

Thursday, 23 January
Tommy got a bad cough. Getting his hair cut, no doubt. Great strike threatened all over the country.[36] We are turning into Bolsheviks. Serious times ahead. Revolution in Portugal: attempt to put former King Manuel on throne again.[37]

Friday, 24 January
Did a little brass cleaning at night and Agnes did a little stair washing. Tommy still got a bad cough so got him a bottle each of cod oil and chemical food.[38] Britain's Air Force leads the world: at the beginning of the war we had 166 aeroplanes and at the finish we had 21,000. In 1914 we had 45 seaplanes, and 1,300 at the finish. In 1914 we had seven airships and have now 103. In August 1914 we had four RAF squadrons. At end of war we had over 300.

---

32 Thomas Cairns Livingstone.

33 Lily and Jack Ferguson were Thomas' niece and nephew.

34 The 'car' was a tramcar.

35 Sinn Fein, the victors of the December 1918 election, established the Dáil Éireann and declared independence, sparking the Irish War of Independence.

36 Trade union leaders called a strike in support of the 40-hour week, which was intended to absorb the workers being demobilised into the workforce without causing unemployment. The usual working week before the First World War was 54 hours.

37 The activities of the monarchists led to civil war.

38 Cod liver oil was widely used for its health benefits; chemical food was an iron tonic.

Saturday, 25 January

Took a walk in the afternoon to the Langside Library. Tommy's cough still very bad. Agnes sewed a tab on my jacket.

Sunday, 26 January

Up in the early dawn, and went to church. We did not go out again as it rained and snowed and misbehaved generally. Tomorrow, everybody goes on strike: no tramcars, no gas, no water, no policemen, no nothing.[39] Help!

Monday, 27 January

Tommy's cough seems a little easier. I seem to have a touch of the cold. The town was full of loafers, I mean strikers, today. The great 40-hour strike has begun. The trams are still running, however. Thousands out on strike all over the country. Bolshevism.

Tuesday, 28 January

About 40,000 on strike in Glasgow. My throat sort of husky. I have evidently got a touch of the cold. We are now allowed three-quarters of a pound of sugar per head for a week. Allied armies strength on the Western Front on 11 November 1918 was 6,427,100 men.

Wednesday, 29 January

My voice not quite so deep as yesterday. Tommy still has a cough. Strike spreading in Glasgow. Strikers threaten to stop the tramcars. Where are the police? 100,000 idle in Belfast.[40] These are the piping times of peace.[41]

---

39 The general strike, which brought Glasgow to a halt, was in support of the 40-hour week.

40 The 40-hour strike had spread to the north of Ireland.

41 The phrase is from Shakespeare's *Richard III*.

Thursday, 30 January

Tommy's cough easier. My voice is quite normal now, but I'm going to have a sore nose. The strike situation is getting serious. Electric power cut off from public works at Port Dundas Station.[42]

Friday, 31 January

Wild scenes in George Square today with the strikers.[43] Riot Act read by the proper official. Documents torn from his hands, and he gets bashed with a bottle. Mounted police charge with batons, and about 50 people qualify for the hospital. I went to the square at night for a constitutional, but kept a wary eye on police. The soldiers arrive, fully armed, steel helmets etc. So I gradually faded away. I'm afraid there will be bloodshed.

Saturday, 1 February

Thousands of troops drafted into Glasgow today. All public buildings, stations and bridges have sentries with fixed bayonets and 'tin hats'. In the afternoon, I took Tommy and Agnes into the square to see the unusual spectacle. Troops billeted in the Post Office, municipal buildings and all round about. The hooligans, loafers or strikers kept quiet. The three strike leaders, Gallacher, Kirkwood and Shinwell arrested.[44] We got safely home. There must be a hundred or so shop windows smashed in the town. We are the people.

Sunday, 2 February

Took a walk round the town before dinner. The military seem to be in complete possession of the town. Sentries round the gas works and tramway works at Coplawhill.[45] More power to their arm. Trust a few of the Bolsheviks to get shot.[46]

---

42 Pinkston Power Station in Port Dundas, to the north of the city centre, provided power to the tram system, street lighting and other municipal enterprises.

43 The Battle of George Square saw the trade unionists who were agitating for a 40-hour week pitted against the police and army, who saw the unrest as a potential revolution. The police baton-charged the demonstrators in George Square, which was ringed by the army, and the crowd retaliated. The following day, troops occupied the city to keep order.

44 William Gallacher, David Kirkwood and Emanuel Shinwell were the leaders of the Clyde Workers' Committee, which co-ordinated the campaign for a 40-hour working week.

45 Coplawhill is to the south of the city centre.

46 This appears to be a rumour; there are no official accounts of shootings.

Monday, 3 February

Dull day and very cold. Agnes keeping herself warm by working in the wash house all day. Glasgow sort of quiet this week, and the 10,000 troops with tin hats, machine guns, bayonets, rifles, barbed wire and trench mortars have evidently put the fear of death into the hooligan strikers. I rejoice accordingly. The trades unions now back the strike and demand the release of the Bolshevist, demented, mad strike leaders.[47] They are evidently optimists. Troops promise protection to men willing to work.

Tuesday, 4 February

Five tanks arrive in Glasgow. The minister here tonight. He embraces Tommy (great joy). Agnes ironed all night. I went over to Calder Street library for a little.

Friday, 7 February

Cleaned a few articles of brass, such as pokers, shovels etc. Agnes did some baking. Belfast still without gas or tramcars.[48]

Saturday, 8 February

Jean here in the early afternoon.[49] So we had a little music etc. I escorted Jean to 10 p.m. train from Queen Street. Bought a new shaving stick tonight. 'Gibb's superfatted cold cream' kidney.[50]

Sunday, 9 February

Before dinner, I took a walk out to Ruglen and back.[51] 'It was there I spent my childhood days, Gathering wulks on Cathkin Braes.'[52] About 6 p.m., Josephine and Pa arrived.[53] We adjourned to the room and had some sacred music etc.

---

47   Gallacher, Kirkwood and Shinwell were among those arrested on the previous Friday.

48   Workers were still striking in Belfast in support of a 40-hour week.

49   Jean Crozier.

50   Gibb's Superfatted Cold Cream Soap was a moisturising soap that helped to avoid razor burn. Kidney here means kind or brand.

51   Thomas' brother Sam and his family stay in Rutherglen, which is pronounced 'Ruglen' by some locals.

52   In this parody of a sentimental song, 'wulk' is a Glaswegian pronunciation of whelk, or sea snail.

53   Josephine is Thomas' sister, who lives with their father Joseph in Bridgeton, in the east of Glasgow.

The Battle of George Square

Glasgow's reputation as the centre of Red Clydeside began during the First World War, but the most important event in that phenomenon was the Battle of George Square on Friday, 31 January 1919, a day known as Bloody Friday, or Black Friday. The day, which saw one of the worst riots in the history of Glasgow, began with a dispute over the trade union campaign for shorter working hours, which had been backed by widespread strikes across the city. The rioting provoked a swift and decisive response from the British government, which flooded the city centre with soldiers and tanks to prevent further gatherings of militants and to diffuse the possibility of what the Secretary of State for Scotland called 'a Bolshevist uprising'. The government may have feared revolution, which had already happened in Russia in 1917 and was then occurring in Germany in the aftermath of war, but the Glasgow trade unionists, in the main, would have been happy with a 40-hour week rather than turning the world upside down.

The roots of the riot lay in the campaign for a shorter working week. Before the First World War, the standard working week was 54 hours. At the end of the war, national negotiations had agreed a 47-hour week for the engineering and shipbuilding industries, to be introduced in 1919. On Clydeside, a Joint Committee of shop stewards, members of the Scottish Trades Union Congress and the Clyde Workers' Committee wanted to campaign for a 30-hour week. When the Glasgow Trades Council joined the campaign, the demand was altered to a 40-hour week, which was nevertheless opposed by most unions, including the Amalgamated Society of Engineers. The objective of the campaign was not social revolution but sharing the limited amount of work (caused by the post-war recession) more widely among the increased number of workers (caused by the demobilisation of troops).

31

On Monday, 27 January 1919, more than 3,000 workers held a meeting in St Andrew's Halls in Granville Street to help decide the issue, and 40,000 people struck work later that day. By the Friday of that week more than 60,000 workers were on strike, and many of them gathered in George Square that day to hear Sir James Watson Stewart, the Lord Provost of Glasgow, deliver a response from the government to the unions' request for the government to intervene in the dispute. The riot began while Emanuel Shinwell and David Kirkwood of the Clyde Workers' Committee were inside the City Chambers with the Lord Provost. The cause of the riot is disputed: some say it began with attempts by the strikers to stop trams passing through George Square, while others blame the police for making an unprovoked truncheon charge on the demonstrators.

Whatever the immediate cause of the riot, the noise brought the two trade unionists out of the chambers, where Kirkwood was knocked to the ground by police and he, Shinwell and fellow activist Willie Gallacher were immediately arrested and charged with 'instigating and inciting large crowds of persons to form part of a riotous mob'. The crowd tore the notes from the hands of Sheriff MacKenzie before he could complete his proclamation of the Riot Act. Running battles took place between the police and the strikers, with iron railings and glass bottles being co-opted as improvised weapons against the police truncheons. The police were unable to gain the upper hand, and the workers headed for Glasgow Green, where they intended to hold a demonstration.

Fighting continued across the city centre that day and into the night, and police managed to arrest 12 people. Robert Munro, the Scottish Secretary, and David Lloyd George, the Prime Minister, decided to send in the army, and 10,000 soldiers from English regiments, with tanks, a Howitzer and machine guns, arrived on Friday night to quell what the authorities feared could become a revolution. In George Square, a 4.5-inch Howitzer was dug in at the City Chambers, and Lewis guns were mounted on the roofs of the General Post Office and the North British Hotel. Elsewhere in the city, the Cattle Market in the Gallowgate became a tank depot, and armed soldiers stood guard at docks and power stations.

The subsequent trial of the three trade unionists for incitement to riot ended with Shinwell and Gallacher being jailed for five months, and Kirkwood acquitted. All three went on to glittering careers in trade unions and politics.

The Riot Act of 1713

The Riot Act of 1713 authorised local authorities to declare that any group of twelve or more people was 'unlawfully, riotously, and tumultuously assembled together', and that they should disperse within one hour or face penalties, which could mean execution. The Act – formally titled 'An Act for Preventing Tumults and Riotous Assemblies, and for the more Speedy and Effectual Punishing of the Rioters' – came into force on 1 August 1715, and remained on the statute books until 1973. The phrase 'reading the Riot Act' referred to an official reading out a warning, set out in the text of the Act, to an unruly mob. Without the warning, any prosecution under the Act would have failed. The warning read: 'Our Sovereign Lord the King chargeth and commandeth all persons, being assembled, immediately to disperse themselves, and peaceably to depart to their habitations, or to their lawful business, upon the pains contained in the Act made in the first year of King George, for preventing tumults and riotous assemblies. God Save the King!' Black Friday was one of the last occasions on which the Riot Act was invoked; it was last proclaimed in Birkenhead in August 1919.

Monday, 10 February
A mouse taking liberties in our coal bunker, so I nailed up a hole with a small board. A lady from the kirk came in at night for our contribution to the 'cleaning fund'.[54] The strike seems to be about over on Clydeside.

Tuesday, 11 February
Andrew's wife up for her tea tonight. Her wee chap has a very bad cough, and vomited all over the shop.[55] Clydeside strike squashed.[56] Work resumed.

Wednesday, 12 February
We have a select company tonight. When I got home, Hetty had arrived, also Mrs Cormack and the two wee girls. Nannie Gordon dropped in later on. We had a great time with singing etc. Mrs Cormack did 95 per cent of the singing. I did the serious, heavy sort of music, and Nannie did some of the light, fluffy, popular kind of stuff.[57] They all away about 11.30. I accompanied Nannie to the Yellow Car at Allison Street.[58]

Friday, 14 February
Agnes put a straight edge on my trousers. The rocking chair was showing signs of distress, so I put a necessary screw nail in same.

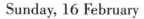

Saturday, 15 February
Cold day. Rained, snowed and sleeted all the time. Not out at all. Belfast now under the military.[59] High time.

Sunday, 16 February
Nice sort of day. Before dinner, I took a walk through Queen's Park and Shawlands, along Dumbreck Road, and car back from Fleurs Avenue. It brought

---

54   Thomas always seems politely cynical about the motives of church emissaries.

55   'All over the shop' is a Glaswegian phrase meaning 'all over the place'.

56   The Clyde Workers' Committee called off the strike on 10 February, after winning assurances that the working week would be cut from 54 hours to 47 hours.

57   Thomas played the piano and sang.

58   Glasgow tramcars had coloured panels to indicate their routes.

59   Belfast was placed under military control after a four-week strike deprived the city of electricity, gas and transport. The strike was in support of a 44-hour working week.

back old times again." Agnes worked hard all day. J. being a gentleman, just smoked.

1905
to
1910

Monday, 17 February
Bitter, cold day. Agnes in the wash house and rubbed 'cloots' at night with a hot iron.[61] Tommy very sick. Kept him in bed all day. Is it . . . ? Or is it . . . ? More grey hairs on my head.[62] The military are now away from Glasgow.

Wednesday, 19 February
Tommy at Hengler's Circus in the afternoon with his ma.[63] I got my hair cut tonight. Tempting providence, I call it.[64] The Belfast strike is squashed and peace reigns once more.[65] Erin go bragh.[66] Tramcars running, and gas and electric power now on.[67] God save the King.

Thursday, 20 February
Mild sort of day. Tommy back to school. Got a letter from Duncan, who is in Salonica.[68] He is well and cheery, which gives me pleasure. I cleaned the covers and jelly pans with Silvo tonight.[69] Agnes bought me a new pair of slippers, coloured like the coat of Joseph.[70]

Friday, 21 February
Dirty, dull day. Took a walk out to Langside Library at night, and a walk home again. The influenza is very bad again all over the country.[71] British Army at the time of the Armistice was the biggest in the world, at 5,680,247 men.

---

60 Thomas is evidently recalling his days of courting Agnes, shown in that day's drawing, with the dates 1905 to 1910. The area he has been walking is south of Ibrox, where Agnes was living with her family at the time.

61 'Cloots' are cloths, used here to mean clothes.

62 Thomas and Agnes are obviously concerned by Tommy's illness, which might be the dreaded influenza.

63 Hengler's Circus was in Sauchiehall Street, where the ABC Cinema later stood.

64 Thomas is indulging in the popular belief that having a haircut is likely to bring on cold weather, just as carrying an umbrella is sure to keep the rain at bay.

65 The strikers reluctantly returned to work after troops moved in to operate the gas and electricity plants and to run public transport.

66 Irish Gaelic phrase meaning 'Ireland for ever'.

67 In Belfast.

68 Salonica, now known as Thessaloniki, is a port in northern Greece. During the First World War, it was the focus of the attack on Bulgaria, one of the Central Powers.

69 Silvo was (and still is) a brand of silver polish.

70 The story of Joseph and his 'coat of many colours' is told in the book of Genesis.

71 The Spanish-flu pandemic, which lasted from March 1918 to June 1920, killed an estimated 50 million people worldwide.

Saturday, 22 February

At night I went out and bought two ounces of 'thick black' at 8d per ounce.[72]

Sunday, 23 February

In the afternoon, we all took car to Maryhill and went to the Western Necropolis.[73] We looked for poor Jenny's grave but could not find it.[74] After all, what did it matter? Jenny is gone, and I still mourn the loss of my dearest friend.

Monday, 24 February

We had a night of music. I brought my typist, Jenny Galloway, home with me. My two nieces, Lily and Isa, likewise my nephew Jack also up. Jenny sang a few pieces, and she can sing. I did the piano trick. I saw the Ferguson clan on to the Yellow Car at Govan Street, and then put my own little girl on her car at Bridge Street. All clear about 11.30 p.m. Amir of Afghanistan murdered (who cares?).[75]

Wednesday, 26 February

Dirty, wet day. Nellie Hamilton up in the afternoon, intimating that Andrew is at home.[76] Broke up an old wash board for firewood.

Thursday, 27 February

Agnes took a run out to Ruglen to see Nellie. Tommy kept the house until I came in at tea time. We got our gas bill. It will be handy as a pipe-light.

Friday, 28 February

A female lady who collects money for the kirk was up tonight for a hour or so. As I think more of the kirk than anything else, she got her cash.[77]

---

72   Thomas smokes 'thick black' tobacco in his pipe.

73   The Western Necropolis, in the north-west of the city, is one of the largest burial grounds in Glasgow.

74   Jenny Roxburgh died in November 1918.

75   Habibullah Khan, who had kept his country neutral during the Great War, was assassinated while on a hunting trip on 20 February.

76   Andrew Hamilton, a former office boy in Thomas' workplace, married Nellie in 1915. They lived in Rutherglen. Andrew fought and was wounded in the Great War.

77   Thomas is being sarcastic.

Saturday, 1 March

In the afternoon, I took Tommy down to the Art Galleries and educated his mind on the various works of art.[78] Agnes went into town in afternoon. She bought herself a new blouse.

Sunday, 2 March

Rained and snowed most all day. We did not go out at all. Sat in and burned stones, dross, slate etc that we pay 2/3 a bag for.[79] 'Controlled Coal'.[80] Wrote Duncan. He is in the canteen in or about Salonica. Keep the old flag flying.[81]

Monday, 3 March

Agnes very busy getting ready for the wash house. I pasted pictures in my scrap album.[82]

Tuesday, 4 March

Andrew up at night. He took supper with us and departed about 9.30. He is discharged from hospital, but is still very lame. Agnes baked a cake at night.

Wednesday, 5 March

Second Lieutenant C. Maxwell MC and Miss Maxwell up tonight.[83] Miss Maxwell is a teacher in Tommy's school.[84] We had a pleasant evening, and they left after 10.30 p.m. Agnes not keeping well.

Thursday, 6 March

Rained all day. Consternation in our little household today. Agnes all out. Unable to get up. Sore all over, head extra sore, and can't eat. What is it? Tommy kept from school to look after the house. I am greatly put about.

---

78 Kelvingrove Art Gallery and Museum.

79 Inferior coal, with many impurities.

80 The government had nationalised the mines during the war, and controlled the coal supply.

81 'Keep the Old Flag Flying, Boys!' was a patriotic song written by L.H. and W.G. Thorpe in 1917.

82 Thomas has been keeping a scrap album of material connected to the war, and is either still updating it or only now getting round to pasting items into it.

83 Claude Maxwell and his sister Miss Maxwell are friends of the family.

84 Victoria Primary School in Batson Drive, Govanhill. The school still stands.

Friday, 7 March

To my great joy, Agnes managed up this forenoon. She is a little better but very weak. She even baked at night, and ironed some of my soft, socialist-looking collars.

Saturday, 8 March

Poor Wee Tommy laid up for repairs. When I got home at dinner time, he was in bed.[85] Sore head, can't eat, vomiting and so on. We kept him amused as best as we could, and can only hope he is not developing anything worse. I took a turn out at night, bought two new 'clays' and the game of Tiddleywinks to keep Tommy amused.[86] Agnes keeping better, very done up at night.

Sunday, 9 March

Tommy seemed better, so we let him up at night. Sam, Nellie and John here for the evening.[87] They left about 10 p.m. Tommy twice sick at tea time. He is evidently not just right yet. Agnes greatly worried.

Monday, 10 March

Tommy quite cheery but kept him in bed all day. We think it is the influenza. I seem to have a touch of the cold myself.

Tuesday, 11 March

Tommy still in bed. His cold seems worse. We had all to go to Greenlodge tonight, but I could only go. Brigton having a big night.[88] The nice young man Foster was there, and his friend Menzies, the singist.[89] Mr Menzies did some singing. Lily accompanied him on one song (quite enough). I managed home at 12.40 a.m. Everybody sleeping.

Thursday, 13 March

Tommy coughed a good bit during the night, but seems a little better today. He is still in bed. I will be glad when he is up and about again. Agnes keeping well. I put a needle in the sewing machine tonight and anointed it with oil.

---

85   Dinner time was in the middle of the day (Thomas works every Saturday morning), and tea time was in the early evening.

86   Clays were clay pipes, and Tiddleywinks is a game, first produced in 1888, in which players flick small discs into a cup or target.

87   Sam was Thomas' brother, married to Nellie.

88   'Brigton' is a local pronunciation of Bridgeton, a district in the east of Glasgow. Thomas' father Joseph lives there, alongside Thomas' sister Lily and her family.

89   Thomas uses a nonsense word, 'singist', to mean singer.

Friday, 14 March

Great rejoicings - Tommy got up and is feeling fine. Agnes went down to Ibrox at night. I saw the largest airship today on its trial trip.[90] The greatest in the world. Clyde-built. It came over Govanhill, so Tommy and Agnes saw it likewise.

Saturday, 15 March

Went out myself after dinner, through Queen's Park and Shawlands, and back by Cathcart. German Army is to be limited to 100,000 men, and the mercantile fleet is to be given up to help feed the Germans, so commands the Allied Peace Conference.[91]

Sunday, 16 March

Took Tommy out after dinner. His first appearance out. We went round by the Hangingshaws and got some country air.[92]

Monday, 17 March

Bright and sunny, but very cold. This is the 17th of Ireland.[93] Following his majesty King Geordie, I did not drown the shamrock.[94] Agnes and Tommy out for a little in the afternoon. Mrs Dunn up here in the afternoon, but she did not get in. The school-board officer was also up.[95]

Tuesday, 18 March

Agnes and Tommy went out to Ruglen in afternoon. I went straight from my work, and we had our tea at Sam's, then we all went to his choir concert held in the Evangelistic Institute.

Wednesday, 19 March

Snowed, rained and sleeted all day. Very cold and dirty. Agnes feeling frisky, evidently, as she went to the washing house. Not so frisky when I got home. Her throat was sore, and she has lost her voice. She tried glycerine and got back a percentage of it.[96]

---

90 The airship R34 was built at Beardmore's airship sheds at Inchinnan, on the south bank of the Clyde.

91 The peace conference at Paris.

92 Hangingshaw was a village in Cathcart, to the south of Glasgow.

93 St Patrick's Day.

94 In April 1915, King George V pledged that no alcohol would be consumed by the Royal Household until the war was over. Thomas appears to be upholding this commitment.

95 The school-board officer checked that missing pupils were not playing truant.

96 Glycerine was used as a medicine for sore throats and coughs.

Thursday, 20 March

Agnes worse tonight. She took a hot drink, bathed her feet and went to bed early. She is evidently taking the 'flu'.

Saturday, 22 March

Agnes worse still. So left word in the morning for the doctor to call. When I got home the doctor had been. Agnes very fevered. It is the dreaded influenza. She has to eat nothing, only drink. She had a very bad day of it. I did some shopping at night in Sam's shop, and put Tommy to bed when I got home.

Sunday, 23 March

Agnes a little easier. The medical man up. Says her temperature is down, which is so much to the good. She is allowed a little food, but her appetite is not extra keen. I did not manage to church today.[97]

Monday, 24 March

Agnes as well as can be hoped for. The doctor up at dinner time. She is to eat as much as she can, which is not very much. Josephine came up at night. Nearly cracked my skull at business today.

Tuesday, 25 March

Agnes very low spirited, melancholy, dumped. No appetite, everything hopeless and grey. Even the way I do the housework doesn't please her. It's very sad. The influenza poison is in her system, evidently.

Thursday, 27 March

Agnes up at dinner time. After tea, she went to bed and had a most unholy time with her head. I had

---

absolutely to hold her down. The lines of care are on my manly forehead.

Saturday, 29 March
Agnes up all day. She is in a very pessimistic mood. Not so well as she thought she would be. Hungary given over to Bolshevism.[98]

Wednesday, 2 April
Agnes went out for the first time. It made her very tired. Put a patent patch on Tommy's bath tonight to make it watertight.

Friday, 4 April

I got a letter from Duncan. He is well. Tommy got a holiday, as it is the education authority election.[99] Agnes bearing up well, but not yet quite well. Tommy seems to have developed a bad cold. British forces in southern Russia in a dangerous position.[100]

Saturday, 5 April
Father dropped in at tea time. I walked him home and went up for about 10 minutes. The lassies seemed to be having a good time. Tommy's cold seemed to be worse. Is it the 'flu'? Agnes completely done out at night.

Sunday, 6 April
We entertained tonight. Mr and Mrs Carmichael and family in for tea. We had music, and Wee Alex scraped his fiddle and made some wonderful sounds. Tommy seems all right again.

Monday, 7 April
Agnes doing quite a lot of work now. I took a walk out to Ruglen, had a look in at the Institute and had a word with the 'heid yin'

---

98   Communists led by Béla Kun took control of the capital and announced the establishment of the Hungarian Soviet Republic.

99   Schools were used as polling places for elections to the education authority.

100 British forces had been sent to south Russia and Ukraine to support the White Volunteer Army, which was battling the Red Army.

APRIL, 1919.

Monday 7
(97-268)

Very mild blowy day. Agnes doing quite a lot of work now.

I took a walk out to Ruglen, had a look in at the "Institute" and had a word with the "heid yin" Dan Rodger.

Have developed a bad sort of cold.

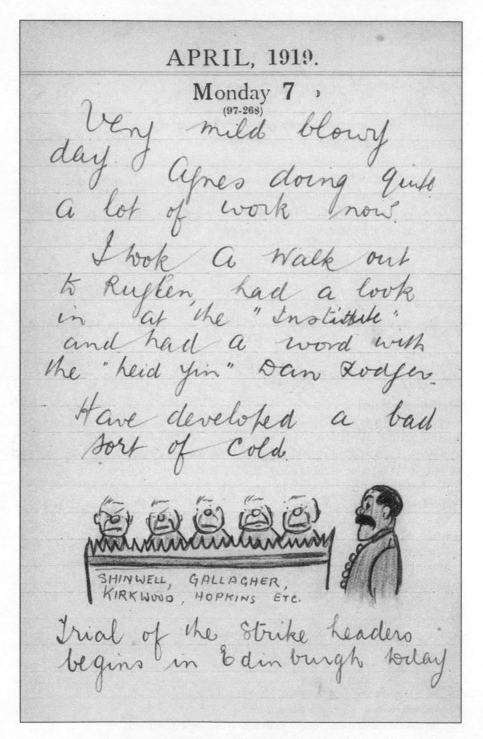

SHINWELL, GALLAGHER, KIRKWOOD, HOPKINS ETC.

Trial of the strike leaders begins in Edinburgh today

Note: Harry Hopkins was the Glasgow secretary of the
Amalgamated Society of Engineers

Dan Rodger.[101] Have developed a bad sort of cold. Trial of the strike leaders begins in Edinburgh today.[102]

Tuesday, 8 April

My cold no better. Head very stuffed. What's it going to be?[103] We made up a parcel tonight for Duncan. Agnes ironed most all night. She is improving.

Wednesday, 9 April

Agnes back to her usual routine. She got up in the morning and made my breakfast. She went to town in the afternoon with Mrs Carmichael. Tommy lost his cap, and I broke my Yale key. Agnes cleaned the room at night.[104] Don't know how my cold is going. It seems to be in my chest now. My-oh-my. The Allies chased from Odessa by the Soviets. British troops being sent to Archangel.

Friday, 11 April

Agnes still seems to have the cold. Saw Jean Crozier tonight in Stockwell Street when I was getting home. She came home with me. The 'no weel' feeling has now worn off me.[105]

Saturday, 12 April

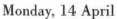

Agnes tempted providence by washing the floor.

Sunday, 13 April

Agnes went to church all by herself. I took a run out to Stobhill Military Hospital in afternoon to see Andrew, but he was out.[106] Agnes not so well at night. She retired early. An unsatisfactory sort of day.

Monday, 14 April

Had a headache all day. But we went at night to the Cinerama.[107] The Carmichaels went with us. There are now no female drivers on the Glasgow tramcars.[108] Their day is done.

---

101 The Evangelistic Institute. The Glaswegian phrase 'heid yin' mea[ns] Daniel Lusk Rodger was the president of the institute.

102 The trial followed the events in George Square in January.

103 Simply a cold, or influenza?

104 The front room or parlour.

105 'No weel' is a Scottish pronunciation of 'not well'.

106 Andrew Hamilton.

107 The Cinerama stood at the corner of Victoria Road and Cuthbertson Street.

108 Glasgow Corporation Transport Department had employed women as tram drivers and conductors to replace enlisted males.

Tuesday, 15 April

Agnes played all night with the sewing machine.
Serious riots in India.[109]

Thursday, 17 April

*Agnes enjoying herself in the wash house
all day. Cleaned the room windows.
Tommy stopped school for his Easter
holidays. He gets all next week.*

Friday, 18 April

Stopped today for the spring holiday. I have got Saturday and
Monday off, the first time since I started work that I got two
days for Easter. Strikers trial finished in Edinburgh. Shinwell
gets five months, Gallacher three months.[110] They got off lightly.
Bolsheviks have captured Sevastopol from the Allies.[111]

Saturday, 19 April

I am off the chain today. Took a run down to the Art Galleries
before dinner. At night we all had a walk through the Queen's
Park and finished up with a look into the 'pictures' at
Shawlands.[112]

Sunday, 20 April

We ate an egg, seeing that this is Easter Sunday. We all went
to Springburn Park after dinner.[113] I knocked a wasp off Agnes'
nose, but it gave her a nip. We were speaking to Nin Henderson
and his wife on our way home.[114] We arranged a night for them to
visit us.

Monday, 21 April

*I am off the chain again today. Took a walk into
town before dinner and saw all the crowds trying to
get cars for Rouken Glen etc.[115] In the afternoon, we*

---

109 Riots followed the massacre by British and Gurkha troops of 379 Sikhs at Amritsar
     in the Punjab.
110 The strike leaders had been accused of incitement to riot. Kirkwood was acquitted.
111 The Allies continued to fare badly at the hands of the Red Army.
112 The 'pictures' is a Glaswegian term for the cinema. Shawlands Picture House stood at
     1045 Pollokshaws Road.
113 Springburn Park is in the north of the city.
114 Ninian Henderson was Agnes' uncle.
115 The cars were tramcars, and Rouken Glen is a public park to the south of Glasgow.

*all went into Paisley and ended up the day with a
visit to the Palace.[116]*

Tuesday, 22 April

Tommy coughed all last night so we got little sleep. Took a walk
round by the Hangingshaws and Mount Florida at night. Tommy is
not looking too well. I would rather look well. Bolshevik revolution
in Turkey.[117]

Wednesday, 23 April

Tommy spent another night spluttering. He also evidently has
the cold. We are getting alarmed, so I hied him round to the
doctor after tea time. The doctor looked down his throat and said
it was a cough, also he had adenoids.[118] We got a bottle. Agnes
whitewashed the bathroom.[119] She's game.

Thursday, 24 April

Tommy coughed all last night, so our sleep was at a minimum.
He did not cough quite so much today, but his nose is running
and he seems to have a right bad cold. Agnes finished out the
scullery.[120] Italy giving trouble at the Peace Conference. She
wants Fiume.[121]

Friday, 25 April

Tommy very feverish all night, and coughed. Kept him in bed. His
nose is running and his eyes are sore. He has got spots around his
ears. I rushed for the doctor at night. Yes, it is the measles. Poor
wee man. We are sort of worried now.

---

116 Paisley is a town to the west of Glasgow. The Palace was either a music hall or a
cinema.

117 As the former empires of the Central Powers unravelled, many states descended into
revolution.

118 Enlarged adenoids (lymph glands at the back of the nasal passages) can make
breathing difficult.

119 The toilet. The Livingstones did not have a room with a bath.

120 A scullery was a small room off a kitchen used for storing food, crockery and utensils,
and sometimes for preparing food or washing dishes.

121 Fiume was a small territory in what is now Croatia, close to the Italian border.

Saturday, 26 April

Tommy very restless all last night. He coughed a lot. Doctor up early. Temperature high, no food but milk and water. He is all covered now with spots. Father here in afternoon. He did not wait long, evidently afraid of catching the measles. I took a walk to the library at night. Read all the medical books there and came home greatly comforted (?).

Sunday, 27 April

Tommy coughed something awful all last night. Not much room on him now for any more spots. He is getting hungry now, and seems cheerier. The doctor up today. Tommy's temperature is now 99 degrees. A severe type of measles, the doctor says, but no complications so far. I feel a bit easier in my mind now. Tommy not yet ready to eat any food, although he would like to. He did not cough quite so much this afternoon, so hope he will have a quiet night.

Monday, 28 April

Tommy improving. Doctor up and says he may now eat. Great rejoicing from Tommy. I took a run over to Greenlodge for a little. Italy leaves the League of Nations. Japan threatens to do the same.[122]

Tuesday, 29 April

Tommy slept better last night. His cough not so bad now. Doctor up and is quite well pleased. Tommy to get sitting up now. Got a new key for the one I had broken. It cost me 1/6.[123] Agnes took a run up to Nin Henderson's to postpone their visit.

Wednesday, 30 April

Tommy slept like a top last night, so did we all of us. Tommy seems to be improving now. His cough not quite away yet. Agnes out on her own tonight, so I stayed in and read good moral stories to Tommy.

---

122 The League of Nations was set up in January 1919 by the Paris Peace Conference, to promote peace and security after the Great War.

123 Seven and a half new pence.

Thursday, 1 May

Doctor up seeing Tommy for the last time. He is still improving. Agnes did a washing at night. I went out for a walk, but the May dew came on, so I went into Calder Street library. Today's military situation: Egypt is quiet. In India the Punjab is still disturbed. Sebastopol was evacuated by the French on Tuesday.[124]

Sunday, 4 May

Jumped out of bed this morning at the 'skeech of day' and took a walk to Queen's Park etc before breakfast.[125] Not out again, as it rained all day. Agnes broke the Sabbath by cleaning out the pantry and I assisted. Tommy got up in the afternoon. He enjoyed the sensation and we were pleased to see him making his usual noise.

Wednesday, 7 May

I saw the famous 52nd (Lowland) Scottish Division in town, just back from the war.[126] Agnes cleaned out the room tonight. I worked late. Italy into the Peace Conference again. Peace terms presented to Germany.

Thursday, 8 May

Field Marshal Sir Douglas Haig presented with the Freedom of Glasgow today. so I saw him.[127] Six aeroplanes buzzed overhead. Tommy out today for the first time. Seeing he was feeling better, Agnes bought him a new crane to amuse him.

Saturday, 10 May

Took Tommy out for a walk in the afternoon. We favoured the Queen's Park. We had Nin Henderson and wife up for tea tonight. We had some violin and piano stunts. They departed 12.45 a.m.

---

124 The Red Army continued its defeat of the Allied Forces in Russia.

125 The 'skeech of day' means the break of dawn.

126 The 52nd (Lowland) Division had served in Egypt, Gallipoli, Palestine, France and Flanders.

127 Haig (later Earl Haig) had been commander of the British forces during the Battle of the Somme, the 3rd Battle of Ypres and the victories leading to German surrender in 1918.

MAY, 1919.

2nd after Easter.

Sunday 4

(124-241)

Jumped out of bed this morning at the "skeech of day" and took a walk to Queens Park etc before breakfast.

Not out again as it rained all day practically.

Agnes broke the Sabbath by cleaning out the pantry and I assisted

Tommy got up today in the afternoon.

He enjoyed the sensation and we were pleased to see him making his usual noise.

Monday, 12 May
Working late. When I got home, Josephine was in. She is thinking of starting a business as a draper in her late employer's shop (who is bankrupt). Agnes in town in afternoon. Business = new hat. Allies are evidently going to attack Petrograd.[128]

Tuesday, 13 May
The joiner man in today and put in pane of glass. We got our lum swept.[129] The sweep took off our 'whirly' and did not put it back on again.[130] Consternation. Working late at night.

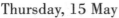

Wednesday, 14 May
Nellie (Sam's wife) here at tea time. Agnes saw her off at Ruglen Road. I then went round and consulted my doctor. I thought I had an ulcer on my leg. I hadn't. Great relief. I then took Tommy and got his hair cut. To finish up my round of gaiety I went back to my work and slaved till 10 p.m. Soot coming down our lum.

Thursday, 15 May
We all went out at night to see Claude Maxwell and his sister. He is now 'demobbed'. Full moon 2.10 a.m. (lucky moon).

Friday, 16 May
We got our new lum today. It is not a 'whirly'. Will it do?

Saturday, 17 May
We all out at night. Investigated the quarries at Giffnock and came back by Cathcart.[131] Three American seaplanes leave Newfoundland to fly to Europe via Azores.[132]

---

128 The Allies were continuing their war against the Red Army.

129 'Lum' is a Scots word for chimney.

130 A 'whirly' is a metal cap for a chimney pot, which rotates with the wind and draws smoke up from the fire beneath.

131 Giffnock is a district to the south of Glasgow. The quarries supplied much of the blond sandstone used in the construction of the city.

132 Three American Curtiss NC flying boats attempted the first transatlantic flight, landing in a number of places en route, in May 1919. Plane NC-4, commanded by Lt Commander Albert Cushing Read, completed the journey, but NC-1 and NC-3 were less successful.

Sunday, 18 May
Took Tommy out today. Car to Govan, then along the Clyde to Renfrew, crossed over the funny ferry there and car home.[133]

Monday, 19 May
Lifted my salary as usual. Worked late at night. British naval squadron chases Bolshevik warship in Baltic.[134] The British aviator 'Hawker' starts on his flight over the Atlantic.[135] The American seaplane C4 reaches Azores.

Tuesday, 20 May
This is the King's Birthday holiday. Very warm, sunny day. Agnes spent the day in the wash house.[136] Before tea I took a walk out through Ruglen and had a seat in the Overburn Park. After tea I went out to Pollokshaws and dropped into a picture house, the Camphill.[137] No word yet of Hawker and his companion Grieve.

Thursday, 22 May
Tommy very restless all last night. We wonder what is going to happen now. His neck not so bad today. Agnes took him into town in afternoon and he got a new suit and a 'Glengarry'. I worked late.

Saturday, 24 May
We all went into town in the afternoon. I bought a new hairy soft hat of a greenish-brownish shade. I used to get three hats for the same money. Having a copper or two left, we all went to the Camphill Picture House at night.

Sunday, 25 May
Hot, sunny day. We all dressed in our best, Tommy in his new suit etc, and went to Pollok Estate. Had a good seat there then walked along Dumbreck Road to Ibrox. We went up to Whitefield Road folks for a while and got home at 10.30.[138] Tommy complains of earache when he goes to bed.

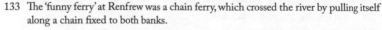

---

133 The 'funny ferry' at Renfrew was a chain ferry, which crossed the river by pulling itself along a chain fixed to both banks.

134 The British Navy continued their support of the anti-revolution forces in Russia.

135 Harry Hawker, chief test pilot and designer for Sopwith, and McKenzie Grieve attempted the first non-stop transatlantic flight.

136 No public holiday for Agnes.

137 The Camphill Picture House stood at 7 Baker Street. Camphill is a district to the south of Govanhill.

138 Members of Agnes' family lived at 37 Whitefield Road, Ibrox.

Monday, 26 May

Bought a pair of hair brushes today and a new pipe. Agnes evidently feeling frivolous, as she went over to the doctor and paid his bill.[139] Working late tonight. Hawker and Grieve have been picked up in the Atlantic by a Danish trading steamship, so their attempt fails.

Tuesday, 27 May

Bought a new shaving brush for three quarters of a dollar.[140] We get ready tonight for the whitewash man. Spring cleaning has started.

Wednesday, 28 May

Man in tonight whitewashing. He got 4/- to himself when finished.[141] We then washed paintwork etc. Ceased fire at 12 p.m., then tea, then bed. Feeling tired. Kabul bombed by British.[142] The American seaplane C4 arrives at Portugal. So America has flown the Atlantic first.[143]

Tuesday, 3 June

Agnes and Tommy went down to Ardrossan this morning to get our summer residence. To my great joy, Agnes had secured a room with attendance for the sum of £3 10/- for the fortnight. Agnes went into the wash house at night.

Wednesday, 4 June

My birthday. I'll soon be 30. Some rain today. This is Derby Day. I lost 2/-. Agnes in wash house all day and ironed all night. At night I went round by the Hangingshaws, Mount Florida and Queen's Park. Was speaking to Mr Cormack on his cabbage patch.[144]

Thursday, 5 June

Agnes, Mrs Carmichael and Tommy at the Majestic.[145] I went out myself about 9 p.m. Some shows on in Butterbiggins Road, so I dropped in and saw all the fun of the fair.[146] Met my wife and family there, so we all came home together.

---

139 There was no National Health Service until 1948.

140 A 'dollar' was a slang term for a crown (five shillings).

141 Four shillings (20p).

142 The Third Anglo-Afghan war was to end in Afghanistan's independence from the UK.

143 This may have been the first crossing, but it was not the first non-stop crossing.

144 His allotment in Queen's Park.

145 The Majestic Cinema stood at 110 Smith Street (now Inglefield Street), Govanhill.

146 The 'shows' is a Scottish expression for a funfair.

Friday, 6 June

Got my hair cut tonight.

Saturday, 7 June

Some very heavy rain today. Getting
ready for the holiday season. Mr
Carmichael went to his plot at night in
Queen's Park, so I honoured him with
my company.[147]

Sunday, 8 June

Very stormy day. We all dressed in our finest and got blown the
length of Queen's Park. Josephine and Pa arrived about tea time,
and departed about 9 p.m. Josephine seems to be doing well in
her new business.

Tuesday, 10 June

This is the one and only anniversary.[148] Agnes at the dentist twice
today. The second time, she got a 'shoogly' tooth extracted.[149] Mrs
Gordon and Ella dropped in this afternoon. As Agnes was going
out, they dropped out again.

Wednesday, 11 June

At night I took a walk through Toryglen and watched the 'gowfers',
and then on to Ruglen and watched the 'boolers'.[150] Agnes ironed
all night and then collapsed all out. She needs her holiday.

Thursday, 12 June

Agnes and Tommy at the Majestic. Got my new golf jacket today,
made by Thomas Arkieson for 45/-. Wrote Duncan at night.

Friday, 13 June

*Ella Gordon here at
tea time to see if we
needed a bag. She
brought one in case.
She went away about
8 p.m. We had a busy
night packing up.*

---

147 Mr Carmichael also has an allotment in Queen's Park.

148 Thomas and Agnes were married on 10 June 1910.

149 'Shoogly' is a Scots word for loose or shaky.

150 Golfers and bowlers.

Saturday, 14 June

This is the day of days. Downed tools at 12 noon and rushed home
to get ready for our holidays. We favoured the Caledonian Railway
and took the 2.14 train, Ardrossan bound. We got down in comfort.
Got in a few messages, then the landlady had tea for us.[151] After
that we strolled along the beach to Saltcoats. Weather the very
best and very hot.

Sunday, 15 June

Before breakfast I took a walk round by the castle. After breakfast
we all dressed in our best and sailed forth to give the natives a
treat. The rain came on five minutes later, and rained hard for the
rest of the day.

Monday, 16 June

Raining as hard as ever this morning, and kept it up all day. High
wind blowing. We out for a little in the forenoon. We met Herbert
Maxwell.[152] After tea I went down to the one and only picture
house and booked seats.[153] We spent the night there. Very sad
weather.

Tuesday, 17 June

*Fine, sunny day. After dinner, we took a
walk to Saltcoats.*

Wednesday, 18 June

We all went to Fairlie today. Had our tea there then
visited the glen. We met Hetty and Meg in Fairlie.
They were house hunting. We got back about 5.30,
had our tea then went down to South Beach station
and saw Hetty and Meg in the train.

Thursday, 19 June

*Wet morning, but cleared up. High wind
all day. In the early morning I went
down to the docks. In the evening we went
round by the waterworks. The wind is most
annoying.*

---

151 The usual holiday arrangement was to rent a room in someone's house, then buy the
     groceries ('messages', in Glaswegian) for the landlady to cook your meals.

152 Herbert was Claude Maxwell's brother.

153 The Lyric Cinema stood at 59-61 Princess Street.

Saturday, 21 June
Sunny day, but most cussedly windy. Took Tommy down to the docks in the forenoon. Afternoon we had a look in at Saltcoats (funny folk there). After tea we had a country walk. I have developed a husky throat.

Sunday, 22 June
Cold, bleak day, and a hurricane blowing. Small rain falling almost all the time. Before breakfast I went down and saw the *Viper*, now about to resume its pre-war duties.[154] After dinner, I walked out myself to Seamill and back. The German fleet interred at Scapa, scuttled by the German crew.[155]

Monday, 23 June
Blowing a hurricane all the day long. In the afternoon we got blown to Saltcoats. Sand flying something wicked. We went to the pictures at night for a rest.

Tuesday, 24 June
We went to Largs today. Nice and sunny, but pretty windy. We got home by tea time. After tea we went up the Dalry road and back by the shore.

Wednesday, 25 June
Warm, sunny day. The first real summer day we have had. We took a walk over castle hill in the forenoon and had a seat in the south beach. We went to Saltcoats at night and listened to the band, and then went out in a motor boat.

Thursday, 26 June
Tommy and I had a walk this forenoon along the sands to Saltcoats. We then met Agnes at the castle and had a seat. Nice and sunny, but blowy. Our landlady was away a drive to Ayr today, and brought Tommy back a nice ball.

Saturday, 28 June
Nice sunny day, but a hurricane blowing. After tea, word was to hand that 'peace' had been signed, so we went down to the boats to see the decorations, rockets etc.

---

154 The TS *Viper* was a triple-screw passenger ship built by Fairfield in Govan in 1906 and operated by the Burns Line.

155 The German High Seas Fleet, which had been interned at the British naval base in Scapa Flow, Orkney, was scuttled on the orders of the German commander, Admiral Ludwig von Reuter, who did not want the fleet to be handed over to the navies of the Allied countries.

Sunday, 29 June

This is our last day in Ardrossan. After dinner we did a country walk trying to get away from the wind. NBG.[156] We spent the night packing up. We are all brown and healthy. It would have been an ideal holiday if there had been no wind, but we got fresh air.

Monday, 30 June

I got up at an early hour, and got the 7.37 Caledonian home. The wind as usual trying to blow the station away. Went home at dinner time and opened up the house. Everything in good order. Agnes and Tommy got home before 2 o'clock. Got all my clocks started at night, then out for a stroll. Amen.

Tuesday, 1 July

Nice, sunny, warm day, of course, now that my holidays are over. Was speaking to Hetty in town today. They have secured a house in Fairlie in August for the holidays. To cheer me up I worked late tonight.

Wednesday, 2 July

Government says we have all to rejoice on the 19th July for the 'peace'. Let us be glad (by command). We all went to the Cinerama tonight. The R34 starts this morning its flight to America.[157]

Sunday, 6 July

Warm, sunny day. After I had broken my fast, I took a walk to Shawlands and had a seat in Pollok Estate. After dinner, we all went out to Clarkston and back by Giffnock. We did not manage to church today. SOS call from the R34. She is evidently in difficulties.

Monday, 7 July

Agnes in the wash house this afternoon. The R34 arrived in New York yesterday morning. She was getting short of petrol, but managed all right. Time for voyage: 108 hours.[158]

Thursday, 10 July

Hetty and Jean in when I got home at tea time. Got shaved today by a barber. First time in 10 years. I did not like it.

---

156 No bloody good.

157 The R34 airship, built on the banks of the Clyde, began its attempt to be the first aircraft to fly westwards across the Atlantic.

158 The R34 landed at Long Island with almost no fuel left. Thomas' diary failed to mention British aviators Alcock and Brown, who made the first non-stop transatlantic flight (from east to west) in June 1919.

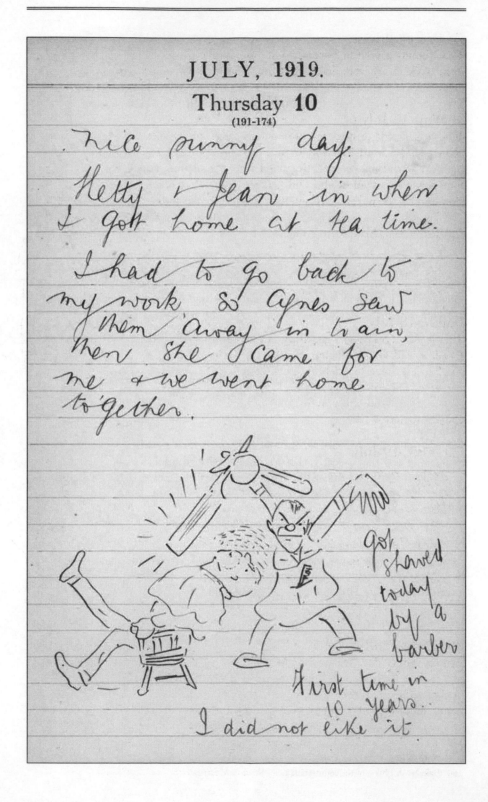

JULY, 1919.

Thursday 10
(191-174)

Nice sunny day.
Hetty & Jean in when
I got home at tea time.

I had to go back to
my work so Agnes saw
them away in train,
then she came for
me & we went home
together.

got shaved today by a barber

first time in 10 years.
I did not like it

Friday, 11 July
Took Tommy a visit to Sweeney Todd after tea time, and then I
went back to my work and did some sweated labour. Coal going up
again.

Sunday, 13 July
Took a walk out to Ruglen in forenoon. Called up at 200 Main
Street. Had a word with Uncle Willie. Mina is in England for a
holiday, so did not see her. Resumed my walk to Burnside,
then home by Croftfoot and Old Cathcart. R34 arrives
Rome today. New York to England by air, time 75 hours.

Monday, 14 July
*We went out at night by 100 Acre Dyke, then
into Cathcart and took the car home. New office
boy started at my work.*

Friday, 18 July
This is Fair Friday, so I got away at 1.15 p.m.[159] After tea,
I took a walk out to Ruglen. See by the notices that the
Ruglen folk have to celebrate peace tomorrow, hang out
flags etc. The town bells will be rung at 8 a.m. and 12
noon, and a band will play in the Overtoun Park. I must go to
Ruglen tomorrow.

Saturday, 19 July
*Seeing this is 'Fair Saturday', I am
off the chain. We did not go out until
the afternoon. We then went out with
Mrs MacKenzie, Willie and Maggie
ditto. We meandered 100 Acre Dyke, then
Willie MacKenzie took our 'pictures'.
After that, they came home with us for
tea. When they went away, I took
Agnes and Tommy to the Majestic.*

Monday, 21 July
Bright, breezy day. This is Fair Monday so I have a holiday. We
took car to Netherlee and then motor to Eaglesham. We had tea
at that village and then walked to Ballagioch and back.[160] We got
home about 6 p.m. We then went to the Cinerama. We went up to

the MacKenzies on our way back to see how our photos had turned
out.

Tuesday, 22 July

Agnes and Tommy at Coatbridge in the afternoon. I went out
from my work by the 5.33 p.m. train. Daisy and I pulled some
rhubarb, which we took home. Poor wee Tommy got his wee finger
bashed in the carriage door going out. Yorkshire miners out. Mines
flooding. Men from the Navy manning the pumps.[161]

Wednesday, 23 July

Agnes was in the wash house. I went a walk at night, 100 Acre
Dyke way. Agnes bothered just now with neuralgia etc. Coal is now
2/5½ for a cwt.[162]

Thursday, 24 July

Beautiful weather. Very warm. We went to the Queen's Park.
For the sum of 1/1 we were allowed into the enclosure at the
bandstand and heard a concert party doing its best. If Agnes'
neuralgia had allowed her, she might have enjoyed it.

Friday, 25 July

The last letter I sent to Duncan returned today, so he is evidently
'demobbed'. When I got home, Mr and Mrs Carmichael were in.
They are going to Furnace to stay, so they had supper with us.[163]
After they departed, we cut up rhubarb for jam.

Saturday, 26 July

Father here for dinner, then I took Tommy and him a walk, or
rather a car drive, to Cathcart.

Sunday, 27 July

Took a walk in forenoon to Rouken Glen and back. After dinner,
I had a seat in Queen's Park. About 10 p.m. Mr and Mrs
Carmichael came in, and then Mrs MacKenzie and Maggie and
Willie. A farewell party, so to speak. All away 12.30 a.m. We
made jam today.

Tuesday, 29 July

We went to the Queen's Park at night and heard the band for a
small fee. We got a chair each.

---

161   Yorkshire miners were striking against revised rates of pay. The dispute lasted four
      weeks.

162   Around 23 pence a hundredweight.

163   Furnace is a village on the north shore of Loch Fyne, Argyllshire.

Saturday, 2 August

Father here for dinner. He gave me the welcome intelligence that Duncan had just got home, demobilised, safe and sound. So I was very pleased. After tea, I went home with Father, got his bag, and Duncan and I put him on to the Irish boat at the Broomielaw.

Sunday, 3 August

I went to the Queen's Park in the afternoon. Duncan up tonight about 5 p.m. His first visit for 13 months. He is none the worse of his life in Macedonia, Serbia etc. The land of crabs, centipedes, ants, snakes, beetles, worms, toads and everything nasty.

Monday, 4 August

This is the day that Glasgow celebrates Peace, so I have a holiday. We went out in the forenoon and squeezed our way onto Saltmarket Bridge, and saw the military procession. After dinner we went to the Queen's Park and saw fireworks and then to town and saw the decorations. After tea, to Queen's Park again and saw more fireworks, and then to town again and saw the great illuminations in the square. We got home about 11.30 p.m.[164]

Wednesday, 6 August

Agnes in town this afternoon. She called in at factor and paid the rent. I broke a few sticks at night. Tommy growing too big for his bed. So I knocked a hole in the end of it to let out his feet. I'll finish it some other night.

Friday, 8 August

Another fine day. I don't feel so fine, though. Seem to have a cold and my head very sore all day. Did some joiner work at night. Finished Tommy's bed and added a sort of draw-bridge to the bottom thereof to rest his feet thereon.

---

164   Following the signing of the Treaty of Versailles in June 1919 (one of the treaties that officially ended the Great War), there were Peace Day celebrations on various dates in the towns and cities of the UK. The square was George Square.

The slow return to peace

The Armistice on 11 November 1918 may have ended the fighting, but life was slow to return to normal after the conclusion of the First World War. Across Europe, the pieces of the former Austro-Hungarian Empire and other peoples declared themselves independent countries, and a variety of unions were formed. For example, between the Armistice and the end of November, Austria, Czechoslovakia, Hungary and Latvia declared themselves republics, and in the following month the Kingdom of Serbs, Croats and Slovenes (later known as the Kingdom of Yugoslavia) and Iceland proclaimed their statehood; in addition, Transylvania united with Romania. The following year began with the Spartacist uprising in Berlin, which sparked an attempted Communist revolution, and the opening of the Paris Peace Conference, which was intended to smooth the way for a new world order matching the needs of the victors.

In Britain, industrial relations were unsettled, as both the employers and the unions struggled to find jobs and working practices that could accommodate both the trade depression that followed the war and the hundreds of thousands of demobbed soldiers expecting to return to their former trades and professions. The government tried to balance a very slow demobilisation programme, to allow the labour market to absorb as many returning soldiers, sailors and airmen as possible, with the demands of servicemen stranded in their barracks, sometimes far from home, who were demanding to be released from service and returned to their families and neighbourhoods.

Rationing continued for up to two years after the end of the war. Margarine was rationed until 16 February 1919, jam until 15 April 1919 and uncooked butcher meat until 15 December 1919. Butter was rationed until 30 May 1920 and sugar until 29 November 1920. The Ministry of Food, which presided over which foods were rationed and what individual allowances should be, was closed on 31 March 1921 after more than four years of regulation. The scheme was judged a success, according to *The Times* on 2 May 1919:

> Both the Food Ministry and the nation have every reason to be proud of the success of rationing. From the moment the coupon method was instituted, and was accompanied by a scientific method of food distribution, discontent vanished and complaints were rare. We believe no country in the world which has resorted to compulsory rationing has equalled or even approached the smoothness with which the change was made in liberty-loving England. It was a brilliant example of administrative improvisation.

There were also severe shortages of some foods, and coal and town gas (which was derived from coal) were scarce for many years, partly because of a series of industrial disputes involving the miners.

Glasgow held its civic peace celebrations on 4 August 1919, shortly after the peace treaty that officially ended the war was signed at Versailles by Germany and the Allied powers on 28 June 1919. The celebrations included a parade of servicemen from Glasgow Green to Charing Cross. In the city parks, dance music was played in the bandstands, and there were displays of fireworks in Glasgow Green, Kelvingrove Park, Queen's Park and Bellahouston Park. Around this time, a committee to build a war memorial to Glasgow citizens who died in the service of their country was set up and began gathering funds. In 1922, the committee appointed Sir John James Burnet to design the monument, which is in the form of a truncated obelisk, flanked by two lions (sculpted by Ernest Gillick). The granite Cenotaph, which is 30 feet tall and includes a sculpture of St Mungo and the city's coat of arms, was constructed at the east end of George Square, in front of the City Chambers, and unveiled by Earl Haig in May 1924.

As Thomas notes in his diary, once the war was over the street lighting was gradually increased to its previous level of illumination and the injunction on speaking foreign languages over the telephone was ended.

Saturday, 9 August

Tommy's birthday. Eight years old. I celebrated it by lying in bed
all day. Not well at all. Been working too hard, I think.

Sunday, 10 August

Got up as usual this morning. Got a headache so took an aspirin
powder.[165] To further the cure I took some cascara.[166] As the day
wore on, I improved and feel all right now. Took a walk before
dinner to the docks. The police would not let me into Prince's
Dock – and I thought the war was over. After dinner (dumpling
etc) we all took car to Rouken Glen. Home by Giffnock quarries
and Cathcart.

Monday, 11 August

Agnes spent a few hours in the wash house at night. Government
going to be very stern with 'profiteers' (so it says).[167]

Tuesday, 12 August

Agnes in wash house all day.
Mrs MacKenzie and William
going to plot at night, so we
went with them.[168] We dug up
a few potatoes and divided
them. We all had tea with
the MacKenzies. Willie
MacKenzie gave me some live
cartridges.[169]

Saturday, 16 August

Very hot day. Sweltered in the Queen's Park after noon. We then
wandered through Shawlands and home by Queen's Park. Great
riots in Derry.[170]

---

165 Aspirin was first marketed in 1899.

166 Cascara is a laxative derived from a species of buckthorn.

167 The government was to introduce the Profiteering Act in November 1919, to punish
     those who made unreasonably large profits when supplies of everyday articles were
     uncertain.

168 The 'plot' was their allotment, probably in Queen's Park.

169 Many returning soldiers brought home their arms and ammunition.

170 Nationalists rioted after being refused permission to march to the city's historic
     walls.

Monday, 18 August

Took Tommy out at night to the Queen's Park. We went into the plot and examined the cabbages, leeks etc.[171] Filled in our ration form at night.[172] And they say the war is over.

Thursday, 21 August

Agnes and Tommy in town in afternoon. Tommy got a new gun for his late birthday. We are now allowed to converse in divers languages through the 'phone.[173] The war is over for nine months now. British squadrons defeat Russian Bolshevik navy.[174]

Friday, 22 August

We lifted the room carpet at night and I cleaned the kitchen and scullery 'fenêtres'.[175] Food going to be dearer than ever this coming winter. Tommy's gun is now broken (perhaps as well). Times are hard.

Saturday, 23 August

In the afternoon I did a big walk to Crookston via Paisley Road and back by Cowglen Road. Took car home from Pollokshaws. After tea we all went through Queen's Park and finished up by having a seat in the Shawlands Picture House. It's the gay life.

Sunday, 24 August

Before dinner I went to the Queen's Park for a little quiet meditation. After dinner, we all took car to Cambuslang. The old wooden bridge over the Clyde there burned down during the week, so we saw the smouldering ruins.

Monday, 25 August

Rained all day. We threw furniture in and out the room at night. Cleaned blinds etc and got things ready. There is a man coming tomorrow with a whitewash pail. Bought two pairs of nether

---

171 The Livingstones appear to have taken over the allotment belonging to the Carmichaels.

172 Rationing of butcher's meat continued until December 1919, butter until May 1920 and sugar until November 1920.

173 Holding telephone conversations in languages other than English had been banned, so that they could be monitored by the authorities.

174 British Navy ships were providing support for the White Russians in their attack on Petrograd.

175 Thomas is using the French word for windows.

undergarments in readiness for the coming winter.
Britain no longer leads in shipbuilding.[176]

Tuesday, 26 August

We had a youth up at night who rubbed the room ceiling with
whitewash. He departed 24 pence the richer. He is evidently not
a profiteer. He only wanted 1/6. Noble youth. We had Duncan for
tea tonight. Glad to get him back again from the Eastern Front.

Wednesday, 27 August

Hung up all the old masters in our parlour suite. We are getting
ship shape now.

Thursday, 28 August

Agnes and I rose at an early hour, and beat the carpet in the
village green.[177] The grass was very wet, so Agnes, Tommy and I
took it out again and gave carpet another touch up. At night we
well and truly laid it.

Saturday, 30 August

Took a walk out in the afternoon to see Josephine's shop, where
they sell little bits of frills and fluffs. Lily's boy is home on leave.
After tea, we all went out through Queen's Park, Shawlands and on
to Merrylee Road and into Cathcart, and car home.

Monday, 1 September

Sent my niece Lily a postcard permitting her and Johnny to visit
us on Wednesday night. This is the day Tommy had to start school
again, but by gracious permission of His Majesty King George the
Fifth, he gets another week. Tommy thinks kings have their uses.

Tuesday, 2 September

Sunny and very warm. Josephine called
into my business address to let me
know that Lily was desolate she could
not come out on Wednesday night. We
went to Majestic at night, but were
refused admittance, so we transferred
our custom to the Cinerama.[178]

---

176 America became the leading shipbuilding nation.

177 The back court.

178 The drawing suggests that the film showing at the Majestic, *The Girl Who Stayed at
Home* (an American film directed and written by D.W. Griffith), was unsuitable for
young Thomas.

Wednesday, 3 September

When I got home at night, James Cook was in.[179] He is not yet demobbed. We sat in and cracked.[180] Agnes in the wash house most of the time.

Friday, 5 September

Tommy went to school today to be entertained. This is the school's 'Peace' celebrations. He got a medal and refreshments etc. Lily and Johnny here tonight. Johnny and I disarmed the cartridges I have, so Agnes is now easy.

Saturday, 6 September

After tea we all went through Queen's Park into Shawlands and home by the River Cart and Mount Florida. Tommy wore his medal.

Sunday, 7 September

Quite forgot to go to the kirk this morning. After dinner we all went to the Botanic Gardens. First time since I was a boy. Tommy goes to school tomorrow. Very sad.

Monday, 8 September

Dull and warm. Have got a bad cold. My nose running like a tap. I'm evidently not well. With great joy (?) Tommy resumed school today after his holiday.

Friday, 12 September

Sinn Feiners giving a lot of bother in Ireland.[181]

Saturday, 13 September

In the afternoon I took a walk over to the very genteel library at Pollokshields, where the knuts can read the papers for nothing.[182] My cold not quite better yet. Great police and military raids all over Ireland against the Sinn Fein rebels.[183]

179 James Cook was a relative of Agnes.

180 The Irish term 'craic' or 'crack' means lively talk or discussion. It is used widely now, but Thomas probably heard it from his Irish relatives.

181 Westminster outlawed the Irish Dáil (parliament) set up by Sinn Fein that day.

182 A 'knut' is someone who takes particular care over his appearance. Popularised by the music-hall song 'Gilbert the Filbert, the Colonel of the Knuts'.

183 Government action against Sinn Fein continued. An unofficial policy of reprisals had been put in place earlier in the month against the rebels.

Sunday, 14 September

*Took a walk into town in the afternoon as far as
Kelvinbridge, where my respected Uncle Sam used
to be a coal merchant (see engraving). When I got
back. Duncan and Father were in.*

Tuesday, 16 September

At night, Tommy and I went up to the plot. I dug up a few 'tatties',
dug a grave for them and then buried them. Agnes came up and
we took home some turnips.

Saturday, 20 September

Got a postcard from Sam intimating that a small boy was born in
his house yesterday. Agnes' cold getting no better, but she is quite
cheery.

Sunday, 21 September

Agnes much worse, and not so cheery. Her voice is almost gone
and she seems altogether dumped. Looks like the influenza again.
A most miserable day. Filled in our new ration cards tonight.

Monday, 22 September

Agnes seemed better at dinner time. Tommy and I went to the plot
at night and brought home some potatoes and undersized turnips.
Put rubber heels on my boots at night. Feel now like 'Spring
Heeled Jack'.[184]

Wednesday, 24 September

Having a parcel of towels for Nellie, I went out to the shop to give
them to Sam and to congratulate him. He was not there. He had
been off all this week with pneumonia. I went out at night to see
him. He was very ill, so I came home very anxious. I saw the wee
baby. Nellie's doing well, but she is worried about Sam.

---

184 Spring Heeled Jack was a character from English folklore who was reputed to jump
     extremely high.

Thursday, 25 September
Agnes took a run over to Josephine's at night. I'm getting very
worried about Sam.

Friday, 26 September
Agnes went out at night to Ruglen. Sam much worse and very
delirious. After hearing Agnes' report I almost prepared for the
worst. Poor old Sam.

Saturday, 27 September
I can hardly think to write this day. In afternoon I went out to see
Sam. He was still delirious. Nellie had been up to see him for the
first time, and was very upset. I gave up hope when I saw him. I sat
with him for almost an hour, and it broke my heart to watch him. I
arranged to come back at night to sit up with him, but just before
10 p.m., Willie Kirk and Ina came up. Sam was dead. He died at
6.15 p.m., just about an hour after I had left him. I just feel this
is the worst and heaviest blow I have ever felt. Sam away. I can't
believe it.

Sunday, 28 September
Went out to Ruglen. Duncan and I and Nellie's brother John and
Will Kirk arranged about the funeral etc and at night I went into
town and put the death in the papers. Poor Nellie. God has been
hard to her.

Monday, 29 September
This is the autumn holiday. Rained all day. Went out for Duncan
in morning, then we went to the cemetery and arranged there.
Agnes went out to Ruglen in afternoon. Duncan here for his tea.
The saddest holiday ever I had.

Tuesday, 30 September
Dull day, and some rain. Agnes baked tonight for tomorrow. Felt
my nerves going at night, so I went out to steady myself. I can't
help thinking of last Saturday when I sat with Sam, and I can't
think I'll never see him again. However, the walk settled me a
little, but I still feel very shaky.

Wednesday, 1 October
Sam buried today in Rutherglen Cemetery. I can say no more, but
it is very hard. Mrs Gordon came up in forenoon and took Tommy
to Ibrox, so that Agnes and I could attend the funeral. I feel now
that I could drop my diary, give it up altogether.

Thursday, 2 October
Fine sunny day. Agnes went out at night to Ruglen to see Nellie.
Nellie getting up now and keeping a little better.

Friday, 3 October
Fine weather. Agnes collapsed tonight completely. The reaction,
I think. She fainted away two or three times. As for me, I feel
absolutely crushed.

Sunday, 5 October
In the afternoon, we went out to the cemetery, and then called in
at Mill Street for a little. Nellie up now, and the baby seems to be
getting on all right.

Monday, 6 October
*The great railway strike is now over.[185]
Men all back to work. I took Tommy
out at night to get his hair trimmed. The
barber gave me a fag to pass the time.
Nasty articles, fags.*

Tuesday, 7 October
Duncan home with me at tea time. Lily and Isa also out for tea.
Tommy getting new poetry and song books at school now. He gets
them free, gratis and for nowt.[186]

Wednesday, 8 October
Agnes spent the day doing the family washing in the wash house,
and ironed at night. I pasted pictures in the war album. Tommy
recited all night. I think he has got another new book at school.

Thursday, 9 October
Sunny day. Agnes ironed all night. Tommy sang all night. Another
new book, I suppose. Agnes bothered with her mouth just now.
Can't sleep at night for it.

Saturday, 11 October
I went up to the plot and dug a few 'pommes de terre'. Mrs
Cormack wasted some of my time on the way home by speaking
to me.

---

185 The railway unions had struck against an attempt by the government to standardise
wages across the country, which would have meant a cut for some grades of workers.
The strikers won their case.

186 'Nowt' is a Scottish and north-of-England expression meaning nothing.

Monday, 13 October

Agnes consulted her tooth specialist and arranged a meeting with him. I'm not jealous. In the afternoon she went out to see Nellie. The one and only 'Pussyfoot' spouting in Glasgow tonight.[187] He is going to abolish whisky. In case I might shoot him, I did not go to hear him.

Thursday, 16 October

Very cold today. My Great War album is now finished. Agnes says: 'Thank Goodness.'

Friday, 17 October

Agnes consulted the dentist man. She came away six teeth short. Her jaws feeling tender at night.

Sunday, 19 October

Nice, sunny, warm day. Up early this morning as I was going to church: Communion.[188] In the afternoon I went out to Ruglen. Met Will Kirk and we both went up to cemetery. None of us very cheerful. Willie has lost his dearest friend and I have lost a brother. I then went up to see Nellie for a little. She says her brain is benumbed with her loss, and I can well believe it. Wee Sammy doing well. He has added about a dozen ounces to his weight this week.

Wednesday, 22 October

Agnes went to her dentist in the forenoon. The last pull. When she came home she couldn't say 'A noisy noise annoys an oyster' or 'Sister Susie sewing shirts'. It is very sad. Man sentenced in Glasgow to be hanged.[189] How cheery.

Friday, 24 October

Working late. Seeing the war is over, there are one or two extra lamp posts lit in Robson Street and one in Morgan Street. Glory be!

Monday, 27 October

Sunny, but cold wind. Tommy not at school. So we had a visit from the officer. Agnes spent the evening

---

187 William 'Pussyfoot' Johnson was an American Temperance campaigner.

188 Thomas, although not a regular churchgoer, attended the quarterly Communion services.

189 James Adams was found guilty of the murder of Mary Doyle or Kane.

in the wash house. I carried one or two articles down.

Wednesday, 29 October
Very cold day. Took Agnes and Tommy at night to the Housing Exhibition.[190] We fell in with Lily, Isa and Willie. Morgan Street illuminations now on pre-war standard.

Friday, 31 October
This is Hallowe'en. As I worked late tonight I did not manage out 'goloshin".[191]

Saturday, 1 November
We all went to Shawlands Picture House at night. Sugar is going to be 8d per pound on Monday.

Monday, 3 November

Paid the blood-sucker his rent today. Agnes went out at night herself to Ruglen to see Nellie. I stayed in with Tommy and meditated on things in general. Half a million miners on strike in USA.[192]

Tuesday, 4 November
Dirty, cold, wet day. As a favour, I washed Tommy tonight.

Saturday, 8 November
We all went out a walk in the afternoon, Maxwell Park direction. The gas is very poor in quality just now. Half the light and double the price.

Sunday, 9 November
We had a dumpling today in honour of tomorrow. I ate my portion with relish. Agnes making preparations – she goes over the top tomorrow (washing day).

---

190 The Housing, Town Planning, etc (Scotland) Act 1919 gave local authorities the power to build council housing. The exhibition gave people a chance to see what kind of housing might be available.

191 'Goloshing', usually known in Glasgow as 'guising', was dressing up for Hallowe'en and visiting neighbours to perform a song or joke in return for sweets or small change.

192 The United Mine Workers, which had agreed a wage-freeze during the war, was now campaigning for a substantial rise.

Monday, 10 November

Agnes rose 'de bonne heure' and went down to the wash house. I watched her from the window in case she would be kidnapped and then hopped back into bed. Lily and Isa sent a little token this morning of their love and esteem to Agnes, this being her birthday. She is now over —.[193] Tommy off school today, having a cold. Hetty and Daisy here when I got home.

Tuesday, 11 November

Very cold day. At 11 a.m., 11 November 1918 the Armistice was signed. Today at 11 a.m. throughout the British Empire, all work ceased for two minutes in silent remembrance. 'The Great Silence.' We lost a good friend also on that day a year ago, so our thoughts went back in silent remembrance to Jenny Roxburgh.

Wednesday, 12 November

Working late tonight. Lily and Isa here at night. Murderer executed in Glasgow yesterday.[194]

Thursday, 13 November

Working late at night. French president in Glasgow today.[195]

Sunday, 16 November

Snowed heavily all forenoon. We did not go out at all. Kept fires going all day in room and kitchen. It was cold. Signs of a thaw at night. It will be a mess.

Monday, 17 November

The great thaw on today. Rained in buckets. However, anything better than frost and fog. Tommy back at school today after a week's rest. The house feels a bit warmer now.

Tuesday, 18 November

Rained all day. Working late at night.

Thursday, 20 November

Raw cold day. Snow and sleet, rain and everything bad. Bought a new pipe today. Had a most terrific

193 Agnes was celebrating her 40th birthday.

194 James Adams was hanged in Duke Street Prison.

195 President Raymond Poincaré.

fall today in town. Every bone nearly broken, all dislocated and internally injured. Went to a quack and got Arnica.[196] Drunk some and got relief. Worked late at night.

Saturday, 22 November
Dull and mild. Very wet and stormy. Got myself a new umbrella today. Spent all afternoon putting Phillips soles and heels on my boots.[197] We all went to the Kelvin Hall exhibition at night. Don't feel so well today. Effects of the fall, no doubt.

Tuesday, 25 November
Took a night off, and took my wife and family to the Majestic. Coal is to be cheaper.

Wednesday, 26 November
Working late again. Agnes and Tommy down at Ibrox at night. Gas is going to be cheaper (perhaps).

Friday, 28 November
Bad escape of gas in kitchen. SOS call to plumber. We had to turn the gas off. Candle illuminations at night.

Saturday, 29 November
The man who mends gas pipes came up and took away the erring pipe, plugged the hole and thus gave us the use of the gas. Amen! Hallelujah!! We all went into town in the afternoon and Agnes got herself a set of 'furs'.

Sunday, 30 November
The kitchen gas makes me sad, so lit a good fire in the dining room and flitted there for the evening. Tommy has got the weekly cold.

Monday, 1 December
Working late. Got Tommy a new overcoat today. It is a hairy one. Nellie and her baby here in afternoon. away at tea time. Coal is now 1/11½ per bag. Lady Astor, our first lady

---

196 Arnica is a herbal anti-inflammatory.

197 Phillips was a manufacturer of rubber soles and heels.

M.P., takes her seat in Parliament today.[198]

Tuesday, 2 December
Working late, of course. Father here at tea time. Duncan working late also, so called in at his place on my way home and took him home for supper. He took Pa home.

Wednesday, 3 December
Had a night off, so took Tommy down to the exhibition of Science and Industry.[199] We got duly elevated and entertained.

Friday, 5 December
Working late. Agnes and Tommy in town in afternoon. Agnes got new shoes and Tommy new boots, in which his feet, though large, will have a large supply of room.

Saturday, 6 December
We got word from Coatbridge yesterday that Mr Crozier very ill, so our visit is postponed.

Sunday, 7 December
Rose early and gave Agnes a cup of tea. Good man. After dinner we all had a walk by Shawlands and back by Cathcart. After tea, feeling in the mood, we all went to Greenlodge and spent an uproarious evening.

Monday, 8 December
Not working late, so sat in and feasted my eyes on my wife and family. Agnes cleaned the flues of the kitchen range today so that we can have more coal.

Friday, 12 December
Cleaned all the windows at night. The world comes to an end next week, says a daft Yankee scientist.[200]

Saturday, 13 December
We dressed in our best and went to Ibrox, had our tea, and then had a musical evening. The young man of Nannie was there.

---

198 Nancy Astor was the first woman to sit as a Member of Parliament. (Constance Markiewicz was the first woman elected to the House of Commons, in 1918, but she did not take her seat.)

199 The British Science Exhibition was held in the Kelvin Hall.

200 American meteorologist Albert Porta predicted that the union of six planets would create a magnetic current that would cause the sun to explode.

Sunday, 14 December

Dull day. After dinner, I took a walk to Cowglen Road and Crookston. After tea, Duncan came up, then Agnes' cousin James Cook. He is now demobbed, so Duncan and he 'fought their battles o'er again'.[201] They dismissed about 11 p.m.

Tuesday, 16 December

Dry day. Dull and misty. The world ends tomorrow night? Here's luck!

Wednesday, 17 December

To celebrate the end of our earth, we went to the Majestic at night. When we went to bed we were greatly relieved that the old world was still buzzing round the same old way. Next prophet, please!

Thursday, 18 December

I shifted the piano at night to another position. Agnes is rearranging the furniture. Tommy lost another tooth today.

Friday, 19 December

Got my hair cut then went and had a bath.[202] Cleaned a few brasses at night. The Sinn Feiners attempt to assassinate Lord French in Dublin.[203]

Saturday, 20 December

Dirty day, very heavy rain at night. We all went to Bow's at night and had a walk round.[204] Everybody seems to have plenty of money and they were very busy. We got a few articles to the value of about a dozen drachmas.

Sunday, 21 December

Josephine here at night, also my father. Some thunder and lightning after we got to bed.

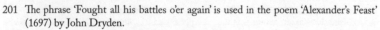

---

201 The phrase 'Fought all his battles o'er again' is used in the poem 'Alexander's Feast' (1697) by John Dryden.

202 Thomas probably went to the Govanhill Baths in Calder Street, which had both a swimming pool and separate rooms with baths for men and women.

203 The Irish Republican Army attempted to kill British General John French in his car at Phoenix Park, Dublin.

204 Bow's was a large furniture and household goods shop in High Street, central Glasgow.

Monday, 22 December

Dull day, rain and sleet. Plumber up today and put on our kitchen gas. Great rejoicings. Agnes spent the day in the wash house. I went down at night and wringed the wringer.

Tuesday, 23 December

Cold dirty wet day. Mr Baxter presented me with a ham today, which I presented at night to my rejoicing wife and family.[205] Tommy wants Meccano for his Christmas.[206] Sent Christmas cards tonight to all my loving friends.

Wednesday, 24 December

Presented Tommy at night with his Meccano. I showed him how to build with it.

Thursday, 25 December

Had a whole holiday today, the first since I started working.[207] Played with Meccano in the forenoon. After dinner, Willie MacKenzie and I went to the plot and carried back about a ton of potatoes.

Friday, 26 December

Tommy got a book from his uncle Bob of Coatbridge and hankies from the girls. My head is very sore and my throat is husky. Evidently I've got the cold.

Saturday, 27 December

Not feeling so well today. Nose running good-oh. The Carmichaels home from Furnace for the New Year, so Willie MacKenzie and I carried down our bed and left it in the MacKenzies so that they could get a sleep. Agnes presented me with a new scarf tonight, bless her. Ten years ago today, my step-mother died.[208]

Sunday, 28 December

Stayed in bed most all today. My nose still in a liquid state.

---

205 Alexander Baxter Senior was the senior partner of Paterson, Baxter and Company, Thomas' employer.

206 Meccano is a construction set with metal pieces that can be joined together with bolts and nuts to make mechanical toys and objects.

207 Most people worked at least a half-day on Christmas Day, which was not celebrated particularly in Scotland.

208 Jane Weir, the third wife of Joseph Livingstone, was Thomas' step-mother.

Monday, 29 December

Spent most of the day in bed, not quite as well as I might be.
Agnes went over to Ruglen and saw Nellie. Cleaned the room
brasses, so there is a kick left in me yet.

Tuesday, 30 December

Went to my work today, but only running on one cylinder, as it
were.

Wednesday, 31 December

Got away at 1 p.m. for my holidays. After dinner I took a stroll
to Greenlodge and then had a look through the People's Palace.[209]
At a late hour Mrs Carmichael and Peggy dropped in. They went
away before the magic hour. We then settled down to wait. Thus
ends the year 1919. A year of bitter loss.

---

209 The People's Palace, now a social-history museum, was built on Glasgow Green in
      1898 to provide a museum and picture gallery for the inhabitants of the East End.

1920

For Thomas and his family, life in 1920 continued much as before, with minor illnesses, domestic mishaps and an extended family full of ups and downs. Prodigious amounts of walking kept them fit, and an enjoyable holiday in Largs gave them some respite from the overcrowded city.

In Britain, industrial unrest continued, with strikes and the prospect of strikes disrupting transport and the fuel supply. Unemployment was rising after the mini-boom that had followed the end of the war, and food prices were inflating. There was also great concern about events in Ireland, where violence and murder were becoming increasingly common. Both Thomas' and Agnes' families came from the north of Ireland, so he has a keen interest in the unfolding saga that leads to the partition of the island and the establishment of the Free State.

In the wider world, the Poles continued to fight the Russians, a proxy battle between western capitalism and eastern Bolshevism.

Thursday, 1 January
'A Guid New Year tae ye all.' Nice frosty day. The start of my
holidays. Nobody 'first fitted' us. We donned our best and went to
Coatbridge by 2.20 train from the Cross. We took Hetty and Jean a
walk. Mr Crozier keeping better now. We came home by late train
from Sunnyside.

Friday, 2 January
Father came here for the day at 12 noon. Mr Gordon, Nannie and
her young man here after 6 o'clock. They gave Tommy a book
for his Ne'erday.[1] We had a song or two from Nannie. All of us
sober.

Saturday, 3 January
Last day of my holidays. Took a walk into town in the afternoon.
Was speaking to Mr Gordon. We went out at night to see the
'pictures'. They were a trifle too busy for us, so we came home.

Sunday, 4 January
Took a walk into the Queen's Park and Shawlands after dinner.
Mrs Carmichael in for a little in the afternoon. We had a visit from
Hetty Cook, now Mrs Mossman, her man and baby.[2] Quite pleased
to see them.[3]

Tuesday, 6 January
Agnes in wash house all day. When I woke this morning I was
deaf. Consternation. Never to hear her voice again.

Wednesday, 7 January
Still hard of hearing. Called in at a chemist
I know. R. Dickson, who gave me some quack
medicine. Agnes filled my ear with a fizzing
drink and hoped for the best. Very sad.

Thursday, 8 January
Agnes, Mrs Carmichael and Tommy at the Cinerama in the
afternoon. Feeling deaf as ever, I consulted my doctor, who
cured me in a few minutes. Great rejoicings. Agnes went
down to Ibrox herself at night.

---

1   'Ne'erday' is a Scottish contraction of New Year's Day.

2   Hetty Cook was Agnes' cousin.

3   Thomas is indulging in understatement.

Saturday, 10 January
We all went at night to see Hetty Cook, now Mrs Mossman, at
Dennistoun. Her baby is to be christened tomorrow. Germany at
last ratifies peace treaty.[4] Kiss now, and be friends.

Sunday, 11 January
I took a walk in afternoon by Hangingshaws and Mount Florida.
Duncan up tonight. Also Mrs Carmichael and Peggy to say farewell
and have a final heart to heart talk.

Monday, 12 January
Helped Tommy to build a crane with Meccano. Agnes got a new
apron from Tommy today. For her Xmas, I suppose.

Tuesday, 13 January
Times are hard.

Thursday, 15 January
Took a run over at night to Ruglen to see how Nellie and the wee
chap were keeping. Agnes and Tommy in town this afternoon. Put
rubber soles on Tommy's boots in order to cheat the cobbler.

Friday, 16 January
Took Tommy to interview the Govanhill 'Sweeney Todd'.[5] Shifted
the piano to a new site in the room. Agnes nearly choked herself
at tea time. I got a shock (so did Agnes).

Sunday, 18 January
Following my usual custom, I went to church (Communion) today.
Agnes came later on. Tommy kept house. Duncan here at night.
I don't feel so well tonight. After I went to bed I had to rise and
walk. My nerves were shaking me to pieces. Oh help.

Monday, 19 January
The old plumber up today sorting our gas. Finally, I hope. Feeling
a bit shaky still, I consulted my medical man at night. I am
evidently run down with various worries, work etc. I got a bottle of
'panel juice'.[6] Shifted the piano again, and cleaned all the spoons.
We entertain tomorrow.

---

4   Germany's ratification of the Treaty of Versailles brought the Paris Peace Conference
     to an end, and inaugurated the League of Nations, which was to guard the peace.

5   Thomas means the barber, referring to Sweeney Todd, a fictional Victorian barber
     who killed his customers, robbed them and made them into pies.

6   People with long-term health issues were assessed by a panel appointed by the
     National Heath Insurance Medical Service, which provided some sick pay. Thomas is
     making a humorous reference to this system with the term 'panel juice'.

JANUARY, 1920.

Monday 19
(19-347)

The old plumber up
today sorting our gas.
finally. I hope
feeling a bit
shaky still I
consulted my
medical man
at night. I am
evidently run
down with
various worries
work, etc.
I got a bottle
of "panel juice"

Shifted the
piano again at
night, and cleaned
all the spoons.
We entertain tomorrow.

19/1/10 Maxwell · t in George Sqr Election.

Tuesday, 20 January

Had a headache in afternoon. Took an aspirin tablet, which did the trick. Having a big night. We entertained all Greenlodge except Isa, who was otherwise engaged. They departed about 11 p.m. I felt no bad effects.

Wednesday, 21 January

Agnes washing the family linen in the house made for the purpose, to wit – the wash house. To reward her, I took her and Tommy to the Majestic. We came home duly thrilled and elevated. I'm feeling a bit better.

Thursday, 22 January

Agnes finishing her wash house labours today. My nerves seem to be improving. My cold still hanging about.

Friday, 23 January

Agnes using the hot iron all night. Have a tight sort of feeling in my chest.

Saturday, 24 January

After dinner, felt very sleepy. No doubt the effect of the bottle I take. Seems to be chloroform. Lay down in bed till tea time. After tea I went round and saw the man of medicine. My chest quite sore. Doctor says the cold will go away in due course. Got another bottle as before. Here's tae ye.[7]

Sunday, 25 January

Stayed in bed a good part of the day. Doctor says I need sleep. Mrs MacKenzie came up for a little. I'm feeling a lot better today. My chest all right again.

Monday, 26 January

Agnes in town in forenoon to see her dentist. She has to go back in three weeks. Helped Willie MacKenzie up with the bed they had borrowed. Mrs MacKenzie also in for a little. Don't feel so well. Cold in my head pretty bad.

Tuesday, 27 January

Agnes seems to be dumped a little. She has had an anxious time.

---

7   A Scottish toast, more associated with a different type of bottle.

Wednesday, 28 January
My nose seems to be in a liquid sort of state. Put caoutchouc heels on Agnes' boots and then we adventured to our favourite picture 'howff'.[8]

Friday, 30 January
Agnes went down to Ibrox after dinner and was home at tea time. Went to my doctor and got a new bottle. A tonic this time.

Saturday, 31 January
A hurricane of a day. Shortly after dinner time, thinking a little fresh air would do me no harm, I took a walk round the dike numbering 100 acres.[9] I got plenty of air, bags of it.

Sunday, 1 February
Terrific hurricane during the night. Thunder, lightning, wind and rain. Agnes in a fever about it. TCL calm and collected. I'll need to get Agnes a bottle. Duncan here at night. He was not very well.

Monday, 2 February
When I got home, Hetty Cook (Mrs Mossman) and her wee baby were in. He is a nice wee fellow. James Cook arrived later on. Hetty had a very bad cold.

Tuesday, 3 February
We all at Greenlodge tonight for our tea. Got home 11.25 p.m. Nice moonlit night. Am quite vigorous again. Tommy got a cough. Maybe the whooping variety? Who's Hooper? We kept him off school today and yesterday.

Wednesday, 4 February
Agnes in washing house all day. Seeing I'm keeping so well, we all went to Majestic at night. A man murdered in Queen's Park recreation ground.[10] He stayed round in Robson Street. Great excitement.

Friday, 6 February
Agnes got a touch of the cold. I am top dog now. Was over an hour getting home from my work. Agnes in a fever. She thought I

---

8   'Caoutchouc' is another name for natural rubber; 'howff' is a Scots word for meeting
      place.

9   The Hundred Acre Dyke was an area of grassland in Cathcart, in the south of the
      city.

10   Henry Senior, aged 35, of 50 Robson Street in Govanhill.

was waylaid and assassinated. Great joy when I turned up. Agnes ironed all night. My health is now excellent.

Saturday, 7 February

After I went to my work this morning a suspicious looking character tried to get in, and Agnes threw him down the stairs. We all out by Shawlands in afternoon. We were speaking to Claude and Herbert Maxwell.

Sunday, 8 February
Took a walk myself after dinner, round by Pollokshields and Crossmyloof direction. Agnes and Tommy went to the kirk at night and I worshipped at home. No visitors tonight. This will never do.

Monday, 9 February
Visited the Italian nobleman who trims my hair, and allowed him to cut a little there from.

Tuesday, 10 February
Agnes took a run down to Ibrox tonight. I stayed at home and protected it. Bad characters going about. The Queen's Park murderers arrested in Belfast. Two men and two females.[11] Agnes got her pocket picked in car tonight, but only her hanky was taken.

Thursday, 12 February
Agnes cleaned the windows tonight (I'm ashamed to say). I cleaned spoons and room fire brasses. Ten years ago today, Agnes and I secured our first house, at 20 Morgan Street.

Wednesday, 18 February

We amused ourselves at night with cards, Meccano etc.

---

11 James Rollins, Albert Fraser, Elizabeth Stewart and Helen White were arrested on suspicion of murdering Henry Senior.

Sunday, 22 February
Took a walk after dinner by Paisley Road and home by
Pollokshields. Duncan and Pa here at tea time. A little later
James Cook arrived.

Tuesday, 24 February
This date 10 years ago, Agnes and I had our tea in Cranstons,
then went to the Pavilion pantomime.[12] Tonight we had our tea at
home (much better) and then went to the Majestic.

Wednesday, 25 February
Took Tommy round to the hair specialist after tea. Agnes at
dentist in the afternoon. She has to go back next Monday. Our tax
collector from the kirk up at night. After she went, Agnes spent
the night ironing things.

Thursday, 26 February
Sugar is very scarce.

Friday, 27 February
We all went into town at night. In a frivolous sort of mood, we
went into the Grand Central Picture House.[13] A female asked me
the time there, but my 'gold hunter' is laid up for repairs.[14]

Saturday, 28 February
Blowing a gale all day. We went out in the afternoon. Got blown
through the Queen's Park and then into a Rouken Glen car. We sat
tight and did the circular tour.

Monday, 1 March
Agnes went to her dentist and got her last tooth abolished. She has
to go back in about a fortnight. I cleaned all the spoons and jam
pan at night. Lily rung me up today. Johnny is now a free man and
they are going to visit us.[15]

---

12   There were a number of Miss Cranston's Tearooms in Glasgow, founded by Catherine
     Cranston, which offered good food in pleasant surroundings. A number of the
     tearooms had been designed by Charles Rennie Mackintosh. The Pavilion Theatre is
     in Renfield Street.

13   The Grand Central was at 18-22 Jamaica Street. The building still stands, now used
     as an amusement arcade, the Sub Club and the Classic Grand music venue.

14   A hunter watch is a pocket watch with a hinged cover to protect the glass. Thomas is
     suggesting that his watch is gold, implying some wealth.

15   Lily is Thomas' niece. Her husband has been demobbed.

The silver screen

The first dedicated cinemas in Glasgow were all in Sauchiehall Street: the Charing Cross Electric Theatre, at 500–516, opened in May 1910 (now a casino); the West End Electric Theatre, at 535, opened in June 1910 (now Charing Cross Post Office); and the Glasgow Picture House, at 140, opened in December 1910 (now part of the Savoy Centre). As the popularity of 'going to the pictures' increased, every district of the city had its own cinemas. The Cinematograph Act of 1909 gave local authorities powers to license cinemas, and the increasing popularity of the medium is reflected in the fact that Glasgow Corporation issued more than 50 licences in the years 1910 and 1911. Most of these new cinemas were in the crowded districts in the east and south of the city, where they quickly replaced the music hall in the affections of the locals. These cinemas included the BB Pictures in Commercial Road, Gorbals; Pringle's Picture Palace in Watson Street; Annfield Halls at 699 Gallowgate; and the Whitevale Theatre, also in Gallowgate (all now demolished). The third wave of cinemas was built in the city centre, where large audiences with more money were an attractive incentive to provide plush surroundings, including tearooms and confectionery stalls.

La Scala, with seating for 1,000 people, opened at 147–163 Sauchiehall Street in 1912 (now a bookshop), and suburban cinemas with capacities of 1,500 and more began to appear, such as the BB Cinerama at 201 Victoria Road in 1922 (now demolished). By the Depression years, Glasgow had more than 130 cinemas, more per head than any city outside America. Green's Playhouse, which opened in 1927 at 126 Renfield Street, had 4,368 seats, making it the largest cinema in Europe at the time (later the Apollo; now demolished). Glasgow was 'Cinema City'.

Going to the movies began before the days of dedicated cinemas, of course. The first recorded showings of moving pictures was in December 1896, in an unlit shop unit in – where else – Sauchiehall

Street (location unknown), and in Walter Wilson's Colosseum Warehouse in Jamaica Street (now demolished). E.H. Bostock began showing films as part of the programme at his Scottish Zoo and Variety Circus in New City Road in 1897 (now demolished), and Arthur Hubner introduced moving pictures to the variety performances in Hengler's Circus at 320–330 Sauchiehall Street in the same year (now part of the ABC music venue). Later, Hubner transferred this attraction to the Britannia Music Hall at 113–117 Trongate (later the Panopticon). George Green introduced moving pictures into his carnival in the Old Barracks Yard (off Gallowgate near Barracks Street) and at Vinegarhill (off Gallowgate near Millerston Street).

The quality of these shows was not of the standard expected now. The *Glasgow Herald*, looking back at the history of cinema in Glasgow in August 1937, noted:

> The crude pictures of those early days gave little
> indication of the films as we know them. The
> defectiveness of the mechanical transmission of
> the action photography to the screen persisted over
> a considerable period. The flickering was a great
> difficulty, not overcome satisfactorily even a decade
> later. Still, there was more than mere novelty in the
> attraction of the living picture even in its infancy,
> and when comedy sketches were added to the scenic
> subjects, it throve in spite of all its blemishes.

The Glen Cinema disaster, which Thomas noted in his diary, occurred in Paisley on 31 December 1929. During a children's matinee show, a freshly shown reel of nitro-cellulose film was put back in its metal box, when it began to billow thick black smoke. The smoke filtered from the spool room into the auditorium, where about 1,000 children were enjoying the show. Panic set in, and children began to stampede towards the fire escape that led to Dyers' Wind. What began as a panic ended in disaster, as the door would not open. Not only was it designed to open inward; it was also padlocked. A total of 70 children were crushed to death in the worst cinema disaster in British history.

There is a plaque on the building, which is now a furniture shop, indicating that there is a memorial to the children in Hawkhead Cemetery in Paisley.

With thanks to the Scottish Cinemas and Theatres Project (www.scottishcinemas.org.uk).

Saturday, 6 March

Seeing that it is spring time, I went out to Ruglen and had a word with my tailor. Took home a pattern book to go into at my leisure. It's a serious matter now, getting a suit.

Sunday, 7 March

I went to church in the forenoon. After dinner I took a big walk by Shawlands and Cathcart. After tea we all went to church, subject: 'Isaac who digged the wells.'[16] Quite a round of pleasures I've had today.

Monday, 8 March

Agnes in wash house all day. Went out to my tailor and showed him what sort of suit I wanted. I'll get it in about three months, and I think it will cost less than a hundred pounds.[17] These are the days.

Tuesday, 9 March

Agnes ironed all night and I took a run down to Ibrox. Food is going up in price again. Put in an application for 30 pounds of sugar for making jam. These are the stirring times.

Thursday, 11 March

Agnes took a run out to see Nellie in the afternoon. I played Agnes a game of cards and got duffed. I am not feeling extra well tonight.

Friday, 12 March

Did not feel like rising this morning, so stayed in bed all day. Got up at tea time.

Saturday, 13 March

Stayed in bed till dinner time. Head sore, nose running and spluttering generally. Looks as if I have a touch of the cold. Poor fellow.

Sunday, 14 March

Up all day. Head sore, but not so bad generally. Agnes and Tommy at church in the morning. Bright cold day. Duncan and Father here at night.

---

16   See Genesis, chapter 26.

17   Thomas is exaggerating both the price of his suit and how long he will have to wait.

Monday, 15 March

Went to my work today feeling 'wonderful'. When I got home, Tommy not so well, sore head. Put him to bed a little earlier. A little later, Agnes feels bad, so she goes to bed a little earlier. Looks as if she has the cold.

Tuesday, 16 March

My head still stuffy. Agnes and Tommy not so bad again. Threaded some spools for Agnes at night, and tried to assist her by doing some sewing on the machine. She was not much assisted.

Saturday, 20 March

After dinner, I took a walk round by Mount Florida. Got some real butter to my tea tonight. It was made years ago, I think, but it was fine.

Sunday, 21 March

Agnes not able to rise in the morning. I fed her in bed, but she revived somewhat after dinner time and got up. Thinking a little fresh air and a walk would do her good, and it being a nice day, we went round the 100 acre and home by Cathcart. She felt a bit fresher at night.

Monday, 22 March

Sugar up today to 10 pence per pound. Before the war we got seven pounds for one shilling. Agnes at dentist in forenoon. Got measured for her new ivories. To encourage free trade, I bought Tommy a gun. 'Made in Germany.' Agnes in wash house at night. I went down for a little and did a wee bit 'caw'.[18]

Tuesday, 23 March

Agnes washed all day in the lethal chamber down by the back green. She ironed all night. To encourage her, I gave her a little music.

Wednesday, 24 March

Dull sort of day, some rain at night. Agnes went and had a consultation with her medical man at night. He gave her a bottle and I put her under observation, so to speak. After this, she went down to Ibrox.

---

18   The Scots word 'caw' means to turn, so Thomas was turning the clothes mangle.

Thursday, 25 March

Agnes does not seem so well today. I cleaned the brasses and Agnes ironed all my collars and much abused hankys.

Friday, 26 March

Agnes at her dentist in the forenoon and got a 'fit on' in a dental sense. We frivolled at the Majestic at night. Folk being murdered every day in dear old Dublin.[19]

Saturday, 27 March

Tommy and I out for a walk in the afternoon round by Pollokshields. Saw eggs today at 2/9 per dozen. Of course I used to see them at 11 pence per dozen.

Sunday, 28 March

Took a walk into the city, up by Charing Cross and back by New City Road. Had a quiet evening at home. Agnes read a love story and I read my Bible.[20] Tommy studied the world's history.

Monday, 29 March

Not keeping well, so went to doctor. He gave me a powder which seemed very powerful. I have a touch of flatulence and a pain in my side. Tommy in bed sick. He has the cold. Duncan here at night.

Wednesday, 31 March

Agnes at dentist in forenoon and got a final fit on. Tommy up today. Agnes consulted her medical man tonight. He wants to see me again. I'm evidently not well. Took a walk out by Ruglen at night.

Thursday, 1 April

The minister and elder gave us a visit tonight. We did not discuss football or horseracing. Gave the kitchen pulley pole a coat of white enamel.[21]

---

19 There were many disturbances in Ireland at the time, and the first of the Black and Tans (former British soldiers recruited by the Royal Irish Constabulary to suppress Republicans by any means necessary) had arrived on 25 March.

20 Thomas may be joking about the Bible.

21 A pulley is a metal frame with horizontal wooden poles used for drying washing. It is raised and lowered on a rope that runs through pulley wheels attached to the ceiling.

Friday, 2 April

Got away at 1 p.m. for Easter holidays. Agnes went into dentist in afternoon and got her teeth. She does not feel at home with them. I went to doctor at night and got examined for my pain. Not the heart or lungs, just flatulence. Got a bottle. Took a run over to Greenlodge myself at night.

Saturday, 3 April

Dull, cold day. Some wind. I am on holiday. None of us anywhere today. Agnes not keeping well yet. The bottle doing its work right well with me. Took a walk in afternoon by Pollokshields and through Pollok Estate. Think I am going to get better.

Sunday, 4 April

Dull, gloomy day, no wind at all. Wet evening. Feeling better today than I have been. Being Easter Sunday, I ate twice my usual allowance of egg. Took a walk today, down by Govan, along Craigton Road into Paisley Road and had a seat in Bellahouston Park. Looked like rain, so car home.

Monday, 5 April

Being a holiday, I did not go to my work. Instead of going to the coast, we took the car to Paisley then walked down to Renfrew and came home again. Mr and Mrs Mossman and the baby came in about tea time. Gordon sung a song about a certain diver. I carried the wee fellow to the car and saw them duly off. The medical bottle causing me some uncomfortable moments.

Tuesday, 6 April

Resumed work again. Mrs Gordon and Ella here when I got home at tea time. After they left, Agnes went to the wash house and finished up dead beat, hardly able to crawl to bed, in fact. She is not well.

Wednesday, 7 April

Agnes consulted the family doctor today. He is coming up on Friday to examine her. Jack over when I came in at tea time, with a bag belonging to me. Isa came in later on. Tommy and Jack went to the Queen's Park in the afternoon. A policeman checked them for sitting on a seat.[22] I saw Isa and Jack away at 10.45.

---

22   The Glaswegian word 'check' means to tick off or chastise.

APRIL, 1920.

Wednesday 7
(98-268)

Bright day. Cold
wind. Agnes consulted
the family doctor today.
He is coming up on
Friday to examine her.
    Jack over when I
came in a wee time with
a bag belonging to me.
Pa came in later
on. Tommy, Jack went
to the Queens Park
in the afternoon.
                A Policeman
                checked them
                for sitting
                on a seat.
                    I saw Isa
Jack away 10.45.

7/4/10   at dentist.

Thursday, 8 April
Agnes ironed all night and not so cheerful. I cleaned the brasses.
The stairhead walls whitewashed today. Up go the rents!

Friday, 9 April
Doctor had to be up today, but did not turn up. I went to the shop
at night for him and requested his attendance. He came up and
examined Agnes. She is not well. Took Tommy to the barber.

Tuesday, 13 April
Dull, wet day. Daddy Longlegs being shown
in Dixon Halls, and Agnes having a notion
to see it, off we went.[23] I didn't like a
certain notice hung up, so I left them in a
comfortable seat and went home. Spent part
of the evening in a profitable manner by
giving the pole more white enamel.

Friday, 16 April
Agnes consulted at night with the gentleman
who looks after her physical welfare. She got
another bottle. What she needs is blood and
a month's holiday.

Saturday, 17 April
Agnes and I took a gentle walk out to Rutherglen and
up the Stonelaw to Burnside and car home. Tommy
did not come, as he preferred to go out with some of
his hooligan pals. After tea I gave the Langside Library a look up.
Tommy very tired at night and says he has earache.

Sunday, 18 April
Rose earlier than usual today. Communion in our kirk, so off I
went. Agnes joined me at half time. Fine day, though a trifle blowy
and coldish. After dinner, we all went to Cathcart by the Giffnock
quarries. Tommy complained of a sore b***y today. No prizes
given for the missing word.

Monday, 19 April
Went to the baths tonight and got a fresh coating of godliness. To
amuse and instruct Tommy, I built a Meccano model at night.

---

23 *Daddy Long Legs* was an American film made in 1919 starring Mary Pickford.

Tuesday, 20 April

Tommy's class got photoed at school. Agnes in wash house at night. Nannie Gordon looked us up at night. Put new rubber heels on my old boots at night.

Friday, 23 April

Agnes consulted her doctor. 'Continue the bottle.' I played with Meccano. Agnes cleaned out the room, getting her hand in for spring cleaning.

Saturday, 24 April

Tommy and I visited the Art Galleries in the afternoon. After tea, we all went out by Newlands way and home by Cathcart. Smallpox getting very bad in Glasgow.[24]

Sunday, 25 April

Agnes and Tommy at church in the forenoon. After dinner I took a turn round by the Hangingshaws and Mount Florida. After tea, James Cook dropped in. He has now started work.

Monday, 26 April

Agnes met Lily in town in afternoon. Agnes is getting a new costume. I went to kirk at night, and booked seats, I mean took a seat for the next six months.[25] Played Agnes at cards when I got home, and licked her.

Tuesday, 27 April

Hetty Mossman and baby here in afternoon, but away before I got home. We went to Majestic at night. Sinn Feiners try a demonstration in the square today, but get chased by the police.[26]

Wednesday, 28 April

Didn't like the look of inside of door of big clock, so painted it white. Tommy smashed the jelly dish tonight. Great grief.

Thursday, 29 April

Agnes and Tommy went to Coatbridge this afternoon. Looked inside the big clock tonight and then painted door a brown shade.

---

24 Glasgow's 1920 smallpox outbreak affected 542 people, of whom 113 died.

25 Thomas was paying his seat rent, which reserved a seat in the church for his use.

26 The 'square' was George Square in central Glasgow. Some of Glasgow's substantial Irish population supported the Sinn Fein rebels.

Friday, 30 April
Cold, windy day. Some hail showers. Hail gentle spring. Gave the clock doors another lick of paint. Call me early, Agnes dear, for I'm to be Queen of the May.[27]

Saturday, 1 May
I took a walk out to Ruglen in the afternoon. Hetty in when I got back. She and Agnes went out for a little after tea to see the shops etc. Chiefly shops where they sell hats etc, likely. Saw Hetty away from High Street station, 9.30 p.m.

Sunday, 2 May
Took a run over to Greenlodge in the afternoon. Josephine in bed with the influenza. Duncan came back with me for tea. Father in when we got back. Feel as if I have taken a cold. Sneezed a lot.

Monday, 3 May
My niece Lily and her boy friend here at night. We enjoyed ourselves in a nice respectable manner.

Tuesday, 4 May
Agnes at Dennistoun in afternoon seeing her cousin Hetty Mossman. She visited the wash house at night and did some hard work there. I took a walk round by Newlands and home by Cathcart.

Wednesday, 5 May
Agnes continued her labours in the wash house until interrupted in the afternoon by the arrival of Mrs and Ella Gordon. I had their company at tea.

Thursday, 6 May
Agnes took a run over to Greenlodge in the afternoon to see how Josephine was getting on. She is up now. Agnes not keeping so well herself, but did a night's washing.

Friday, 7 May
Shaved myself at night. Filled in 'bullets' for *John Bull*.[28] £1,000 prize for me.

Saturday, 8 May
The great and only Beatty reviewing the Boys' Brigade today, so we saw him en route.[29]

---

27 Thomas is paraphrasing the first verse of Tennyson's poem 'The May Queen' (1833).

28 *John Bull* was a weekly magazine that published a word puzzle called 'Bullets'.

29 Admiral of the Fleet Sir David Beatty was a First World War naval hero. The Boys' Brigade was founded in Glasgow in 1883.

Wednesday, 12 May
Tommy got his school group photos today. He looks not so bad.
Agnes' new dress arrived tonight, and then we all toddled to the
Majestic.

Thursday, 13 May
Working late at night. 113 cases of smallpox in hospital. Time I
was getting vaccinated.

Friday, 14 May
Took Tommy over to doctor and both got
vaccinated. Tommy collapsed after the
operation, so I led him gently home.
Took a run over to Greenlodge at night.

Monday, 17 May
Wet night. Got our lum swept. Agnes went
over tonight and got 'vaxinated'. Tommy seems
feverish. Sugar up to 1/2 per pound today.

Tuesday, 18 May
Working late. Tommy off school today, seeing he has a 'pock'.[30]
My arm beginning to feel sore now.

Wednesday, 19 May
Agnes' arm not showing much sign yet. Tommy's and mine at
the juicy stage. In spite of my wounded arm, I cleaned the room
windows at night.

Thursday, 20 May
Agnes over at Josephine's shop in the afternoon and came home
laden with a few purchases. Agnes' arm looks as if it might
develop. She cleaned some windows at night, which should help
to circulate the smallpox stuff.

Friday, 21 May
My arm sore under the oxter.[31] Agnes' seems to be doing all right.

Saturday, 22 May
Took a run over in afternoon to Josephine's shop. Speculated in a
couple of pairs of socks. Agnes in town afternoon with Tommy. A
pair of shoes for herself and boots for Tommy. I took a look into
Langside Library at night. Agnes a little sick with the vaccination.

---

30   A 'pock' is a raised red bump with a yellow centre filled with pus.

31   'Oxter' is a Scots word for armpit.

Sunday, 23 May

Hurrah! Summer at last. Great sunshine and heat. I went to church in the forenoon. After dinner, Tommy and I explored the quarries at Giffnock. Took a walk myself at night the length of Burnside.

Monday, 24 May

Another perfect day. Agnes in wash house all day, in spite of her sore arm. I did my bit by working late. Rents are to go up 40 per cent.

Tuesday, 25 May

This is a holiday. Beautiful weather again. We took car to Dalmuir and meandered along the canal to Old Kilpatrick.[32] We went into the glen and sat down and sucked oranges. Got the train home. Wound up the day by patronising the Cinerama.

Wednesday, 26 May

Two men hanged in Glasgow this morning.[33] Their day's work is done. Hot summer day. Agnes in town this afternoon regarding her costume. I worked late. Agnes upset boiling water on her foot tonight. She made an exclamation. Queen Mary born this day 1867. She's nae chicken.

Thursday, 27 May

Pouring wet day. Summer is over and gone away. Agnes is in town this afternoon, business – new hat. Left it to be trimmed. To pay for it I worked late.

Friday, 28 May

Worked late again. Agnes in town this afternoon and got her hat home. It seems all right.

Saturday, 29 May

A showground on in Queen's Park recreation ground in aid of the 'broken men', so we spent some of the afternoon there.[34] I made some money on some immoral game and lost more. Took Tommy on the roundabout. At Langside Library at night.

---

32   The Forth and Clyde Canal.

33   James Rollins and Albert Fraser were hanged in Duke Street Prison for the Queen's Park murder.

34   'The broken men' was a popular term for those wounded or incapacitated by the war. The phrase comes from the title of a poem by Rudyard Kipling.

Monday, 31 May

Agnes and Tommy went to Dennistoun in the evening to the
Mossmans. I went straight from my work. Wee man Mossman in
good form. Our last and final 'bawbee' tram fare.[35] Ichabod.[36]

Tuesday, 1 June

The halfpenny car fare is now abolished and letters cost two pence
for postage. The war is evidently not yet over. Went out to Ruglen
and got a fit on.[37] When I got back the man was finishing the
kitchen and lobby whitewashing. He fined us 5/-. I helped Agnes
to wash paintwork and tidy up generally. We got to bed sometime.

Wednesday, 2 June

Took Tommy to the barber after tea, then went back to my
work. When I got home, lady from the kirk was in for her usual
donation. This is Derby Day. Agnes and I backed the wrong
'hosses'. 3/- gone.

Thursday, 3 June

Agnes and Tommy went down to Largs in the morning to look for
a holiday residence. They got back about 10.30 p.m. They had
succeeded well. She met the two Henderson girls from Montrose
Street down there and spent the day with them.

Friday, 4 June

Agnes a done woman. Tired out. I did some shopping. Got unto
myself a new pair of boots, a new cap and a new hairy sort of soft hat
of a kind of blue colour. I took a walk out as far as Cathcart at night.

Saturday, 5 June

Went out to Ruglen in the afternoon and brought home my new
braws.[38] Now I'll be a knut. Agnes took Tommy into town after
tea. He got a new blazer and shorts. We spent about a thousand
pounds this month.[39]

Thursday, 10 June

On 10 June 1910 Agnes and I got married. Indeed we did. In
honour of the occasion we went to the Majestic at night.

---

35 Glasgow Corporation Transport Department withdrew the halfpenny fare from 1
    June 1920. A 'bawbee' was a Scottish halfpenny.

36 Biblical character whose name means 'the glory is departed'. Also features in Robert
    Browning's poem 'Waring' (1842).

37 For his new suit.

38 'Braws' is a Scots word for one's best clothes.

39 Thomas is exaggerating, of course.

Saturday, 12 June

In the afternoon I took a walk through Queen's Park and into the Langside Library to see the latest in religious literature.[40] At night assisted Agnes. I myself sewed 10 buttons on Tommy's trousers.

Sunday, 13 June

After dinner, we dressed Tommy in his best. Agnes put on her new costume, new hat and new shoes. I donned my new suit, new boots and new hairy hat and we went over the top. We got out by Pollokshaws, Merrylee Road and Cathcart. The military was not called out, nor the fire brigade, so we got safely home again.

Monday, 14 June

Agnes took a run over to Josephine's shop in the afternoon and got a few necessaries. Agnes and Tommy presented me with a fountain pen for my birthday. Got my hair cut to make me look well. I may 'click' at Largs.[41]

Wednesday, 16 June

Blazing hot day. Left my work at 1.30 p.m. We took our final meal in Morgan Street and got the 4 o'clock train to Largs. Train pretty quiet, so travelled in great comfort. Our address for the next 14 days is 3 Sandringham, Largs, care of Mrs Gates. We had our tea by 6 p.m., then a walk around. The shows not yet away. Unfortunately they collect a rough crowd.

Thursday, 17 June

Fine sunny day, very warm. In the forenoon I took a walk to Fairlie and back.[42] Broke my good new house pipe. Tommy got unto himself a yacht. There is a fine pond near us. Agnes went up to see the Hendersons in the afternoon. I basked on a seat and smoked. Then a great thunderstorm arose, and a most terrific downpour. Tommy and I fled. I left my stick on the seat. After tea we all went to the Picture Pavilion.[43]

Friday, 18 June

Another hot day. Went out before breakfast and bought two long clays.[44] After breakfast I bought a new walking stick, and then

---

40 Thomas is probably borrowing far less edifying books.

41 To 'click' is to attract a romantic partner.

42 Fairlie is a village three miles south of Largs.

43 Probably the Largs Picture House (later the George) in Waterside Street.

44 Clay pipes.

took Agnes a walk along the Bowen Craig Walk.[45] We saw some
girls dooking.[46] Tommy stayed at the pond with his boat. After
dinner we motored to Wemyss Bay and back.[47]

Saturday, 19 June
Hot, sunny day. Took a walk myself to Fairlie. Had a seat on
the shore and then got the train back. Tommy sailed his boat all
forenoon. In the afternoon we all went to Douglas Park and got to
the top, 600 feet up. After tea I went myself the same walk, only
higher up. Agnes went round to the pond where Tommy lives. We
are having the good weather.

Monday, 21 June
One or two showers, but turned out a sunny, warm afternoon. In
the morning I climbed up the mountains and over to the Greta
waterfall.[48] Forbidden ground, but don't tell. In the afternoon we all
took the train to Fairlie. Explored the glen, examined the tadpoles
and had a seat on the shore.[49] Train back to Largs. We went to the
pictures at night. I'm getting sunburnt.

Tuesday, 22 June
Cold, dull day, blowing a hurricane. In the forenoon, Tommy and
I took a walk the length of the monument.[50] I sat and smoked and
Tommy made castles of sand. Agnes met us later on. After dinner
we all went up the 'red road' a few miles.[51] We wore our big coats
today. After tea we went to the pictures for a rest.

Wednesday, 23 June
Fine day. A trifle blowy. In the forenoon I
took the law into my own hands and climbed the
mountains behind Cock-ma-Lane.[52] After dinner we
all went out to see the profiteer's – no, I mean
the Prophet's – Grave and motored back.[53] After
tea we all went round by the Largs memorial.

---

45   To the south of the town, leading to the monument known as The Pencil.

46   Sea bathing.

47   Wemyss Bay is a village and port ten miles to the north of Largs.

48   The Greta Falls are in the hills – hardly mountains – inland of Largs.

49   Fairlie Glen is a picturesque area inland of the village.

50   The monument to the Battle of Largs in 1263, known as The Pencil, from its shape.

51   Routenburn Road was known as the 'red road' from the colour of the soil.

52   Cock-ma-Lane is a former shepherd's cottage on the hill behind Largs.

53   The Prophet's Grave marks the burial place of William Smith, a minister of Largs
     who died during the Black Death in the seventeenth century. It stands in Brisbane
     Glen.

Thursday, 24 June
Fine day, but inclined to be dull. After breakfast we went to the station to meet my niece Lily, who has come down for a day and a night. We had a cup of tea in the one and only 'McKay' and then we climbed to the top of Douglas Park.[54] After dinner we all had a walk up the Glen road. After tea we had a seat in the minstrel place.[55] Tommy stayed out and sailed his boat.

Friday, 25 June
Took a walk to the 'Pencil' before breakfast. We were all out for a little after breakfast, as far as the 'Noddle'.[56] Came on heavy rain. Home again. I dropped in at the library, looked around and dropped out again. After dinner we escorted Lily away to the station. We went to the pictures at night.

Saturday, 26 June
Fine day. In the forenoon I walked up the 'red' road and back by the shore. After dinner we all meandered along to Fairlie and got a motor back. A magnificent evening, so we climbed the heights of Douglas Park and had a look at Paddy's Milestone.[57] Tommy got a new pair of sandshoes.

Sunday, 27 June
Rained all day. A compete washout. Being near the end of our stay, and being in a fit state of mind, we visited the cemetery. After tea, rained worse and worse.

Monday, 28 June
Nice forenoon. Took a walk to Fairlie. Had a seat and a smoke, then took the train home for dinner. After that, the rain came on for the day. Agnes' two cousins, Agnes and Susan Henderson, up about 3 p.m. After we had our tea, we all went to the pictures.

Tuesday, 29 June
Blowing a hurricane all day, and a bit cold. In the forenoon, I took a walk up the 'red' road and back by the shore. After dinner we went up the Glen road. Seeing it was so stormy, we went to the pictures at night.

---

54   McKay was presumably a hotel or a tearoom.

55   The 'minstrel place' was presumably a music hall.

56   The Noddsdale Water is a stream to the north of the town.

57   Paddy's Milestone is a jocular name for Ailsa Craig, an island in the outer Firth of Clyde. It is around the halfway point of the journey between Belfast and Glasgow, hence the nickname.

Wednesday, 30 June

Dull sort of day, and blowy. Took my last walk round about Largs.
We then got ready for home. We got the 1.45 for St Enoch and were
home about 4 p.m.[58] We found the old house intact. After tea I took
a walk out to Ruglen and called in at my tailor. My trousers don't fit
me very well. Was home about 9 p.m., and so ends our holidays.

Thursday, 1 July

Dirty, wet day. Started work this morning. Called round at my
doctor after tea to give an account of myself. Took a run out to
Greenlodge with the cases.

Friday, 2 July

I cleaned all the windows at night. Feeling strong, Agnes put up
the bed hangings and fresh window curtains.

Saturday, 3 July

Dull sort of day. After dinner, I took a walk out to Ruglen for my
misfit trousers. After tea we took a walk round by Langside. Passed
a picture show we had never been in, so in we went and sampled it.
We saw a certain funny personage called Charles Chaplin.[59]

Sunday, 4 July

Beautiful, warm, sunny day. We had a long lie. After dinner
Tommy and I went as far as Clarkston. We tried a new road back,
and walked along the railway line to Muirend and got on to the
road by the bridge there. Pa here about 6 o'clock, then Duncan
and Tommy Semple arrived.

Monday, 5 July

*Did some late work at night.
When I got home, James Cook
was in. Tommy at the Queen's
Park boating pond in the afternoon
sailing his yacht.*

Wednesday, 7 July

We all went over to Greenlodge tonight. Duncan going to Ireland for
his holidays, so like a gentleman I lent him my bag and carried it
over to him. We got home at 12.10 a.m. Walked all the way.

---

58   St Enoch Station stood on the east side of St Enoch Square.

59   The most recent Charlie Chaplin film in July 1920 would have been *A Day's Pleasure*,
     released in December 1919, in which Chaplin takes his family for a day out in their
     ramshackle Model-T Ford. Misadventure and hilarity, of course, ensue.

Saturday, 10 July

In the afternoon I took a walk to Carmunnock via Netherlee and Busby, and back by Mount Florida. At night I took a run out to Dennistoun to see James Cook and Gordon Mossman. No one in. This is the Orangeman's Walk in Glasgow today.[60] Everybody in the town seems drunk tonight.

Sunday, 11 July

After dinner, Tommy and I took a walk down to the docks and saw boats. We then crossed over the ferry (gratis now) and walked up to New City Road via Charing Cross, and got the car home.[61] James Cook and Gordon Mossman here at night. They brought their canary. We take it in change till they come back their holidays. Gordon and I took a walk out by Cathcart before supper.

Monday, 12 July

Dull, wet, depressing day. To cheer us up, we went to the Majestic 'opera' and saw the melancholy *Gladys*. After that I took a turn up to Dennistoun to see how James Cook and Gordon were getting on. They are grass widowers at present. Hetty is at the coast. I managed home at midnight.

Tuesday, 13 July

Alexander Baxter, senior partner of my firm, died today. Agnes and Tommy took a run down to Ibrox in the afternoon, and got home 9.30 p.m. I made my own tea, then took a walk in Queen's Park direction.

Wednesday, 14 July

I took Tommy round to the Italian gentleman who removes hair. Helped Agnes at night. Cleaning brass work etc. My head seems to be very sore tonight.

Friday, 16 July

This is Fair Friday, so it rained all day practically. Put on my suit of sober black, hard collar and hard hat, took train to Hillfoot and attended my old boss's funeral in Old Kilpatrick Cemetery.[62] Motored back to Killermont and got car home.

---

60 The Loyal Orange Order celebrates the Battle of the Boyne (1690) each year on or about 12 July in both Scotland and the north of Ireland.

61 Thomas and Tommy would have crossed the river on the Clyde Street Ferry (Springfield Quay to Clyde Street, Anderston) or the Hyde Park Ferry (Springfield Quay to Hydepark Street).

62 Both these locations are in the town of Bearsden, to the north-west of Glasgow.

Saturday, 17 July
Showery sort of day, but fine on the whole. I'm still on holiday.
Before dinner I took a walk into Pollok Estate, had a nice seat and
a smoke. Very quiet there. After dinner, we all took car to Rouken
Glen, had a walk through, and then car to town, and home again.
After tea, we went to Queen's Park to see view from the flag pole.
I've seen better from the window.

Sunday, 18 July
Rose at 7 a.m., gave Agnes a cup of tea (and myself) then hied me
to the flag pole of Queen's Park to see the magnificent panorama. It
was pretty hazy. After breakfast we took car to Burnside, meaning
to see the great view from Cathkin. It rained and it poured, so back
we came. After dinner we took car to Netherlee and meandered to
Clarkston and Busby. More heavy rain. Not at church today.

Monday, 19 July
Still on holiday. We rose early, and got an early train to
Craigendoran then steamer to Innellan.[63] Very warm day. Mr
Crozier and I took a walk the length of the pier then looked into
the Royal Hotel and tasted the 'mineral waters'.[64] After dinner we
went out with the girls. We got the steamer back about 7 p.m.

Wednesday, 21 July
*We all went over Cathkin at night. Midges
seemed very partial to me at times.*

Friday, 23 July
Tommy at the pond in Queen's Park with wee Leitrim
and his pa sailing 'Shamrocks'.[65] At night, cleaned the
room windows and overhauled the boots.

Saturday, 24 July
*My small nephew Jack Ferguson was here
today to get a bag strap. The gas man over
today to examine the gas leaks. To wind up the
Fair, we all went to the 'Carnival' in the Kelvin
Hall. We went into the circus and saw cowboys do
wonderful things with whips. We also tried some of*

---

63   Craigendoran is near Helensburgh on the north bank of the Firth of Clyde, and
     Innellan is near Dunoon to the west.

64   Or possibly something stronger.

65   *Shamrock* was the name of the five yachts with which the Glasgow grocer Sir Thomas
     Lipton unsuccessfully attempted to capture the America's Cup.

*the gambling affairs and came home with
three half-pound boxes of chocolates.*

Monday, 26 July
Terrific rain at frequent intervals. The man who
mends gas stoves here today, and mended one
more. Agnes in wash house at night. I went
back to my work for protection. I took Tommy
with me.

Tuesday, 27 July
Agnes washed the family clothes all day in the wee kirk in the
back green. We got a note yesterday from the factor, increasing our
rent about 33 per cent. To cheer us up we went to the Majestic at
night.

Wednesday, 28 July
James Cook here at night. He is just back his holidays. The
Shamrock fails to lift the 'Cup'.[66]

Thursday, 29 July
Speculated tonight in a can of 'Irish Paddy' paint. I'm going to do
some work.

Friday, 30 July
Gave the kitchen mantelpiece a touch up of Sinn Fein paint
tonight.

Saturday, 31 July

*Gave the kitchen another lick of rebel paint.
After tea we took a walk through Queen's
Park and Shawlands. Passed a picture house
and, as they were letting people in (on
payment of a small fee) in we went.*

Sunday, 1 August
Took a run up to Dennistoun before dinner to see our
friends Mossman after their holidays. After dinner
we went along the Cowglen Road, up another road to
Kennishead, and back another road. We forgot to go
to church.

---

66 The American yacht *Resolute*, captained by Henry Walters, beat *Shamrock IV*,
captained by Sir Thomas Lipton, in the 1920 America's Cup.

Wednesday, 4 August
Got my 'Colonial' pipe back today from the menders. Got a note from the insurance people today warning me that my policy was running out. I'll see to it. Seeing it is a dirty night, we go to Majestic.

Thursday, 5 August
A paid my fire and burglary insurance today, so housebreakers are now at liberty to pay me a visit. We went out to Dennistoun at night to see the Mossman family.

Friday, 6 August
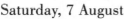

The factor up for his rent. We killed him and buried him under the hearth stone. Brought home a tin of white paint. Tommy and I took a walk round 100 Acre Dyke ce soir. Are we going to war with Soviet Russia?[67]

Saturday, 7 August
Took a walk about Queen's Park after noon. Tommy got a gun for his birthday (which is Monday). I spent the evening showing him how to shoot.

Sunday, 8 August
Wakened in the early morn, meaning to go to the church and see what like it is. Rain very heavy, so hopped back to bed. Turned out a better day, so had a seat in Queen's Park after dinner. Pa here at tea time.

Monday, 9 August
Tommy's birthday.[68] After tea, I paid my barber a visit and got my curly locks shortened. Agnes in washing house all day. Made a start tonight at the paint slinging. Painted scullery roof and shelf white.

Wednesday, 11 August
Rose at 6 a.m. and did some more artistic work in the scullery. Hetty and baby here after noon, so Agnes and them out a wee walk. Gordon in at tea time. He gave me a pair of 'snitchers' to keep Agnes in order.[69] After tea, Gordon, Tommy and I shot the old

---

67   Poland and Russia had been at war since April, and Russia had just recognised the independence of Lithuania and was about to recognise Latvia and Estonia.

68   Tommy was nine years old that day.

69   The 'snitchers' were handcuffs, perhaps brought back from the Great War.

gas mantle to pieces, then I put on a new one. Wee Billy has now got a tooth about a month old.

Thursday, 12 August
Very dull day, but warm enough. Our sugar ration is up this week to 12 ounces per head, and bread is going to be dearer. Played myself in scullery tonight. Agnes is getting impatient.

Friday, 13 August
Rose at 5.30 a.m. and played at paint man in scullery. When I came home at night, donned suitable clothes and dived into scullery again and finished it. Hallelujah! Amen!! Gordon came up for a little at night. He left me some paint and varnish, and a smaller size in 'snitchers'. Agnes can slip out of the other pair. We saw the airship R33 tonight. Agnes made some plum jam.

Sunday, 15 August
Took Tommy to the forenoon church. Duncan up at night. Broke my pipe in kirk today. Spliced it with string.

Monday, 16 August
We have a big night on tonight. Josephine, Lily, Isa and Jack, John Martin and the English girl, Lydia McIntyre.[70] We had a great night.

Tuesday, 17 August
Rained morning, noon and night. A tremendous rainfall.
Great floods all over the country. We got a circular from the factor, proving that he is a poor, misjudged man regarding the increase in rents. We caught a mouse tonight.

Wednesday, 18 August
We all at Dennistoun tonight seeing Hetty, Gordon and the wee Mossman. Another mouse massacred today.

Thursday, 19 August
Cleaned the 'snitchers'. Everybody is going on strike on Monday and no cars will be run. Rent strike. Factor, beware.[71]

---

70   John Martin later married Lily Ferguson. Lydia McIntyre was evidently a friend of the Ferguson children.

71   The strike was called to oppose the rent rises announced by the Glasgow Property and Factors Association, and to highlight the fact that few property repairs had been carried out since 1914.

Friday, 20 August
Fine day, sunny and warm. Agnes in town today laying in a stock
of new carpet.

Saturday, 21 August
After dinner we went into town and got Tommy a new school bag
and various other articles. After tea, Agnes went back to Bows
with a basin which was too big, but the place was shut. After that,
we all had a walk to Queen's Park.

Monday, 23 August
This is the great day. By command of the Bolsheviks the
workmen strike today. No cars run in Glasgow. Being fond of
factors, I worked as usual.[72] Tommy started school today. Mr
Gordon here in the afternoon. We all at Greenlodge tonight. Had
to walk home, of course. Got a note from the assessor, estimating
our net rent 15 guineas.

Tuesday, 24 August
Glasgow sober now, tramcars running and everybody at their work.
Put size in the bathroom as I am going to paint it.[73] It is a sweet
smelling compound.

Wednesday, 25 August
Summer again. Warm sunshine. We all celebrated at
the Majestic. When we got home, I dived into the
paint pot and got a start made with the bathroom
floor. The Poles routing the Red Russian Bolshevik
Soviet Army.[74]

Thursday, 26 August
Donned my overalls at night and finished
the painting operation. Will varnish it next.
The Lord Mayor of Cork in prison on hunger
strike. Said to be dying. Let him die.[75]

---

72   While Thomas dislikes factors, he dislikes 'Bolsheviks' and strikers even more.

73   'Size', also called 'distemper', is an undercoat that helps paint to stick to brick or
     plaster surfaces. It is generally made from animal-hide glue.

74   Polish forces, fighting to preserve the independence of their country, defeated the Red
     Army in the Battle of Warsaw.

75   Terence MacSwiney, the Sinn Fein Lord Mayor of Cork, had been arrested on charges
     of sedition and placed in Brixton Prison, London, where he began a hunger strike.

Friday, 27 August

Took a walk at night by the Queen's Park. There's going to be a big coal strike, so we will get no coal.[76]

Saturday, 28 August

Good weather continues. Wouldn't mind if I was in Largs just now, or even Ardrossan. After dinner, boarded a car for Jordanhill and wandered on to Anniesland and got car home again.[77] We saw a big fire at Dixon's, at the 'rows', four or five houses burned.[78] When we got home I varnished the bathroom.

Tuesday, 31 August

Agnes took a run down to Ibrox in the afternoon. Her aunt is not keeping very well just now. After tea, we went to see how the Majestic was faring. Wonder what I'll paint now. Wild fighting all over Belfast.[79]

Wednesday, 1 September

The lady from the kirk in tonight on her usual business. Agnes made some damson jam tonight. Fighting continues in Belfast: 24 killed so far.

Thursday, 2 September

Got a postcard from Hetty Mossman. They are coming over on Sunday. We removed the covers that have ornamented (?) our wall for 10 years and put pictures in their place.[80]

Friday, 3 September

Mrs Gordon and Ella in when I got home at tea time. Tommy and I went out for a walk. Coal is now 2/10 ½ per bag. Wirra! Wirra![81]

---

76 The miners were threatening to strike over their claim for a pay rise. The government, as a trade depression began to make itself felt, did not want to increase the miners' wages.

77 Jordanhill and Anniesland are districts in the north-west of the city.

78 William Dixon's Govan Ironworks at Hutchesontown featured a row of single-storey houses known as 'Collier's Raw'. The ironworks was known as Dixon's Blazes.

79 The Black and Tans were carrying out reprisals against communities all over Ireland, and the Republicans stepped up their campaigns against the Royal Irish Constabulary.

80 The 'covers' were copper dome-shaped plate covers.

81 An Irish expression of sorrow or deep concern.

Monday, 6 September

Laid in five bags of coal. As the Boy Scouts say, "Be Prepared." Having a little loose change left, we 'blewed' it in the Majestic.

Tuesday, 7 September

Agnes in the wash house from early dawn till dewy eve.[82] A Miss Paterson from the close up at night for the loan of our steps.[83] Took a walk at night, the length of Langside Library.

Friday, 10 September

Took Tommy down after tea, and the hair man performed an operation for sixpence. I then took a walk out Langside way. Looks as if the miners are going to strike.

Tuesday, 14 September

Drew the black line round the bathroom tonight. Assisted Agnes by fixing a needle in the sewing machine.

Thursday, 16 September

Getting nippy in the morning. Broke my pipe tonight. Squared matters by mending my Sunday walking stick. Gave Tommy some hints on arranging his stamp album.

Friday, 17 September

Mended Tommy's bed tonight and tinkered with boots etc. Got my hair cut and got myself a bottle of hair juice to calm my untidy locks. The miners climbing down a bit.

Saturday, 18 September

This is pay day so, having plenty of money, we went down to the Housing Exhibition at night.[84] Saw various nice and wonderful things. We speculated there in a wonderful sort of knife. It skins apples, cores apples, peels potatoes, makes chip potatoes, cuts your corns and I suppose can be used as a safety razor and patent pipe-lighter. Tommy collected a couple of thousand circulars and catalogues.

---

82   'From early dawn to dewy eve' is a standard Victorian phrase, origin unknown.

83   A neighbour from the same common staircase borrowed Thomas' stepladders.

84   An early version of the Ideal Home Show, held in the Kelvin Hall.

Sunday, 19 September

As usual, we all went to church after breakfast.[85] After dinner, we walked out to Ruglen, took car to Burnside, up East Kilbride Road, and down through the Calderwood, then turned to the right and landed near Cambuslang. Escaped home on the car. Tommy and I arranged some stamps in his album at night.

Monday, 20 September

The papers say living is going to be much dearer this winter. To cheer us up we took a turn in at the Majestic. Looks very like a coal strike.

Thursday, 23 September

Agnes ironed all night. The papers say that the great coal strike hangs by a thread.

Friday, 24 September

The coal strike postponed for a week. Summer time put back for a month, by order of the government. Got my autumn holidays today. Agnes ironed and baked all night.

Saturday, 25 September

Very dull day. Tommy and I went down to the Art Galleries in the forenoon. Hetty and Gordon and wee Billy here at tea time. Agnes and Hetty went out for a little. Gordon and I played at 'Bad men's pictures'.[86] Then we disembowelled the piano and cleaned it.

Monday, 27 September

On holiday today. We all went to Coatbridge by 2.20 train from Cross. Daisy, Tommy and I went out for a little. We got 9.50 train back. A gentleman the worse of liquor travelled in same compartment. Not liking his appearance, we shifted. On arriving home, I found I'd left the big key at Coatbridge. The situation was saved with Carmichaels' key and I was forgiven.[87]

---

85   Thomas is being facetious when he writes 'as usual'.

86   They played cards. Games of chance are frowned upon in some denominations.

87   The Livingstones' front door was apparently fitted with both a Yale lock (Thomas has referred to his Yale key before) and a mortice lock operated by a 'big key'. There was evidently a spare set of keys in the Carmichaels' house, across the landing.

Tuesday, 28 September
Resumed my occupation today of making money to keep the family going. Sent out the SOS call to Coatbridge for our key. At night we went to the Royal Opera House in Carfin Street and saw the one and only 'Pearl White'.[88] We came back with the Carmichaels. They are just newly back from Furnace.

Wednesday, 29 September
Father here at tea time. Josephine arrived from her shop afterwards. The great coal strike is in the balance, the paper says.

Thursday, 30 September
Got our key back from Coatbridge. Now I'll be able to lock the door and sleep at night. Took a run up to Dennistoun myself at night with the canary. No 'Vicky!' now. We are broken hearted.

Friday, 1 October
We mended the binding of a large volume of the Scriptures to leave in our pew in the kirk. Since January 1919 there have been murdered in Ireland: 111 policemen. Up Dublin! Up Morgan Street!

Saturday, 2 October
After tea we took car to Pollokshaws, then walked along Cowglen Road. We took the wee road round by the castle, then down the Crookston Road, and car into the town.[89] Coal strike postponed for a fortnight.

Sunday, 3 October
We all went to the church this morning and walked all the way. After dinner, we had a walk through Queen's Park and a look in at the glass house, where they grow winter flowers. Tommy at the Sunday School. He said his text there twice. Good boy.

Monday, 4 October
Bought three shirts today of a heavy make. Getting ready for the winter. We went to the Majestic at night to see what like it was.

---

88   Pearl White was an American film star of the silent movie era. She starred in two films released in 1920: *The White Moll* and *The Thief.* Thomas is being humorous about the Royal Opera House.

89   The castle is Crookston Castle.

Tuesday, 5 October

We all went to Greenlodge for our tea. Duncan goes away tomorrow night to Belfast. He has started a business there with another ticket writer.[90] My relations are getting fewer.

Saturday, 9 October

We all went to the Health and Housing Exhibition at night. This is its last night. Tommy carried The Weekly Record but the Man of Big Aggie was unkind.[91] We bought a little lamp that gives light, at the cost of about a halfpenny per 100 years, or thereabouts.

Sunday, 10 October

We all jumped up early this morning. With my assistance, Agnes and Tommy managed to morning church. I stayed at home for this once. This is the Sunday I usually see a baby being sprinkled, but nothing doing today, to Agnes' disappointment. Tommy at Sunday School today at 3 o'clock. After dinner, I took a walk down to Govan. When Tommy got back we all meandered into town, Charing Cross, Woodlands and Great Western Road.

Monday, 11 October

We all went to our usual 'howff' tonight. Belfast fighting again. Pussyfoot in Glasgow to make us all teetotal.

Tuesday, 12 October

Agnes did some baking tonight. I pasted 'dabities' in my album.[92] Tommy head boy in the class now. Smart boy, Tommy.

Wednesday, 13 October

Lily and Isa here tonight, also John Martin. Miners reject the government offer. Looks like a strike.

---

90   Ticket writers were sign-writers who produced advertising notices for shop windows, restaurant walls and similar sites.

91   This was a typical newspaper promotion of the time. If you carried a particular paper, you might be stopped by a representative of its publisher and given a prize, often of cash. Of course, many bought – and displayed – the papers, and few were rewarded.

92   'Dabities' or scraps were small coloured illustrations that children would collect between the pages of an old book. The word was later used to mean transfers, or pictures that could be transferred from paper to skin, like temporary tattoos. In this case, Thomas is probably referring in his usual humorous way to a scrapbook of newspaper cuttings or a stamp album.

Saturday, 16 October
We all took a walk this afternoon to Shawlands, Newlands and Cathcart. The great coal strike starts today. Export of coal stopped. Serious times ahead.

Sunday, 17 October
Agnes and I at church today. Mass.[93] In afternoon, we all round by the 100 Acre Dyke and back by Cathcart. Jenny Galloway here tonight, a surprise visit.

Monday, 18 October
We are rationed in coal again. One bag this week. Sugar allowance cut to eight ounces per head owing to the strike. Works closing down, tramways threaten to strike, railways make strike.[94] A lively time, my masters.[95] To drown our sorrows, we went to the Majestic.

Tuesday, 19 October
Put on my overcoat today. Several agents up tonight, soliciting my vote, so I made them all happy. Glasgow is going back to war lighting, owing to the strikes.

Thursday, 21 October
Put iron soles on Tommy's boots and plates of a finer make on my own. Tramway men decide tonight whether to strike or not.

Friday, 22 October
Bought myself a magnificent overcoat today. Tramway men don't go on strike. Railway men say they will go on strike on Sunday. Cheery times.

Sunday, 24 October
After breakfast I meandered through Queen's Park. After tea we all went to Ibrox. Put on my new overcoat. Fine spectacle. Railway strike off. Winter time starts in the early morning, so back went the clocks.

---

93 Agnes and Thomas attended Communion, not Mass. He is being humorous, in a way that might have offended some conservative Presbyterians (who attend Communion) or Roman Catholics (who attend Mass).

94 Workers in the public sector, fearing that they may also be denied a wage rise, supported the striking miners.

95 Thomas may be echoing the title of a Jacobean stage play, *A Mad World, My Masters*, written by Thomas Middleton around 1605.

Monday, 25 October

Agnes in wash house all day. Took a constitutional myself at night, round by Maxwell Park way. The coal strike may be settled soon. The Mayor of Cork died in prison after hunger striking 74 days. Foolish man.

Tuesday, 26 October

Tommy fell today on road to school and knocked his face and knees off. Very sad. We drowned our sorrows in the Majestic at night. The King of Greece died. A pet monkey bit him.[96]

Thursday, 28 October

Thomas not yet at school. His injuries progressing favourably. The coal strike practically settled. Ballot next week.

Saturday, 30 October

All Ibrox here at night, including Nannie's 'block'.[97] A sort of Hallowe'en party.

Monday, 1 November

Tommy resumed his scholastic duties today. We spent the evening much as we did on 27 April this year. Tomorrow is polling day.

Tuesday, 2 November

As a dutiful citizen, I registered my vote. New dead heads for the town council. As a dutiful citizen (female) Agnes did the same. At the same time we voted wet or dry.[98] Tommy had a holiday.[99] Miners vote today to work or not to work.

Wednesday, 3 November

Took Tommy out at night and got his hairs shortened. Went out then to my tailor in Rutherglen and got a pair of trousers he was due me. Pussyfoot gets knocked out at the polls.

---

96 King Alexander of Greece died of sepsis after being bitten by two monkeys. He was bitten while defending his dog, which had been attacked by a monkey in the Royal Gardens in Athens.

97 'Block' is a Glaswegian pronunciation of bloke, so this was Nannie Gordon's boyfriend.

98 Under the provisions of the Temperance (Scotland) Act of 1913, local veto polls were held to allow citizens to vote for or against local Prohibition. From the early 1920s, a number of districts, such as Cathcart and Whiteinch, became 'dry areas'. These polls were abolished only in 1976.

99 Tommy was off because his school was being used as a polling place.

Thursday, 4 November
The coal strike now over. Polished the jam pan.

Tuesday, 9 November
Agnes in wash house all day. Father here after noon, but did not tarry as I was working late.

Wednesday, 10 November
This is Agnes' birthday. She did not feel well at all today. Tommy got a new pair of trousers. I worked late.

Thursday, 11 November
This is the day we congregated in the square, two minutes' silence. A most impressive spectacle. The 'unknown warrior' buried in Westminster Abbey.[100] We all went to the Mossmans' at night.

Friday, 12 November
Coal is now three shillings a bag. If I bought 100 tons it would cost me £500.

Saturday, 13 November
Sugar can now be got for 11d per pound.

Monday, 15 November
A hurricane raged all night, so Agnes got no sleep. To show my sympathy, I slept very little. The day turned out just as bad. To calm her nerves, I took her to the Majestic at night.

Tuesday, 16 November
Gave Tommy a few lessons tonight on long division. He seems very slow at it, but had a glimmer of it when I had finished with him.

Wednesday, 17 November
At night, Tommy and I went to the Kelvin Hall 'Engineering Exhibition'.[101] *We were duly amazed at*

---

100 The exhumed corpse of an unidentified British solider who died on the Western Front was reburied in Westminster Abbey on 11 November 1920. The text on the grave (taken from Second Chronicles, chapter 24, verse 16) reads: 'They buried him among the kings, because he had done good toward God and toward his house.'

101 Among the many attractions of the Shipbuilding and Engineering Exhibition were the passenger car of the R36 airship that was being constructed at Inchinnan, Renfrewshire, by William Beardmore & Co., and the PK mechanical arm and hand, being developed by the same firm in its Temple Works in Anniesland, Glasgow.

the wonderful things we saw. We had to walk home most of the way, to Tommy's delight and my sorrow.

Thursday, 18 November

On and after this date, workmen's fares are abolished on Glasgow tramcars. Workmen have to pay full fare like ordinary poor people. I fear a revolution.

Saturday, 20 November

We went into town in the afternoon, and I bought a (whisper) gold chain. Yesterday was pay day.

Sunday, 21 November

We all went to church this morning. In the afternoon we walked out to Rutherglen and visited the cemetery. Sad memories of 1914 and 1919.[102] At night I took a walk over to Greenlodge and walked home.

Monday, 22 November

Very thick fog all day and seemed worse than ever at night. We all went out at night and looked for the Majestic. We found it. Mrs Carmichael sat with us, and Peggy.[103] Fourteen British officers murdered in Dublin by Sinn Feiners.[104]

Wednesday, 24 November

Worked late at night. Old Mrs Brown, of the next close, has just died, and Miss Campbell, our ancient dairy wife, has done the same.

Friday, 26 November

Agnes got the cold very bad. Sore head, sore throat, sore ears etc etc etc etc, but she bore up and did some baking at night. Gave her a hot drink when she retired.

---

102 Thomas' sister Lily died in October 1914, and his brother Sam died in September 1919. Both were buried in Rutherglen Cemetery.

103 Peggy was Mrs Carmichael's daughter.

104 On Sunday 21 November, the Irish Republican Army attacked eight addresses in Dublin, killing 12 British Army officers, some of whom were intelligence agents. Two members of the Royal Irish Constabulary Auxiliary died when they were caught up in one attack.

Saturday, 27 November

Gordon Mossman, Hetty and the wee man all here tonight. Gordon brought two brass shell cases. Something for me to keep clean.

Monday, 29 November

Tommy off school all day with the cold. Sugar now decontrolled, so can buy a ton of it if I want, but I don't. Sinn Fein outrages in Liverpool. Several warehouses burned.[105]

Tuesday, 30 November

This is the day I don the kilt, being the day of St Andrew. Tommy examined at school for eyesight. He passed. Father over in the afternoon, with a most alarming story of Isa. She is very ill. I went over to Greenlodge on my way home. Isa pretty bad with influenza and anaemia. Fifteen 'Black and Tans' murdered in Cork.[106]

Wednesday, 1 December

Agnes went over to Greenlodge at night. Isa seems a little better. I stick in stamps in her absence.

Thursday, 2 December

The female up in the afternoon for the usual religious contributions. Agnes complains that my various pipes crowd the mantelpiece, so I put a little rack up to keep them together.

Saturday, 4 December

Took a walk in the afternoon to Calder Street library. Tommy unearthed his Meccano and built a windmill.

Sunday, 5 December

Agnes and Tommy went to the church in the forenoon. In the afternoon we all out by Shawlands and Langside. Agnes and Tommy took a run down to Ibrox. I went to Greenlodge to see Isa. She is still in bed, but seems to be improving.

---

105 Twenty large warehouses were attacked by arsonists in Liverpool on 20 November, as part of an Irish Republican Army campaign against economic targets on the British mainland.

106 The Irish Republican Army ambushed a patrol of 18 Royal Irish Constabulary Auxiliaries in Kilmichael, County Cork, killing 17 of them.

NOVEMBER, 1920.

Monday 29
(334-32)

Tommy off school all day with the cold.

Very loch night indeed.

Sugar now de-controlled so can buy a ton of it if I want but I dont.

A TON OF SUGAR.

Sinn Fein outrages in Liverpool Several warehouses burned.

Monday, 6 December
Frosty and very foggy. At great danger to life and limb, we ventured to the Majestic tonight, but got safely there. Got in two bags of coal today. Three shillings each.

Tuesday, 7 December
Agnes spent the latter part of the day in wash house. I showed Tommy how to build Meccano.

Wednesday, 8 December
Agnes in wash house nearly all day. Post offices were first established in 1464. I don't have any stamps from that period.

Thursday, 9 December
Agnes went over to Greenlodge after noon. Isa seems to be getting along nicely. Agnes ironed all night and, to my sorrow, cleaned windows. She is threatening to get the kitchen whitewashed.

Friday, 10 December
Agnes engaged a man to whitewash. I'm going to emigrate.

Saturday, 11 December
We all at Dennistoun tonight visiting the Mossmans. Wee Billy walking about now. The south of Ireland under martial law.[107]

Sunday, 12 December
I got up at 7.30 a.m., made a cup of tea for Agnes and myself, lit the fire then hopped back to bed. After a bit, Agnes got up and made the breakfast. I got mine in bed like a gentleman. I did not get up till about 2 p.m.

Monday, 13 December
The man of paint here at night, whitewashing the kitchen. He did it for a double florin.[108] He made a good job of it this time. When he finished we had the usual aftermath to clean up. City of Cork burned.[109] Millions in damages.

---

107 The British government proclaimed martial law in counties Cork, Kerry, Limerick and Tipperary on 10 December.

108 A florin was a two-shilling coin, so the tradesman charged four shillings (20p).

109 The Black and Tans, in retaliation for Irish Republican Army attacks, set the commercial centre of Cork alight on the night of 11 December. More than five acres of the city were destroyed, and £20 million of damage done.

Tuesday, 14 December
We went to the Majestic at night. On this day, the Glasgow District
Subway opened in 1896, the year I started to work.

Wednesday, 15 December
Agnes cleaning out the room tonight. Not liking the general
appearance of the room bed mattresses, we heaved them into the
midden.[110]

Thursday, 16 December

*Anticipated Christmas tonight by
presenting Tommy with a stamp album.
I polished the room brass work. Agnes
busy about the room.*

Friday, 17 December
Isa here when I got home at tea time. I was pleased to see her so
far recovered. Tommy went himself to barber today. I also went all
by myself. Tommy walloped into his stamp album at night.

Sunday, 19 December
Rose as usual this morning at 7 a.m. Made ourselves a cup of
tea, lit the fire and hopped back to bed. After breakfast, I took
a walk out to Ruglen, up to Burnside and home by Croftfoot and
Mount Florida. Wind in the west, but pretty raw, and very dirty
walking.

Monday, 20 December
Agnes in the washing house all day, and it rained,
and it rained, and it rained, and it rained, and it
RAINED. Likewise, it was very cold. Not a good
'drying day', in washerwife talk. Unemployment
getting very serious.[111] Bread a farthing down today.
Hallelujah!

Tuesday, 21 December
*We all went to Majestic at night.
Farrow's Bank has failed, but my money*

---

110 The 'midden' was the bin shed in the back court of the tenement.

111 After a post-war boom in the economy, as destroyed ships, factories and houses
were replaced and world trade resumed, Britain was thrown into the beginning of
a depression. This was caused by the continuing decline in the traditional industries,
where there had been little investment for a decade, and a loss of exports to new
competitors.

is otherwise disposed of." Tried a patent vacuum
cleaner that Mrs MacKay sent up. NBG.

Wednesday, 22 December
Agnes still walloping about the room. I helped a little, a very little.
Brought home a half bottle of the best.[113] We had a small raffle in
the office. I won.

Thursday, 23 December
Took a run up to the Mossmans, and on my way back dropped into
Greenlodge. Isa keeping well, and at her work. Got home at 11.25
p.m. Addressed a few cards then.

Friday, 24 December
Sent all our kind friends little messages of love today. This is
Christmas Eve. Agnes gave me my tobacco for nothing. Isa phoned
me today that Josephine's shop had been broken into during the
night and about £50 worth of goods stolen. She could not say if
the place was insured. A serious loss indeed. Agnes finished the
cleaning tonight. At least, I think it is finished.

Saturday, 25 December
Wishing you a merry Christmas. I have a whole holiday today.
Took a walk over to Greenlodge in the forenoon to see what
further news there was of the burglary. Nothing fresh. Had a look
in at People's Palace on way home. Had my usual Xmas dinner,
then spent the afternoon taking in Xmas presents (maybe). Our
total collection: two cards. We did not go to the pantomime this
Xmas.

Sunday, 26 December
Went to church this morning, after my usual manner. Agnes got
a touch of the cold and is a little fatigued after her labours, so
she did not go out. After dinner I took a walk round the town.
Tommy at Sunday School. Gave the clocks their final wind-up of
the year.

Monday, 27 December
We got a few more cards. We all went to the Majestic at night,
seeing this is Boxing Day. Tommy troubled with a certain looseness
of the bowels. It will be the turkey we didn't have.

---

112 Farrow's Bank suspended payments on 20 December, and a trial of the directors
     uncovered severe financial mismanagement on their part for the previous ten years.

113 This would have been a half bottle of whisky.

Wednesday, 29 December

Tommy got a New Zealand stamp today from Isa that I don't have. Agnes ironed at night and put up curtains. I cleaned windows. Tommy still bothered, so Agnes took a run round to the doctor, who gave her a bottle. I am getting all my good resolutions looked out. I put them all carefully past, on 2 January of this year.

Thursday, 30 December

Cleaned the silver, including the cake basket. It's getting near the New Year. Tommy a little better. His chief diet is milk.

Friday, 31 December

Got away at 1 p.m. for the holidays. Did not go out at all again. James Cook up to see us at night. He gave Agnes a box of chocolates, Tommy a story book, and the head of the house tobacco. He went away at 11.30. We then got ready for the midnight hour. Amen.

1921

For Thomas and his family, repeated illnesses and shortages of coal and gas made domestic life challenging, but frequent long walks in the country and visits to the cinema kept their spirits up. Thomas developed his interest in stamp collecting, and Tommy continued to do well at school and Sunday School.

In the United Kingdom, miners and others struck work against reductions in wages. The administrative areas of Northern and Southern Ireland were established on 3 May, under the Government of Ireland Act 1920, with elections to the two parliaments following soon after. The continuing conflict between Republicans and Crown forces dominated the headlines for much of the year.

Internationally, peace treaties made the world seem a safer place.

Saturday, 1 January

At 12.01 this morning we trooped into the Carmichaels and wished them 'many o' them'.[1] We had a cup of tea etc, then back again at 2.30. After a short interval in bed, we got up. We went out to Coatbridge by 2.40 train from Buchanan Street.[2]

Monday, 3 January

Took a stroll in the forenoon to Josephine's shop to see how the burglary had fared. She told me she was insured, so it's not too bad. After dinner, I went along to the Majestic and booked three seats of the best. We then took a turn round town. After tea, we went to the Majestic, seeing we had seats booked. My holidays are now over.

Tuesday, 4 January

At work as usual today. Tommy's inside in a puzzling condition. We managed to make him swallow some castor oil to try to help matters.[3] Played Agnes a game or two, and she might have won but didn't.

Wednesday, 5 January

Tommy's inside works getting more normal-like now.

Thursday, 6 January

Agnes spent most of her time in the wash house. Tommy getting his meat now.

Saturday, 8 January

Rained in buckets all day. We took Tommy into town in afternoon and, got him an oilskin and sou'wester. Have a touch of the cold. Tried a 'Little Victor Inhaler'.[4]

---

1   The full toast would have been 'a good New Year and many of them'.

2   Buchanan Street railway station, which was closed in 1966.

3   Castor oil was a popular laxative.

4   The Little Victor Inhaler, which was placed in the nostril and sniffed, released menthol and other fumes into the nose. Its manufacturer claimed that it 'destroys harmful germs, gives immediate relief, and promptly cures cold in the head, nasal catarrh, throat irritations &c.' It was made by Cockburn and Co. Ltd, 130–140 Howard Street, Glasgow.

January 1921.

Sunday 9. Rained + Stormed
All day. not out at all.

Monday 10. A terrible wet day
up till dinner time. and
rain again at night.
Took a run down to
throp at night to see my
dentist. as I have an
old tooth or two I am
thinking of giving up.
As it was after 7 pm when
I got down, I got a
reprieve. Tommy getting some
use for his old tins

Tuesday 11. Dirty nasty day.
Went down to my
dentist after tea in
good time and got
one or two old
roots uplifted.
Survived and
walked home

Wednesday, 12 January
My gum slightly swollen, so did not go to my work.

Thursday, 13 January
My face not so bad, so went to my work. Agnes tried some new fancy baking tonight.

Friday, 14 January
Bought a new pipe today of a strange shape.

Saturday, 15 January
Took a walk to Langside Library in the afternoon. After tea we all took a little turn out. The slump in prices is beginning.

Sunday, 16 January
Agnes and Tommy in church in the morning. In the afternoon, we all out by Mount Florida and Cathcart. Not being satisfied with my new pipe, I resurrect my old 'Colonial'.

Monday, 17 January
Assisted at night by cleaning the spoons. Dug up my old hard hat, and wearing it this dirty weather.[5]

Tuesday, 18 January
A certain lady called Mrs Dunn here all afternoon.[6] She was very much 'de trop'.[7] We are having a big night. Josephine, Lily, Isa and Jack here for tea. After that, John Martin, his brother Willie and Willie's chum David arrived.

Wednesday, 19 January
Pay day. Spent the evening studying some new stamps. That's how my money goes.

Thursday, 20 January
First Thursday after Pay! Cleaned kitchen window at night. Picked a lot of stamps off the approval

---

5   Thomas' 'hard hat' is a bowler.

6   Mrs Dunn may have been a neighbour.

7   Too much or excessive.

8   Thomas is mimicking the pre-printed entries in diaries, such as 'First Sunday after Easter'.

sheets.[9] *Brushed all the boots in the house tonight.*

Friday, 21 January

Got a postcard from Hetty Crozier saying that representatives from Coatbridge would be over to see us on Saturday. Got a phone message from Hetty Mossman that representatives from Dennistoun would be over to see us on Sunday. My late typist Anna Boyd dropped in to see me this evening at my work.

Sunday, 23 January

This is Communion Sunday at our kirk. Agnes went herself. I, being in an evil humour, did not go. Gordon Mossman, Hetty and little Billy here at night. James Cook came a little later.

Monday, 24 January

Got a letter this morning from little 'Willi' in Germany with some more stamps.[10] 'Hoch, hoch!'[11] Not out at night. Got a postcard from Maxwell asking us out on Thursday. Trade very bad. British submarine *K5* sunk with all onboard.[12]

Tuesday, 25 January

Agnes in the wash house in afternoon and at night. Bought myself a new pair of boots. Tommy still bothered with toothache, so off to the dentist. He got two teeth out, which will be a relief.

Thursday, 27 January

We all at Langside tonight seeing my old friend Claude Maxwell and the rest.

---

9   Stamp dealers would send sheets of stamps 'for approval', and clients would keep the ones they wanted, and return the rest with payment for the chosen ones.

10   Thomas was developing a network of friends in other countries, and trading stamps with them. It is remarkable that, just three years after the end of the Great War, Thomas has a pen pal in Germany.

11   Literally 'High! High!' in German, used here to mean 'Hurrah! Hurrah!'

12   HMS *K5* was lost off the Scilly Isles on 20 January while travelling to a mock battle in the Bay of Biscay. All 57 hands were lost when the submarine dived but did not resurface.

Friday, 28 January

Had a terrible pain in my side yesterday. Thought I had pneumonia. It is much better today. Got it rubbed last night.

Monday, 31 January

Got my 'fast turning white' hair cut tonight. Germany has to pay, as War Reparation, £11,300,000,000 payable in 42 years, and a 12 per cent tax on exports.[13] I'll be getting no more stamps from 'Little Willy' of Crefeld.[14]

Wednesday, 2 February

Tommy into a new class at school. Standard the four.

Saturday, 5 February

Put on a clean collar, then we all went to Dennistoun to have tea with the Mossman family. Regret to mention I made a slight rent in Hetty's blouse. I must have been too frisky. Factor up today and got his rent.

Sunday, 6 February

Felt off colour. Didn't eat much dinner. Took a walk round Pollokshields and came back in good form for my tea. I likewise enjoyed my supper. Hallelujah!

Monday, 7 February

To give my hard working wife a rest, we went to Majestic at night. Called in at Claude Maxwell's place in forenoon. Saw both Claude and Herbert. They come to see us next Thursday.

Tuesday, 8 February

Agnes in the washing house all afternoon and night. I stayed in and amused myself in various ways.

---

13   These reparations were part of the Treaty of Versailles, signed by Germany and the Allied and Associated Powers on 28 June 1919, and later negotiations. The final payments were due to be made in October 2010.

14   Crefeld, known as Krefeld after 1929, is in western Germany, near Düsseldorf.

January 1921

Friday 28.
Some pain today and
very stormy. Had a terrible
pain in my side
yesterday. Thought I
had pneumonia.
It is much better
today. Got it
rubbed last night.

Saturday 29.
Dislocated my
shoulder blades
this morning brushing
my hair. Very sore
all day. Did not
go out this afternoon.
Dull day.

Sunday 30. Took Agnes
and Tommy to church this
morning. A nice sunny

Thursday, 10 February
Claude Maxwell up about 8 p.m., also his brother Herbert, likewise his two sisters. We got on all right.[15]

Friday, 11 February
Agnes' arm does not seem any better. Either a strain or rheumatics. Railway strike threatened.

Saturday, 12 February
We all at Ibrox tonight. Got some more stamps today from 'Willy'. He does not like Lloyd George.

Sunday, 13 February
Agnes went to church this morning all by herself, which gave me an uneasy conscience all day. After dinner, we all went out a walk by Shawlands and Cathcart.

Monday, 14 February
Hetty Mossman here in afternoon. Gave Tommy his first lesson on the piano at night.

Wednesday, 16 February
Daisy and Peggy here when I got home. They taught me some new card games.

Saturday, 19 February
Agnes' arm giving her trouble. She washed the floor and brushed five pairs of boots, to my everlasting shame and degradation. She took Tommy into town at night, and got him a new pair of boots.

Sunday, 20 February
Agnes not well at all, so she lay in bed. As I am a very unsatisfactory sort of housewife, she got up at dinner time.

Monday, 21 February
Tommy seems very bad with the cold. We gave him some castor oil. Agnes and the Carmichaels out at night. We took Tommy into our bed at night. Not very comfortable, so Agnes hopped into Tommy's bed. I don't think she slept very well.

---

15   Thomas is understating how well they got on.

Tuesday, 22 February

Tommy seemed much better, but kept him off school. Tommy at his Sunday School soiree tonight, and as this is his first, Agnes went with him. They got home about 10 p.m. It had not been a very swell affair.

Wednesday, 23 February

Agnes in the wash house all day. Tommy and I went to Majestic at night, to see a certain "Button Belonging to Alf".¹⁶ Agnes' arm pretty sore at night, so I gave it a bit of a rub.

Friday, 25 February

Agnes went to her doctor in the evening to see what the matters were with her arm. The verdict was 'muscular rheumatism'.[17]

Saturday, 26 February

After tea, I went to the Mitchell Library and studied various devout and elevating literature.

Sunday, 27 February

We all attended divine worship this morning. We had a special service – the unveiling of the war memorial.

Monday, 28 February

Tommy back at school again. We all went at night to our picture howff. Six Sinn Feiners executed in Cork this morning.[18]

Tuesday, 1 March

Tommy in disgrace tonight. He broke our best jelly dish at tea time. I gave him some five finger exercises to do on the piano. Wild night in Cork last night. Six soldiers murdered.[19]

---

16   *Alf's Button* was a British silent film, directed by Cecil M. Hepworth and released in May 1920. One of the buttons on Alf's pyjamas was made from the metal of Aladdin's lamp. When he cleans it, a genie appears. Thomas seems to have worked this into his drawing.

17   Later known as fibrositis, and now referred to as fibromyalgia. Symptoms include muscular pain, debilitating fatigue, sleep disturbance and joint stiffness.

18   Six men were executed by firing squad after being convicted by a military court. Five were found guilty of waging war against the king, and the sixth of possession of an unlicensed revolver.

19   In retaliation for the previous day's executions, the IRA shot and killed 12 British soldiers in separate incidents in Cork.

Thursday, 3 March
At tea time Mrs Carmichael dropped in to see if Agnes would like to go to a concert in St Andrew's Halls.[20] Agnes went.

Sunday, 6 March
I went out for a 'donner' after dinner.[21] We entertained on a large scale at night. Our company included Mr and Mrs Carmichael, Peggy and Alec of same name, Mrs MacKenzie, Jeanie, Willie, Maggie and her boy. I think they all enjoyed themselves.

Monday, 7 March
Isa dropped in when we were at our breakfast, to our alarm. She said my father was very ill and Lily was no better, so Agnes went over in the afternoon. She got home about 9.30. Things not so bad as I thought.

Tuesday, 8 March
I went over to Greenlodge at night to see the invalids. Father not so well tonight, and very despondent. He shook hands with me when I was going away and said he would never see me again. I don't know what to make of it. The doctor said there was not much wrong with him. Prince of Wales in town today, so I saw him.[22]

Wednesday, 9 March
Isa phoned me this forenoon that Father was worse and Lily had had a relapse. So Agnes went over again in the afternoon. She got home 10.45 p.m. Father past recovery.

Thursday, 10 March
Agnes took Tommy over to Greenlodge in afternoon and I went straight from my work. Mary (my sister) opened the door. I have not seen her for about nine years. Father practically unconscious all the time now. It is pneumonia. The end seems very near now. Agnes and Tommy had to go home without me. Josephine, Mary and I sat up all night with the poor old man. He lay just as Sam did, 18 months ago.

Friday, 11 March
Arrived home this morning about 7 o'clock. Agnes already up and had the fire lit. Took my breakfast and then to my work. Phoned Isa in the forenoon, to learn that Father had died about 9.30, just three hours after I had left him. It was not unexpected, but it was

---

20 St Andrew's Halls, which stood in Granville Street, near Charing Cross, was destroyed by fire in 1962. Its façade is now the western entrance to the Mitchell Library.

21 A 'donner' (usually written 'dauner') is a Scots word for a walk or stroll.

22 The future King Edward VIII and, after his abdication in 1936, Duke of Windsor.

a blow all the same. A father is always a father. I went over to
Greenlodge after dinner. Duncan was in, having come over from
Belfast that morning. He was in before Father died. We made
a few arrangements. Agnes and Tommy also came over in the
afternoon. 'The love of life is a powerful instinct.'

Saturday, 12 March

Agnes up early this morning, baking cakes etc for the funeral,
which is today, and then we got over to Greenlodge. There about
12. We got to the cemetery about 1.30 and buried him in my
step-mother's grave. She died over 11 years ago. They are now
united. Sam's and Lily's graves are quite close, so in death they
are all not far away. Mary going home to Edinburgh, so I put her
on train at Queen Street 7.45 p.m. Then looked for the Irish boat
timetable, as Duncan goes back to Belfast tonight. Lily got up
today and seems to be keeping better. We got home at last about
10 o'clock, I think. Mrs Carmichael dropped in. She had got all
our messages. Agnes says a good neighbour is a blessing, to which
I heartily agree. She sat for a little with us. We are all feeling very
tired, and I think I'll now go to bed. 'The darkness of death is like
the evening twilight.'[23]

Sunday, 13 March

Did not go out at all. Taking a rest. Agnes took a run down at
night to Ibrox.

Monday, 14 March

Agnes in the wash house afternoon and evening. Took a run over
myself to Greenlodge at night to arrange some affairs. Mary's wee
girl Jean there. Six Irish rebels hanged in Dublin this morning.[24]

Tuesday, 15 March

Went over at night to the Foresters and closed my father's affairs
there.[25]

Wednesday, 16 March

Wrote to my father's cousin in New Zealand letting him know the
sad news. Agnes took a run over to Greenlodge in the afternoon.
No one in, so she went to the shop and saw Josephine.

---

23   Thomas is quoting John Paul (1763–1825), a German Romantic novelist and story
     writer.

24   Six IRA prisoners were executed by hanging in Mountjoy Prison.

25   Joseph Livingstone had been a member of the Ancient Order of Foresters, a friendly
     society founded in 1838 that provided insurance, sick pay and funeral grants.

Thursday, 17 March
My niece Lily and my niece Jean in when I got home. A very nice little girl is Jean. I went home with them all the way, and brought back the box of joiner's machinery.

Friday, 18 March
Took a run over to Greenlodge at night and brought over the desk, with the assistance of John Martin and my nephew Jack.

Saturday, 19 March
Agnes and I went to Bows in the afternoon and bought some bedding etc. Tommy stayed at home. I examined contents of the tool chest at night.

Sunday, 20 March
Tommy and I went out for a little in the afternoon. Wrote a letter to Mary. Looks as if we were in with each other again. Mr and Mrs Mossman and Wee Billy here at night.

Monday, 21 March
Agnes in town in afternoon about a new costume and hat. Got the 'money' from the bank today and went over to Greenlodge at night with it, but got no one in.[26] Wrote Duncan today.

Thursday, 24 March
Lily and her boy Johnny here tonight, also Wee Jean. Lily and Jean stayed overnight as all Greenlodge are at Fairlie. Jean entertained us at the piano, and Johnny Martin had to go home himself.

Friday, 25 March
The day all Good Christians eat hot cross buns. I stopped tonight for my Easter holidays. Lily, Jean and Johnny here again at night. Lily and Jean again wait overnight. Bought myself a new hairy hat.

Saturday, 26 March
Jean and Lily away this morning. Took a walk round by Pollokshaws in the forenoon. In the afternoon we all went to the Hampden, a new picture house.[27]

Sunday, 27 March
After dinner, we all went out to Ruglen and visited the cemetery where Father, step-mother, Sam and Lily all lie asleep, awaiting the final call.

---

26   Thomas has evidently closed his father's bank account.

27   The Hampden Picture House, which stood at 91 Westmoreland Street, Govanhill, opened in December 1920 and closed in 1969. Now demolished.

Monday, 28 March

This is the spring holiday. Rained in torrents all day. We all went to Coatbridge by 2.20 train from the Cross and home by 10.08 from Sunnyside. Tommy got some foreign stamps from Daisy, so I wangled one or two for myself. Mr Crozier not looking well at all.

Wednesday, 30 March

Agnes in wash house in forenoon and ironed all night. The kitchen blind out of order, so Agnes got a new one, which turned out to be too short.

Thursday, 31 March

Agnes went into Josephine's shop in afternoon and saw Lily and Wee Jean. Josephine living at Fairlie. Agnes got presented with a nice blouse, in appreciation for all she has done etc. When she came home, she continued the ironing. All the miners go on strike tonight.[28] Very serious times.

Friday, 1 April

This is the day you say 'ma gowk'.[29] I gave my ankle a sprain at my work, and at night discovered I couldn't walk, and was exceedingly painful. Agnes gave it a hot bath and bandaged it. All miners on strike now.

Saturday, 2 April

Couldn't go to work today with my injured ankle. Stayed in bed till tea time. The pain not so bad.

Sunday, 3 April

Got up as usual, but spent the day chiefly in resting. At an early hour I put all the clocks forward one hour as we are now into summer time. Agnes not keeping well at all, and I'm not any help to her.[30] Mrs Carmichael in for a little to see how I was keeping.

---

28 The coal-mining industry, which had been nationalised during the Great War, was returned to private hands on 1 April 1921. The government had resisted cutting wages before that date, to avoid a coal strike, but the private owners made clear their intention to reduce costs.

29 Thomas is referring to the Scots tradition of 'Hunt the Gowk', the equivalent of April Fool.

30 Thomas may occasionally make breakfast and polish the brasses, but – for whatever reason – he does not wash and iron laundry, shop for groceries or cook meals.

Monday, 4 April

Managed into my work, and feel no ill effects so far. Agnes did some baking and ironing at night. Coal situation very serious. Many pits are now flooded, and the railways may strike next.

Tuesday, 5 April

When I got home at night, quite a company had arrived. Lily, Wee Jean, Johnny Martin and Jenny Galloway. Shortly after, Isa arrived. It was an unexpected visit from Jenny.

Friday, 8 April

Brilliant sunshine all day. Saw the great eclipse of the sun. The Triple Alliance decides to strike in support of the miners, so we are undecided about going to Fairlie.[31] I took a run over to Greenlodge to discuss the matter there.

Saturday, 9 April

The railway strike to take place on Tuesday, so they say. We decided to risk Fairlie. Saw Agnes and Tommy off by 11 a.m. train, and I followed by 1.10 train. Tommy and Jack met me at the station. After dinner we all went to Douglas Park in Largs, and after tea Josephine, Agnes and I took a walk by West Kilbride shore. The government calls for volunteers, and calls out the naval and military reserves. Many pits flooded.

Sunday, 10 April

Agnes, Tommy, Jack and I in Fairlie Glen after breakfast. After dinner, we all went a good distance towards West Kilbride. After tea, Josephine and I walked to Largs and back.

Monday, 11 April

Came up myself by 8.22 a.m. train. Agnes and Tommy staying down yet. Posted Tommy down his other pair of boots. Feeling a bit melancholy at night. Went into St Enoch Station at 10 o'clock and met Jack. Went home with him and stayed at Greenlodge all night. Josephine came up today, and Lily and Wee Jean went down. So Agnes will have company.

---

31   The Triple Alliance was the united front of the transport, rail and mining unions.

Tuesday, 12 April

Staying all by my lonesome now. Sandpapered my desk tonight. I'm going to give it a coat of lacquer or stain. Some of the mines being pumped again. Tramway men threaten to strike.

Wednesday, 13 April

Got two postcards this morning from Agnes. Stained my desk at night, and wrote a long letter to Agnes. Everybody is going on strike on Friday night.

Thursday, 14 April

Isa phoned me this forenoon to see what I thought of the strike situation. I advised that they should all return on Friday night in case. I got a postcard from Tommy and a letter from Agnes. Made a start at night with tidying up. Cleaned all the windows and washed the kitchen floor.

Friday, 15 April

Rose at 6 a.m. and tidied up the kitchen. Got a letter from Agnes at my work saying they would be at home tonight and would I meet them. I would. Word this evening that railways and transport strike is off. The Triple Alliance is split. Went to St Enoch Station to meet the crowd. Jack was there. They arrived about 6.20 p.m. Put Lily and Jean into a cab, then took my dearly beloved and the wee chap home. Spent the evening holding her hands.

Saturday, 16 April

We can't get coal now at all. So laid in some planks of wood. Got the money today for my father's old age pension, so went over to Josephine's shop with it in the afternoon.

Sunday, 17 April

Agnes and I at church this forenoon, at Communion. After dinner we went round by the pits, but found all quiet there.[32]

---

32 The family probably toured the collieries of Cambuslang, near Rutherglen.

Monday, 18 April

We got in some coke today, as we are not allowed any coal at all.[33]
We went to the Majestic at night. The miners are furious with
railwaymen.

Tuesday, 19 April

Agnes and my niece Lily at Dennistoun this afternoon, visiting
Jenny Galloway. Agnes got home just as Tommy and I had finished
tea. Sawed some planks of wood. The coke is burning fine.

Wednesday, 20 April

Agnes spending the day in the wash house. Could get no coke today,
so examined our coal supply and find we are not so badly off.[34]
Seeing we have a gas stove, the authorities allow us no coal at all.

Thursday, 21 April

Got two half-bags of coke today, and
it is very bad stuff. The kitchen blind
collapsed today and nearly killed my poor
wife. I put the blinker up again at night
and guarantee it will stay up for all time.
Got some pineapple after dinner, and have
a slight pain in the belly tonight. There
may be a connection between the two. Agnes
ironed all night.

Friday, 22 April

Tommy got a stiff dose of the cold, so he was not out today. Wrote
Duncan a letter tonight, so that's off my mind. Miners and masters
met today again, so we will wait and see.

Saturday, 23 April

Tommy not out, owing to his cold. Took an airing myself in the
afternoon. After tea, I walked out to Ruglen via Carmunnock Road,
Croftfoot and Blairbeth.

Sunday, 24 April

Took a large dose of castor oil last night, which made me doubtful
about going to kirk today. After dinner, we all went out by
Merrylee Road and Cathcart. After tea, still feeling vigorous, we
all went out Cowglen Road, Crookston and home by Ibrox.

---

33 Coke is what is left once coal is heated to produce coal gas (used for heating and
lighting).

34 The Livingstones' coal supply would have been kept in the coal bunker in the
kitchen.

Tuesday, 26 April

Agnes spent the entire day in wash house and back green. Nice warm, sunny day. A 'guid dryin' day'.[35] I cleaned the kitchen and scullery window then went out for a walk by Hangingshaws, Carmunnock Road and back by Mount Florida. Got a note from the factor intimating another slight increase in rent.

Wednesday, 27 April

Tried to mend the big easy chair. Not being a practical upholsterer or a blacksmith, I gave it up. Agnes has got a very bad cold. The coal strike not yet settled.

Thursday, 28 April

Agnes went over to Josephine's shop in the afternoon. She got home just as Tommy and I were finishing our tea. Tackled the easy chair again and got on much better. Will perchance finish it tomorrow. We got a postcard from Hetty Mossman asking us out on Sunday.

Friday, 29 April

Agnes took Tommy into town in the afternoon to get him a new suit. He got it. Spent the evening at the easy chair … and made good progress with it. Coal deadlock continues, and the government is considering extending summer-time another hour to save daylight.

Saturday, 30 April

Finished the easy chair this afternoon, as far as the joinery work is concerned. After tea we all had a walk round by Pollokshaws.

Sunday, 1 May

We all went to church this morning. We watched some elders being created. I was not among them. After dinner, we meandered out to Ruglen then took car to Dennistoun and had tea with the Mossmans. We all went out a walk by the canal.[36]

35 Thomas is adopting the Scots to record that the weather provided good drying conditions for the family laundry hanging on the washing lines in the back court of the building.

36 The Monkland Canal, which ran to the north of Dennistoun on the route now taken by the M8.

Monday, 2 May

The gas pressure is now reduced owning to lack of coal. To cheer us up we went to the Majestic. Agnes tried to bake with the fancy gas.

Wednesday, 4 May

Police van attacked in High Street by Sinn Feiners. A police inspector shot dead. We all went to Greenlodge at night. The car we got had come through Sinn Fein Abercromby Street and was badly damaged. A priest had been arrested in the locality.[37]

Thursday, 5 May

Took a walk round by Pollokshields at night. About 30 Sinn Feiners arrested in connection with yesterday's outrage. Agnes has made a start with the spring cleaning.

Friday, 6 May

All the Glasgow dockers out on strike this afternoon.[38] We are in very serious times. Agnes cleaned out the scullery, and washed the ceiling and walls etc. Got word from Coatbridge that Agnes' uncle is very ill.

Saturday, 7 May

When I got home at dinner time, Tommy was in himself, Agnes having gone off to Coatbridge. Tommy and I took our dinner and then took a tram down to Bellahouston Park. Agnes arrived home about 9 p.m. She found her uncle in a very grave condition and fears the worst. All shipping held up in the Clyde. The gas is now very poor. D--- this strike.

Sunday, 8 May

Rose at early dawn and went to church. After dinner, took a walk down to Princes Dock and saw armed guards etc. After tea, we all went out by Giffnock quarries and home by Cathcart.

Monday, 9 May

Sawed a couple of planks tonight for firewood. The water off when I got home. To our joy it went on again about 9 p.m. Agnes did some fancy baking

---

37 Irish Republicans ambushed a prison van outside Duke Street Prison in an attempt to free IRA member Frank Carty. Inspector Robert Johnson was shot dead and Detective Sergeant George Stirton wounded. Father Patrick MacRory of St Mary's in Abercromby Street was among those arrested, and a crowd smashed windows and attacked trams in Gallowgate.

38 The dock workers, as part of the Triple Alliance, were on strike in support of the miners.

with the fancy gas. Everybody going on strike, and trade going to the dogs.

Tuesday, 10 May
We had company tonight. Josephine, Isa, Jack and Wee Jean Carlyle, also John Martin. Nannie Gordon also dropped in, having ridden over on her bicycle. My throat very stiff and husky, so I gave it a gargle at night.

Wednesday, 11 May
Got word this morning that Agnes' uncle, Mr Crozier, had died at an early hour. Our friends are gradually going. Took a run up to Dennistoun myself at night and let Hetty and James Cook know of the sad event. Agnes in wash house all day. The Scottish railways threaten to strike on Friday.

Thursday, 12 May
Agnes went out herself in afternoon to Coatbridge. The strike situation is very serious. Next week we are only getting gas during meal hours, and are not allowed either coal or coke. Agnes brought home a small paraffin stove.

Friday, 13 May
Bought myself a hard black hat for the funeral tomorrow. Took a walk round by Pollokshields at night and looked at the gas works. The strike getting worse and worser.

Saturday, 14 May
Took a day off my work to attend Mr Crozier's funeral. We took the car out and were there about 1 p.m. Some rain fell. We left Tommy at home. He stayed in with Peggy Carmichael. James Cook and Ed Campbell at funeral. We got home about 10 p.m. feeling very saddened. I was very vexed for the girls. I know their feeling too well.

Sunday, 15 May
Agnes not very well at all, and not in a very communicative mood. Tommy and I went out for a little before Sunday School time. When we got back, the Mossmans had arrived. After tea, Gordon and I took a walk to Crookston Castle, climbed up said castle and viewed the lands. We got back in good time for supper. Wee Billy upset the ink bottle all over my desk, the wee heathen. We are only allowed gas at meal times now.

Monday, 16 May

Dull day, wet night. Jean Crozier in to see me at business today regarding a lawyer. I took her to a reliable man. Spitted my leg with a packing needle at my work. Agnes put the fear of death into me, saying it would likely develop into blood poisoning. Oh, my.

Tuesday, 17 May

Sawed wood today and cleaned the oil lamp. Damn that strike. Trade going to the dogs. Took a turn round Polmadie at night.

Wednesday, 18 May

Agnes got a hundredweight of coke today. Fearful and wonderful stuff, but hope for the best. Took a turn up to Dennistoun at night with a paint-pot and brush belonging to Gordon. Played a game of draughts and licked him. This is going to be a bad financial year for me.

Thursday, 19 May

Took a walk round by Giffnock at night to cheer me up. We got a bag of coal today for five shillings. Strafe the miners.

Friday, 20 May

Only allowed four hours of gas per day now. None after 6 p.m., so had to light our old oil lamp tonight. Tommy away to a Boys' Brigade social tonight. Agnes and I went out ourselves and dropped into the Hampden.

Sunday, 22 May

At night we all went over Cathkin, and got devoured by midges.

Monday, 23 May

This being a holiday, I did not go to my work. Warm, sunny day. I took a walk over Cathkin before dinner. After that we took car to Baillieston, then motor to Coatbridge. Came home by same way.

Thursday, 26 May

Agnes in wash house all day. Feeling vigorous, she washed the floor at night. Glasgow dockers intimate their willingness to start work again on their own terms. Great battle in Dublin. Custom House burned.[39]

---

39   Dublin IRA units occupied and burned the Custom House in Dublin, the
     headquarters of local government in Ireland.

Friday, 27 May

Took a walk at night to Carmunnock, back by Busby and Clarkston. The coal conference sits today, trying to end the strike. The Glasgow dockers will be allowed back on the masters' terms only. Hear, hear.

Saturday, 28 May

I got a letter from Duncan. He wants the tool chest. We are getting an increased supply of gas from today. We lit the gas at 10 p.m. and got a fine light. After tea, we all took a walk round by Shawlands and looked in at the Camphill Picture House.[40]

Monday, 30 May

Lloyd George threatens both miners' leaders and owners with the gaol if the strike is not settled.[41] Bought a new paper dial for kitchen clock for sixpence. Cleaned a lot of brass work at night. Spring cleaning is in hand. Hard times ahead.

Tuesday, 31 May

Put the new dial on the kitchen clock, and used many strange words doing so. Agnes up to the eyes in work. Got a letter from Japan with some stamps for my collection. Banzai!

Wednesday, 1 June

The man here whitewashing the kitchen at night, so I was put into the room, out of the road. He departed the richer by about a dollar. Agnes then washed most of the paintwork and I put up the kitchen clock.

Friday, 3 June

Weather a regular scorcher. After tea we all meandered round 100 Acre Dyke. We walked on to Ruglen, through Overtoun Park and down Stonelaw. We spoke to Jessie Keith in Ruglen.[42] She is married now. A big dog evidently liked us, as it followed us from the Hangingshaws into Ruglen, then deserted us. We had to have plumber up today regarding the kitchen gas pipe. The army reserves now disbanded.

---

40   The Camphill Picture House stood at 7 Baker Street.

41   Lloyd George was Prime Minister.

42   Thomas may have known Jessie Keith from his schooldays in Rutherglen.

Saturday, 4 June

My birthday. Heat wave continues. Hetty and Meg dropped into my work today. Hetty said she would pay us a visit in the afternoon. Tommy at his Sunday School trip. He got a tinny.[43] This is his first trip and he was quite excited. Hetty arrived about 4.30. After tea we all went round by 100 Acre Dyke. Tommy's trip there, saw Tommy and brought him out, then we all walked to Ruglen. We took car home from Ruglen, then we all went into Queen Street and saw Hetty away by 9.25 train.

Sunday, 5 June

Agnes and Tommy went to church in the morning. I stayed at home and tidied up, in a sort of way. After dinner we took car to Lambhill, and walked along the canal to Cadder, then Bishopbriggs and car home.[44] Agnes did not enjoy the walk. After tea we took a stroll by Queen's Park and Shawlands.

Friday, 10 June

On Friday 10 June 1910, Agnes took me 'for better or worse'. The lady who collects for our kirk in tonight, so I went out for a walk. Looked in at Langside Library, looked out again, and home. The lady who collects for our kirk still in when I got home, but did not delay after that. She is a bit of a blether. The miners have to ballot next week.

Saturday, 11 June

Hetty and Jean here today. Tommy went into town this afternoon with two of his pals. With some misgivings I let him go, but he got safely home. Amen. After tea, we went out for a little with Hetty and Jean. They looked chiefly at shops that pander to the vanities of the gentle sex. Tommy did not come with us.

Sunday, 12 June

After breakfast I dressed like a gentleman and walked myself to Pollok Estate. Josephine and Jack here for tea. We then took a walk to Pollok Estate. Tommy got a prize from his Sunday School teacher – *Tom Brown's Schooldays*, for text repetition. More than I ever got.

---

43   A 'tinny' was a tin mug, which could be hung on the shoulder on a string.

44   The canal was the Forth and Clyde Canal.

Monday, 13 June
Agnes in wash house morning, noon and night. Got our census
paper today. A wonderful document. Wild weekend in Belfast.
Murder and battle. 11 killed.[45]

Tuesday, 14 June
To celebrate our anniversary (which was last Friday), I took Agnes
to the Majestic. Tommy did not come as he preferred to play
about. Fighting renewed in Belfast.

Wednesday, 15 June
Agnes spent the entire night bashing into the room. More people
killed in Belfast riots. Miners ballot today.

Thursday, 16 June
A blazing hot day. Agnes up to her neck spring cleaning the room.
She had the room carpet outside and beat it. I assisted a little at
night by cleaning the wallpaper with some patent material like
putty. It did not so bad.

Friday, 17 June
Agnes cut the room carpet down the middle. I stained the desk
and wee stool. Broke my pipe today.

Saturday, 18 June

At night we wandered into Shawlands.
I bought a new pipe of a quaint
design. We then wandered into a house
of pleasure near Shawlands. Miners'
ballot result – 'Still to strike'. Dear
help us.

Sunday, 19 June
Agnes went to Communion this morning. Tommy's Sunday School
now closed for the season. After dinner we went to Old Cathcart
by Carmunnock Road. Back by car. Feeling still the need for
exercise, I took a walk at night to the Gorbals Water Works.[46]
Home by Barrhead and Paisley. Got home about 10.30. Agnes
thought I had fallen in. Filled up the census paper by candle light.

---

45   On Sunday 12 June, three members of the Royal Irish Constabulary (RIC) were
     shot by the IRA on Falls Road in Belfast. One of them died. Uniformed RIC and
     Black and Tans arrested and murdered three Catholic men in north Belfast. During
     the following two days, Loyalist gunmen killed six more Catholics and the IRA
     assassinated three Protestants.

46   The waterworks were in the hills to the south of Barrhead.

Monday, 20 June

Paid the gas bill. Having some change, we went to Majestic. Agnes sewed the room carpet together, making it look like a new one.[47] She then polished the furniture. The miners want everyone to strike.

Wednesday, 22 June

Agnes took Tommy into town this afternoon for more boots. She then took a run up at night herself to see Hetty. King and Queen in Belfast today, opening new Parliament. They were not assassinated.

Thursday, 23 June

Dull day, but a very nice night. So I went me to Carmunnock a walk. Agnes carried home some char today with Mrs Carmichael, which was too much for her.[48] Agnes made rhubarb jam.

Friday, 24 June

When I got home at tea time, Agnes completely done out. Her back giving her terrible pain, and feeling very shivery, she went to bed, absolutely helpless. I cleaned the kitchen and scullery windows.

Saturday, 25 June

Agnes worse, and pain very bad. No appetite. Tried hot fomentations after dinner.[49] Irish troop train wrecked yesterday by Sinn Feiners, five soldiers killed.[50]

Sunday, 26 June

Agnes not any better, so Tommy went for the doctor. He says it is lumbago, and recommends hot fomentations and aspirin.[51] The aspirin relieves the pain a little.

Monday, 27 June

Kept Tommy off school to act as housemaid. Agnes a little easier, but very weak. She has had no sleep yet. Doctor up at dinner time. She has to keep bed

---

47 Agnes would have stitched the outside edges of the carpet together, so that the worn areas would be at the edges and the centre would look new.

48 'Char' is similar to coke.

49 'Fomentations' are hot compresses or poultices.

50 On 23 June IRA volunteers ambushed a troop train in County Armagh. A mine beneath the train derailed it and killed four soldiers of the 10th Royal Hussars, two drivers and sixty-three horses. Thomas is mistaken about the date of the attack.

51 'Lumbago' is a term used to describe lower back pain.

all week. Got her up long enough to
make her bed, and then boiled her
bedding. Another coal conference on.

Tuesday, 28 June

Agnes' pain not so acute. Josephine here at
tea time. So she made the tea and Agnes'
bed. Agnes has never slept yet. Coal strike
over after lasting three months.

Wednesday, 29 June

Tommy back to school. Doctor up tonight, thinks Agnes will get
better. Agnes getting very melancholy for want of sleep.

Thursday, 30 June

Agnes got up tonight for about three hours. She got a little sleep
last night. Isa up tonight with Ella Carlyle. Mrs Carmichael in
tonight for a little. She has done more for us than our nearest and
dearest friends.

Friday, 1 July

Agnes up for five hours tonight. Mrs Carmichael
washed the lobby and stairs. Saw Hetty and Jean
in town today, told them that Agnes was confined to
bed. Hetty has not yet come to see her. Washed the
kitchen floor at night, with many a text on my lip.

Saturday, 2 July

Agnes got up at 4 o'clock and stayed up till 10. She is evidently
getting better. Took a run out for an hour after tea for some fresh
air. Saw a big volume of smoke in the town, like a fire. Big prize
fight in America: Carpenter knocked out by Dempsey.[52]

---

52   Jack Dempsey knocked out George Carpenter in the fourth round to win the
     heavyweight boxing championship. The fight report took up the first 13 pages of the
     New York Times.

Sunday, 3 July

Agnes managed up at noon. Gordon Mossman and Wee Billy dropped in before dinner to see Agnes. Tommy and I went into town to see remains of the great fire in Argyle Street. Two firemen had been killed.[53] Josephine up at night with my niece Ella from Edinburgh.

Monday, 4 July

Agnes up after breakfast, and stayed up all day. Jean Crozier here at dinner time. Agnes out today for the first time. Tommy not at school today as he stopped for holidays last Thursday. Miners making a start now.

Tuesday, 5 July

Lily here when I got home. She went away shortly after tea. I took Agnes and Tommy at night to see the 'great fire'. We watched the men demolishing the walls. I would not like to be a demolisher. Agnes feeling chirpy.

Wednesday, 6 July

Got Agnes a bottle of homeopathic liquid to drink. Guaranteed to kill or cure. Took the wife and family to a house of amusement to help forget our sorrows. Smuts and De Valera confer on the Irish Troubles.[54] Got a letter from New Zealand.

Thursday, 7 July

Went into Carmichaels at night to superintend and assist in the hanging of their oil paintings. We all had supper there.

Friday, 8 July

Agnes made the breakfast today and did quite a lot of work. Coal selling now four to five shillings a bag. Got a letter from Austria with a fine collection of stamps. De Valera to meet Lloyd George.

Saturday, 9 July

Agnes washed the floor, so she is improving. In afternoon we took the car to the new estate at Netherlee, called 'Linn'.[55]

---

53   Firefighters Frederick True and James Farquharson died while quelling the blaze at Bowman's Economic Stores, on the east corner of Miller Street and Argyle Street.

54   Jan Smuts, the Prime Minister of the Union of South Africa, was acting as a potential peacemaker between the United Kingdom government and Éamon de Valera, leader of Sinn Fein and Prime Minister of the outlawed Irish parliament.

55   Glasgow Corporation bought the Linn estate in for £10,000 in 1919 and laid it out as a public park. The Linn Park was opened in 1921.

July, 1921.

Saturday 9th July.
Dull sort of day but
a terrific heat in the air.
Agnes washed the floor so
she is improving.
In the afternoon we took
the car to the new estate
at Netherlee. called "Linn".
After tea we took a walk
through Shawlands

Sunday 10th July
Sun blazed all day
Thermometer 107°
in the sun.
This is the way
to dress for
comfort. Went
to Maxwell Park
to bask in the
sunshine, but
came home before
I went up in
a flame. After
tea we all went
to Rouken Glen.

Sunday, 10 July

Sun blazed all day. Thermometer 107 degrees in the sun. This is the way to dress for comfort. Went to Maxwell Park to bask in the sunshine, but came home before I went up in a flame. After tea we all went to Rouken Glen.

Monday, 11 July

We toddled to Majestic tonight. The price of coal fixed at 3/9 a bag. All murder to stop in Ireland today at 12 noon.[56] To celebrate the event, Belfast has a big riot. 21 persons killed.

Wednesday, 13 July

Bright day. Agnes feeling all right now. She cleaned the kitchen windows. Took a walk to Calder Street library at night. Came home by the Wee Park.[57] A band in it, and saw Mr Carmichael.

Friday, 15 July

This is Fair Friday, so struck work at 1 p.m. Took some cascara last night for a certain tightness, so feel a decided looseness today. At night we had a walk through Queen's Park and Shawlands.

Saturday, 16 July

Fair Saturday. Very heavy rain during the night and this forenoon. Have a holiday today. Took a notion to see Paisley, so I went there in forenoon. Got a bit of a soaking on the road, so went into the museum to dry. At night we went to Queen's Park and had a look in at a certain picture house in Shawlands.

Sunday, 17 July

Great heat wave on again. Took a walk in forenoon down to the docks and admired the water. In the afternoon took Agnes and Tommy a walk to the Gorbals Water Works.

Monday, 18 July

Still on holiday. Turned out a day of tremendous heat. Had our dinner early and meandered out to Busby via Netherlee. We had a seat in Busby Glen and then we pushed out to Carmunnock and home. To get a rest, we had a seat in the Majestic. Mine explosion at Uddingston, three men killed.[58]

---

56   A truce between the UK government and the Irish forces was signed on 9 July, to come into effect at noon on 11 July. Thus ended the Irish War of Independence.

57   Govanhill Park.

58   Three miners were killed and one fatally injured in an explosion at the Blantyre Ferme Colliery in Uddingston in the early hours of 18 July.

Wednesday, 20 July

Got a nice selection of stamps today from a man in Finland. We all up at flag pole of Queen's Park at night.

Friday, 22 July

We asked the Carmichaels in for an evening. We gave them a lesson in card playing, then I elevated their souls with a little music. Mrs MacKenzie also in.

Saturday, 23 July

In the afternoon I took a walk through Queen's Park, then went into Langside Library and perused divers journals. After tea, took Agnes and Tommy a walk through Queen's Park, into Shawlands and along the Cart into Mount Florida.[59]

Tuesday, 26 July

We went to the Majestic place at night. Got a nice selection of stamps from St Helena (where Napoleon spent his holidays).

Wednesday, 27 July

Agnes in wash house all day. Finished my letter to New Zealand. The powers that be have given us full use of the gas. The strike is over.

Thursday, 28 July

Posted my letter to New Zealand, also two of my diaries, which I insured for £10. Agnes ironed all night.

Friday, 29 July

Packed my father's tool chest, which I intend sending to Duncan. He evidently thinks he is a joiner. Here's luck.

Monday, 1 August

Paid the factor his extortionate dues, and with the balance we hied to the Majestic at night.

Thursday, 4 August

Made unto Agnes a couple of footboards for the wash house. She gave Mrs Carmichael one of them.

---

59   The 'Cart' is the River Cart.

Friday, 5 August
Tommy at Linn Estate this forenoon with some pal or other. Agnes and I out for a walk at night. Tommy preferred other company.

Monday, 8 August
Got my hair cut this evening, then had a hot bath.

Tuesday, 9 August
This is Tommy's birthday. Ten years old today. We bought him a wonderful pocket-knife, so hope for the best. Mrs Gordon, Ella and wee chap here at tea time. We heard that Mrs Dunn of Ibrox is dead.

Friday, 12 August
Working late again and took Tommy in with me. Sent box of tools off to Duncan.

Saturday, 13 August
Stopped today for my holidays. Took a small walk in afternoon. After tea we went into Shawlands and into the picture house there.

Sunday, 14 August
After breakfast I walked to Shawlands Cross, took car to Thornliebank, then walked to Gorbals Water Works, turned into Barrhead Road and home by Nitshill, and car back from Pollokshaws. We all went to the Mossmans' for tea.

Monday, 15 August
This is the first day of my holidays. Sun shone all day. One of the best. I took a walk in forenoon to Stonelaw Woods. After dinner we all went to Paisley. Agnes admired the shops and I admired the girls.

Tuesday, 16 August
Very wet day, so we did not go to the coast. I took a run into town before dinner. After dinner I went into town again for some literature. After tea I took a walk through Linn Estate.

Wednesday, 17 August
Dull morning, but dry, so we ventured forth in holiday mood. Took car to Dalmuir then car to Balloch. Heavy rain by this time. We went through Balloch Park and admired Loch Lomond. We had tea in Balloch Castle. Had a look round the village, rain now off, and got home the way we came. Got a wonderful collection of stamps from Latvia this morning, by registered post.

Friday, 19 August

Dull morning, but we ventured forth. Walked to the Broomielaw and boarded the *Isle of Skye*.[60] She left at 9.30 and we got to Lochgoilhead about 2 p.m. The sun blazing by this time, and an almost cloudless sky. We had tea in a little wooden shed and got boat back again at 3.30 p.m. She crawled into the Broomielaw about 8 o'clock. We are all sunburnt.

Saturday, 20 August

Dull and warm. I took car to Clarkston, then tramped on to Eaglesham. Sat down there on a seat, which bore the inscription 'Village rest, protect it'. Had a smoke, then proceeded on my way to Ballagioch. Walked across the moor for an hour and arrived at Kingswells. Turned on to a footpath there, which took me to Loganswell. Then Newton Mearns via the Mearns. Took the motor from there to Eastwood Toll. Got home about 5.30 p.m. Hetty and Daisy had just arrived. We all sat in.

Sunday, 21 August

Shortly after breakfast Duncan paid us a surprise visit. He is over from Belfast for a few days. He had dinner with us, then I took him to the Linn Estate. Jack Ferguson arrived before we got back, then Isa Ferguson and Lydia MacIntyre. We put up the notice 'House Full' then, and got on with our tea. Agnes had her hands full, I tell you.

Monday, 22 August

Tommy's holidays are over, so off to school he went. I did not venture a country walk, but spent the forenoon in town, including a visit to the Mitchell Library. Dull afternoon, so just loafed about. At night we went to the Majestic.

Tuesday, 23 August

Beautiful day. Sun blazed all day. Girded up my loins and started out. Clarkston first, then Busby. After a few miles, turned up a wee road that eventually took me to Hairmyres station. Dropped in to see the station master, whom I know well, but found he was on holiday, so I pushed on to East Kilbride. Called in at Miss Balfour's shop, and had a cup of tea and a crack. Walked back by East Kilbride Road and Burnside. Got home about 6. Agnes very annoyed as I had evidently gone away without intimating my destination. A man in Jerusalem sends me stamps. Oh help!

---

60   The *Isle of Skye* was a paddle steamer operated by Buchanan Steamers.

Wednesday, 24 August
Dull sort of day. Took a walk into town this forenoon. Called in at a place where suits are made and got a few patterns. I then called at a place where snap-shots are developed and got some belonging to Jean Crozier. After dinner, Agnes called in at Josephine's shop. I took a walk out to Ruglen and got a quotation from my tailor. He lost. At night we all went to the Cinerama.

Thursday, 25 August
We all out at Coatbridge by 10.35 train. Hetty took our photo in the back garden, but have my doubts. After tea we all went round by the Lochs.[61] This has been a real holiday for Agnes. Great airship disaster. R38 blows up over the Humber. 44 lives lost.[62]

Saturday, 27 August
The last day of my holidays. Took a walk through the Queen's Park before dinner. Gordon, Hetty and Wee Billy here at night. We had some music, and I played Gordon at cards, and he beat me. We are now getting coal for 2/6. Population of Scotland on 19 June 1921: 4,882,157. England, same date: 37,885,242.[63]

Monday, 29 August
A very sad day this. Resumed my business duties once more. Agnes in wash house all day, and made jam all night. I worked late to make up for my holidays.

Tuesday, 30 August
We all at Majestic at night then I went back to my work. To guard against possible assassination and robbery, I took Tommy with me. Gunmen busy in Belfast. 18 people killed in the streets.[64] Terrible times.

Wednesday, 31 August
I worked late and Agnes made another ninepence. Tommy had a pal of his in at night, seeing it was wet. Got a postcard from the man in Vienna. He promises more stamps. Good man. The lady from the kirk in at night.

---

61 Lochend Loch and Woodend Loch, in what is now Drumpellier Country Park.

62 The airship R38, on its fourth flight, failed structurally and burst into flames over Hull before crashing into the Humber, killing 44 people.

63 These figures are from the 1921 census.

64 Street battles in Belfast left nine Protestants and nine Catholics dead.

Thursday, 1 September

Last night was the official end of the Great War.[65] Now I can breathe easy. Feeling the need of a little relaxation, we all at Majestic at night.

Friday, 2 September

Took Tommy down at night and left him in charge of the barber, with strict instructions to cut his hair like a gentleman. To get some good air into my lungs I took a walk to Rouken Glen. Military in charge of Belfast.

Sunday, 4 September

After breakfast, I did the Carmunnock – Busby – Clarkston walk. Beautiful day of sunshine. Tommy starts his Sunday School once more. He says he is going to join the Band of Hope.[66] Good boy. Took a walk over to Greenlodge at night. No one in, so took a walk back again. Taught Agnes how to sing a hymn at night.

Thursday, 8 September

Got measured for a new suit at T. Arkieson. Working late at night. Another ninepence for Agnes.

Friday, 9 September

Another warm day. Called in at Tommy Arkieson and got a fit-on. Did some late work again. Tommy went to the Band of Hope tonight. He did not seem enthusiastic when he got home. Battle of Flodden 1513.[67]

Sunday, 11 September

Wild, stormy wet forenoon. Cleared up in afternoon, so I took a walk to Linn Estate and admired the waterfall. Came home by Carmunnock Road.

Monday, 12 September

Agnes went to the wash house at night, and I worked late. I brought home a geranium plant presented to me by Mr Sutherland.

---

65 The United States formally ended the First World War by declaring peace with Germany.

66 The Band of Hope was a temperance organisation for working-class children, who took a pledge of total abstinence.

67 The Battle of Flodden Field was fought in northern England between an invading Scots army under King James IV and an English army. The English won.

Wednesday, 14 September

Got a phone message from my niece Isa that my sister Mary was
through from Edinburgh, and all Greenlodge would come out
to see us at night. They duly came. Mary and her son Tommy,
Josephine, Jack, Isa, Lily and her boy John. Mary sang us a few
warbles, I played a few bars, and we told some funny stories. Then
we said: 'Farewell, remember me.'[68]

Friday, 16 September

Sorted Tommy's school bag, mended Agnes' shoes and broke some
wood. Agnes did some sewing. Tommy at Band of Hope and got
his pledge card.

Saturday, 17 September

Jean here from Coatbridge shortly after dinner. We took her a walk
to Shawlands and home by Cathcart and Newlands. Tommy is
going to join the library, so I filled in the form for him and wished
him good speed. Jean left by 10 p.m. train from Queen Street, so
we all went to the station with her. I had to carry Jean's case, but
on the way to station discovered I had forgotten it. Consternation!

Sunday, 18 September

Left the house in the forenoon, took car to Baillieston then walked
to Coatbridge with the overlooked case. Agnes entertaining Nannie
Gordon and her boy when I got home. Was wearing my new suit
today.

Tuesday, 20 September

*Tommy took his first book out of the library.
It dealt with boats.*

Wednesday, 21 September

Agnes bought a pane of glass, frosted design, and I
fitted it to scullery window at night. The Japanese man's
brother sent me a letter today from Shanghai. He is going
to send me some stamps. Banzai!

Friday, 23 September

Stopped work tonight for the autumn holiday. Did some putty work
in the kitchen to keep out small animals. Terrible explosion in
German chemical works. About 1,000 killed.[69]

---

68   This phrase occurs in *Hamlet* and a number of traditional songs.

69   Around 600 people died in an explosion in the BASF fertiliser factory at Oppau on
     21 September. About 80 per cent of all buildings in the town were destroyed, leaving
     6,500 homeless.

Saturday, 24 September

Fine day. Took a walk through Queen's Park in forenoon. At night we all went to the pictures at Shawlands. On our road home, we went into the shows at Butterbiggins Road. To show Tommy my skills as a marksman, I had a shot. I missed.

Monday, 26 September

This is the autumn holiday. Brilliant sunshine all day, and as hot as any day in summer. Hetty and Daisy arrived before noon. After dinner we all did the Carmunnock – Busby – Clarkston walk.

Friday, 30 September

Agnes out at night with Mrs Carmichael to the Alhambra to see *The Blue Lagoon*.[70] I stayed at home with Tommy and played games with him.

Saturday, 1 October

Got some more stamps from my man in Vienna. At night I did a walk to Newlands and Cathcart. Agnes did not get out except for messages.

Sunday, 2 October

Took a walk into town (instead of going to church, which I regretted ever after). Summer time ends at midnight, so with a sad heart and a tear in my eye, I put back the various clocks one hour.

Monday, 3 October

We were awakened in the wee sma' hours by hearing Tommy diving out of his bed in his sleep. I dived out of my bed and saved his life. We were paralysed. I'm going to handcuff the child to his bed tonight.

Tuesday, 4 October

In the early morning, Tommy rose up in his bed, but I had string tied all around him. We wakened up, and saved him from being hanged. It's getting a problem. My good friend in Denmark sent me today a nice selection of 'labels'.[71]

---

70 The Alhambra Theatre stood at the corner of Waterloo Street and Wellington Street. Alhambra House, a modern office block, now occupies the site. The play was based on a romance novel of the same name by Henry De Vere Stacpoole (1908).

71 In stamp-collecting terminology, a 'label' is any philatelic item not valid for postage.

September, October.

Friday 30ᵈ Sept

Nice warm sunny day
just like summer.
Tommy off school yesterday
and today. He has a
very bad cough.
Agnes out at
night with Mrs
Carmichael to the
"Alhamba" to
see th "Blue
Lagoon"
I stayed
at home with
Tommy., and played games
with him. He washed the
dishes as I was disabled.
Cut my finger in a
nasty manner at my
work. Put the child to
bed about 10 p.m.
Agnes home 10 45 p.m.

"Be fit for more than the thing
You are now doing."

Wednesday, 5 October

Agnes went to the Majestic herself at night, as she is in need of a little diversion. Started to make a patent top for Tommy's bed. When Agnes got home she was all out with the cold in her head, dead beat, non compos mentis. Great alarm and consternation in our happy little home.

Thursday, 6 October

Finished the 'life guard' for Tommy's bed (with some little assistance from Agnes). Agnes bathed her feet at bed time and went to bed in a sad condition.

Friday, 7 October

Agnes much better today. Did not do much at night, which means I did nothing.

Saturday, 8 October

We all did a little walk before tea. After tea, Agnes went out for a message or two (a wing for a certain hat) and Tommy for a new book.[72] I stayed in and tried over some wonderful music I had brought in.

Monday, 10 October

We all went to the Ideal Home Exhibition at night. Disaster in Firth of Clyde yesterday morning. The Laird Line steamer *Rowan* run into, cut in two and sunk. 36 lives lost. She was sailing from Glasgow to Dublin.[73]

Wednesday, 12 October

Not getting a big enough smoke in my old pipe, I speculated in a new one with a larger seating capacity, so to speak. It is more satisfactory. Josephine dropped in at tea time. She gave Tommy a nice case for carrying £s notes etc.

Friday, 14 October

Went out to Greenlodge at night myself. Tommy has given up the Band of Hope.

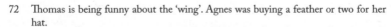

72 Thomas is being funny about the 'wing'. Agnes was buying a feather or two for her hat.

73 SS *Rowan* sank off the Rhinns of Galloway, near Corsewall Point, with 34 casualties. Eight members of the Southern Syncopated Orchestra, a London-based jazz band, died.

Sunday, 16 October
Agnes and I went to church in forenoon, Mass being celebrated. Tommy stayed at home. I took a walk to Linn Estate for some fresh air. We all went to Ibrox after tea.

Monday, 17 October
We saw a fine eclipse of the moon last night. We all went to Majestic at night, and I put on my new slippers, which cost 10/6, when I got home.

Wednesday, 19 October
Agnes and Mrs Carmichael away to some church function at night. I did some joiner work in the coal bunker to render it mouse proof.

Thursday, 20 October
Paid the gas bill today to our profiteering Corporation.[74] Got a few more stamps from the man in Latvia (if you know where that is).

Sunday, 23 October
Agnes and Tommy went to church this morning. I stayed at home to welcome them back on their return. In the afternoon we went through Queen's Park, and home by Maxwell Park and Pollokshields. After tea, Agnes took a run out by herself to see Hetty Mossman. Gordon Mossman out of his old job, but has been working in Birkenhead for some weeks past.

Tuesday, 25 October
Took a walk out to Langside Library at night. Agnes sewed all night, and then she ironed all night.

Wednesday, 26 October
Agnes flitted to the wash house at night. Having nothing better to do, I built a certain noisy erection with Tommy's Meccano.

Thursday, 27 October
Agnes in washing house all day, then went out at night to see Hetty Mossman. The 'event' is not far off.[75]

---

74   Gas was supplied by Glasgow Corporation.
75   Hetty is pregnant for the second time.

Crime and punishment

Like every large city, Glasgow has had its fair share of shocking murders, and Thomas recorded three of them in his diaries. The newspapers of the time referred to them as the Queen's Park Murder, the Whiteinch Murder and the Go cart Case, and all resulted in the death penalty for the perpetrators. The first of the three had a particular significance for Thomas and his family, because the victim lived very close to their home and was killed in the nearby Queen's Park, where they regularly walked and listened to music at the bandstand. For Thomas and his contemporaries, murder trials made sensational reading, not least because the verdict could lead to another death.

On 3 February 1920, Henry Senior, 35, of 50 Robson Street in Govanhill, walked the short distance from his home to Queen's Park, he told his mother, to meet a lady friend. The park was well known as both a lovers' lane and a place of prostitution. Senior did not meet his date but did encounter Helen White, who engaged him in conversation. Senior did not know that the attractive woman was part of a criminal team who were targeting well-dressed and presumably wealthy men, so he was completely taken aback when James Rollins, 22, emerged from bushes and attacked him, claiming to be outraged at Senior's conduct with his partner. Rollins' accomplice Albert Fraser, 24, then appeared, and battered Senior to death with a revolver. Rollins, Fraser, White and another woman stole their victim's coat, shoes and money, then fled the country. The police followed the men's trail to Belfast and arrested Rollins and Fraser in a cave outside the town. An address on a piece of paper in Rollins' pocket led police to a house in Belfast, where they arrested White and Elizabeth Stewart. The women agreed to turn King's Evidence, and both men were found guilty of murder at a trial in April 1920. Rollins and Fraser were hanged in Duke Street Prison on 26 May 1920.

161

The body of Elizabeth Benjamin, 14, was found in the back court at 67 George Street (now Medwyn Street), Whiteinch, in October 1921, with her hands tied behind her neck and a wound to her head. The police found the girl's purse and attaché case, which led to the arrest of William Harkness, 31, a driller, and his wife Helen McLeary or Harkness, 28, of 67 George Street. During the trial, in January 1922, when 70 witnesses appeared for the Crown, the pair were accused of murdering Elizabeth Benjamin by suffocation in order to steal money she had been collecting, door to door, on behalf of her father's business. The jury took 26 minutes to reach a unanimous verdict of guilty against both accused, with a strong recommendation to mercy on behalf of the woman. On 18 February, Helen Harkness was reprieved and sentenced to life in prison. Three days later, her husband was hanged in Duke Street Prison.

John Johnston, 13, was on his usual round, delivering newspapers in the Whifflet district of Coatbridge, on 20 June 1923. When he came to the house at 2 Newlands Street occupied by Mrs Annie Young, a widow, he was invited into the room rented by her lodgers, John Newell, his wife Susan Newell, 30, and Janet McLeod, 8, her daughter from a previous marriage. Susan Newell, who was alone in the room at the time, strangled the boy and stole the little money he had on him. The next day, Susan and her daughter took the body, wrapped in a rug and placed on a go-cart (a bogie made from pram wheels and a plank of wood), and set off for Glasgow. A witness saw the boy's head inside the rug, and alerted a policeman. He arrested Susan Newell, who blamed her husband for the murder. Their trial began in Glasgow on 18 September 1923. John Newell was able to prove that he was away from home on the two days of the murder and attempted disposal, and his wife stood alone in the dock. The jury, by a majority verdict, found Susan Newell guilty of murder, and she was hanged in Duke Street Prison on 10 October 1923. She was the last woman to be hanged in Scotland.

There were 22 people hanged in Glasgow in the twentieth century, all for murder. The first 12 were hanged in Duke Street Prison. By the time that closed in 1955, the site of executions had moved to Barlinnie Prison. Duke Street Prison, which was built on the site of the old House of Correction, opened in 1823 as the Town and County Bridewell, serving Glasgow and the Lower Ward of Lanarkshire. When Barlinnie opened in

1882, Duke Street became a women's prison, but it retained its accommodation for men on remand. In the distant past, executions were performed in public at Glasgow Cross, outside the Tolbooth. When the Justiciary Building opened at the foot of Saltmarket in 1812, executions were first performed in Jail Square (now Jocelyn Square), facing Glasgow Green. From 1865, hangings took place in private, inside Duke Street Prison. That function moved to Barlinnie in 1928 and remained there until 1960, when the last hanging in the city took place.

The City of Glasgow Police was formed in 1800, the first force to be established in Scotland. By the start of the twentieth century, the force employed 1,355 officers (of whom 187 were Irish, 26 English and three foreign), who were responsible for the safety of the 761,712 people in the city. It appointed its first detectives in 1904 and its first women constables in 1915. In 1921, the force bought two police cars; these were reserved for emergencies, and constables and officers were expected to walk or travel by tram during their investigations. In 1926, three years after the third murder reported by Thomas, the force introduced an innovative system for recording the modus operandi of each persistent criminal in Glasgow.

Monday, 31 October

This is Hallowe'en, so we hied us to the Majestic. I did not go out with the 'goloshans'.

Tuesday, 1 November

We got a postcard from Dennistoun today, saying that a small Mossman, female species, had been born there last Sunday. Tommy has a holiday from school. The municipal election on, Agnes and I, being dutiful citizens, and citizenesses, and having the welfare of our Great City at heart, went to Tommy's school and voted for the right man. The ballot being secret, I cannot tell you his name. A young Jewess has been found murdered in Whiteinch.[76]

Wednesday, 2 November

Labour has received a decided 'dull thud' at the elections. Glory be! Agnes took a run out to Dennistoun to see mother and child.

Friday, 4 November

The factor called today, and robbed us in his usual cheery manner. We all at a party tonight in the Carmichaels. We dooked for apples and had various games, and a little jigging for those who could.[77] We came away about 1.15 a.m.

Saturday, 5 November

Agnes went up to Dennistoun in the early forenoon, and brought Wee Billy Mossman home with her. I spent the afternoon looking after him. Agnes took him home at night. I got some stamps from South America, which I arranged in her absence.

Tuesday, 8 November

We entertained all Greenlodge tonight, including Johnny Martin. Agnes got an apron of many colours from them. My throat is very husky tonight. I suppose I have got the cold.

---

76   The body of Elizabeth Benjamin, aged 14, was discovered in the back court of 67 George Street (now Medwyn Street), Whiteinch. Her hands were tied behind her head.

77   Dooking for apples involves dropping a fork held in the mouth into a tub of water in which apples are bobbing. The object is to spear an apple. 'Jigging' is dancing.

Wednesday, 9 November

Did not get much sleep during the night, so I stayed in bed all day. Got up at tea time. Feeling not so bad. Tied a bandage round my sick throat.

Thursday, 10 November

Got up after breakfast and went to my work after dinner.
Agnes not feeling well at all. Sore throat, sore head, stiff neck
etc. Tommy brought his pal up at night and played various
games with him. This is the birthday of my well beloved.

Friday, 11 November

This is the day of the 'two minutes' silence'. At 11 a.m. on this
date three years ago, we also lost a friend, dearly beloved.

Saturday, 12 November

We all at Langside, visiting the Maxwells. We would have been
better at home, as we all have the cold. On this date 206 years
ago, Glasgow's first newspaper was published.[78] Unfortunately, I
have mislaid my copy.

Monday, 14 November

Agnes went to the wash house for the day. I bought myself a bottle
of oil of the cod, to renovate my constitution. Here's luck, and
here's tae ye.[79]

Tuesday, 15 November

Worked late at night. The great nations are not to build any
warships for 10 years.[80] So the millennium has come. Amen! Yea,
so be it. Hallelujah.

Monday, 21 November

Working late at night. Got a letter from New Zealand today with
some very interesting enclosures.

Thursday, 24 November

*Agnes at Josephine's shop in the afternoon. She made
a few purchases, including some khaki handkerchiefs
for Tommy. Agnes got a beautiful new aluminium*

---

78   The *Glasgow Courant* was first published on 14 (not 12) November 1715. It lasted
     less than a year.

79   Two toasts usually associated with stronger beverages.

80   The International Conference on Naval Limitation, which opened in Washington
     DC on 11 November 1921, agreed a number of treaties designed to improve world
     security.

*teapot from Tommy in honour of her late
birthday. I also celebrated the occasion by
buying myself a beautiful new loose-leaf
stamp album. Great rejoicings in the family
circle. Worked late tonight. Agnes turned
very ill tonight, and collapsed after supper.*

Friday, 25 November

*Agnes very ill during the night, so
Tommy had to go for the doctor in
the morning, and stay off school into
the bargain. Doctor arrived at dinner
time and will be back tomorrow for
another examination. Agnes in bed all
day. I washed the floor at night
and made myself useful.*

Saturday, 26 November
Doctor up today, and will come back on Monday and see what
developments there are. Tommy doing his share of housekeeping.
Took a run into the library at night for some literature to cheer up
my poor wee wife. Belfast in the hands of the gunmen. Tramcars
blown up and about a score killed during the week.[81]

Sunday, 27 November
Agnes in her bed all day. Did a little amount of household work
and a large amount of stamp arranging in my new album.

Monday, 28 November
Doctor up this forenoon. He is better pleased. The haemorrhage
has practically stopped. Agnes made the dinner today, but of
course went back to bed again.

Tuesday, 29 November
Agnes inclined to be sick in morning and not inclined for any food.
Sent Tommy back to school at dinner time. I worked late at night.
Mrs Carmichael in for a couple of hours at night, and made the bed.

Wednesday, 30 November
Got a letter from Estonia with a few stamps. Agnes up nearly all
day. The doctor made his last visit tonight. Agnes just about right
now. Fresh air, a tonic and rest to finish the cure. The lady from the
church in for a few hours at night. Feeling very tired and worn out.

---

81   A total of 30 people were killed during episodes of violence in Belfast between 21 and
     25 November.

Poor old man. I managed to do some work on my new stamp album.

Thursday, 1 December
Agnes up now. Got her a tonic, 'Fellows' Syrup' and a loaf of
Fleming's bread to put … I mean to build her up again.[82] Did
some good work with my stamp album at night.

Friday, 2 December
Agnes has arranged with a lady to do a washing. Tommy got a
penny at school today for good writing.

Saturday, 3 December
Agnes improving. She washed the floor today. I have a touch of
toothache.

Monday, 5 December
We all went to the Majestic at night. My cold all right, but Agnes
sneezing like 10 men and a wee fellow.

Tuesday, 6 December
*The Irish Question settled at last.
Ireland to be called the Irish Free State.
Went down to the dentist at night and got
a tooth out. Had a long wait there and did
not get home till 10 p.m. Agnes in a fever
and imagining vain things.*

Wednesday, 7 December
My gum bled all night, and looked as if it would
bleed for ever. So I went down this forenoon to my dentist. He
saved my life.

Thursday, 8 December
Agnes and I cleaned the windows between us. Agnes
then ironed, and I proceeded with my stamp arranging.
Post offices were first established in 1464. On looking
over my collection, I find I have no stamps of that date.

Friday, 9 December
*Tommy still got a cough, so I hauled him
round to the doctor, who sounded him and thinks
him all right, and advises cod liver oil.*

---

82 'Fellows' Syrup of Hypophosphires' was marketed as a tonic and promised to 'accelerate
convalescence' and 'restore energy and vitality'. It contained iron and other minerals.

Saturday, 10 December

We all went to the Cinerama in the afternoon to see Charlie in The Kid.[83] I spent the evening with my stamps.

Sunday, 11 December

I rose early and went to the kirk. Put on my hard (very hard) hat to give it an airing. We all had a walk through the Queen's Park in the afternoon. Tommy then went to Sunday School. I stuck stamps at night, then my mounts gave out. Then I was stuck.

Monday, 12 December

Not out at night. Stamps again. I have laid in a fresh supply of mounts, also some extra pages for the album. Agnes cleaned out the press, to get her hand in for the New Year.

Tuesday, 13 December

At night, wasted my time as usual sticking in stamps. Have got the length of Poland now. Where the piano players come from.

Wednesday, 14 December

Agnes visited the wash house for the day. Bought an ounce of herb mixture in Queen Street and smoked a pipeful. I'm not going to smoke another pipeful. Not again. Measured the kitchen floor and drew various plans at night. We go tomorrow to get some linoleum.

Thursday, 15 December

Agnes and Tommy met me in town at 5 p.m. We went to Bow's Emporium and got some linoleum (inlaid variety) for the kitchen. Also a couple of yards for the scullery. Agnes visited at night and I played at stamp albums.

---

83   Charlie Chaplin wrote, directed and starred in *The Kid* (1921), a silent comedy drama featuring Jackie Coogan as his adopted son and sidekick.

Friday, 16 December
Tommy complained of neuralgia at night, but he revived soon after.
I spent the entire night digging tacks out of the various floors.

Saturday, 17 December
After dinner, I got started to the linoleum. Mr Carmichael assisted me up till 6 o'clock. After tea I got it finished, that is about 10 p.m. I sounded the 'last post'.

Sunday, 18 December
Feeling very stiff and sore after my hard work. I cut out the
linoleum for the scullery and fitted it in.

Monday, 19 December
Tommy is now top boy in his class.

Wednesday, 21 December
Agnes, Tommy and Mrs Carmichael at a matinee at the Cinerama
this afternoon. Finished sticking stamps in my album tonight.

Thursday, 22 December
We addressed a few Christmas cards to our dear
friends.

Friday, 23 December
Being near Xmas, I presented Tommy with an air gun and taught him how to shoot. Cleaned the windows when I wasn't shooting.

Saturday, 24 December
On holiday today, so I took a walk to Linn Park in the forenoon. To make a suitable target for Tommy's gun, I stole the bread board, and Agnes had to buy a new one.

Sunday, 25 December
This is Christmas Day, so I wish you a merry one. Being Sunday,
I had to be merry canny like. We all had a walk through Queen's
Park after dinner. Tommy presented his Sunday School teacher
with a box of chocolates. Played a little music at night suitable for
the season.

Monday, 26 December

On holiday today. Tommy and I scored bulls eyes all day long. After tea we all went to the Majestic. Tommy received a postal order this morning from Duncan (5/-) for his Christmas.

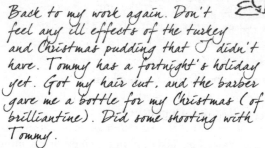

Tuesday, 27 December

Back to my work again. Don't feel any ill effects of the turkey and Christmas pudding that I didn't have. Tommy has a fortnight's holiday yet. Got my hair cut, and the barber gave me a bottle for my Christmas (of brilliantine). Did some shooting with Tommy.

Thursday, 29 December

Cleaned the kitchen and scullery windows at night. We fitted in a new hearth waxcloth, and Agnes ironed all night. Got a selection of stamps from a firm in Germany.

Friday, 30 December

Got my New Year holidays today. Agnes cleaned the silver cake basket at night and I watched her.

Saturday, 31 December

Last day of the year. Took a walk through Queen's Park then on to Rouken Glen and back by Linn Park. Admired greatly the various waterfalls. We are now expecting our neighbours from next door to visit us at 12.01 a.m. And so ends 1921, a year of loss, trials and tribulations. Grant that next year may be better.

1922

For Thomas and his family, the year 1922 continued to bring mixed fortunes, and a range of illnesses and mishaps to be dealt with and overcome. The political situation was more settled at home, with the exception of a strike and a lock-out, and the continuing birth pangs of the modern Irish state. Abroad, the fallout from the apportionment of the Ottoman Empire among the victors of the Great War caused conflict in the Balkans, and there was strife in China. Thomas, a one-man League of Nations, attempted to generate world peace through exchanging stamps with fellow collectors around the globe.

Sunday, 1 January

Shortly after midnight, we were 'first fitted' by the Carmichael family: Mr and Mrs, Alex and Peggy. We sat round the festive board and then Mrs MacKenzie and Willie arrived. About 2 a.m., Jeanie came in. Everybody away at 2.50 a.m. A wild morning of wind and rain. We all got to bed sometime after. None of us ventured out, so we passed the day quietly and peacefully.

Monday, 2 January

Fine, sunny day but bitter cold wind. Glasgow is looking clean and tidy after all the rain. We all went to Coatbridge by 2.18 train from the Cross.

Tuesday, 3 January

Started work today, but stopped at 1 o'clock. Sunny day. We all went to Rouken Glen in the afternoon. After tea, we celebrated the New Year in the Majestic.

Wednesday, 4 January

Working full-time now. Agnes and Tommy in town in the afternoon.

Thursday, 5 January

Agnes and Tommy went to Dennistoun in the afternoon to see Hetty Mossman. She was not in, but Agnes learned that she was away to Stobhill Hospital to see her brother James. Agnes went again at night herself to see Hetty. Poor Jimmy is very ill indeed, with haemorrhage. Not much hope for him.

Saturday, 7 January

Hetty Mossman, baby and Wee Billy here for dinner. After dinner Agnes and Hetty went to Stobhill to see James. I stayed with Tommy and Billy. When they got home, they didn't have much hope for James. He is very weak, and far gone. Agnes went home with Hetty about 7 o'clock and got back 10. She then went to see Mrs Carmichael, who has got the influenza.

Sunday, 8 January

After dinner, I took a run out to Stobhill to see James. The poor chap very weak and far gone, but I have hopes that he will pull through. He was very pleased to see me. When I got home, Agnes and Tommy went to Dennistoun to give Hetty the news. The Irish Parliament ratifies the Peace Treaty and that disturber of the peace, beaten, resigns.[1]

---

1   The Anglo-Irish Treaty, which had been signed in London on 6 December 1921, was
     ratified by the Dáil Éireann after long debate on 7 January 1922 by a vote of 64 to
     57. Éamon de Valera resigned as President of the Republic, throwing pro- and anti-
     Treaty politicians against each other and setting the stage for the Irish Civil War.

Ireland in the 1920s

Thomas had a keen interest in events in Ireland, because he and his wife had their roots in Lurgan, near Belfast, and because he was in touch with family members in that part of the island. His brother Duncan, who had lived between Belfast and Glasgow, settled in Belfast with his partner Maud and began a business as a sign-writer. Thomas, as a Presbyterian, a social conservative and a loyal Unionist (his father, after all, was a member of the Orange Lodge), took the side of the Unionists and made clear his loyalties in his diary entries detailing 'the Troubles' attending the birth of the Irish Free State.

The early years of the Anglo-Irish War (1913–22) were often obscured by the more violent and murderous clashes of the First World War, but the events in Dublin on 24 April 1916 echoed around the world. The Easter Rising, as it became known, saw around 1,000 members of the Irish Volunteers and Irish Citizen Army take control of more than 20 key points around the city, including St Stephen's Green, the Four Courts, the Jacob's Biscuit Factory (next to Dublin Castle, the epicentre of British rule) and the General Post Office. Patrick Pearse, calling himself the Commandant-General of the Irish Republican Army (IRA), declared that Ireland was an independent republic. Elsewhere in Ireland, other rebel groups attempted to seize power.

The plain people of Ireland were not roused to action by the republicans, and the British Army soon had each group of rebels contained. The Crown forces then began a systematic bombardment of each group, using field artillery and HMS *Helga II*, a patrol vessel anchored in the River Liffey. This onslaught destroyed much of the centre of Dublin, including the records and archives of Ireland stored in the Four Courts. After six days of fighting, and the deaths of 134 British soldiers and policemen, 64 rebels and 220 civilians, Pearse surrendered. Using the Defence of the Realm Act, the British authorities court-martialled 160 rebels and executed 15 of them as traitors. The British devastation of the city and the choice of punishment for the insurgents swayed Irish public opinion towards the rebels, and created 15 republican martyrs.

Sinn Fein, the republican political party that had been systematically infiltrated by the IRA, won an overwhelming victory in the December 1918 General Election, winning 73 of 105 seats. The candidates had stood on the policy that they would not take their seats in the House of Commons in London (which they did not recognise as having legitimate power over the Irish people) but would instead convene themselves in Dublin as an Irish parliament. This new Dáil Éireann first met in January 1919, unrecognised by Westminster. Outside of parliament, the IRA targeted members of the Royal Irish Constabulary (RIC) and British intelligence. The following year, the RIC began employing recruits from mainland Britain, who became known as the Black and Tans; because of shortages of uniforms, they were dressed in a mixture of police and army clothing. The new recruits soon acquired a reputation for reckless and brutal violence against the Irish.

Once more, the politicians gained the upper hand, and Westminster passed the Government of Ireland Act in December 1920. This proposed two self-governing statelets in the north and south of Ireland, both subservient to Westminster on matters relating to the Crown, foreign affairs, international trade, currency and defence. One year later, after more violence on both sides, and the signing of the Anglo-Irish Truce (in July 1921) and the Anglo-Irish Treaty (in December 1921), the parliaments in both Dublin and London agreed that the 1920 legislation should be put into effect. In January 1922, the Irish Free State (Saorstát Éireann) was established as a Dominion within the British Empire, with King George V as head of state. Less problematically, the government of Northern Ireland had been established in May 1921, within six counties of the province of Ulster, where the majority of the population were loyal to the British Crown.

Following the establishment of the Free State, those anti-Treaty elements of the IRA who insisted on a 32-county republic, free of all ties to Britain, occupied the Four Courts in Dublin in April 1922, and when pro-Treaty forces of the same organisation attacked them in June 1922, the Irish Civil War began. After 11 months of internecine fighting, the war was over, the IRA disbanded and the Free State settled down to build a working economy.

Wednesday, 11 January
We went to the Majestic at night. The influenza has started in Glasgow again.

Thursday, 12 January
Agnes went to Stobhill in the afternoon to see James, then took a run up to Hetty Mossman. When I got home at tea time, Tommy had a sore head, and then he vomited. He felt better after. We gave Tommy castor oil at bed time.

Friday, 13 January
Kept Tommy off school. Got some more stamps from Germany. Agnes did some baking at night.

Saturday, 14 January
We had company this afternoon. Hetty, Jean, Meg and Daisy arrived about 4 p.m. The afternoon and evening was chiefly spent in crack. I accompanied them into town for the 10.16 train from the Cross. I went straight on to Dennistoun to see Hetty Mossman for the hospital pass. Nobody in, so I came home.

Sunday, 15 January
I went to Stobhill, got in without the pass. James seems to be getting up his strength a little. Gave him some biscuits and bread and fresh butter.

Monday, 16 January
Snow general all over Scotland. Some fell today, about six inches in Glasgow. Agnes imagined herself an Eskimo and spent the day in the wash house. I did not venture out at night. Tommy thinks this fine weather!!!???

Tuesday, 17 January
Snow still yards deep. Stuck the thermometer out of the window at night, and it sank to 27 degrees. Very cold indeed. I did not let the fire go out when I came home at tea time.

Wednesday, 18 January
Clearer and going to thaw. We all went to the Majestic at night.

Thursday, 19 January

Rain in torrents. 'Sna' sna', flee awa'.'[2] Agnes met Hetty Mossman
in the afternoon and they went to Stobhill. Poor James seems to be
very far through. No more visiting to be allowed on account of the
flu epidemic. Tommy went to the library at night.

Friday, 20 January

We got word today from Ibrox that their intended visit is off.
Nannie has the flu and the baby is not well. Great fire in North
British Railway Goods Yard in High Street. Five lives lost, and
damage estimated £1,000,000.[3]

Saturday, 21 January

Students have a great day in town in aid of the unemployed. In the
afternoon, Tommy and I out for a little. We saw the students, and
they saw us. Agnes and Tommy went into town at night for gloves.
Tommy had lost his. They also viewed the great fire.

Sunday, 22 January

Like a dutiful husband, I went to church. After dinner I walked
out to Ruglen, up East Kilbride Road and down the Calderwood.
After tea, Agnes went out to Dennistoun to see Hetty Mossman.
Poor James died today.

Monday, 23 January

*Most terrific cold day. Saw my niece Isa
this forenoon and put off their intended
visit owing to James' death. Took a violent
pain in my back today, so off to doctor at
night. He says lumbago. Bathed my feet
at night and took aspirin.*

Tuesday, 24 January

I stayed in bed most of the time. Got up in the
afternoon, and we all went to the MacKenzies' at night. Agnes took
a run over to the Mossmans' in the afternoon.

Wednesday, 25 January

In bed most of the day. Agnes went into town to let the firm know
how I was.

---

2   A Scottish saying: 'Snow, snow, flee away.'

3   High Street Goods Station stood at the corner of High Street and Duke Street,
     operated by the North British Railway Company. To the south, on the former site
     of Glasgow University, stood the College Goods Station, operated by the London,
     Midland and Scottish Railway Company.

Thursday, 26 January

In bed as usual. James Cook buried today, but I was unable to go to funeral. Agnes called out at Dennistoun in forenoon with our wreath, and the one from Coatbridge.

Friday, 27 January

Not so well at all today. Felt alarming symptoms. Agnes sent for the doctor.

Saturday, 28 January

Feeling a little better, I got up at dinner time. Doctor came up later on, says it is the flu and orders me back to bed. To bed I accordingly went, feeling very uneasy.

Monday, 30 January

Tommy back at school today. He was off all last week with the cold. Doctor up to see me at dinner time. My temperature normal and I have to get up tomorrow afternoon.

Tuesday, 31 January

My niece Lily up to see me in afternoon. I rose about 3 o'clock, a little wobbly no doubt. Tommy went to library and got me a book. I sat up till about 9 p.m. Feel very depressed.

Wednesday, 1 February

I rose about 2 o'clock. Agnes went to the wash house in the afternoon. Still got the depressed feeling.

Thursday, 2 February

Got up before dinner. Mr Carmichael gave me in a magazine. Josephine to see me in afternoon. The uneasy feeling not so bad tonight.

Friday, 3 February

Rose much earlier. Went round to my doctor at noon. He certifies me well and fit for work. Got a bottle of juice to tone up shattered system. Called in at Calder Street library for some literature. Finished the book after dinner, so Tommy got me another. The uneasy feeling now gone.

Sunday, 5 February

Was out for about an hour today to see if I could walk. I managed. I am taking Bovril now for my supper.

---

4   This 'beef tea' was invented in 1871 by a Scot called John Lawson Johnston, and marketed under the name 'Johnston's Fluid Beef'. It was renamed Bovril in 1886.

Monday, 6 February
Started work today. I managed in a way, but pretty well done up at night. Hetty Mossman and her baby here at tea time.

Wednesday, 8 February
Dirty, wet day. A tramcar ran away going down High Street. Nobody killed.

Thursday, 9 February

Tommy got the fountain pen he wrote for. So many coupons and so much cash. He is a proud wee man. To celebrate the event, we all went to the Majestic at night.

Friday, 10 February
Didn't feel so well tonight, but improved later on. Looks like civil war in Ireland.

Saturday, 11 February
Got a note from my old friend G. Ferguson. He accepts my invitation to come out and see me. One of the 'old brigade'. In the words of the song, I often ask myself, 'Where are the boys' etc.[5] All dead and scattered, so I'm pleased to see one of them in the flesh again. Tommy's pen is still working.

Sunday, 12 February

Agnes and Tommy went to church this morning. I stayed at home and mismanaged as usual.

Monday, 13 February
Got an assortment of stamps from Norway. Tommy's Sunday School soiree on tonight, so Tommy took his ma to it. Wrote Duncan a letter.

Tuesday, 14 February
Met my old friend G. Ferguson this evening at Eglinton Toll, then took him home for tea and had a crack over old times. He stays in Cambuslang. Got my two diaries back from New Zealand, also a letter, likewise a good selection of stamps from Germany.

---

5   Thomas is referring to the song 'The Boys of the Old Brigade', written in 1901 by the American composer William Paris Chambers, rather than the later Irish Republican song of the same title.

Wednesday, 15 February

Our good friends the Carmichaels have got a new piano, so we all went in at night and I consecrated the instrument. It suited my delicate touch all right.

Thursday, 16 February

Agnes spent the evening usefully in ironing, and I spent it usefully (or otherwise) in stamp arranging.

Friday, 17 February

Got an illustrated paper today from New Zealand. The minister dropped in for a little tonight, and Tommy got embraced as usual.

Saturday, 18 February

Took a walk myself in afternoon round by Pollokshields. The female Whiteinch murderer has got a reprieve but her husband hangs on Tuesday.[6]

Monday, 20 February

Paid the thieving Corporation today its gas bill. Having a shilling or so left, we went to the Majestic.

Tuesday, 21 February

The murderer Harkness hanged in Duke Street Prison this morning. Agnes at a church social tonight with Mrs Carmichael.

Wednesday, 22 February

Received a letter from Duncan. All Greenlodge here tonight. Josephine and Jack for tea and the rest (including Johnny) later on. Great American airship disaster. Airship *Roma* destroyed, 35 lives lost.[7]

Friday, 24 February

Mrs MacKenzie measured Tommy tonight for pyjamas. I got my hair cut.

---

6 William and Helen Harkness were found guilty of murdering Elizabeth Benjamin at the High Court at Glasgow, and sentenced to death. Helen Harkness' sentence was commuted to penal servitude for life.

7 The *Roma*, the largest semi-rigid airship in the world, crashed in Norfolk, Virginia, during test flights on 21 February. The hydrogen-filled craft touched high-voltage electricity lines and burst into flames. From then on, airships were filled with helium. A total of thirty-four people were killed and eight injured.

Saturday, 25 February
Wild, stormy day. Soot blowing down all over the place. I took
a walk in the afternoon to Langside Library. Landru, the French
Bluebeard, executed this morning.[8]

Monday, 27 February
*Got some stamps from Denmark and the Irish Free
State. Mrs MacKenzie up at night with Tommy's
new pyjamas.*

Tuesday, 28 February
Tommy had a holiday from school, seeing that Princess Mary is
being married.[9] Agnes celebrated by going to the wash house. I
wrote to New Zealand at night.

Wednesday, 1 March
Agnes in the wash house this forenoon. I did the usual folding
of clothes with her at night. Got some fine stamps from a certain
Lithuanian.

Friday, 3 March
Got a large number of stamps from Belgium today. The lady of the
kirk here at night.

Saturday, 4 March
Took a look in at Calder Street library this afternoon. After tea we
had a walk to Shawlands. Saw the Waverley Picture House, was
tempted and fell.[10] It is a fine wee house.

Wednesday, 8 March
Agnes in town this afternoon with Mrs Carmichael. A man up at
night to move our gasolier by about a yard. He did it all right, so
we gave him 5/- sterling. No appetite for dinner today. The pain
still there, so I went to the doctor at night, and got him to listen
to my inside works moving. Nothing alarming. The stomach and
a touch of the liver. I got a bottle. 'Tis a relief.

---

8   Henri Désiré Landru was found guilty of murdering ten women (and the teenage son
     of one of them) whom he had romanced and swindled between 1914 and 1918 in
     Paris. He went to the guillotine in Versailles on 25 February.

9   Princess Mary, the third child and only daughter of King George V and Queen Mary,
     married Henry Charles George, Viscount Lascelles, the elder son of the fifth Earl of
     Harewood, in Westminster Abbey.

10   The Waverley stood at 19 Moss-side Road, Shawlands. It is now the Tusk bar and
     restaurant.

February 1922

Saturday 25 Feby
50°   53°   43°

Wild stormy day
Soot blowing down
all over the place.
Pouring wet
night. Took a
walk in the
afternoon to
Langside Library.
Landru, the French Blue-
beard executed this morning

Sunday 26 Feby.
43°   57°   43°

Very stormy day Heavy
rain morning and evening.
A slight thunderstorm at
night. We all went to
Church in the forenoon.
After dinner we were
out by Thornliebank,
and through Giffnock,
home by Cathcart.

"Poverty is no disgrace to a man,
but it is very inconvenient."

Thursday, 9 March

Agnes in a very depressed state tonight. She is not very well.

Friday, 10 March

Don't feel very well tonight. Think I'm going to have the cold. My
nephew Jack here at night.

Saturday, 11 March

The great engineering lock-out starts today.[11] Took a walk in the
afternoon along Carmunnock Road and back by Linn Park. I find
that I have got the cold. Tennant's Stalk fell down yesterday. Four
men killed.[12]

Sunday, 12 March

We did not go to church. My nose is in a liquid condition.
Tommy went to Sunday School. He has to get a prize for being
able to repeat 'Matthew, Mark, Luke, John etc'.[13] I can't do it
myself.

Tuesday, 14 March

Agnes cleaned some windows today (to my sorrow) and baked at
night (to my joy). I polished the jam pan. The Bolshevik Rand
Rebellion crushed.[14]

Wednesday, 15 March

Called in at Eglinton Street and brought my Lithuanian editor
home for tea.[15] He had expressed a wish to see my stamp
collection, so he saw it. I am very pleased to see anyone finding
it of interest. I saw him away at Eglinton Street Station 9 p.m.

Friday, 17 March

Agnes did a big ironing at night. Tommy got his hair cut.

---

11   The Amalgamated Engineering Union, concerned that many of its members were
     unemployed, banned overtime working. The employers responded by locking the
     factory gates on 11 March.

12   'Tennant's Stalk' was the local nickname for the giant chimney at the St Rollox
     chemical factory owned by Charles Tennant and Company. It was struck by lightning
     in March 1922 and had to be dynamited down. Tennant is not to be confused with
     Tennent, the Glasgow brewing dynasty.

13   Tommy is presumably able to recite the names of the books of the New Testament.

14   The Rand Rebellion was an armed uprising by white miners in Witwatersrand,
     Union of South Africa, sparked by intensified exploitation by their employers. More
     than 200 people were killed when state forces confronted the strikers.

15   Thomas may be calling this man his 'editor' because he has been translating letters to
     and from Thomas' stamp-collecting correspondents.

Tuesday, 21 March
Speculated in a box of dominoes, with which we played at night.

Thursday, 23 March
Agnes went to Coatbridge herself this afternoon. I played Tommy
at dominoes at night.

Friday, 24 March
School-board election today, so Tommy has a holiday. Agnes and I
voted before tea.

Saturday, 25 March
Hetty and Meg in this afternoon. Glasgow Subway closes today.[16]
Summer time starts.

Sunday, 26 March
I went to church myself this morning. In the afternoon we went
out a walk. At night we all went to Greenlodge. Got home 11.35,
having to walk. Tommy got his prize at the Sunday School, a nice
little pocket knife.

Monday, 27 March
Great Labour rout at the school election. To celebrate it, we got to
the Majestic this evening.

Tuesday, 28 March
When I got home at tea time, Gordon, Hetty, Billy and baby were
in. Gordon's home from England, and out of work.

Wednesday, 29 March
Agnes and Mrs Carmichael at the Colosseum this afternoon.[17] We all
in the Carmichaels' at night, and had a little music.

Thursday, 30 March
We got the lum swept this morning.

Friday, 31 March
*Put a patent of my own on gas meter so that it
can be easily turned on or off. We don't want to
be suffocated some night.*

---

16   The privately owned Glasgow District Subway found itself in financial difficulties
     and closed on 25 March 1922. Glasgow Corporation bought the subway system and
     reopened it in July 1922.

17   The ladies were visiting the Glasgow Colosseum on Jamaica Street, a drapery and
     clothing warehouse, rather than the similarly named Coliseum picture house in
     Eglinton Street.

Sunday, 2 April
After dinner, I took a walk to Rouken Glen by Giffnock and back by Thornliebank. Nannie Gordon and her boy here at tea time.

Wednesday, 5 April
My voice is very husky and I have a very sore head. Called in on my way for a crack with the Lithuanian priest Petrauskis. Got a stamp or two. Agnes ironed all night.

Thursday, 6 April
Agnes baked at night and made candy.

Friday, 7 April
Isa here at night. The elder left our admission tickets today for Sunday Mass.

Saturday, 8 April
We all went to Dennistoun in the afternoon. Tommy brought his boat for a race between it and Wee Billy's. No water in the pond in Alexandra Park, so race is postponed. Gordon Mossman still idle.

Sunday, 9 April
Agnes went to church herself. This is the Communion. In the afternoon, we all went a walk by Queen's Park and Cathcart.

Wednesday, 12 April

All the Carmichaels in at night. Wee Alex had his fiddle and I had my piano. Enough said.

Thursday, 13 April
Tommy off school now for Easter. He went a picnic in the afternoon some place out by Cathcart.

Friday, 14 April
Hot cross bun day. Likewise Good Friday. Likewise bank holiday. Rained all day and night. I stopped work today for the Easter holidays. Got my hair cut.

Saturday, 15 April
Had a holiday today, so it rained all day. After tea we all went to the Majestic.

Sunday, 16 April
This is Easter Sunday. After tea, I took a walk to Ruglen and made myself melancholy with its associations.

Monday, 17 April
This is the spring holiday. Nice sunny day. Took a walk myself in the forenoon to Linn Park, and back by Carmunnock Road. After dinner, to give Agnes and the child some exercise, we took car to Rouken Glen and walked from there to Paisley, about six miles. After tea, to give Agnes and the child a rest, we went to the Majestic.

Tuesday, 18 April
Holidays over. Nice sunny day. Duncan is over from Belfast for a holiday.

Wednesday, 19 April
Agnes went to wash house at night. She complains now of a very sore throat. Tommy has a sore nose, and his face is swollen with it. I took a run over to Greenlodge at night. Duncan, Lily and Jack just up from Fairlie.

Thursday, 20 April
Duncan here at tea time, and Josephine came later on.

Saturday, 22 April
The Mossmans all here in the early afternoon. We went to Queen's Park for our regatta. Tommy's boat won, so Gordon gave him the VC. Gordon and I then went a walk to Giffnock and Cathcart. After tea, Gordon knocked spots off me at shooting.

Monday, 24 April
Bleak, cold, showery day. Josephine and Duncan here at tea time. Duncan sails tonight for Belfast.

Friday, 28 April
I went to Langside Library at night. Got some more stamps this morning from Latvia, including a 1,000 rouble stamp (Russian).

Saturday, 29 April
Tommy and I went to the Art Galleries in the afternoon. At evening we took a walk through Queen's Park and into Shawlands. We dropped into

an auction there and saw some wonderful bargains. Agnes' neck very sore, so I rubbed it gently at night.

Sunday, 30 April
Tommy and I took a walk down to the docks after dinner, and looked at boats.

Monday, 1 May
This is Labour Day, but did not take a holiday. The bakers are now on strike, so we will starve. We went to the Majestic at night. Civil war in China.[18]

Tuesday, 2 May
I took a walk at night to Linn Park etc. Was speaking to an old friend, Florrie Peden. Unfortunately she was with her man, to say nothing of her son and heir. I got home 10.20 p.m., Agnes beginning to think I was lost.

Wednesday, 3 May
Isa and Jack here at night. Jack licked me at shooting. Youth tells.

Thursday, 4 May

Tommy got presented at school by the headmaster with a pencil for having the most marks. Smart boy, Tommy. Agnes had been into a shop and booked a wardrobe. I go tomorrow to inspect it, and give my official sanction.

Friday, 5 May
Agnes met me at Paisley Road Toll at 5.30 p.m. and I looked at the wardrobe. It will do, so I gave the man the money and told him to carry on. I cleaned the room windows at night, and Agnes ironed a couple of hundred collars for me.

Saturday, 6 May
Spent the afternoon painting the scullery ceiling. To straighten my back, we all went to the Majestic last house.

Sunday, 7 May
I went to church myself in the morning. Five little cherubs were sprinkled there with holy water. After tea, we all went out, Giffnock quarries direction, climbed over the railway and home by Cathcart.

Monday, 8 May
Went to my work naked, that is, without my overcoat. Summer has begun.

Tuesday, 9 May
Our wardrobe arrived this forenoon. A fine place to put my Sunday hat. Helped Agnes to wash the dinner service. We are going to be spring cleaning. Ah, me!

Wednesday, 10 May
The paint man whitewashing the kitchen when I got home. We presented him with four silver shillings on his retreat.

Saturday, 13 May
After dinner, I meandered round Shawlands and Cathcart. After tea, Agnes and I went to town and I got a new hat and a new pair of boots. Agnes treated herself to a new pair of shoes.

Tuesday, 16 May
All Ibrox here at night, including Nannie's boy. Agnes' uncle not yet working, owing to the lock-out.

Saturday, 20 May
After tea we walked round by Shawlands and Cathcart. Saw some optimistic men angling in the Cart. I walked for a little but saw no fish.

Monday, 22 May
This is a holiday, so of course I did not go to business. Took a walk through Queen's Park in forenoon. After dinner we all went to Coatbridge. P&O liner *Egypt* sank in fog off French coast. 112 lives lost.[19]

---

19   *Egypt* was on a voyage from the Thames to Bombay (now Mumbai) when she was rammed, in thick fog, by the French liner *Seine*.

Tuesday, 23 May

Working late. Agnes in Josephine's shop in the forenoon, and in the afternoon went into town with Tommy and got him a new suit. We lifted the room carpet at night.

Wednesday, 24 May

Working late. Took down the pictures when I got home. Agnes beat the carpet today, with the assistance of Mrs Carmichael.

Friday, 26 May

Agnes at Josephine's shop this afternoon and got some feminine articles. We laid the carpet at night well and truly.

Monday, 29 May

Working late. Horatio Bottomley sentenced to seven years for cheating the British public.[20]

Tuesday, 30 May

Agnes in wash house. I work late. On and after this date, Tommy sleeps in the room.[21]

Wednesday, 31 May

Tommy went to Queen's Park with his boat at night. Agnes and I went to the Majestic. Murders still going on in Belfast, the 'City of Terror'.[22]

Friday, 2 June

Agnes went down to Largs (Mrs Carmichael with her) and, after much travail, managed to get a house for our summer holidays.

Sunday, 4 June

Took a walk to Pollok Estate after dinner. At night we all went to Greenlodge. Seeing as this is my birthday, I bought myself a new pipe yesterday.

Monday, 5 June

Agnes and Tommy presented me with a swell walking stick for my birthday. My friend, the Lithuanian priest, drops in to see me at tea time. He gave me Russian stamps (5,000 roubles).

---

20   Horatio Bottomley, a former MP, was found guilty of fraud, perjury and false accounting after his John Bull Victory Bond Club, a forerunner of Premium Bonds, defrauded thousands of savers.

21   Tommy, who has been sleeping until now in the kitchen, where his parents also sleep, is moving to the front room or parlour.

22   Thomas is repeating a phrase used by the more colourful newspapers.

Thursday, 8 June

Agnes in the wash house this forenoon, and ironed all night. I cleaned all the windows then took a run up to Dennistoun to see how the Mossmans were getting on. Gordon is still idle.

Friday, 9 June

Agnes busy as a bee, so I took a little walk myself at night.

Saturday, 10 June

This is our anniversary. We all went to Pollok Estate after tea.

Sunday, 11 June

I was up about 7 a.m. and, after a cup of tea to Agnes and a cup of Bovril to myself, I galloped round Old Cathcart and Carmunnock Road. Agnes and Tommy went to church. After dinner, we went to Linn Park.

Monday, 12 June

We all went to the Majestic at night. Got two letters and Father's diary back from New Zealand.

Tuesday, 13 June

The holidays are drawing near. Mr Carmichael assisted me into St Enoch Station at night with some of our luggage. The great engineering lock-out over. The men allowed back. Out for 13 weeks.

Wednesday, 14 June

Agnes and Tommy off this forenoon to Largs. Mrs Carmichael and Peggy go with them for a few days. I went to St Enoch and, with many a sigh, put them into the 10.20 a.m. train. As I did not sleep last night, after tea I went over to the doctor, who gave me a bottle to regulate my 'Little Mary'.[23] Sent Agnes a love letter.

Thursday, 15 June

Got a postcard from Agnes announcing her safe arrival, which cheered me up. Met Claude Maxwell today, who gave me a dozen silk collars. At night, took a walk in the Queen's Park.

---

23 Thomas is referring to the play *Little Mary* (1903) by J.M. Barrie, where the phrase refers to the stomach.

Friday, 16 June

Seeing Agnes is away. I put on my good hat today. Got a letter from Agnes. I wrote her and sent Tommy a postcard. Worked late.

Saturday, 17 June

This is the day I get my holidays, so I quit work at 12.30. Came home, packed up, donned my hairy waistcoat, took my umbrella and rain coat, and set out on my summer holidays. I got the 3.15 train, and had a comfortable seat. Agnes met me at Largs. After our tea we went to the station, and saw Mrs Carmichael and Peggy away.

Sunday, 18 June

Rained a lot today. After dinner we went out, but the rain chased us back. Agnes got a stiff neck, so I hied myself to the chemist for some rub-juice and applied same to Agnes' neck. The first day over. Feeling a bit melancholy, but hope for the best.

Monday, 19 June

Took a walk to Fairlie Glen and back this forenoon. In the afternoon we all went out the Wemyss Bay Road, and had a seat by the water. The sun very warm now. It has been a fine day.

Tuesday, 20 June

Blowing a hurricane this forenoon. Took a walk to the Pencil and back. Turned out a nice sunny day. After dinner, we went to Fairlie Glen, and took motor back. Agnes bought a pair of bellows to keep our fire going. After tea we went to the pictures.

Wednesday, 21 June

Went to Douglas Park in the forenoon. Hetty Crozier coming down for a week, so we all went to the station and met her about 4.40 p.m. After tea, we all took a walk round by the Pencil. Dull, cold, showery and windy.

Friday, 23 June

In forenoon I went to the Pencil and Douglas Park. After dinner, Agnes and Hetty went to Fairlie. Weather not so bad today.

Saturday, 24 June
Took a walk to Fairlie Glen in the forenoon, and the train back. In the afternoon we had a seat at the yacht pond. At night we had a walk up the 'red' road and back by the shore. Tommy did not come as he was sailing his boat.

Sunday, 25 June
Took my usual walk this forenoon round by the Pencil. We all went to Fairlie Glen in the afternoon and got motor back. After tea we had a walk along Brisbane Road. Dull, cloudy and windy.

Monday, 26 June
In the forenoon, Tommy and I tried our hand at putting and then took a sail over to the Cumbraes on a motor boat. After dinner we all lay in the Douglas Park and got sunburnt. After tea we did the Bower Craig walk. We met G. Ferguson and his wife. He is here for a week. Exactly 10 years ago we met them in Rothesay.

Tuesday, 27 June
Bright and sunny. In the forenoon, I went to Bower Craig and Douglas Park. In the afternoon, Hetty, Agnes and I walked up the Glen road and got the motor back. Tommy busy with his boat. After tea we went to the pictures.

Wednesday, 28 June
Showery day. Tommy and I putting in the forenoon, then I walked to Bower Craig. In the afternoon we all took a turn at the front. Hetty goes home today, so we all saw her away by 5.50 train. After that we took a walk to the front. Met Guy Ferguson and his wife, and went a walk by the Bower Craig with them. Civil War in south of Ireland. Battle in Dublin.[24]

Thursday, 29 June
Nice day. In the forenoon I walked to Fairlie by the shore and back by the road. In the afternoon we all walked to Fairlie and got motor back. I went myself to the pictures at night to hear the great pianist.[25] Agnes did some packing.

---

24 On 28 June fighting broke out in Dublin between units of the Irish Republican Army that supported or opposed the Anglo Irish Treaty. This conflict, which marked the start of the Irish Civil War, effectively ended the violence in Northern Ireland by distracting Republican and nationalist activists from the continued British presence in the north of the island.

25 In the era of silent films, each cinema employed a pianist to provide suitable soundtrack music.

Friday, 30 June

Our last day in Largs. Tommy and I carried the hamper to station then Agnes and I carried the rest. We got a train at 3.20 and travelled home very comfortably. We got home all right, and had our tea with the Carmichaels. Mr Carmichael and I went into station at night for the luggage.

Saturday, 1 July

My holidays are now over. Irish rebels routed out of Dublin by Nationalist army. The great war, bedad.

Sunday, 2 July

Took a walk before dinner to Pollok Estate. At night I went to Linn Park and Clarkston. The Subway re-opened today by the Glasgow Corporation.

Monday, 3 July

Got into harness once more and resumed my business worries. Tommy's school holidays have just started. To cheer us up, we go to the Majestic at night. De Valera in charge of the Irish rebels.[26]

Tuesday, 4 July

Agnes in the wash house today. I went out at night to see my friend Father Petrauskis at Mossend.[27] He moved me to the chapel and the Holy of Holies, then we smoked cigars etc. I came home with my pockets full of Lithuanian stamps.

Wednesday, 5 July

Agnes spends this day in the wash house and irons all night. Tommy getting a big boy. He went to the Cinerama himself at night.

Sunday, 9 July

After tea we visited the Mossmans at Dennistoun. Gordon is still idle. We got home at 11.40 p.m. Walked all the way.

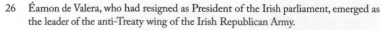

---

26 Éamon de Valera, who had resigned as President of the Irish parliament, emerged as the leader of the anti-Treaty wing of the Irish Republican Army.

27 The Reverend Joseph Petrauskis was an assistant priest at the Holy Family Church in Mossend, Lanarkshire, from 1920 until he died in 1934, attending the Lithuanian community there.

Monday, 10 July

I went to the Majestic myself at night. The German mark is now down to '10 a penny'.[28]

Wednesday, 12 July

Dull day. Agnes met Jean Crozier in town this afternoon. They had tea in the Ca' d'Oro.[29] Some swish. They were here when I got home at tea time. I saw Jean away by 9.26 train from Queen Street. We had to leave car as it went on fire. Agnes made jam tonight.

Thursday, 13 July

Took a run over to Greenlodge, but nobody in. I then strolled through the Green and listened to the band.[30]

Friday, 14 July

This is Fair Friday, so I away from business about 1.20. Beautiful day of heat and sunshine. Took a walk in the afternoon through Busby and Carmunnock. After tea, took Agnes and Tommy to the Majestic.

Saturday, 15 July

This is Fair Saturday, so I'm off the chain. Gordon Mossman up for me about 9 a.m. to go our walk, so the pair of us took the car to Clarkston, walked to Eaglesham, Ballagioch, Kingswell, Newton Mearns and Eastwood Toll, then we took the car home. Got home about 5.30. Hetty and the two small Mossmans there. We all saw them partly home at night.

Sunday, 16 July

Dull, showery day. However, seeing it's the Fair, we took the motor to Eaglesham and walked from there to East Kilbride. We got a wee mouse trap on wheels called a motor back to Burnside and then got a decent tramcar home.

Monday, 17 July

I am still on holiday. We took 11.15 a.m. train from the Cross to Coatbridge. The girls took us a walk by the canal and through

---

28   Germany entered a period of hyperinflation in July 1922. The price index accelerated during the next 15 months, with price increases running faster than the presses could produce new notes of ever larger denominations.

29   The Ca' d'Oro tearoom was in the building, now known as the Ca' d'Oro, at the corner of Gordon Street and Union Street. Like many other tearooms in Glasgow at the time, they were fashionably decorated and targeted at women. The name comes from a palazzo in Venice, the House of Gold.

30   The 'Green' was Glasgow Green.

the park.[31] Got a postcard from Duncan. He makes holiday at Portstewart.

Tuesday, 18 July
Business as usual today. Agnes not well enough to rise this morning, but went to the wash house in the afternoon and did an ironing at night. I went a walk by the Hangingshaws and Cathcart direction.

Wednesday, 19 July
Tommy at Queen's Park in the afternoon, yachting with a pal. Received stamps from Belgium today.

Friday, 21 July
Took a walk over Cathkin and got home 10.20 p.m. Agnes very busy. The rebels driven out of Limerick and Waterford.[32]

Saturday, 22 July
After tea, Agnes and I walked out by Shawlands and Cathcart. Agnes very sick at night and went to bed without supper, which made me very sad.

Sunday, 23 July
I took a walk in the afternoon to Pollok Estate, Dumbreck Road and home by Paisley Road. Sixth Sunday after Trinity. First Sunday after the Fair.

Tuesday, 25 July
All Greenlodge here tonight for tea except Jack, who is at a boys camp in Carlisle. All clear at 11.20 p.m.

Thursday, 27 July
Agnes and I went to the Queen's Park and listened to the 'entertainers'. Tommy did not come with us. He is getting independent.

Friday, 28 July
With a tear in my eye, the rent was paid today. With the change left over, we sought consolation in the pictures. Mrs Carmichael now home from Furnace. She gave Agnes a cup and saucer with the arms of that village painted thereon.

---

31   The 'canal' was the Monkland Canal.

32   The forces of the Irish Free State defeated the anti-Treaty brigades of the Irish Republican Army in the towns of Limerick and Waterford on 20 and 21 July.

Saturday, 29 July

We all at Dennistoun to see our friends the Mossmans. Gordon has
now got prospects of work. We went to Alexandra Park, and tried
races on the pond with the wee yachts, and then had a walk round
the park. I don't like Dennistoun.

Sunday, 30 July

Tommy and I took a walk to Pollok Estate in the afternoon. We
were invited into the Carmichaels'. I gave them sacred music and
elevated their various souls, and then we had supper with them.

Monday, 31 July

Agnes spent the day in the wash house. Tommy out with a chum,
and did not come home till 9.50 p.m., which is too late for a small
boy. We spoke severely to him, and I sent him to bed without any
supper. Felt uneasy at my own supper, so we gave him a bite in
bed.

Thursday, 3 August

All Ibrox here for tea, except Ella, who is working in
Grangemouth. Mr Gordon is still idle. We did a little shooting with
Tommy's gun and then some music with Tom's piano. The German
mark is now about 1,000 to the pound.

Friday, 4 August

Agnes and I went to the Majestic. Paid the fire and burglary
insurance today.

Sunday, 6 August

Thundery, but we ventured out to Clarkston. We got as far as
Waterfoot, but the big drops began to fall, so we got on to a motor
back to Clarkston, then the car and then down the rain came.
A terrific deluge, with thunder and lightning. It was so wet we
could not leave the car at our destination, but went into town
and managed into another car home. Agnes went to bed early,
disgusted with everybody.

Tuesday, 8 August

A small boy called Bruce Meldrum came up at night to see
Tommy.

Wednesday, 9 August

We all out by Shawlands tonight and back by the Queen's Park.
This is Tommy's birthday, 11 years old today. Agnes took him
into town this afternoon, as he wanted one or two parts for his
Meccano.

Thursday, 10 August
Agnes and I went to the Queen's Park at night, and listened to the entertainers. We met the Carmichaels and Mrs MacKenzie on the way back. Mrs MacKenzie invited us up, so we spent the evening there.

Saturday, 12 August
I had a walk through Queen's Park. Irish rebels routed at Cork.

Monday, 14 August
Agnes went to the wash house at night. Tommy takes a book from the library. The reading season has begun. I had a walk to Linn Park and back via Netherlee and Carmunnock Road.

Tuesday, 15 August
Agnes in the wash house. Irish rebels recapture Dundalk.

Wednesday, 16 August
Agnes got an invitation for Dunoon next week. Took a turn to library at night.

Thursday, 17 August
Pasted some pictures in my scrap album. Tommy got a bath. Heard a commotion at our street corner and looked out the window. There had evidently been a fight.

Friday, 18 August
This is the jubilee of the Glasgow tramcars, so they are all wearing a wee flag today."[33]

Saturday, 19 August
After tea we all took car from Thornliebank, and walked up the wee back road to Rouken Glen. Took car home.

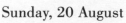

Sunday, 20 August
I went to church this forenoon. After dinner, I had a walk to Linn Park. Agnes getting ready for Dunoon.

33   The first trams ran on 19 August 1872, on a route from St George's Cross to Eglinton Toll, operated by the Glasgow Tramway and Omnibus Company. Glasgow Corporation took over the operation in 1894.

Monday, 21 August
I got the passports for Dunoon, and gave them to Agnes at dinner
time. She and Tommy were waiting at the car. They went away
by 1 o'clock train via Craigendoran. I took a walk to Linn Park
at night, but no one to welcome me home. Went to bed in a
melancholy mood.

Tuesday, 22 August
*Dined in town today. Wrote a love
letter to Agnes at night.*

Wednesday, 23 August
Getting back my good cheer again. Was invited in
to have tea with the Carmichaels tonight. Got a
postcard from my well-beloved.

Thursday, 24 August
*Got a letter from Agnes. She is enjoying
herself, so is Tommy. I sent her another
letter, and a postcard to Tommy. Michael
Collins, Free State Commander, shot dead in
County Cork yesterday.*[34]

Friday, 25 August
Got word that Agnes and Tommy come home tonight.
Great rejoicings. After tea I washed the floor and tidied
up a little. My one and only due at Queen Street Station
about 9 o'clock, so I went in and met her. I likewise met
Tommy. They were looking well, but pleased to be home
again. The house is homelike once more.

Saturday, 26 August
Got a letter this morning from Austria. The postage on it was
600 kroner, about £25 (old value).[35] Took a walk over to Eglinton
Toll in the afternoon for a few pipes. After tea we all went to the
Majestic and then had a walk afterwards.

Monday, 28 August
*Tommy started school today. Poor child. Miss
Maxwell is now his teacher. I went to Queen's Park*

---

34   Michael Collins, Commander-in-Chief of the National Army, was killed in an
     ambush by anti-Treaty republicans at Béal na mBláth, near his family home in
     County Cork, on 22 August.

35   Austria was also experiencing a period of rapid inflation.

at night and Agnes made jam. Got some fine old stamps from Norway this morning.

Tuesday, 29 August
Took a run up to Dennistoun at night to see the Mossmans. Gordon got started work today after about six months' idleness.

Wednesday, 30 August
Very warm day, a regular heat wave. Agnes spent it in the wash house. Chilean liner wrecked. 300 lives lost.[36]

Thursday, 31 August
Got a great collection of stamps from Poland today. I am getting a world-wide connection. I have had letters from Austria, Germany, Turkey, China, Japan, Palestine, Czechoslovakia, Denmark, Norway, Finland, Latvia, Estonia, Belgium, Argentina.

Sunday, 3 September
Took a walk before dinner to the Queen's Park. Stuck in stamps most all day.

Monday, 4 September
Delightful weather. Sunny, calm and warm. Agnes and I had a walk round the 100 Acre Dyke at night our two selves. Tommy preferred to play about, so we let him. The Greek army wiped out by the Turks. More trouble in the Balkans.[37]

Tuesday, 5 September
I gave the piano a good polish tonight. Disaster at Whitehaven Pit. 39 killed.[38]

Wednesday, 6 September
We entertained the Carmichael family, also Mrs MacKenzie and Jeanie. Willie dropped in about midnight. Wee Alex played his fiddle and I accompanied on the piano. It was great. All clear 12.30 a.m.

---

36   More than 200 passengers and crew died when the Chilean steamship *Itata*, sailing from Valparaíso to Coquimbo, foundered in a storm off Coquimbo on 28 August 1922.

37   The final stages of the Greco-Turkish War (1919–22) were being played out. The war, which began when Greece was awarded parts of the former Ottoman Empire at the conclusion of the Great War, ended in October 1922 with the Treaty of Lausanne, which restored the lost territories to the victorious Turkish forces.

38   An explosion of firedamp (methane) in Number 1 pit at Whitehaven, Cumbria, killed 39 miners on 5 September 1922.

Friday, 8 September

Great air race, London to Glasgow. I saw half a dozen airplanes at night.[39] Took a run to Langside Library at night. Wrote a letter to Duncan.

Monday, 11 September

Saw a big fire in town today. The 'Veritas' gas mantle building on the Clyde side.[40] Got some stamps from Denmark.

Tuesday, 12 September

Very wet day. Tommy is a 'Son of Temperance', so he went to a meeting tonight of that clan. He was elected an Assistant Scout.[41]

Wednesday, 13 September

We all went to the new Cinerama at night. It is a fine building.[42]

Thursday, 14 September

Got a letter from Duncan. Tommy had a small boy up tonight called Matthew Graham.

Friday, 15 September

Got a good selection of 'labels' from Vienna. Took a walk tonight. In my absence, the lady from the kirk was in, and delayed Agnes grievously. Turks on the warpath. Smyrna burned, thousands massacred.[43]

Sunday, 17 September

Mr Gordon here at tea time. He is not yet working.

Monday, 18 September

Agnes in the wash house. Got a postcard from friend Bobinski in Warsaw. British troops and guns landed at the Dardanelles against Johnny Turk.

---

39 Thomas witnessed the first King's Cup air race, an annual event supported by King George V to encourage the development of light aircraft. The route of the first race was from Croydon Aerodrome to Glasgow and back. It was won by Frank Barnard, chief pilot of the Instone Air Line.

40 The Glasgow branch of Falk, Stadelmann & Company, manufacturers of the Veritas gas mantle, was at 260 Clyde Street.

41 The Order of the Sons of Temperance was established in New York in 1842 and introduced to Britain in 1842. It campaigned against the evils of drink.

42 J.J. Bennell opened the new Cinerama at 201 Victoria Road on 7 August 1922. He transferred the name from a smaller cinema at the corner of Victoria Road and Cuthbertson Street, which had opened in 1912.

43 Smyrna is now known as Izmir.

1922

Monday 11 September

Dull cold day.
Saw a big fire in
                    the
            town to day.
        the "Veritas"
        gas mantle
        building on
    the Clyde Side.

            Got some
            stamps
from Denmark this
morning. Did not go
out at night.
Agnes not feeling so
well so she had her
supper in bed.

Tuesday, 19 September
Got a wonderful collection of stamps from Poland. Agnes ironed all night.

Wednesday, 20 September
Agnes at Ibrox in the afternoon. I paid a visit to the gentleman who cuts hair, and let him do his worst.

Friday, 22 September
Looked in at Langside Library. Wrote my foreign friends with the fancy names.

Saturday, 23 September
Very nice day. We all went out at night. Queen's Park, Shawlands and Cathcart. A charming night and a charming walk.

Tuesday, 26 September
All Greenlodge here at night. Got Tommy a new up-to-date atlas.

Wednesday, 27 September
Mended Tommy's school bag and helped Agnes to cut up rhubarb for jam. Revolution in Greece. King Tino loses his job.[44] He can go to the 'burroo'.[45]

Thursday, 28 September
Agnes in town with my niece Lily getting a new coat for the winter.

Sunday, 1 October
Tommy and I went to Busby and explored the glen. After tea we all went to church. Three years ago on this date, Sam was buried.

Monday, 2 October
Worked late at night. Brought Tommy with me as guard.

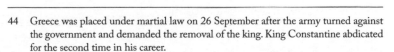

44   Greece was placed under martial law on 26 September after the army turned against the government and demanded the removal of the king. King Constantine abdicated for the second time in his career.

45   'Burroo' or 'broo' is a Glaswegian term derived from 'employment bureau', where people could search for work. Unemployed people are still said to be 'on the broo'.

Thursday, 5 October

Father Petrauskis up seeing me tonight. He admired my stamp collection. We cut up rhubarb at night.

Friday, 6 October

Worked late at night. Took Tommy with me. Agnes made rhubarb jam.

Saturday, 7 October

I took a walk to Carmunnock and Busby in the afternoon. Beautiful in the country. We all went to Majestic at night.

Sunday, 8 October

Agnes and Tommy went to church in the forenoon. After dinner we all had a walk by Maxwell Park and Queen's Park. Tommy joined a new Sunday School in Robson Street tonight. Nannie Gordon and her boy here at tea time.

Monday, 9 October

I have a bad cold. Bathed my feet and took a small hot drink.

Tuesday, 10 October

Tommy at his secret society's meeting at night.[46] My cold gets worse. Am diving into cod liver oil now, and hope for the best.

Wednesday, 11 October

My nose running good-oh. Turkey signs the agreement, so peace reigns once more in the East.[47]

Friday, 13 October

We went to the Majestic at night. My legs feel sore. Have I got the flu?

Saturday, 14 October

Thinking that fresh air would do me good, we went this afternoon to the Queen's Park and Shawlands. Agnes bought a brace of towels there. I felt pretty well done up, so home we came. I took a small reviver, and did not go out again.

---

46   The Order of the Sons of Temperance had secret hand grips, passwords and rituals similar to the Freemasons.

47   The Armistice of Mudanya was signed on 11 October, concluding the Greco-Turkish War.

Sunday, 15 October

Stayed in bed for a rest nearly all day. My devoted wife attended to all my wants. I rose up about 5 p.m.

Monday, 16 October

Got a nice selection of stamps from Holland. My cold seems a little better.

Wednesday, 18 October

Agnes ironed all night. I called in at Eglinton Street and got some new Lithuanian stamps.

Thursday, 19 October

We went to the Ideal Home Exhibition. For a shilling we bought a wonderful gas lighter. It will light the gas 10,000 times (so it says).

Friday, 20 October

The kirk lady here this afternoon for a donation to Mr Tainsh's Jubilee Fund.[48] We donationed. The Coalition Government has resigned. Out Lloyd George, in Bonar Law.[49]

Sunday, 22 October

Nice sunny day. Feeling vigorous, so I took a walk to Linn Park and back. Took a run over to Greenlodge at night.

Monday, 23 October

Agnes met me in town about 5 o'clock and I got a pair of boots. When we got home, discovered the boots were not 'mates'.

Tuesday, 24 October

Agnes took Tommy into town this afternoon to get him a new overcoat. Got my badly matched boots exchanged.

---

48   John Tainsh was the minister of the Tron United Free Church in Dundas Street, Glasgow, where the Livingstone family worshipped.

49   The coalition government of David Lloyd George had been in power since December 1916, latterly only with the support of the Conservatives. After a series of scandals, the Tories withdrew their support, the coalition fell and Andrew Bonar Law formed a Conservative administration.

Wednesday, 25 October
Got a nice selection of stamps from Austria. Majestic at night.

Thursday, 26 October
When I got in, Lizzie Campbell (Nin Henderson's wife) was in along with Mrs Donald, a cousin of Agnes' on the Henderson side. She comes from Lanark. Agnes has not seen her for about 17 years, so they had a lot to say.

Friday, 27 October
Sunny day, but a bitter cold wind. On went my overcoat at dinner time. "So, blow on, thou wintry wind."[50] Tommy discovered a scratch on his wrist, which seems to be bealing.[51] Agnes bound it up. Tommy collapsed.

Saturday, 28 October
In afternoon, waded among foreign stamps and so forth. After tea, we all had a walk round Shawlands. Tommy got a new pair of gloves. Tommy's wrist still requires attention at night. It is suppurating.

Sunday, 29 October
Frost and fog. I went to church myself.

Tuesday, 31 October
Got some nice stamps from Poland. Agnes in the wash house at night. This is the night we eat nuts and apples and dook. I did the first.

Wednesday, 1 November
Agnes got finished with the washing house today. The German mark stands at 20,000 to the pound.

Thursday, 2 November
Some snow during the night. Going to my work, a blizzard of snow and sleet, same at dinner time, and simply brutal at night.

---

50 Thomas is paraphrasing William Shakespeare, who wrote 'Blow, blow, thou winter wind' in *As You Like It*.

51 Thomas is using a Scots word meaning festering sore, boil or pimple.

Friday, 3 November
We all in at Carmichaels tonight. We had a little music. Revolution in Turkey.[52]

Tuesday, 7 November
Agnes and Mrs Carmichael went to the Princess's Theatre and saw *A Royal Divorce*.[53] Tommy went to his meeting. I stayed at home. An election agent came up to see how my inclinations were. I made him happy.

Thursday, 9 November
Worked late and took Tommy with me.

Friday, 10 November
Tommy's sore wrist much improved. A great event happened on this date some time ago.[54]

Saturday, 11 November
This is the great anniversary, the day of remembrance, the day of two minutes' silence and prayer. I was in the Square at 11 a.m., and it was most impressive.

Sunday, 12 November
Nice sort of day. After dinner I took a walk round the 100 Acre Dyke. Agnes went to church herself at night.

Monday, 13 November
We all went to the Majestic at night. Great earthquake in Chile on Saturday. About 2,000 lives lost.[55]

Wednesday, 15 November
Nice day. General Election today, so Agnes and I duly voted.

Thursday, 16 November
Agnes ironed all night. Great Labour victory in Glasgow and all over Scotland.[56]

---

52 The Ottoman Empire officially ended by vote of the Turkish Assembly on 1 November, and the country was declared a republic.

53 The Princess's Theatre stood at 119 Gorbals Street. The building is now the Citizens Theatre. The play, written by C.C. Collingham and W.G. Wills, told the story of the Emperor Napoleon and his wife Joséphine de Beauharnais.

54 This is Agnes' birthday.

55 The 1922 Vallenar earthquake occurred in the Atacama region of Chile on 11 November 1922. It triggered a tsunami that damaged the coast of Chile and was seen as far away as Australia.

56 The UK election was won by the Conservatives, and Andrew Bonar Law (MP for Glasgow Central) continued as Prime Minister. In Scotland, Labour won 29 seats out of 71, more than any other party.

Saturday, 18 November

Lifted my salary today. Feeling wealthy. I bought a new pipe. At night we all went to the Majestic.

Sunday, 19 November
Nice sunny day. I took a walk round by old Cathcart. Passing a house, I saw an old friend of mine at the window (Mrs King), so I went in for a little. After tea we all went down to Ibrox.

Monday, 20 November

Bought a new pipe of a quaint design. Wrote Duncan at night.

Tuesday, 21 November
All Greenlodge here tonight, including Johnny Martin, the boy of Lily.

Friday, 24 November
Got a good selection of stamps from my friend who stays in Jerozolimski, Warsaw.[57]

Saturday, 25 November
I stuck in a few stamps. After 10 o'clock I took a walk for recreation and fresh air.

Sunday, 26 November

Tommy and I went to church this morning. As we are leaving this kirk, we brought back the large pew Bibles.

Monday, 27 November
We went to the Majestic at night. A few ex-premiers executed in Greece for the Greek disaster in Smyrna.[58] A few British politicians not executed for the Great War.

---

57   Aleje Jerozolimski (literally Jerusalem Alley) is one of the principal streets in Warsaw, Poland.

58   The Revolutionary court sentenced to death six former ministers and military leaders on 27 November; they were executed the following morning.

1922

Thursday   30   November

Windy day. Very
      wet night.

      This is the
      day of
      "St Andrews"

      Called in at.
      Eglinton Street
            tonight
      and saw
            my friend
      St Petrauskis.
      I got some
more Lithuanian stamps

Thursday, 30 November
This is the day of Saint Andrew. Called in at Eglinton Street tonight and saw my friend Saint Petrauskis. I got some more Lithuanian stamps.

Monday, 4 December
Agnes in the wash house all day. After tea we wandered to the Majestic. Wrote friend Bobinski in Poland and friend Gaube in Austria.

Tuesday, 5 December
Stuck in stamps at night. Tommy went to the meeting place of his secret society.

Thursday, 7 December
Repaired the floor of the coal bunker in case our neighbour below gets more than her rightful share of black diamonds.

Friday, 8 December
Gas very poor tonight. Went out for about an hour.

Saturday, 9 December
Went out in the afternoon as far as the Langside Library. Gas getting worse and worse.

Sunday, 10 December
The gas hopeless, so wrote a strong letter to the Corporation. Agnes took a run out at night to see Hetty Mossman.

Monday, 11 December
Three workmen came today and hit the gas pipe in the close a few taps with a hammer, and then went away. The light at night just as bad as ever. To accustom our eyes to the dark, we went to the Majestic.

Tuesday, 12 December
Men dug up our close mouth today, and put in new gas pipes. Brilliant light at night. Hallelujah! Tommy has to draw a map for school, so I gave him expert advice. Agnes working the old sewing machine at night.

Wednesday, 13 December

Agnes doing some hectic work in the room. I assist by putting a polish on the doors. Stop now and again to admire the brilliance of our gas.

Thursday, 14 December

Tommy finished his map. It should get first prize. Put some plates of steel on my boots, to make them last longer.

Friday, 15 December

Helped Agnes to wash our priceless dinner set at night.

Sunday, 17 December

I made the breakfast this morning.[59] To thoroughly digest it, I took a walk round the Dumbreck road. Agnes made the dinner.

Monday, 18 December

Agnes in wash house at night. Speculated in a stamp catalogue. Tommy and I went to the Majestic at night. Polish president assassinated. There are no police?[60]

Tuesday, 19 December

Agnes finished her washing. Being one of the fortunate ones, I lifted my salary today as usual.

Wednesday, 20 December

Cold day. To keep herself warm, Agnes ironed all night. Brought home a tin of paint.

Thursday, 21 December

On my way home, I called in and saw my friend Petrauskis. We are spring cleaning in a sort of way.

Friday, 22 December

Agnes lamed herself today by kicking a pail. The pail is all right. Tommy stopped today for his holidays. He got a fine book as prize for 'excellence in composition'.

---

59   This is such an unusual occurrence that Thomas not only illustrated himself cooking
      but also underscored the word 'I' twice and drew two hands pointing towards the
      letter.

60   Gabriel Narutowicz, first President of the Second Republic of Poland, was assassinated
      five days after taking office. His assassin was a right-wing extremist.

1922

Friday   22 December

Rained all day, and
very stormy night.
            Agnes lamed
            herself today
            by kicking
            a pail
            the pail is all
            right. Painted
            the kitchen
            mantle piece
a nice shade of
grey, and the range
a nice shade of black.
Tommy stopped today for his
holidays. He got a fine book
as prize for "Excellence in composition"

Monday, 25 December
Have a holiday today, seeing that it is Christmas. It rained all day, and blew a hurricane. We went to Majestic at night and let on we were at the pantomime.[61]

Tuesday, 26 December
Wild hurricane during the night. Deluges of rain, thunder and lightning. Let the factor know that our chimney had a kink owing to the weather.

Wednesday, 27 December
A man came up today to sort our kitchen gas pipe. Didn't think that this would help our lum, so I spoke gently to the factor for an explanation. He explanated a mix up of names. Agnes and Tommy at Ibrox tonight with various gifts.

Thursday, 28 December
A man came up and amputated the fractured part of our chimney can. The treatment to be continued at a later period. Got a Xmas card from my friend in Warsaw.

Friday, 29 December
I assisted at night by cleaning the kitchen brasses. Think I'll stop keeping a diary.

Saturday, 30 December
On holiday today. Rained all forenoon. Dry after dinner, so I took a walk to Linn Park. Agnes gave the stair its last wash for the year.

Sunday, 31 December
The last day of the year. We took an extra-long lie this morning. I made a cup of tea about 8 a.m., then back to bed. After a late dinner, I took a walk round the Queen's Park. We now await the new year, and hope for the best. Amen.

61 'Let on' here means 'pretended'.

1923

For Thomas and his family, 1923 continued to present health and domestic problems that dogged their steps. However, they found plenty of time for their hobbies of visiting the picture house and walking in the country. This year, they added indoor golf and listening to the wireless to their pastimes. Thomas and his family were on the ball, since broadcasting arrived in Glasgow this year, and they were among the first to 'listen in' on the primitive radio sets that were available. Stamp collecting continued, and an astute purchase of some German marks made Thomas a millionaire, if only hyperinflation hadn't made his currency speculation a poor investment. At home and abroad, incidences of unrest seemed to figure less, with the Irish Civil War coming to an end and the League of Nations promoting peace in Europe.

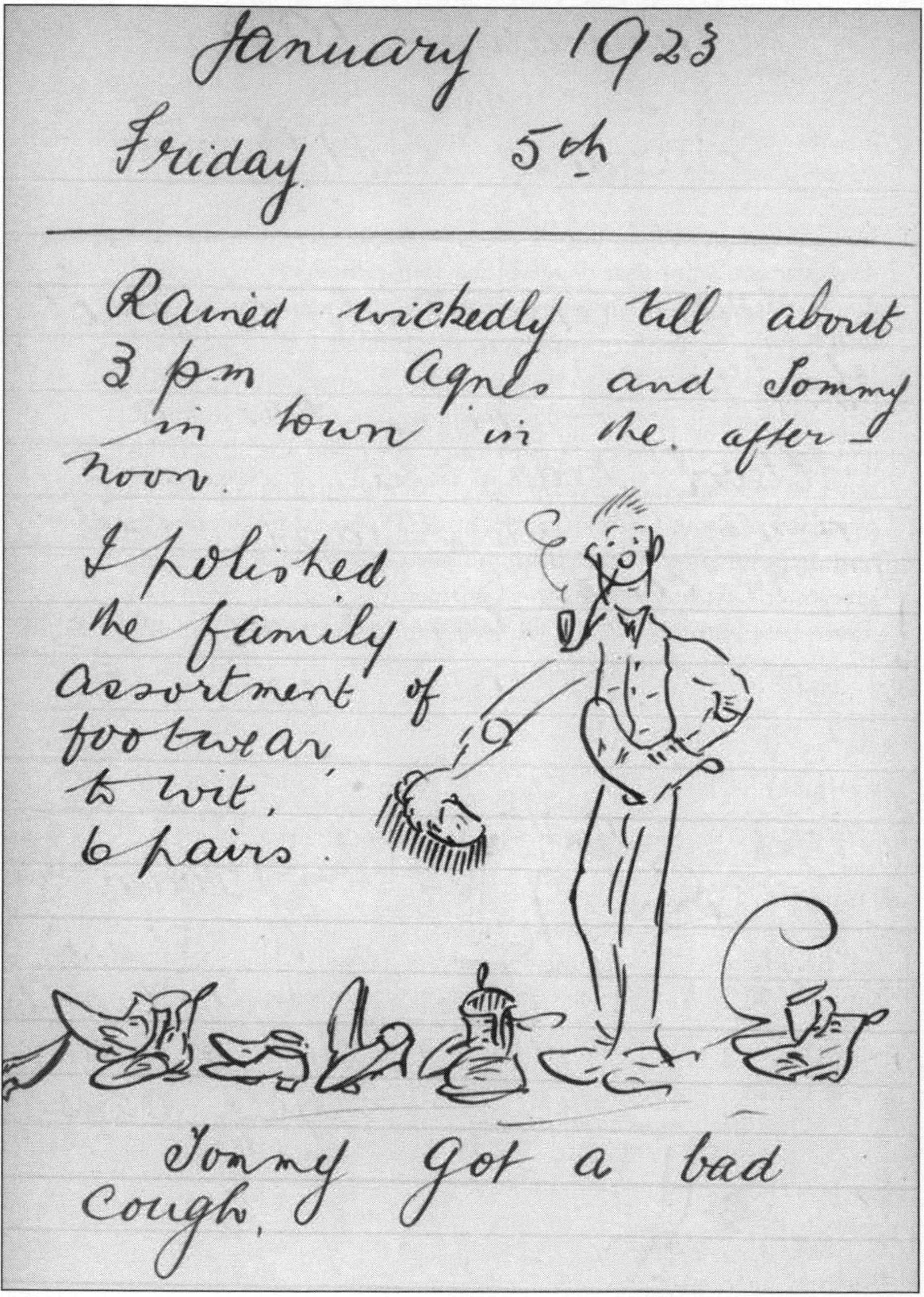

January 1923

Friday   5th

Rained wickedly till about
3 pm   Agnes and Tommy
in town in the after-
noon.

I polished
the family
assortment of
footwear,
to wit,
6 pairs.

Tommy got a bad
cough.

Monday, 1 January
At a very early hour this morning, we all went into the Carmichaels' and wished them all the compliments etc. We got back at 3.45 a.m. On holiday today. We all went to Coatbridge by 3.25 train from the Cross.

Tuesday, 2 January
Started work today. Stopped at 1 o'clock. We finished up our holidays with a visit to the Majestic.

Wednesday, 3 January
Mrs Gordon, Ella and the wee chap here tonight. Agnes in the wash house.

Thursday, 4 January
Tommy had a school mate up after dinner. They played with Meccano. Said small boy had tea with us. Started to shape some boards for a new golf game.

Friday, 5 January
Agnes and Tommy in town in the afternoon. I polished the family assortment of footwear, to wit six pairs.

Tuesday, 9 January
We have now got our lum on. We spent the evening at Greenlodge.

Wednesday, 10 January
Gave up the golf game. I'm not a joiner.

Thursday, 11 January
Mr Gordon here in the afternoon. He gave us a golf ball from Nannie. Went to a joiner man I know and gave him the golf game and wished him god speed.

Saturday, 13 January
Got a letter from Vienna, with stamps and a collection of Kroner notes. Money is no use in Austria. Also some stamps from Warsaw. Tommy not feeling very well, a boil on his forehead is giving him trouble. Hetty, Meg and Daisy here in the afternoon.

Sunday, 14 January
Tried my hand at surgery and operated on Tommy's boil with a needle, and hope for the best.

Monday, 15 January
Tommy in bed till after dinner. We are quite worried about the
lad. We played games at night to cheer us up. Got some stamps
from Germany.

Tuesday, 16 January
Agnes in the wash house. Wrote to New Zealand. Memel invaded
by the Lithuanians.[1]

Wednesday, 17 January
More boils on Tommy, so Agnes took him round to the doctor
at night. Doctor says he is all right. They will go away. We are
mightily relieved thereby.

Thursday, 18 January
I cleaned the kitchen windows tonight. The German mark stands
at 110,000.

Saturday, 20 January
*Tommy and I had a walk in the
afternoon. After tea, I went into
Calton and looked round the barrows,
but did not see what I was looking
for – to wit, a putter.*[2]

Sunday, 21 January
Still being without a kirk, I did not go to that place of
entertainment. Feeling the need of fresh sweet air, took a tramp
round Thornliebank, Giffnock, Clarkston and Cathcart.

Tuesday, 23 January
Dull, damp and mild. All Greenlodge here at night. Agnes
was presented with a blouse, Tommy with a book, and I got a
beautiful tie. Isa gave us a few exercises on the piano, nobody
sang and we played a hybrid sort of game of golf with a walking
stick. Fore!

---

1   Memel, in western Lithuania, had been under Allied control since the Great War. On
    11 January an insurrection ousted the Allied forces and restored the city to Lithuanian
    control.

2   Margaret Russell (later McIver) rented static barrows to traders in Moncur Street
    each Saturday. This grew to become the Barras, or Barrowland, the large weekend
    market in Calton.

Thursday, 25 January
Tommy's watch arrived today.[3] Great rejoicings.

Friday, 26 January
Saw the Duke of York in town. He was too busy to speak to me. Maggie MacKenzie of the next close married this evening.

Wednesday, 31 January
I had an evening with my stamp album. The German mark is at 220,000.

Thursday, 1 February
Agnes ironed all night. Tommy's boils appear to be getting better.

Friday, 2 February
Got a letter from Warsaw. This is Candlemas Day.

Saturday, 3 February
Gordon Mossman, Hetty his spouse, Billy the son and heir, and the wee lassie all here at 6 o'clock. We amused them in our usual manner.

Sunday, 4 February
Nice sunny day. Tommy and I went to Linn Park and Rouken Glen in the afternoon. When Tommy and I got back, Mr Gordon was in. He is working now, so we were all very pleased.

Wednesday, 7 February
The sewing machine not working well, so I tried my hand at it. The sewing machine is still not working well.

Thursday, 8 February
The factor here for the rent. Being law abiding, simple minded people, we paid it. Tommy got an atlas at school for excellence in map drawing.

Tuesday, 13 February
Tommy at his meeting tonight. Agnes has finished knitting her scarf.

3   Tommy has presumably been saving up coupons for a watch, as he did for a fountain pen in 1922.

Wednesday, 14 February
Dropped in at night on my way home and had a crack with my
good friend Mr Petrauskis.

Thursday, 15 February
Tommy says he has a sore ear.

Friday, 16 February
Tommy's ear seems to be not well yet.

Sunday, 18 February
Pumped warm water into Tommy's ear and told him it
was now better.

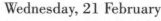

Wednesday, 21 February
Deep snow lying when I got up. Agnes took
Tommy to the Princess pantomime tonight.

Thursday, 22 February
Agnes baked an apple cake at night.

Friday, 23 February
John Callan up tonight to see the
Morgan Street stamp collection. Got
a letter from Poland today. Postage
1,000 marks.

Saturday, 24 February
Bitter cold. Agnes and I went to Rouken Glen, and got some very
fresh air.

Monday, 26 February
Agnes went into town this afternoon and picked wallpaper of an
elegant and chaste design.

Tuesday, 27 February
Some rain as usual. Tommy's ear looking bad
again, so I plied the squirt once more.

Wednesday, 28 February
Agnes took Tommy to the doctor. He looked at his ear
carbuncle. He is to keep from school. Benny Caldwell
up at 8 a.m. to paper the room. He finished at 8 p.m.

Friday, 2 March
Dull forenoon, then rain. Tommy at doctor again. His ear is now all right.

Monday, 5 March
Tommy back at school. Got a letter from Vienna with the usual donation. Postage on it 3,000 kroner. We went to the Majestic at night.

Tuesday, 6 March
Got back my bits of wood from the joiner, so I worked a brace of hours trying to complete it.

Wednesday, 7 March
Called in at Eglinton Street at night and saw my Lithuanian priest. Did some glue work at the golf game at night. It will be finished one of these days.

Thursday, 8 March
Dry day. Called in at a shop today, and got a putter. Spread the 'game' on the floor tonight. We decide it takes up too much room.

Friday, 9 March
Took the golf boards to another joiner, and got them back shortened. We tried a round or two at night. It will do.

Saturday, 10 March
Stained the golf boards.

Tuesday, 13 March
Tommy got his school photo today. Tommy at his club at night. Did a little paint work in connection with the golf game. Put numbers on the board and gave the plate a chaste shade of green.

Wednesday, 14 March
After tea, Agnes took a run up to Dennistoun to see the Mossman family. I spent the evening in the bosom of my stamp album.

Thursday, 15 March
Got a letter from Poland this morning with the usual assortment.

Saturday, 17 March
Mr and Mrs Gordon and wee chap arrived first, then Nannie and
Charlie. Not having a 'listening in' machine, we played at parlour
golf. I am giving the wireless my consideration.

Sunday, 18 March
Tommy went out a walk in the afternoon. He 'clicked' with some
boy and they walked to Carmunnock and Busby. Following in
father's footsteps. Mossmans arrived about 6 p.m. We spent the
evening in music and elevating discourse.

Tuesday, 20 March
Agnes went to a kinderspiel with Tommy and Mrs Carmichael.[4]
She had to leave it, and Mrs Carmichael took her home, all out,
dead beat. She bathed her feet and so to bed. Very sad.

Wednesday, 21 March
Agnes in bed all day. Doctor examined Agnes thoroughly. She has
a severe cold. Has to keep in bed for a few days.

Thursday, 22 March
Agnes' chest very sore and cough bad.

Friday, 23 March

Doctor up again. He thinks Agnes is improving. He prescribes a bottle for her cough. I washed the floor at night.

Monday, 26 March
A warm day at last. Agnes up all day.
Josephine and Lily came in at night to see if we were well. We
weren't. I played Lily a round of golf, and Josephine made the
supper.

Tuesday, 27 March
I'm not well today. At dinner time felt all out, nose running good-
oh. Bathed my feet and had a good anti-prohibition drink and so
to bed.

---

4   Literally, 'kinderspiel' means 'children's games'. Here, it presumably means a concert
     or variety show featuring children and aimed at a mixed audience.

Wednesday, 28 March

In bed all day. Isa and Jack here tonight to see how Agnes was getting on. She seems to be improving. I played my niece and nephew at golf, just to show them how to hit a golf ball, and the correct end of the golf stick to hit the aforesaid ball with.

Thursday, 29 March

Back to my work again. Feeling wonderful.

Friday, 30 March

Stopped today at 4.45 for the Easter holidays. Jean and Daisy in when I got home. The entertaining season has begun. I played Daisy a few games of draughts. Good Friday.

Saturday, 31 March

Spent the forenoon washing the floor. Being a labour of love, I wotted not.[5] At night, we visited the Gordons at Ibrox. Uncle Willie (Agnes' uncle) was there.

Sunday, 1 April

An uncle of Agnes', Mr Peter Henderson, very ill so Agnes went to Tollcross with Nannie Gordon in afternoon to see him. I arranged stamps in her absence, and Tommy went to Sunday School. Josephine dropped in about 6 o'clock.

Tuesday, 3 April

Tommy in town with his ma for a new suit. I put ironworks on Tommy's boots. They should last for another week.

Wednesday, 4 April

At 1 a.m. Tommy frightened us out of our wits by walking into the kitchen. He seemed to be asleep. We let him into our bed, and I went to room. Agnes slept no more. Bought myself a new pipe. Mrs Gordon, Ella and the wee chap here at tea time. All the Carmichaels in at 7 p.m. We played golf, piano, fiddle etc.

Friday, 6 April

Agnes went to the doctor at night. She got a bottle, a tonic, as she is much run down.

Sunday, 8 April

Fine sunny day, but very high wind. Agnes in bed all day after dinner. I out after breakfast, over Cathkin, Carmunnock, Busby

---

5   Thomas seems to mean 'I cared not', but the phrase means 'I knew not'. He may be quoting from the religious poem 'Ballad of the Lost Souls' (1913) by John Oxenham.

and car from Crookston. Not out again. Got my bellyful of fresh
air.

Monday, 9 April

*Tommy went to Buchanan Street Station
with his pal to examine railway engines.
He goes back to school tomorrow.*

Tuesday, 10 April

Agnes very bad when I got home. An awful pain in
her side. Having visions of the worst, I rushed for
the doctor. Our own doctor not at hand, so I got a Dr Murdoch.
Pleurisy, he said.[6] So we poulticed Agnes all night with mustard
etc.[7] Mrs Carmichael and Mrs MacKenzie gave me valuable
assistance. The pain eased somewhat, towards the early hours.

Wednesday, 11 April

Agnes a little easier. The doctor up (our own one) and he says
the pleurisy has stopped. No food but milk. Josephine in at night.
She did a small ironing and made the supper. Mrs Gordon here
at night, Mrs Carmichael also, likewise Jenny Sutherland (who is
coming for a time to assist in the house). I went out for a little at
night for a smoke.

Thursday, 12 April

*Agnes a little easier. Doctor
up and quite pleased so far.
Jenny takes the reins today.
Lily up at night. I had a
smoke in the room.*

Friday, 13 April

Milder sort of day. Agnes getting a little sleep. Doctor up again
and sees no reason for alarm. The elder up tonight with the
Communion cards. We gently let him know 'nothing doing'.

Saturday, 14 April

Doctor up today and expresses satisfaction. Feeling a bit wobbly
today. Smoked in the kitchen for the first time since last Monday.
Mrs Carmichael dropped in after tea. I dropped in to see Mr
Carmichael and had another smoke.

---

6   Pleurisy is an inflammation of the pleura, the lining of the cavity surrounding the
     lungs. It can cause sharp pain when breathing, coughing or sneezing.

7   A poultice is a moist mass of bread or cereal spread on a cloth and held against the
     skin to relieve pain or inflammation. Mustard can be added to provide extra heat.

Sunday, 15 April

Agnes not any worse. Mrs MacKenzie dropped in to see how she was. Agnes was allowed a little fish for dinner today. Entertained to tea Isa and Nannie and Mrs Carmichael. Charles Petrie called at night for Nannie.

Monday, 16 April

Got letters from Lithuania, Denmark and Austria. Had to pay sixpence on the Lithuanian, and I could not read it. Doctor up as usual. Quite pleased with Agnes' condition. Her cough is easier now. Tommy's night out. He went to the Cinerama. Mrs Carmichael made the bed.

Tuesday, 17 April

Agnes still improving. Mrs Gordon and the wee chap up this afternoon. Dropped in to see Petrauskis tonight and he translated the Lithuanian letter.

Wednesday, 18 April

Sunny day, but cold wind. Left off my overcoat today. Doctor up tonight. Agnes got up for about an hour. Josephine here, and made the bed.

Thursday, 19 April

Beastly cold day, so on goes my overcoat again. Jenny, our little maid, cleaned the windows. Agnes up for a brace of hours. She made the bed, with a certain amount of my assistance. I wrote to Peter Henderson tonight. Primrose Day. Who cares?[8]

Friday, 20 April

Doctor up at night. Agnes to be allowed up during the day. She got up for a pair of hours tonight. Mrs Carmichael in for a bit tonight and made the bed. Wrote to my friend in Warsaw. Tommy went to the library.

Saturday, 21 April

Agnes up for about five hours after dinner. I gave Tommy a bath at night.

---

8   Primrose Day is the anniversary of the death of politician and Prime Minister Benjamin Disraeli in 1881. The primrose was his favourite flower.

Monday, 23 April

Doctor up today. Agnes to get up when she likes. So she had her tea at the table, but supped in bed. Miss Wylie dropped in for a bit at night and talked and talked and talked. Had a look at Alex Carmichael's wireless tonight.

Tuesday, 24 April

Got a letter from New Zealand and a photograph. Jenny in the wash house today, so Agnes made the dinner and was up practically the whole day. Was listening in on Alex Carmichael's machine.

Wednesday, 25 April

Agnes up most of the day. The load is gradually lifting from my mind. Gave Tommy's boots an overhaul.

Thursday, 26 April

Agnes up all day except for breakfast. She is gradually getting on to her feet again. The Duke of York is getting married today, so Tommy has a holiday.[9] He went to the art galleries. This is Jenny's last day with us.

Friday, 27 April

Tommy brought home another prize from school. Agnes still getting on, and up all day.

Saturday, 28 April

Doctor up today, and he is allowing Agnes out tomorrow. We went to the Carmichaels' for a little at night and 'listened in'.

Sunday, 29 April

Agnes made breakfast. Took Agnes a little walk for about 40 minutes.

Monday, 30 April

Agnes all done up today. She says I walked her too far yesterday. It is very disappointing. Hetty Mossman and Wee Billy here in the afternoon. Gordon is now out of hospital.

Tuesday, 1 May

Agnes made the breakfast and was out in the afternoon. Tommy now getting swimming at school, at least the first stages. He seems to like it fine. Wrote to New Zealand.

---

9   The wedding of Prince Albert, Duke of York, and Lady Elizabeth Bowes-Lyon took place in Westminster Abbey. In 1936 they became King George VI and Queen Elizabeth. In 1953, she became Queen Elizabeth the Queen Mother.

1923

Tuesday 24 April.

Bright, sunny day, but very cold. Off goes my overcoat again.

Got a letter from New Zealand and a photograph.

Jenny in the wash house today so Agnes made the dinner, and is up practically the whole day.

"Was listening in" on Alex. Carmichael's machine.

Friday, 4 May

Doctor up on his last visit, and pronounces Agnes not so bad. Factor here and got his rent. Worked late at night. When I got home Agnes had got about half of the floor washed, so I finished it.

Saturday, 5 May

Nice warm day. We all went out in the afternoon via Queen's Park and Shawlands.

Sunday, 6 May

Agnes a little bit tired, so did not go out. After dinner I had a walk over to Greenlodge. Lily not keeping in the best of health.

Monday, 7 May

Agnes engaged a lady to do the washing.

Tuesday, 8 May

Tommy posted his answers for a certain competition. He is going to win £100. Agnes did an ironing tonight. I sorted my boots with a new patent liquid leather. The King and Queen are in Italy.

Wednesday, 9 May

Agnes getting vigorous, so she washed the floor. The King and Queen are visiting the Pope now. Where are the police?

Thursday, 10 May

Had a pain in my belly all day. Took a large dose of castor oil at night and sat in the big chair with a hot water bottle under my waistcoat. Feeling relieved by bed time.

Sunday, 13 May

Bright and sunny at times. Dull and wet at other times. Warmer at times. Took a walk to Pollok Estate in the afternoon and had a seat. Basked in the sunshine and thought it fine to be alive.

Monday, 14 May

When I got home, Jenny was in, also Mrs Gordon and wee chap. We tried the Carmichaels' wireless in our house, but couldn't get it to work very well. I went in with Mr Carmichael to his house and it worked better there. Agnes went in about 10 o'clock to Carmichaels' to hear a tune.

1923

Tuesday   15 May

Better day but very
wet night. Tommy at
bathing parade today and
library at night.
        Agnes worked
all night at a fancy
bed mat.

Wednesday   16 May

Bright day but extremely
cold.   Cleaned my pipe
tonight
which did
not sweeten
the atmosphere.
also
mended
Tommy's
school bag

Tuesday, 15 May
Tommy at bathing parade today and library at night. Agnes worked all night at a fancy bed mat.

Thursday, 17 May
Cleaned all the windows. Mrs Carmichael not well, so Agnes in and out.

Saturday, 19 May
Went out in the afternoon for some tobacco and dropped into library in Calder Street. We went to the Majestic tonight. First time since the spring holiday.

Monday, 21 May
This is a holiday. King's birthday. So to work I did not go. Bright sunny day. In the forenoon I went to Linn Park. After dinner we all walked to Linn Park via Carmunnock Road. After tea we went to the Majestic.

Tuesday, 22 May
Agnes not well at all. Sick and fevered. No appetite. She went to bed after dinner. Josephine came in at night. Owing to ill health, Bonar Law resigns.[10]

Wednesday, 23 May
Agnes' inside works seem in a bad way. My nephew Jack here in the afternoon with a ticket for Tommy. Some gymnastics display in which Jack is competing. About 5 p.m. I got the fright of my life by Jack appearing at the office. He said Agnes was very ill and I had to come home. I got home, I don't know how. It was a relief to find Agnes a little better. She had collapsed and had to be carried to bed by Mr Carmichael. Doctor up and says she is fevered and has to eat nothing.

Thursday, 24 May
Doctor up today. Agnes' temperature normal and she feels a bit better, but no food yet except a little milk. Josephine here and did an ironing.

Friday, 25 May
Agnes up again all day. Hallelujah. She has not much of an appetite yet. Tommy sits today his qualifying examinations.[11]

---

10   Andrew Bonar Law resigned as Prime Minister on 22 May and died of throat cancer six months later.

11   These exams determined whether pupils went to a junior or senior secondary school. The former were for less academic students, who were expected to leave school at 15 for a trade, while the more academic students would remain at school longer and be prepared for college, university or white-collar occupations.

Monday, 28 May
Agnes at doctor at night and got a bottle and some good advice.
Fresh air, plenty of food etc.

Thursday, 31 May
Cleaned all the windows at night. Agnes is getting a little
better and is enjoying her food more.

Friday, 1 June
Agnes at Tollcross this afternoon. She washed
the floor, so she is getting on. There being
some shows in the vicinity of Queen's Park, I
had a walk through them at night. 'Walk up.
Ladies and gentlemen.'

Saturday, 2 June
Got a letter etc from Vienna. Tommy went to
the shows in the afternoon and came home in hot
haste with a wee goldfish. I went with Agnes
a few messages. After tea we all went to Linn
Park and finished up at the shows. I had
three shots at the goldfish, but our livestock
was not increased thereby.

Sunday, 3 June
The fish is still alive. We call it Babinski.

Monday, 4 June
Brought home a larger globe for wee Babinski. He
or she will have room to swim now. My birthday.

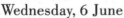

Tuesday, 5 June
Agnes out in afternoon with Mrs Carmichael to see *Flames
of Passion*.[12] My word.

Wednesday, 6 June
Agnes at Tollcross then at Josephine's shop. I dropped in to see
Petrauskis on my way home. Tommy has passed his examinations.
187 marks out of 200. Which is extra good.

Friday, 8 June
Tommy met me in town at night. We bought a
goldfish, a big one, to keep wee Babinski company.

---

12 *Flames of Passion* (1923), directed by H.G. Moody and starring Frank Whitson, was
    a melodrama set in an American lumber camp.

 *Was at library tonight. Consulted a few volumes that refer to fish.*

Sunday, 10 June
The one and only anniversary. Vile day of wind and rain.

Monday, 11 June
Agnes got a new hat this afternoon. Mrs Gordon here in her absence, so did not get in. I went to Carmunnock at night. In my absence the minister called. Agnes and Tommy entertained him. Revolution in Bulgaria.[13]

Wednesday, 13 June
Agnes took a run down to Ibrox in the afternoon. Nanny Gordon and Charles here at night.

Thursday, 14 June
Bright, sunny day. Took a walk at night through Ruglen, over Cathkin and home by Carmunnock Road and Mount Florida.

Friday, 15 June
Cleaned all the windows at night. The German mark now stands at 500,000.

Saturday, 16 June
In the afternoon I went down to Erskine Hospital.[14] Andrew Pettigrew has been lying on his back there for three months with curvature of the spine, a war legacy.

Sunday, 17 June
Tommy and I at Ruglen visiting the old landmarks. Old Ruglen Quay, the Shipyard and the Green Groats etc.[15] A most depressing locality. After we got home, we all went to Dennistoun and visited the Mossmans.

---

13   Armed forces under General Ivan Valkov overthrew the government in what became known as the 9 June Coup d'état. The Communist Party declined to be involved in the uprising.

14   The Princess Louise Scottish Hospital for Limbless Soldiers and Sailors was opened in Erskine, Renfrewshire, in 1916. It was always known as Erskine Hospital, the name it adopted later. In 2000 the original hospital was closed, and three new units were opened elsewhere in the town. It still cares for ex-Service personnel.

15   The quay and the shipyard were in the north of the town, on the south bank of the River Clyde.

Tuesday, 19 June
We went to the Majestic at night. Had some pain in my inside
for some little time, and some blood came tonight, which caused
me some considerable uneasiness. Think I've burst all my inside
works.

Wednesday, 20 June
Consulted my doctor tonight, who greatly relieved my mind.
Nothing to be alarmed about. He gave me a bottle to keep my
inside right. Took a run over to Greenlodge at night.

Friday, 22 June
Agnes went down herself to Largs, and searched the whole village
for a summer house for herself and her good man, to say nothing
of the child. She got a house before giving it up as a bad job.

Saturday, 23 June
We had a walk at night through Queen's Park. We listened for a
bit at the bandstand. Some fine opera stuff being warbled there.

Sunday, 24 June
Agnes being a lady, and I a gentleman, the first named party got
breakfast in bed. Dull, bleak, windy day. We rusticated in Queen's
Park etc at night. The wind played tricks with Agnes' hat.

Tuesday, 26 June
Agnes and Mrs Carmichael at the Coliseum to see some juicy
picture in the afternoon. We are getting the kitchen whitewashed
very soon, so made the preparations tonight. Polished up the
kitchen clock and assisted my sweetheart in washing the dinner
service.

Wednesday, 27 June
Agnes was at school today, as Tommy's teacher wished to consult
her. Benny here at night and put on the whitewash, I being
banished to the room, out of the way. Benny let us off for 3/6.

Thursday, 28 June
At last!!! A real summer day. Sun blazing like a real one. Brilliant
day, real heat. Agnes consulted the headmaster of Strathbungo
School (Tommy's future academy).[16] Mrs Gordon and Ronnie here
when I got home. After tea I went over Cathkin. German mark now
at 750,000.

---

16   Strathbungo Senior Secondary School stood at 83 Craigie Street. The building is now
     St Bride's Primary School.

Friday, 29 June

Blazing hot, sunny day. Tommy stopped at school for the holidays. This is his last day at Victoria School. He came home laden with prizes. He cleared everything, the best scholar in the school. Agnes and I had a walk round by the Hangingshaws.

Saturday, 30 June

I went into town this afternoon, and bought myself a new knife. Agnes will now be able to cut her various corns off. After tea we all had a walk through old Cathcart and Netherlee Road. We met the King family (not the royal family) and had a crack. I knew Mrs King 23 years ago when she was a lassie (Florrie Peden).

Tuesday, 3 July

Some heavy rain this forenoon, but turned out a very warm day. Tommy and Jack playing at golf. Agnes at the shop where the paint is, and bought a pail of the stuff. I went to Greenlodge from my work. Agnes and Tommy there early. We walked home.

Wednesday, 4 July

Got started tonight on the paint job.

Thursday, 5 July

Sweltering heat wave. Got more paint work done. Tommy brought home a dozen 'baggies' or so.[17] There were two survivors at night.

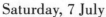

Saturday, 7 July

Dull, muggy day. Heat terrible. Got all the painting finished. Went out for a breath of air at 9 p.m.

Sunday, 8 July

Warm, sunny day. The finest day I have seen for a long time. Did a little varnish work on the shelf this forenoon. Being Sunday, it should be extra shiny. We all went to Ibrox in the afternoon.

---

17   'Baggy' (or 'baggie') minnows are small fish of indeterminate species, often caught in a net rather like a butterfly net and kept in a jam jar.

Monday, 9 July

Dull day, some rain, but still extra warm. Mrs Gordon here in the morning with Ronnie. We kept Ronnie for the day. Agnes went down to Ibrox with the wee chap after tea. German mark is now standing at 1¼ million to the pound.

Friday, 13 July

Blazing hot day. Away at 12.45 for a few days, this being the Fair. Tommy and I at Giffnock quarries in the afternoon. We got a roasting. After tea we all had a walk by Merrylee Road and through old Pollokshaws.

Saturday, 14 July

Fair Saturday, so I do not go to business. Nice sunny day. Gordon Mossman up for me after breakfast. He and I had a walk by Clarkston, Eaglesham, East Kilbride and back by Busby. We got back about 5 p.m. Hetty and the weans were in. After tea, Gordon and I had a walk through the Queen's Park.

Sunday, 15 July

Rained all day. Took a walk myself to Queen's Park. At night it cleared up a little so we took the car to Canniesburn and walked down to Jordanhill and got car home.

Monday, 16 July

Nice sunny day, but pretty breezy. We had a little picnic of our own at Waterfoot. We then meandered back to Busby by the glen, and old print works.[10] We finished the day with a visit to the Majestic.

Tuesday, 17 July

Started work again. Heavy showers all day. Took a walk as far as Ruglen at night. Too wet like to go any further.

Wednesday, 18 July

Agnes and I had a walk to Pollokshaws, Cathcart and through the wee road at Mount Florida Station. One of the 'baggies' died this day.

Thursday, 19 July

Tommy went down to Ibrox himself in the afternoon, a message for Agnes. One of the room chairs in a bad way (the seating accommodation), so I put new webbing on etc.

---

18   The 'glen' was Busby Glen, and Busby Printworks opened in 1796 to print calico and other textiles produced at the town's two mills.

Friday, 20 July
Painted the inside of kitchen press. German mark 1,800,000.

Saturday, 21 July
Got a letter from Warsaw. Willie MacKenzie in for his tea at evening. He just home from his holidays. Agnes, Tommy and I out for a little at night, but the rain chased us home.

Sunday, 22 July
Rained all day. Not out at all. Agnes not well at all. Fainted and so forth. Wish we were away our holidays.

Monday, 23 July
All the Carmichaels home tonight from Furnace. We took them in and gave them their tea. We had some music etc. Wee Alex Dunn came in to have a cut in his skull doctored up.

Wednesday, 25 July
Got a letter this day from Estonia, if you know where that is. Got a pair of white duck shoes for my holidays.[19] Had a walk round by the Cart at night. Very cold wind.

Friday, 27 July
Getting busy at night now, we are going to Largs next week. Cleaned the room windows and mended the case of my telescope. German mark 4,100,000.

Saturday, 28 July
Tommy had a small boy called Taylor in all afternoon. They amused themselves with the air gun. Seeing it was a wet night, we went to the Majestic.

Monday, 30 July
Went at night and ordered a motor car (automobile for short) to take us to the station on Wednesday morning. Then I went over to Greenlodge for the loan of a case.

Tuesday, 31 July
Stopped today for my holidays. I got my hair cut so that I will get all the sun going at Largs. We spent a hectic night packing up.

---

19   White duck shoes are made with unbleached white cotton duck, a sturdy fabric that
      takes its name from the Dutch word 'doek', which means linen canvas.

German mark now stands about 5½ million. In other words, its value is nil.

Wednesday, 1 August
All up early this morning. Our motor car arrived in time, so we drove to St Enoch Station like gentlemen. We got our train about 9.15 a.m., and got our compartment to ourselves right down to Largs. We spent the day basking in the sunshine and admiring the village. Fine, warm and sunny.

Thursday, 2 August
Weather very broken. Agnes and I had a walk through Douglas Park in the afternoon, but got chased by the rain. We went to a picture house at night.

Friday, 3 August
Blowing a hurricane and heavy showers at times. I took a walk to Fairlie in forenoon. Agnes and I listened to a 'Jazz' band at night.[20] Tommy went to the Cadets with somebody.[21] He had not arrived home by 10.30, so I went out to look for him. I got him.

Saturday, 4 August
Brilliant hot, sunny day. We took a walk past Fairlie, and had a seat by the shore. In the afternoon we had a look at the swimming gala here, then Agnes and I putted.

Sunday, 5 August
Nice forenoon. Tommy and I took the 'red road' walk, and back by the shore. The flies enjoyed our company very much. After tea, we went up the Brisbane Road, but a heavy shower made us turn back. We had a seat on the esplanade.

Monday, 6 August
Showery and stormy. After breakfast, I took the Bower Craig walk. After that, we went a little picnic a little past Fairlie. After tea, we took the Skelmorlie Road and then a look at the Cadets. The weather seems to be very uncertain.

---

20   Thomas and Agnes are early adopters of jazz. The word was first applied to music in
     1915 in Chicago, and the first jazz record was released in 1917 in New Orleans.

21   Alvin Sawyer and the Smart Set Cadets were a music-hall act that played a summer
     season in Largs every year from 1909 to 1928. The show featured singing, comedy and
     sometimes ventriloquism.

1923

Sunday   5 August

Nice forenoon. Tommy
and I took the red
road walk
and back by
the shore
The flies
enjoyed our
company
very much.

Very showery
afternoon.

After tea we went up
the Brisbane Road,
but a heavy shower
made us turn back
we had a seat
on the Esplanade.

Not cold by any means

Tuesday, 7 August

Buckets of rain in the morning, but turned out a mild day. In the afternoon, we putted, and Agnes won. We then went along and had a seat at the boat. We spent the evening at the Cadets.

Thursday, 9 August

Glorious weather today. Sunshine of the best. Had a walk myself in forenoon to Douglas Park. A bloodthirsty bee stung Agnes in the hand. In the afternoon we took the motor boat to Millport. We had an hour in that city, then our motor boat sailed us back again. This is the life. German mark 20,000,000.

Friday, 10 August

Another nice day. In the forenoon, I went the 'red road' walk. After dinner we all at Douglas Park. After tea we tried our hands at putting. We then met Nannie Gordon at the train at 8.45 p.m. She is down for the weekend. After a cup of tea we had a walk round by the Pencil. A charming night.

Saturday, 11 August

Blazing hot sunshine all day. After breakfast, I had a seat at the putting green. Nannie and Tommy then joined me, and we putted. We then had a stroll around. After dinner we all went to Douglas Park. Nannie took our photo in various attitudes. While basking on a seat, an impious bee bit my hand. After tea we took motor to Fairlie Glen, and motor back. A perfect day.

Sunday, 12 August

Dull, wet afternoon. I saw and had a stroll with Claude Maxwell in the forenoon. After tea, we all had a walk to the Prophet's Grave.

Monday, 13 August

All of us up at the crowing of the cock. Nannie departed for Glasgow by 7.28 train. We all waved her adieu. After tea we did the putting game twice. At night, we went to the Pencil. Tommy pointed the camera at us and said we were photographed.

Tuesday, 14 August

Nice sunny day. In the forenoon, I was along the Wemyss Bay road. In the afternoon, we putted, then to Fairlie by the shore, and motor back. After tea we succumbed to the putting fever, and then up the 'red road' and had a nice seat. I'm winning now at putting. German mark now 20,000,000.

Wednesday, 15 August
A sad, sad day, but everything comes to an end. Our holidays
draw to a close. Some heavy showers. Took my farewell walk by
the Bowen Craig. After dinner, Tommy and I took our farewell
game on the putting green. We then took our hamper to the
station. For the sum of 1/-, the railway company will deliver
said hamper tomorrow to our home address. We finally got
packed up and got the 3.25 train home. We all had tea with the
Carmichaels, and so ends our holidays. The most enjoyable for
many a year.

Thursday, 16 August
*Back to work. Dull and cloudy. Went to Calder
Street library for a little at night.*

Saturday, 18 August
Very warm, sunny afternoon, so I ventured forth to Cathkin
Braes. When I got there, heavy rain chased me home again.
Dull night, but we managed out for a little.

Monday, 20 August
Tommy had Jack Taylor up at night. Agnes ironing some
articles.

Tuesday, 21 August
Tommy starts his new school today, to wit Strathbungo. We go to
Majestic at night. German mark 30,000,000.

Wednesday, 22 August
After tea, Agnes and Tommy went to town for some school books. I
cut up rhubarb at night.

Friday, 24 August
Stayed in at night, and stuck stamps. Tommy learning French and
Latin.

Sunday, 26 August
Agnes got her breakfast in bed this morning, as she did not feel
100 per cent. All the folk from Ibrox here at night. Mr Gordon is
again idle.

Monday, 27 August
Agnes went to see the eye specialist. She is going to get glasses.
After tea, we went out to see Mrs Mossman.

Wednesday, 29 August
Tommy in town getting more books. Agnes washed all night. Some Italians murdered by Greeks.[22] More trouble.

Thursday, 30 August

Took a walk over Ruglen at night. Was speaking to my old schoolmaster, Mr Scott. Agnes went to town and got her glasses. Italy sends ultimatum to Greece.

Friday, 31 August
Agnes and Tommy in town for a case for Tommy's books and gymnastic shoes. German mark now 53,000,000.

Saturday, 1 September
We meandered into Shawlands at night, then meandered into the picture house of that name. Italy seizes Corfu.

Sunday, 2 September
Brilliant sunshine all day. Tommy and I at Ruglen in afternoon, home by Croftfoot and Linn Park. At night we all went to Ruglen by the 100 Acre Dyke, and got car home. Great earthquake in Japan.[23]

Monday, 3 September

Agnes went to New City Road with her eyeglasses, as they won't keep company with her nose. Think she will need 'specs'. Italy getting very warlike with Greece. Tokyo and Yokohama destroyed in the great earthquake.

Tuesday, 4 September
All Greenlodge here at night. Isa's young man up for the first time, so I made him look very carefully through my stamp collection. We played golf, music etc. Hundreds of thousands reported killed in Japan.

---

22   The Corfu Incident began on 27 August, when the Italian general Enrico Tellini and three of his assistants were murdered by persons unknown in Greece near its border with Albania (effectively an Italian protectorate). Italy demanded the capture and execution of the murderers and, when Greece was unable to do this, invaded Corfu, killing at least 15 citizens. The League of Nations ordered Greece to pay reparations, and Italy to leave Corfu.

23   The Great Kanto Earthquake devastated Tokyo and Yokohama on 1 September, killing more than 100,000 people.

Wednesday, 5 September
Got a letter from Babinski this morning. We all at the Majestic at night.

Thursday, 6 September

Agnes in town and got 'specs' with ear legs on them. Had a word with the Rev. Petrauskis on my way home. Got word today that Andrew Hamilton is dead.

Friday, 7 September
Took the afternoon off and attended Andrew's funeral. Helped to lower him to his grave, my last sad duty. A million German marks now cost a penny.

Monday, 10 September
Mrs Gordon, Ella and Ronnie here at tea time. Got my hair cut. Ireland admitted to the League of Nations. Italy and Greece friendly again.

Wednesday, 12 September
Agnes at Dennistoun at night. Tommy at Cinerama. German mark 465,000,000.

Thursday, 13 September

Rained heavily all morning. Rained heavily all forenoon. Rained heavily at mid-day. Rained heavily all afternoon. Rained heavily all night.

Friday, 14 September
Tommy at the ABC book shop in the afternoon.[24] He came in at tea time with various parts of his anatomy missing. He fell off a car. Poor wee chap.

Sunday, 16 September
Fine sunny day. After breakfast I went my favourite Busby and Carmunnock walk. After dinner Agnes and I went to Sighthill Cemetery. We meant to go to the Necropolis to see Andrew's grave but were too late. Tommy away for a long walk with Jack Taylor.

---

24   The ABC Bookshop was a Glasgow institution for new and second-hand school books for almost a century after it opened in the 1890s.

Monday, 17 September

Agnes in town this afternoon. Left her 'specs' to be mended. The German mark is now 689,000,000.

Tuesday, 18 September

Got word from Dennistoun this morning that a wee girl had arrived. At night, we go to the Majestic. The German mark gone mad: 1,300,000,000 to the pound.

Thursday, 20 September

Agnes in town in the afternoon for her 'specs'. They are now quite satisfactory and are a good fit. Tommy had Jack Taylor up at night.

Friday, 21 September

Got a letter from Babinski this morning, also his photo. If I'm ever in Poland, I'll know him when I see him.

Saturday, 22 September

Had a look round the Queen's Park after dinner. After tea, we all round about Shawlands. Bought a new hat today of a pleasing shade of fawn.

Sunday, 23 September

Carmichael's pipe burst, so I assisted him to destroy the surrounding woodwork in our effort to locate the injury. We located it, and put it in splints. The heartless waterman then turned off the water.

Monday, 24 September

This is the autumn holiday, and a glorious day of sunshine. After dinner, we all went to Carmunnock via Clarkston and Busby, and walked home. No water yet.

Tuesday, 25 September

Water still non-existent, so rung up the factor. It was on shortly after. Agnes made jam tonight. Big pit disaster at Redding Colliery, near Falkirk.[25]

---

25 The Redding Pit Disaster, one of the worst in the history of the Scottish coalfield, occurred in the early morning of 25 September, when water flooded Number 23 Pit and forty miners were killed.

Thursday, 27 September

Received today 600 million marks from Germany for 20 shillings. It was for a friend of mine. I kept 50 millions, so I am a millionaire.

Friday, 28 September

The man who examines the various gas appliances put up a new gas fixture for us. It is high and not extra straight. Mr Carmichael came in to admire it. He showed me the error of my ways in political matters for a few hours. Agnes seemed to be quite annoyed.

Saturday, 29 September

Tommy got another goldfish at the shows. We went to the Majestic at night.

Sunday, 30 September

Beautiful warm, sunny day. Went to Pollok Estate in forenoon. After dinner, Agnes and I went to Mosspark and examined the new houses.[26] After tea, we all went to the Mossmans' and saw the new baby.

Monday, 1 October

Not feeling up to the mark, and not feeling equal to eating a big dinner, I took a large dose of castor oil and went to bed at 2 o'clock. Got my tea in bed, then got up for a little at night. The castor oil was a big success.

← my new pyjamas

Wednesday, 3 October

Agnes at Ibrox in the afternoon. She finds that her aunt is ill and confined to bed.

Thursday, 4 October

Agnes at Dennistoun at night. She and Hetty Cook had been shopping at Josephine's shop. Five miners rescued alive at Redding after being entombed nine days. The German mark now stands at 2,000 million. My 50 million is now worth about sixpence.

---

26   Mosspark, to the south of Bellahouston Park, was one of the first housing estates built by Glasgow Corporation.

Friday, 5 October
Tommy alarmed us by appearing in the early hours at our
bedside. He had walked in his sleep.

Sunday, 7 October
*Took a walk round Maxwell Park after dinner.
Agnes went to Ibrox.*

Wednesday, 10 October
*After my usual allowance of porridge,
my appetite failed me. Quite evidently
I'm not well. Felt better at night. My
50,000,000 marks are now worth a penny.
Mrs Newell of Coatbridge hanged this
morning, the first woman for
70 years.*[27]

Saturday, 13 October
We all at the Housing Exhibition at night. Saw many
things there that I would like.

Sunday, 14 October
Fine sunny day. Agnes and Tommy at church this morning. A new
church, to see what it was like. After dinner, we all went to the
Botanic Gardens and admired flowers and fish.

Monday, 15 October
Agnes at Dennistoun after tea. The baby is doing well.

Tuesday, 16 October
We went to the Majestic tonight. My 50,000,000 German marks
now worth one half-penny.

Thursday, 18 October
The Auld Ruglonian Society having a show on in the Ruglen
Library.[28] I went out at night to see it. Saw various Ruglen
antiquarians etc and came home duly and suitably edified.

Saturday, 20 October
Went across in the afternoon to the Govanhill Library to see the

---

27   Susan Newell (née MacAllister) of Coatbridge was hanged in Duke Street Prison
     in Glasgow after being found guilty of murdering John Johnston, 13. She was
     the only woman hanged in Duke Street Prison, and the last woman hanged in
     Scotland.

28   A 'Ruglonian' is a resident of Rutherglen.

new system of 'open access'.[29] After tea we all went to Shawlands. We went through the Queen's Park. It being so dark, Agnes a nervous wreck when we got out safely. Germany in a terrible condition. The mark now stands at 50 thousand million. My little lot is now worth one farthing.

Sunday, 21 October

Agnes at the new church this morning. New Bridgegate UF Church.[30] Seems a likely church. so she took seats in it. So now we are one of the flock. Tommy went down to Ibrox to see how Mrs Gordon was keeping. Mr Livingstone stayed at home and washed the dishes.

Monday, 22 October

Received a long letter from my worthy friend in Vienna. Agnes went on her visit of mercy to Ibrox. Looks as if Germany is going to split asunder. The Rhineland sets up a republic, and Bavaria stands on its hind legs.[31]

Wednesday, 24 October

Agnes at Ibrox at night. Mr Gordon started work again. The Carmichaels borrowed our steps. Mr Carmichael is going to stick on some wallpaper. My heart goes out to him.

Thursday, 25 October

For one pound you can get 500,000,000,000 marks.

Friday, 26 October

Agnes at Ibrox in the afternoon. Ella is now home from Grangemouth to look after the house. Following my usual custom (to avoid Sunday labour) I brushed all the boots in the house at night.

---

29 Until this change, the entire library stock was behind the counter and borrowers would consult a catalogue and then ask for the book or books they wished to read or borrow. The open access system put most of the collection on shelves in the public area of the library.

30 New Bridgegate United Free Church stood at 69 Dixon Road, a few streets south of Thomas' house. It was designed by the architect John Thomson, son of Alexander 'Greek' Thomson, and opened in 1923. The building is now Govanhill Workspace.

31 The Rhenish Republic was declared on 21 October 1923, during the occupation of the Ruhr by French and Belgian forces. The separatist state collapsed in November 1924.

Sunday, 28 October
We all at our new church this morning, and Tommy went to the Sunday School of said same church at night, and Agnes went herself at night to the aforesaid same church.

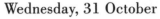

Wednesday, 31 October
Hallowe'en tonight. Jeanie MacKenzie came in at night, so I gave her her Hallowe'en. Agnes at Ibrox. Dirty, wet day at times.

Thursday, 1 November
Wet this morning, which is not very unusual. The kitchen easy chair needing mending in the nether regions. I mended it.

Friday, 2 November
The Carmichaels having a party tonight. We were graciously invited, and as graciously accepted the invitation, and thus lent the festivities an air of refinement and distinction. We had music, singing, dancing, bee-baw-babbity etc.[32] We left at 1.30 a.m. German mark 2¾ billion.

Sunday, 4 November
We all at Mosspark in the early evening. Smoked several cigars and 'listened in'.

Monday, 5 November
Agnes not entirely satisfied with the appearance of the room. I shifted the piano, so it has now got a different appearance.

Tuesday, 6 November
Got a letter from Babinski. He is finding life hard and dreary in Warsaw. We both recorded our vote in the municipal election. Went to the Majestic at night. Some misguided wag threw a firework that made a bang into the corridor, and nearly started a panic. The appearance of the room not yet satisfactory, so back went the piano into its old spot.

---

32 'Bee-baw-babbity' is a Scottish ring dance, with the song also used as a skipping rhyme by children.

Wednesday, 7 November

Bright, cold, sunny day. Hard frost, so on goes my overcoat. I might as well be warm. Our man got in at the election. No doubt my vote had something to do with it. Working late.

Saturday, 10 November

Cold, dirty sort of day. This is Agnes' birthday. I got a letter from Mr Gaube, Vienna, with a nice selection of stamps.
Took Tommy out a walk in the afternoon to Linn Park. I spent the evening sticking in stamps, and Agnes spent it in running out messages.

Sunday, 11 November

This is the Day of Remembrance. Armistice Day. Special services in all the churches, and two minutes' silence at 11 a.m. We went to morning church, Tommy went to his Sunday School, and Agnes and I went to church at night. Amen.

Tuesday, 13 November

Dropped in before tea time and had a word with Petrauskis, and discussed the affairs of Lithuania and Poland.

Wednesday, 14 November

Agnes at Ibrox in the afternoon. Mrs Gordon seems to be pretty ill.

Friday, 16 November

Tommy appeared at dinner time with his wrist and leg all tattered and torn. He had a fall. Agnes put bandages on, and we hope for the best. I got word today that Jack was very bad with boils, so I went over to Greenlodge at night. He was in a sad condition, but the danger was over.

Sunday, 18 November

We all managed to church. After dinner I took a walk round Shawlands. After tea we all went to Greenlodge and found Jack improving.

Monday, 19 November

We all went to the Majestic at night. Nannie Gordon here when we got home. Mrs Gordon not making any headway.

Tuesday, 20 November

I got a postcard from Germany, and the postage amounted to 24,000,000,000 marks. The mark stands at 34 billions to the pound.

Wednesday, 21 November

Looked up Isa today, was told Jack keeping fine. Worked late.

Friday, 23 November

Agnes and Tommy at Cinerama at night. I cleaned the goldfish kennel. and generally enjoyed myself.

Saturday, 24 November

I put the thermometer outside the window this morning. It dropped to 27 degrees. I decided it was cold. Took a walk through Queen's Park in the afternoon. The ponds all frozen. Some folk think they will get skating soon. I don't.

Sunday, 25 November

Agnes and Tommy went to church this morning. After dinner I took a walk by Cowglen Road and Crookston. Passing Ibrox, I called in to see Agnes' aunt, and found her sitting up. Agnes went to church at night. I took a run over to Greenlodge. Jack practically all right now.

Monday, 26 November

Thinking I could see more if I wore glasses. I had my eyes tested this afternoon. Discovered there I couldn't see at all without glasses. So I have secured a pair. Worked late.

Wednesday, 28 November

Poor wee 'Yellabelly' died. Cause of death unknown. It was cremated in the kitchen fire.

Thursday, 29 November

Got my eyeglasses tonight, and managed home without being run over. I will now see all the things I have missed. At night I sharpened the bread knife, brushed a few score of boots, shaved myself etc.

Friday, 30 November

Agnes went to Ibrox at night as her aunt seems a bit worse. This is the day of St Andrew, hence the kilts.

Saturday, 1 December

Went to Calder Street library for a volume. Agnes baked a cake. She is trying for a prize in our church bazaar. As this is a test cake, it turned out a failure. John Maclean, the communist, dead.[33]

Tuesday, 4 December

This is the day you vote 'wet or dry'. Not having studied the question thoroughly, I did not vote. I met Isa about 5 p.m. and took her home with me. Lily came shortly after. After tea John Martin and Jack Archibald arrived.

Wednesday, 5 December

Agnes took her cake to the church at night. We hope to get first prize.

Thursday, 6 December

Polling today in Glasgow, so Agnes and I registered our vote.[34] Brought home five pounds of tea from China that Alex Baxter gave me.[35] Had a Corporation bath before tea.[36] Agnes at the Dixon Hall with her cakes at night, then we went to Ibrox.[37]

---

33 John Maclean MA (1879–1923) was a Scottish schoolteacher and revolutionary socialist, primarily known for his outspoken opposition to the First World War. He was appointed the Bolshevik consul to Scotland by Lenin.

34 The Labour Party won ten of the fifteen Glasgow seats in the 1923 General Election. Glasgow Cathcart, in which Thomas and Agnes lived, returned Robert MacDonald, one of the five Conservative candidates.

35 Alexander Baxter Junior was the senior partner of Paterson, Baxter and Company, Thomas' employer.

36 Thomas had a bath (not a swim) in one of the Glasgow Corporation public baths, probably Govanhill Baths.

37 The Dixon Hall, the former Crosshill and Govanhill Burgh Halls, stands on the corner of Dixon Avenue and Cathcart Road.

Friday, 7 December

Agnes and Mrs Carmichael at a church concert in Jamieson Street.[38]
Great victory for Free Trade in all the election results. Big Labour
and Liberal gains.[39]

Saturday, 8 December

Agnes and Tommy at our church bazaar with
Mrs Carmichael. They came home with one or
two purchases. Tommy had seen a conjuror
there who did some wonderful tricks.

Wednesday, 12 December

Put up a small thing in the scullery with
hooks on it to hang small pots and pans etc.

Thursday, 13 December

My ear very sore all night. Agnes was kept up most
all the time pouring oil down it, sticking thermal wool into it and
placing hot water bottles over it. We enjoyed a little sleep about
6.30 a.m. After breakfast felt all right again. Got a letter from
Duncan to cheer me up.

Friday, 14 December

Tommy got an average of 89 per cent for his three days
examination at school, which is very good. Agnes washed the
dinner service, as New Year approaches. I brushed all the boots in
the house.

Saturday, 15 December

Nice bright day. In the afternoon, Tommy and
I had a walk to Ruglen, up Stonelaw, through
Buchanan Drive and down the Calderwood. I
was spellbound by the beauty of the countryside
as seen through my magic spectacles. I have
missed a lifetime of the beauties of nature.

Sunday, 16 December

Agnes came with me to church at night. I saw the architecture of
the church in a new light.

---

38   Now Coplaw Street.

39   The Conservatives, who had fought the election on the platform of tariff reform, won
     the most seats, but the gains made by Labour and the Liberals resulted in a hung
     parliament.

Monday, 17 December

Agnes at Ibrox in the afternoon. She spent the night washing curtains and ironing collars.

Tuesday, 18 December

Had a crack with Father Petrauskis on my way home. Agnes very busy at night, cleaning out the room etc. I assisted by polishing the poker, tongs and shovel.

Wednesday, 19 December

Being fortunately placed, I drew my usual salary today. We are all right for another month.

Thursday, 20 December

Went out at night to consult with my dentist. Saw a beautiful coloured rainbow round the moon. Managed down to Ibrox just in time, where the dentist gently and painlessly coaxed out my offending tooth.

Friday, 21 December

Winter commences, shortest day. So my timetable says. It is wrong. It commenced this year in January. Very dark, wet day. To get some light on the subject, we went to the Cinerama. Text: *The Wandering Jew*.[40]

Saturday, 22 December

Took a notion to see art, so went to Art Galleries in afternoon. Tommy and Jack Taylor there also. Big fire in Glasgow (Drury Street) tonight. Two lives lost.[41]

Monday, 24 December

Got my hair trimmed tonight so that I would be nice for the festive season. Agnes gave me a very shiny case for my glasses. We received various Christmas cards, also a letter from Babinski.

---

40   A UK film directed in 1923 by Maurice Elvey, based on a stage play of the same name, with Matheson Lang as Matathias. Based on the Christian legend of the Jew cursed by Christ to immortality.

41   At least one boy died when fire broke out in an office in Drury Street. The owner shouted a warning to two young employees, then fled the building. The boys were trapped in the upper floors, above the fire. One jumped to safety, although badly injured, and the other perished.

Tuesday, 25 December

Christmas day, so I have a holiday. Off I went to the country.
Walked to Linn Park, car to Clarkston, walked to Busby and on
to Carmunnock. Snow started on my way home, and fell heavily
all the way. We gave Tommy a book for his Christmas. At night
we went to the Majestic. Still snowing, and about a foot deep.
Heaviest fall for 30 years.

Wednesday, 26 December

Snow lying deep round about us. Very cold
day. Tommy and Jack Taylor at the Carnival
in the Kelvin Hall this afternoon.

Thursday, 27 December

Got a letter from Vienna this morning. My Austrian
friend enclosed his photo. Agnes working very hard
getting ready for the New Year.

Friday, 28 December

Agnes made the ginger wine tonight for
drinking our health at Ne'erday. I did
the usual boot cleaning job.

Saturday, 29 December

Agnes got a very sore head, although I do not
associate it with the picture on preceding page.
I took a run over to Josephine's shop in the
afternoon.

Sunday, 30 December

Agnes' head still bad this morning. So Tommy and I went to
church alone. After the service I interviewed the minister to see
if our transfer lines were to hand. They weren't. Agnes at Ibrox
in the afternoon. When she got home, we went to church, and
were introduced to the elders and got the 'glad' hand
generally.

Monday, 31 December

Got away at 12 noon. Very
wet day. Did not go out
again this year. We spent a
busy sort of evening getting
things ship shape for the New

(w) "Ring out the old."

Year." We expect visitors on or about midnight. A small boy born tonight to Maggie MacKenzie, or I should say Mrs Fraser.

42   Scottish tradition demands that people go into the New Year with all their dishes
     washed, rooms tidy and clean, and all loose ends tied, to ensure good luck in the
     coming 12 months.

1924

Thomas and his family were settling down into life in the 1920s. As always, they were involved in a regular round of visiting and hosting visits of family, friends and neighbours. Tommy, as he became more independent, joined the Scouts and found a fellowship there and in Sunday School. He also showed considerable academic prowess at his new secondary school. The family moved to a more local church, which encouraged the nature-loving Thomas to devote more of his Sunday mornings to indoor worship. Agnes continued to be troubled by illness, her recovery always hampered by worry and overwork. The Livingstones acquired a radio – always the do-it-yourself enthusiast, Thomas built his own case and erected his own aerial – and a newfangled carpet sweeper.

In the outside world, the first Labour government came and went, stirring Thomas only by lowering the duty on tea and sugar, and the League of Nations continued to keep international skirmishes to a minimum.

Tuesday, 1 January

At the witching hour of midnight (I should, rather, say at 12.01 a.m.), we opened the door and in came the Carmichaels. We had a right merry party, and they departed 3.30 a.m. We retired to bed at 4.30 a.m. We all went to Ibrox in afternoon. We sang, played, listened in etc, and got home 12.15 a.m. Got a letter from Duncan this morning.

Wednesday, 2 January

Took a walk out to Ruglen in the forenoon. Called in for a few minutes at 200 Main Street.[1] Home for dinner at 2 o'clock. Agnes took Tommy into town after dinner for a new suit. We finished up our holidays at night in the Majestic.

Thursday, 3 January

At work once more. Josephine and Jack in when I got home. We received various gifts in honour of the season. Agnes received a dressing jacket, I got a pocket book, and Tommy was overjoyed with a book. We played dominoes etc.

Friday, 4 January

Got some newspapers from New Zealand, and Agnes got a letter from Duncan's girl.

Sunday, 6 January

We all at church this morning. After dinner, Agnes took a run down to Ibrox. Her aunt is still improving, and was out for a little. Mrs Carmichael in twice today letting us know how Maggie is keeping. She is very ill indeed.

Monday, 7 January

Tommy back at school. We went to Majestic at night.

Tuesday, 8 January

We all at Greenlodge tonight. Isa met me at 5 o'clock and I went home with her. We played at ping-pong etc. Maggie MacKenzie seriously ill.

Thursday, 10 January

Heavy fall of snow this morning. Started a letter to Duncan tonight.

---

1   Home of Thomas' uncle Willie.

Friday, 11 January
Heavy snow all forenoon. Maggie of the next close still seriously ill. Continued my epistle to Duncan. Will get it finished one of these nights.

Sunday, 13 January
Ground white with snow this morning, then heavy rain wiped it out. We did not go to church. Tommy composed two articles for the school magazine.

Monday, 14 January
Maggie MacKenzie now out of danger. We go to the Majestic at night.

Wednesday, 16 January
Agnes did a little baking at night. A railway strike threatened.[2]

Thursday, 17 January
Agnes at Parkhead and bought a few articles of clothing.[3]

Monday, 21 January
Railway strike started.

Tuesday, 22 January
Dropped in tonight and had a word with the Lithuanian. We have now a Labour government. Ramsay MacDonald, our first Socialist premier.[4]

Saturday, 26 January
Nannie Gordon and Charlie here at night. We played at cards.

Sunday, 27 January
Tommy and I went to church in the morning. Gordon Mossman and Wee Etta here in the afternoon.

Monday, 28 January
Got a letter from my good friend in Vienna. Tommy at pantomime tonight in the Coliseum with Mrs Carmichael and Peggy.

2　The Associated Society of Locomotive Engineers and Firemen (ASLEF) was campaigning against proposals to cut the wages of its members, who were among the lowest paid in the railways.

3　Josephine's shop was in Parkhead.

4　When the minority Conservative administration lost a vote of confidence in the House of Commons, King George V asked MacDonald to form a new government. Labour ruled with the tacit support of the Liberals.

Tuesday, 29 January
Railway strike settled. Went to Mossend at night to see the Rev. Petrauskis. We listened in and examined stamps. I got the 9.32 train home. Agnes very bad with neuralgia.

Wednesday, 30 January
Got a letter from Babinski. My last letter to him has gone astray, so I put a claim through the Post Office. Agnes in bed all day. Tommy and I washed the floor at night.

Thursday, 31 January
Agnes extra bad with her head. Could eat nothing at all.

Saturday, 2 February
Isa here at night to see the invalid, and Jack her boy came in about 9 p.m. The Russian Soviet recognized by Britain.[5]

Sunday, 3 February
Went to church myself this morning. I had a small walk after dinner. Josephine here at night. Ex President Wilson of USA (the country that won the war) has died.[6]

Monday, 4 February
Our washer wife washed the kitchen floor.

Tuesday, 5 February
Agnes shows signs of reviving now. We played at dominoes tonight.

Wednesday, 6 February
Cleaned the room windows at night, and wrote to Herr Gaube. Agnes' head getting clearer.

Friday, 8 February
Agnes out today for the first time, and survived it. The Prince of Wales broke his collar bone today.[7] TCL broke his about 30 years ago. The wee Fraser block christened tonight.[8]

---

5   The new MacDonald government formally recognised the Union of Soviet Socialist Republics on 1 February.

6   Thomas Woodrow Wilson died at his home in Washington DC on 3 February. He was 67.

7   Edward, Prince of Wales, fell from his horse and broke his collarbone while jumping fences at Billington.

8   Maggie MacKenzie's new baby boy.

1924
Tuesday   29 January

Railway strike
settled.
            Very mild day
Went to Mossend
at night to see the
Rev. Petrauskis.   We
listened in and examined
stamps. I got the
9.32 train home.
    Agnes in bed when I
got in very bad with
                neuralgia etc.
                I rubbed her
                head with
                linament. Some
                went into her
                eye, and nearly
                blinded her

Sunday, 10 February

Agnes and Tommy at church. After dinner, Tommy and I went to the Mossmans'.

Thursday, 14 February

Isa has the flu, so Agnes took a run over at night. Dock strike threatened.[9]

Saturday, 16 February

Had a run over to Langside Library in afternoon. Played Tommy a few games of draughts at night and managed to beat him. Dockers' strike now started. All Great Britain affected.

Sunday, 17 February

We all at church this morning. At evening, Agnes went to church herself. When she came home, I went over to Greenlodge. A very stormy night, and a pouring wet one, and I had to walk home.

Monday, 18 February

George (one of our staff) being laid up, I went out tonight to see him. He is a stamp collector, so we passed a pleasant evening. Great explosion at Erith, London. 11 girls killed and a man.[10]

Tuesday, 19 February

A party at Greenlodge tonight (Lily's Sunday School pupils). Agnes went over.

Thursday, 21 February

Agnes in wash house today, first time for a year. She survived (so far). I am going to erect a wireless receiving station, so bought a few parts. I went to Dennistoun at night, and left the wireless with Gordon Mossman to put together.

---

9   The dock workers, who had poor conditions and no job security, were striking for better pay and conditions. The strike disrupted all British imports and exports.

10   The Slade Green Filling Factory had been a munitions factory, but after the war became a privately owned facility for breaking up munitions. The women were working with Verey light cartridges when one exploded, setting off all the other cartridges in the shed. Eleven of the eighteen women working in the shed died along with their foreman in the inferno.

Friday, 22 February

Spent the evening, assisted by strange language,
making a wee box for the wireless.

Saturday, 23 February

Spent the afternoon putting an aerial up in
the lobby. At night we all went to Mossmans',
and I brought home the variometer." I joined
up the machine and listened to America.
Atmospheric conditions bad, so I got more noise
than music.

Sunday, 24 February

Agnes and I at church this morning. Business –
Communion. After dinner, I rigged up the wireless.
Heard a few sounds. Then it gradually faded away.
By night it was dead.

Monday, 25 February

Put a new crystal in the musical box, and
put a few inches on our aerial. Improved it
a bit, so we heard the Tales of Hoffman."
About 9.30, oscillating started, which bust
the show.

Tuesday, 26 February

Our machine without wires doing fine now.
Agnes listened a little in the afternoon, and we
had the Parkhead Silver Band at night.[13]

Wednesday, 27 February

Agnes at a kinderspiel tonight with
Mrs Carmichael. Gordon Mossman
dropped in about 9 o'clock. He examined
our wireless. He thought it was too
wireless, so we put a length of aerial
across the kitchen. Results most
pleasing.

---

11   The variometer, or tuning circuit, was the heart of a crystal wireless set.

12   *Tales of Hoffman* is an opera written by Jacques Offenbach in 1881.

13   Station 5SC – owned by the British Broadcasting Company (a private company)
      – began broadcasting from Glasgow on 6 March 1923.

The early days of radio

Thomas was an early adopter of radio in Glasgow, buying a crystal set in kit form in early 1924 and making his own wooden box to hold the completed machine, which was assembled by his friend and relative Gordon Mossman. This was a primitive receiver with no valves or power supply that took its power from a lengthy aerial wire and was able to drive only one set of headphones. So his early experiences of listening to the news from London or concerts from Europe would be very like someone in the present era listening to a Sony Walkman or Apple iPod, wrapped up in their own world to the great amusement of those around them. Thomas was a great consumer of news, from newspapers and magazines, and music, from his own piano, from cinema organs and orchestras, or from bands in the various parks he enjoyed walking through or sitting in. The radio expanded and enriched the scope of his – and his family's, once other headphones were added – knowledge and experience of the world. This included hearing the unveiling of the Menin Gate Memorial to the Missing, in July 1927, by the King of the Belgians.

The early radio sets were delicate, relying on a small crystal of semiconducting material to extract the signal from the radio carrier wave; the second generation used the more expensive but more reliable vacuum tube valves (which had been developed during the First World War for use in military communications) to carry out the same function. These required a power source, usually a lead-acid battery, which could also be used to drive a loudspeaker, which of course made listening to the radio more of a social experience. The components for these radios, as well as finished sets, were supplied by specialist shops. In Glasgow, the pioneering supplier of radio equipment was the Clydesdale Supply Company, at 134 Saltmarket, where B.M. Levine and his family sold a variety of goods, including bicycles, gramophones, radios and musical instruments. The firm later expanded into other outlets across the city.

Thomas records that he bought his first radio licence for 15 shillings in March 1924. If he had bought a radio directly from the BBC, it would have cost ten shillings. The number of radio licences issued between 1923, when they were introduced, and 1929 shows the great growth of the medium: 1923 – 200,000 licences; 1924 – 600,000; 1925 – 1.2 million; 1926 – 1.8 million; 1927 – 2.2 million; 1928 – 2.4 million; and 1929 – 2.6 million.

The British Broadcasting Company (later Corporation) launched the first regular broadcasting station in the world on 14 November 1922 in London. Over the next few months, stations opened in Birmingham, Manchester, Newcastle, Cardiff, Glasgow, Aberdeen and Bournemouth. The Glasgow station, 5SC, began broadcasting on 6 March 1923 from the attic of Rex House at 202 Bath Street (a plaque on the building records this historic event). This small studio was host to orchestras, pipe bands, choirs and theatre companies, as well as solo performers and presenters of all stripes, sending out music, drama, news, current affairs, sport and other entertainment to local listeners. By the end of 1924, 'relay stations' had been opened in Belmont Street, Aberdeen (2BD), Lochee Road, Dundee (2DE), and George Street, Edinburgh (2EH).

In October 1924, Mr L. Hotine, the engineer in charge of 5SC, wrote about his station for readers of *Amateur Wireless* magazine. He wrote: 'All the engineers at Glasgow are station proud, and we have every right to be, for we do our best to radiate good stuff; but, obviously, as the art has progressed so rapidly, it has been impossible to install new gear all at once. When our dream of new gear and premises is a material fact, we will fearlessly assert that 5SC is second to none, and I guarantee it will be.' He added: 'Our studio is a small one, and is separated from the control room by a partition that is hardly sound proof. Imagine a telephone conversation between us and, say, Sheffield, via London, with a brass band on the other side of the wall. You will say: "I've no doubt you manage." We do, and though we are beset with many difficulties, our life is a happy one.'

Thursday, 28 February
We heard the Savoy up to midnight.[14]

Friday, 29 February
Perishing cold day. Snow blizzard this forenoon. Hard frost at night. Tommy at a Bible examination. The variometer in good form tonight.

Saturday, 1 March
This is St David's Day, so I eat the leek.

Sunday, 2 March
Nice day, but very cold. Felt as if I had the cold this morning.

Monday, 3 March
Cold still most unholy. That is the weather I refer to. Let Mr Carmichael hear the wireless set tonight, and he thinks it all right. Agnes did a lot of baking tonight. We may entertain.

Tuesday, 4 March
Heavy snow this morning, then a hard frost. Paid to the government today 15/-, being the cost of licence for my wireless receiving station. Met Isa at 5 p.m. and escorted her to our house. All Greenlodge being entertained. Tommy sat on Jack's specs so they bust.

Wednesday, 5 March
Foggy, frosty and cold. Took Jack's specs into town to be mended.

Thursday, 6 March
In bed all day with the cold or the flu. Agnes went into town in afternoon for Jack's specs. Cost us 6/-.

Friday, 7 March
In bed till tea time, then I got up. The office boy up to see me shortly after tea time. Josephine is not keeping well, so Agnes went over at night to see her.

---

14   The BBC broadcast a weekly programme of dance music live from the Savoy Hotel in London from 1923.

Sunday, 9 March

Listened (in a sort of a way) to Los Angeles, 6,000 miles away, about 3 o'clock this morning. Up at usual hour. Agnes and Tommy at church. Agnes over at Greenlodge this afternoon. The office boy up to see me about the same time. I am getting on nicely.

Monday, 10 March

Resumed my business connection today. Feeling very shaky, but survived. Agnes took a turn over to Greenlodge in afternoon. The striking works of Big Ben, in the lobby, out of joint, so I put it to rights at night.

Tuesday, 11 March

My cold seems still to linger about, like Sinbad's Old Man of the Sea.[15] Agnes in wash house all day. She managed to scald her arm in an unpleasant manner. She managed to wash the floor at night.

Wednesday, 12 March

Feeling not yet up to the mark (German or otherwise). Pain is all over me, and my head is as stuffy as ever. My, oh my!

Friday, 14 March

I could be feeling better. I heard Ramsay MacDonald, the prime minister, on our wireless. Wrote to my friend in Vienna.

Saturday, 15 March

Got a French stamp catalogue from Warsaw from my good friend Babinski. Agnes in town this afternoon for some footwear. The Prince of Wales nearly killed again. It is quite evident he cannot ride a horse.[16]

Monday, 17 March

My health is back to 100 per cent. We discovered a big crack in the habitation of our golden pets, so transferred them to a large bowl (pro tem). We all at an entertainment in the kirk at night. Trial

---

15   In *Tales of the Arabian Nights*, Sinbad encounters the Old Man of the Sea, who rides on his shoulders and will not let go.

16   The Prince of Wales fell in a point-to-point race at Garth and was kicked in the face by his horse. He suffered concussion and was kept in a darkened room for three weeks.

by Jury.[17] Got a large photo from our New Zealand friends. Babinski's lost letter turned up.

Tuesday, 18 March
The plumber up today, fixing a new pipe in the jaw box.[18] Was speaking to my nephew Jack in town today. Agnes ironed a few hundred collars at night. I'm all right, for a week or so.

Wednesday, 19 March
The joiner up this morning sorting the woodwork of the sink. He made a better job of it than he meant to do.

Thursday, 20 March
Agnes in town this afternoon buying a new globe for the fish.

Sunday, 23 March
I, myself, at church in forenoon. Mrs Gordon and Nannie here before 5 p.m.

Monday, 24 March
Jack Taylor up at night, being coached in Latin by Tommy.

Tuesday, 25 March
Agnes in wash house all day. Dropped in at night for a crack with Father Petrauskis.

Friday, 28 March
The Plymouth broadcasting station opened tonight, so I heard the lord mayor speaking from that town. Agnes dead tired at night.

Saturday, 29 March
Took a walk to Linn Park in the afternoon. Agnes went to town at night. Wrote Mr Gaube.

Sunday, 30 March
Agnes and I at church this morning. Josephine here at night, also Nannie Gordon and Charlie Petrie.

Monday, 31 March
Agnes took a run up to Dennistoun at night to see Hetty Mossman. Tommy and I stayed in. Tommy learned lessons and I footered with the wireless.

---

17   A comic opera in one act by Gilbert and Sullivan.

18   'Jaw box' is a Scottish term for a large sink, particularly in a kitchen or wash house.

Wednesday, 2 April

Agnes and Tommy at pantomime tonight with Mrs Carmichael and Peggy. Mr Carmichael came in about 7 p.m. and we listened in all night.

Thursday, 3 April

Tommy's school examinations in full blast. Cleaned all the windows at night.

Friday, 4 April

Got word from Vienna that my philatelic friend was a po. Wrote him at night in a suitable and befitting manner. Agnes listened in all night to Aberdeen.[19]

Sunday, 6 April

We all went to church this morning. In the afternoon, Tommy and I had a walk round by the Dumbreck Road. Agnes and Tommy went to church at night. I listened to a concert from America this morning at 12.45 a.m. It was an improvement on the last one.

Thursday, 10 April

Agnes at Ibrox in the afternoon. The light of my life is very tired tonight.

Friday, 11 April

Wrote to Babinski tonight.

Saturday, 12 April

Took a walk myself in the afternoon. As I wouldn't take Tommy with me, Agnes was greatly annoyed. After tea, Agnes and Tommy out for a little. A melancholy evening thereafter.

Sunday, 13 April

Snowed all day. Nobody out. Gordon and Wee Billy here in the afternoon. Another melancholy day. Ah, me.

---

19   The BBC's 2BD station began broadcasting from Aberdeen on 17 October 1923.

Monday, 14 April

Agnes in town this afternoon. Tommy's school examinations card shows his marks as 92 per cent. Like father, like son.

Wednesday, 16 April
Tommy stopped school today for the Easter holidays. He did not complain. After tea, Agnes went to town and I cleaned all the windows.

Saturday, 19 April
Wet sort of forenoon. After breakfast, Tommy and I had a walk through Busby and Carmunnock. More rain in the afternoon. After tea we all had a walk by Shawlands and Cathcart.

Sunday, 20 April
Mild day, but pretty windy. We all at church this morning. At night we had a walk through Ruglen, the land of hope and glory.

Monday, 21 April
Brilliant day of sunshine and very warm. We all took car to Barrhead and walked towards Paisley. Agnes got very tired, so we took car to Paisley. Admired all the shops and visited the museum. We concluded by a night in the Cinerama.

Tuesday, 22 April
Back to work again. Jack Ferguson here all day, and away after tea time. Got an Easter card from friend Babinski of Warsaw.

Wednesday, 23 April
"King opens the great exhibition at Wembley." His speech is broadcast, also the Prince of Wales. Agnes and Tommy both heard. As all this happened during business hours, I did not hear. Agnes in the wash house all day. As she was very tired at night, I washed the kitchen floor.

Friday, 25 April
Got a letter from Mr Gaube in Vienna. Tommy at Queen's Park tonight with his yacht.

---

20   The British Empire Exhibition was held at Wembley, Middlesex, from April to November 1924. It was repeated in 1925.

Saturday, 26 April
We all went out after tea, and met Hetty Mossman and the baby in Robson Street. We all had a little dander.

Sunday, 27 April
Gave Agnes her breakfast in bed, then Tommy and I went to church. Beautiful sunny day. So after dinner Tommy and I round the Merrylee Road.

Monday, 28 April
Mrs Gordon, Ella and the wee chap here when I got home at tea time. After tea I escorted Ella to Mount Florida. Agnes escorted the rest of the party to Ibrox. Wrote New Zealand.

Wednesday, 30 April
Tea and sugar going to be cheaper. Nothing off tobacco.[21]

Thursday, 1 May

Agnes and Tommy at the Cinerama tonight. I stayed at home and listened to Faust in ease and elegance.[22]

Friday, 2 May
Tommy got photographed at school today.

Saturday, 3 May
Put a DL5 crystal on my set. Result very good. Mr and Mrs Gordon, Nannie and Charlie here at night. Charlie brought a 'valve' so we had some loud stuff.[23]

Sunday, 4 May
Tommy went to church himself this morning. Tommy got a shilling from his teacher at the Sunday School for doing so well in the examination.

Monday, 5 May
Agnes at Josephine's shop in the afternoon. Had a look in at Calder Street library at night.

---

21 Phillip Snowden, presenting the first Budget by a Labour Chancellor of the Exchequer, on 29 April 1924, reduced the duty on sugar, tea, cocoa, coffee and dried fruits.

22 *Faust* is an opera written by Charles Gounod in 1859.

23 The DL5 crystal extracted the sound signal from the carrier signal; the valve amplified the volume of the sound.

Tuesday, 6 May

Had a crack with Father Petrauskis this evening on my way home. Sorted a loose castor on the easy chair at night.

Thursday, 8 May

Tommy got his school magazine today, with his first literary efforts printed therein. Wrote Duncan tonight.

Friday, 9 May

Received a letter from the factor, permitting me to erect an outside aerial.

Saturday, 10 May

We all had a walk round by Cathcart after tea. When we got home Agnes disappeared into the Carmichaels' until 10.30 p.m.

Sunday, 11 May

Agnes and Tommy at church this morning. After dinner I took Tommy a walk round by Kennishead and Thornliebank. We saw a war memorial being unveiled at latter named village. After tea Agnes and I had a walk round by Thornliebank and Cathcart.

Tuesday, 13 May

Working late, then over across the way and interviewed the neighbours and said I was putting up an aerial. No objections.

Wednesday, 14 May

Agnes in town this afternoon regarding a new costume. Tommy at the swimming pond today. Working late. Laid in a fresh stock of wires for the wireless. Put up a new earth wire at night, and bored a brace of holes.

Thursday, 15 May

Rose up early this morning and fixed up the new aerial from our kitchen window to a stairhead window facing. Tested it at night and found it exceeded my expectations, so down came the old aerial. Mrs Carmichael and Agnes at Majestic. I cleaned the room windows.

Saturday, 17 May

We all at Ibrox. Mr Gordon has made a wireless set but it is a 'dud'. Tommy, Charlie, Nannie and I went out for a little putting.

Sunday, 18 May
Tommy at church this morning. Agnes and I spent the day resting.

Monday, 19 May
This is a holiday. Nice sunny day, but very windy and dusty.
Painted the roof of the scullery white, sorted the linoleum and took
a little turn out before tea. The Majestic at night.

Tuesday, 20 May
Working late. Agnes washed the dinner set in readiness. We spring
clean.

Wednesday, 21 May
Kitchen and lobby whitewashed tonight. I worked late. Tommy got
photographed in the Gallowgate.[24]

Thursday, 22 May
Agnes and Tommy at the Majestic. I worked late. Wrote to Mr
Gaube of Vienna.

Saturday, 24 May
George (a lad of our warehouse), Tommy and
I at the stamp exhibition at the People's
Palace. Took George home for tea, then let
him see my stamp collection. He also duly
admired my wireless set and aerial.

Monday, 26 May
Working late. Agnes in wash house all day. Jack Ferguson has now
started work.

Tuesday, 27 May
Got a letter from Duncan. Worked late. Agnes ironed all night.

Wednesday, 28 May
Majestic at night. Mended Tommy's bag. Letter from NZ.

Thursday, 29 May
Agnes at Largs today, for our summer house. She got home about
6 p.m., tired but comparatively happy. She got a house.

---

24   Street photographers would take photographs of people and – for a fee – post them
the finished print. Some operators had a tame monkey that people could be pictured
with.

Friday, 30 May
Working late. An exhibition of school work in the Kelvin Hall. Tommy there this afternoon. He saw one of his school paintings on exhibition. Maybe he will be an artist.

Saturday, 31 May
Very cold, bleak day. The Cenotaph unveiled today by Earl Haig etc.[25] We heard all the speeches at home. After tea, we went into the square, and had a look at it in the flesh, so to speak.

Monday, 2 June
Helped Agnes to lift the room carpet, then took a walk myself by old Cathcart and Carmunnock Road. When I got home, Josephine was in. She gave me a pair of socks and suspenders for my approaching birthday.

Tuesday, 3 June
Got measured today for a light overcoat. With Mrs Carmichael's assistance, Agnes beat the room carpet, and with my assistance she laid it at night.

Wednesday, 4 June
This is my birthday. Nice sunny day. Agnes bought a new hat. At night, she went to church. The elder here with the tickets for Communion. This is Derby Day, but I'm not interested.

Friday, 6 June
We are resting tonight. At least, I am. Got letter from Gaube.

Saturday, 7 June
Agnes and Tommy in town in afternoon, as Tommy required new shoes. Too wet at night to go out.

Sunday, 8 June
We all at church this morning. As a result of Tommy's religious examinations, he was presented at church today with a prize (books), a certificate and a special prize (a very handsome gilt-edged Bible). We were all quite pleased. I went out for a little at night during a dry blink.

---

25   The Cenotaph in George Square, Glasgow, was the city's monument to its citizens who died in the Great War. It was designed by the Glasgow architect J.J. Burnet.

Monday, 9 June

Agnes went to the wash house for a little at night. Tommy played cricket and I took a walk through Linn Park and old Cathcart.

Tuesday, 10 June

Agnes in wash house for the day. I cleaned the kitchen window, sorted out my boots and listened in. On 10 June 1910 we did none of these things. On that date Agnes promised to love and obey me, etc.

Wednesday, 11 June

Agnes in town in afternoon re her new costume.

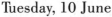

Friday, 13 June

Fine day. I got my new summer overcoat today, and Agnes' new costume arrived this evening.

Sunday, 15 June

Agnes and I at church this morning. Communion. Not out again. Wrote Gaube.

Monday, 16 June

Nice sunny day. Not out at night. Toe sore.

Wednesday, 18 June

Tommy got his hair cut. Went round to the doctor at night and let him see my toe. He says it is 'locked toe'.[26] Have to rest it, bathe it in hot water and paint it with iodine.

Thursday, 19 June

Got a letter from Duncan. We made rhubarb jam tonight.

Saturday, 21 June

Agnes took Tommy into town this afternoon for new trousers. Got a postcard from Babinski. He is in Danzig on holiday.

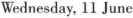

---

26 Thomas seems to be suffering from hallux rigidus, a type of degenerative arthritis of the main joint of the big toe.

Sunday, 22 June
I am resting. So got my breakfast in bed. Agnes and Tommy at church.

Monday, 23 June
Got another postcard from Babinski. Agnes at Josephine's shop in afternoon. My foot getting easier, but not using it much.

Wednesday, 25 June
Agnes finished her wash house task today. Went to doctor at night. He says my toe seems a little better, but to rest a lot yet. Took a small walk.

Friday, 27 June
Got a postcard from Babinski. He wants some literature. Tommy stopped school for the summer. We all out at night through the Hangingshaws and Mount Florida.

Saturday, 28 June
My foot is most desperately itchy. The iodine has taken off the skin, so put on some ointment.

Sunday, 29 June
Breakfast in bed again. Agnes and Tommy at church this forenoon. My foot seemed a little swollen today, which gave me some concern. It gradually got more normal.

Monday, 30 June
Lily here at tea time. I took a walk round to the doctor for more expert opinion. I have to quit the iodine trick for a little and soak the toe with olive oil every night.

Tuesday, 1 July
My summer overcoat is too long, so left it at my tailor's to be abbreviated. We all at Majestic tonight.

Saturday, 5 July
Nice day. In the afternoon we all went to the Queen's Park, and at night the Linn Park.

1924

Saturday　　28 June

Wild wet stormy
day. Coldish likewise

We all out for
a little at night.

My
foot
is
most
desperately
itchy.

The iodine
has taken off the
skin so put on some
ointment.

Sunday, 6 July

Fine warm, sunny day. After dinner, Tommy and I had a walk round by Toryglen. I was at my work in the morning as I wanted to finish a certain task. At night, Josephine and Jack here with Janet Foster. Janet has been in America for about 13 years, and is here on holiday.

Monday, 7 July

Tommy has a bad tooth, so Agnes took him down to Leiper the dentist in the afternoon. He left a vacancy in its place. Tommy's face is now swollen 'un peu'. Wrote Duncan tonight.

Tuesday, 8 July

Had a crack with Petrauskis tonight. He is going to Lithuania for his holidays. Went back to my work at night. Agnes in wash house.

Wednesday, 9 July

Uncle Jack and Uncle Willie here at night. Uncle Jack brought his wireless to test it on my aerial. My machine has it.

Friday, 11 July

Agnes took Tommy to the boot shop for some feet furniture.

Saturday, 12 July

Terrific heat today. In the afternoon it developed into a severe thunderstorm and heavy rain. We did not listen in during the storm. In fact, we kept away from it. Turned out a beautiful night, so we had a walk to Cathcart. Agnes got a 'coat of arms' cup of Millport from Peggy.

Sunday, 13 July

We all donned our best and went to church this forenoon. It is what is called a 'thin' congregation, owing no doubt to the holiday season. Turned out a nice night, so we took a car to Linn Park.

Monday, 14 July

Isa and her young man here about 8 p.m.

Tuesday, 15 July

When I got home at tea time, Mrs Gordon, Ella and wee chap here.

Friday, 18 July

This is Fair Friday, so I quit work at 12 noon. Warm, sunny day. Tommy and I at Rouken Glen in the afternoon. We admired the new boating pond. Duncan and his girl are due from Belfast in the morning.

Saturday, 19 July

Tommy and I out early. We met Duncan and Maud at the Irish Boat about 7.45 a.m., then home to breakfast. We rested till about noon, then Duncan, Maud, Tommy and I at Queen's Park. Josephine here when we got back. After dinner, we all at Linn Park. After tea, Tommy and I saw them off to St Monans from Queen Street Station at 7 p.m.[27] Brilliant sunny day.

Sunday, 20 July

Another perfect day. After tea, we all at Busby exploring the old factory there.

Monday, 21 July

Dull, bleak, cold day. Still on holiday. We went to the Cinerama in the afternoon. Wet night.

Tuesday, 22 July

Back to work again. Heat wave back again. We all at the Linn Park putting.

Friday, 25 July

Agnes met me at Bow's Emporium and we looked at holiday hampers. Thought we would do better in our own district. So hied us to Victoria Road and got one for 10/6. At tea time Mr Gordon dropped in. He had been touring the countryside all day on his bicycle.

Saturday, 26 July

Weather fine today. We all at the Mossmans' for tea. Then a walk through the Alexandra Park.

---

27   St Monans is a village in the East Neuk of Fife.

Sunday, 27 July

Broke my specs, so took a turn into town and left them with the necessary man to be mended.

Monday, 28 July

Agnes met me as I came from my work and we went to the boot shop. I got a pair to fit me with comfort of a most appalling size and shape.

Tuesday, 29 July

Left word with the railway company to lift our hamper tomorrow. We spent a busy hour or two at night packing said hamper.

Wednesday, 30 July

To make me look and feel nice for my holiday, I got my hair cut then a bath. The hamper was duly lifted today by the London, Midland and Scottish Railway, Glasgow and South Western section.

Thursday, 31 July

Paid the factor his rent today, in case he ejected us when we were away. We spent a hectic evening making final preparations for Largs. I think I mentioned before we are going there for our holidays.

Friday, 1 August

Agnes and Tommy away to Largs this forenoon by train about 11.30. I followed later by 5 o'clock train. Arrived Largs about 6.30. Raining in torrents. Agnes and Tommy met me at the station, also a pal of Tommy's yclept Jack Taylor. After tea, Tommy and Jack went to the pictures. Turned out a dry night, so Agnes and I got a walk.

Saturday, 2 August

The real start of our holidays. In the forenoon I went to Bowen Craig. Nice sunny day. After dinner, Agnes and I went to Fairlie by the shore. After tea we tried our hands at putting.

Sunday, 3 August
Rained most of the day. Dry night, so we walked to the Pencil.

Monday, 4 August
Tommy and I putted this forenoon. We went to the Picture House at night.

Thursday, 7 August
Very cold, stormy morning. We boarded the good ship Glen Rosa shortly after 10 a.m.²⁸ Turned out a beautiful sunny day, so we had a fine sail to Rothesay. We spent a few hours in the old familiar spot. Got back to Largs about 6 p.m. We had a walk to the Pencil at night.

Saturday, 9 August
Nice warm, sunny day. In the forenoon, walked to Skelmorlie and motored back. In the afternoon, Agnes and I putted then had a seat in the 'red road'. After tea we all took bus to Fairlie, visited the Glen and motored back.

Monday, 11 August
Dull and windy. Rained nearly all day. In the afternoon we putted. Still wet at night, so to the Picture House we went.

Wednesday, 13 August
Blazing hot sunshine. In the morning I scaled the mountains of the Douglas Park. In the afternoon we putted, then motored to Fairlie. After tea, we once more putted, and did the Bowen Craig walk.

Friday, 15 August
This is our last day. We got the 12 noon train home. We found everything in good order. The plants and the fish of gold all alive-oh, thanks to Mrs Carmichael. Tommy and I went to Linn Park and putted. After tea, I went to town and laid in a stock of literature.

Sunday, 17 August
We all at church today. It rained all day.

---

28 *Glen Rosa* was a paddle steamer built in 1893 and operated by the Glasgow and South Western Railway.

Monday, 18 August

Back at work again. Bright, sunny day. When I got home, Mrs Gordon, Ella and Ronnie were here. I feel as if I am taking the cold, which is absurd.

Tuesday, 19 August

Tommy starts school once more today. We all at the Majestic at night. I have got the cold, which is pure nonsense.

Wednesday, 20 August

My cold very bad. Tommy's school bag minus a handle, so I put one on with some spare aerial wire. He should hear with it.

Thursday, 21 August

Agnes at Josephine's shop in the afternoon. Bought a new clock of the alarum variety.[29] *Agnes made jam tonight.*

Friday, 22 August

Terrific thunderstorm in Govanhill. A chimney head near us struck by lightning.

Saturday, 23 August

My cold is better now. Hallelujah. All the Mossmans visited us tonight. My wireless set now meets with Gordon's approval. Carry on.

Tuesday, 26 August

Agnes in the wash house. Her usual serenity of temper a trifle frayed at night.

Thursday, 28 August

Lily, my niece, dropped in at dinner time for half an hour. She had been making a business call in our locality. Agnes made jam tonight.

Friday, 29 August

Got a letter from Duncan with some of the holiday snap-shots.

---

29   'Alarum' is an antique spelling of 'alarm'.

Saturday, 30 August

Agnes and Tommy in town this afternoon. I stayed in and raised my aerial about a foot at my end. We went to the Majestic at night. Agnes then discovered she had no specs. Tommy had to run home for them.

Sunday, 31 August

Tommy and I went to church. We all at Ibrox at night. We saw the pup.

Monday, 1 September

Agnes did some ironing and I gave the wireless set a little encouragement by listening a little.

Tuesday, 2 September

The Duke and Duchess of York in Glasgow. By means of the wireless, Agnes heard the female York speak. Tommy started swimming at school. Agnes made jam.

Wednesday, 3 September

Mounted police now patrol Glasgow as an experiment. We all at Linn Park. To keep our hand in, we had a round of putting.

Thursday, 4 September

Rose up at an early hour and raised my aerial a bit at the far end to keep small boys 'off the grass'. Agnes made jelly tonight.

Friday, 5 September

Got a letter from Gaube with a £1 note and a note for 500,000 kroner. I cashed last named note for 30/4. Mr Gaube owed me £2 10/-, so we are quits.[30]

Tuesday, 9 September

Agnes in the wash house at night. Made a sort of bookcase for Tommy, to keep his many and various school books. Wrote friend Gaube.

Wednesday, 10 September

Made a start to the couch. Took out all the springs and replaced them, with six extra.

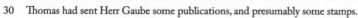

30   Thomas had sent Herr Gaube some publications, and presumably some stamps.

Thursday, 11 September

Got started to the couch again. Put the webbing on couch and sewed the springs thereon.

Friday, 12 September

Finished the couch tonight. Hallelujah. Amen.

Saturday, 13 September

Bright and sunny at times. Raining very heavily at other times. Blowing a hurricane all the time. We meandered out to Millerston in the afternoon to see Hogganfield Loch. We saw it. We went to the Majestic at night.

Sunday, 14 September

We all at divine service this morning. We saw a child getting Christened. On and after this I will require to rise earlier on Sunday morning. Weather very bad. Nannie Gordon here at night.

Tuesday, 16 September

Met my niece Isa about 5 p.m. and took her home with me. Josephine, Jack and Janet Foster were there when we arrived. Lily dropped in next. The next arrival (unexpected) was Mr Gordon. He is idle again. John Martin and Archibald (Jack) next arrived. All away about 10.25 p.m.

Friday, 19 September

Brushed all the boots, as usual. Agnes washed all the stairs, as likewise.

Saturday, 20 September

Agnes went to town in the afternoon for a few articles. Tommy and I went to Linn Park. We spent a few minutes putting. After tea we all went out for a little.

Sunday, 21 September

We all at church this morning. I had my new anthem book with me, so that I could keep my eye (ear?) on the singing.

Tuesday, 23 September

Agnes spent the evening in the wash house.

Wednesday, 24 September

Agnes finished her wash house task today. I laid a little waxcloth in the room at night.

Baden Powell Junr

Friday, 26 September

Tommy goes out at night and joins the Scouts.

Saturday, 27 September

Put wheels on my tool box at night, to lighten the labour of taking it out and in.

Sunday, 28 September

Agnes and I went to church this morning. Our old minister, Mr Tainsh (who married us), was the officiating clergyman.

Monday, 29 September

Autumn holiday. Poured hard all day. We did not go out at all.

Wednesday, 1 October

Tommy went to the Majestic himself at night. We wanted to see Harold Lloyd in *Why Worry?*.[31] Agnes went to Dennistoun after tea to see the Mossmans.

Thursday, 2 October

Agnes went to the Majestic tonight with Mrs Carmichael. Seeing that Peggy was going with them, Tommy also went. I stayed at home and listened in and stuck stamps.

Friday, 3 October

Agnes in town in the afternoon. She bought a new case for Tommy's school books. Tommy at his Scout meeting at night. My toe inclined to be sore tonight.

---

31   *Why Worry?*, which was produced by Hal Roach, was an American silent film released in 1923.

Saturday, 4 October

We had arranged to go to Dennistoun tonight, but Agnes was too ill to go. So Tommy took a run up before dinner and let them know we would not be. Agnes retired to bed after tea. Her head is very bad.

Sunday, 5 October

Agnes quite all right again. Tommy to Sunday School. After tea he went to some Scout meeting.

Monday, 6 October

Agnes not at all well during the night. Raised my aerial to top of window at night. Got a new hat tonight (9/11). Posted a letter for Tommy, for which he owes me 3½d.

Thursday, 9 October

Agnes not well at all. Kept her bed all day. Got Tommy a chain. He fastens himself to one end and his key to the other end. Arthur Fraser in at night, testing his 'phones on my machine.[32]

Friday, 10 October

Received my diary back from Vienna today. Agnes still in bed. A special wireless night in Aberdeen, so asked Mr Gordon up. He came, and we listened all night. He enjoyed it, being an Aberdonian. Tommy at the Scouts.

Saturday, 11 October

Agnes feels better. So she is up all day. Tommy washed the kitchen floor, a Scout-like deed.

Sunday, 12 October

Agnes feeling fine. We did not go to church. After dinner we all walked out to the ancient and royal burgh of Rutherglen. Fine sunny day. Tommy alarmed us at an early hour this morning by suddenly appearing. He was sleeping.

---

32   Arthur Fraser is the husband of Maggie MacKenzie, who lives in the next close.

1924

Thursday 9 October

Agnes not well at
all. Kept her bed all
day. Tommy stayed off
school to look after things
Got Tommy a
chain today. He
fastens himself
to one end
and his key
to other end.
Arthur Fraser
in at night
testing his
phones on my machine.
Later on Hetty and
baby dropped in.
I saw her on to her
Car about 9 p.m.

Wet afternoon and
night.

Monday, 13 October

Agnes very ill during the night. Greatly alarmed, she went round to the doctor. He came over in afternoon and thoroughly examined her. She is a nervous wreck. Got a bottle of nerve juice and tablets to make her sleep. Mrs Gordon and the wee cuss here at tea time. Heard Ramsay MacDonald's speech on the wireless tonight.

Tuesday, 14 October

Agnes not so bad today. She went to the wash house in the afternoon. We are going to have a gas fire put in the room, so a man from the gas place was in, measuring around.

Thursday, 16 October

Cleaned all the windows at night. Put on the earphones and listened to Mr Baldwin stating his reasons why he should be the next prime minister.[33]

Friday, 17 October

I listened at night to friend Asquith, who is standing for Paisley.[34]

Monday, 20 October

Doctor up and gave Agnes another examination. She has to continue the bottle.

Tuesday, 21 October

We went to Majestic at night.

Wednesday, 22 October

Peggy in at night for some musical advice. The pictures too exciting for Agnes so we are not going back.

Thursday, 23 October

Agnes took Tommy to the Scout headquarters for his new uniform. They got home after spending about 25/-.

Friday, 24 October

The man left the various parts of the new gas fire. Some day it will be fitted up. Belfast broadcasting station (2BE) officially opened tonight. So I heard the old country.

---

33   Stanley Baldwin was the Conservative leader in the House of Commons.

34   Herbert Henry Asquith, the MP for Paisley, was the Liberal leader in the House of Commons.

Saturday, 25 October

All Ibrox here about 5.30 p.m. Mr Gordon brought up a new radio set he had made. Not much of an improvement.

Sunday, 26 October

This is Communion Sunday. So Agnes and I went to church this morning. Agnes and Tommy out for a little in the afternoon. I rested my delicate toe. At night, Agnes and I went to church and Tommy went to his Scout meeting.

Monday, 27 October

The doctor up again to overhaul Agnes. He seems a little more pleased. He is not coming back for a fortnight, which seems a great relief to Agnes. I went round at night and got a bottle doubly strong, which will last at least a fortnight. He mentioned that a holiday and Agnes would go well together.

Tuesday, 28 October

Agnes in the wash house during the afternoon and night. Tommy kept guard over her in the hours of darkness. Wrote to Duncan at night. He wants some advice on wireless. I gave it.

Wednesday, 29 October

Agnes finished her washing by dinner time. Sent a postcard to the gas folk saying how glad I would be if they fitted up the gas fire. This is voting day. So we duly voted. The Socialist government has got to go. We got some election results by the wireless at night, which augured very well indeed.

Thursday, 30 October

The Conservatives are sweeping the country. The Socialist government gone now. The man who fits in gas fires got started to ours today. There is something compelling in my love letters to the Corporation.

Friday, 31 October

Our gas fire is now finished. It gives quite a heat, and will save Agnes a lot of work, be cleaner and will give Glasgow a purer atmosphere. Amen. Tommy at a Scout Hallowe'en beanfeast tonight. I cleaned all the windows.

Saturday, 1 November
We all out for a little in the afternoon. The Wembley exhibition officially closed, so we heard the Prince of Wales (wirelessly). After tea we amused ourselves with playing cards. Agnes won.

Sunday, 2 November
We all at church this forenoon. A woman beguiled us into buying tickets for a church concert affair. It cost us 5/- (five shillings, 60 pennies, ¼ of a pound), about four thousand million marks. At night, Agnes went to church herself.

Monday, 3 November
Agnes at Parkhead in afternoon seeing Josephine. At night she attended a Scout meeting for parents. She came home not sure whether she is now scoutmaster general or what not. She is going to give something to the bazaar.

Tuesday, 4 November
Man up today to examine the gas fire. He says what we need now is a larger gas meter. Fortunately, we get it for nothing. A sister of Mrs Gray (the wife next door) in here this afternoon.

Wednesday, 5 November
Agnes baked cakes for the Scout bazaar and after tea took them to Mount Florida.

Thursday, 6 November
Winter has come. Thick yellow fog all day. Tommy at a Scout social doing some 'skivvy' work.

Saturday, 8 November
Agnes and I had a walk round by the Hangingshaws before tea. Tommy spent the entire afternoon doing some work for the Scouts.

Sunday, 9 November
We all at church special service for Remembrance Day. Tommy out for a little after dinner. Before tea, Agnes and I out for a little. At night Agnes took a run out to see Hetty Mossman.

Monday, 10 November
This is Agnes' birthday, the birthday of my sweetheart. The doctor up this afternoon, and gave Agnes another examination. Seems a little more pleased with her condition. Worked late.

Tuesday, 11 November
This is Armistice Day, so I had two minutes' silence in the square. Agnes in the wash house all day. I worked late.

Thursday, 13 November
Tommy spent the night with the Boy Scouts. He is working very hard for that institution.

Friday, 14 November
Mr Gordon dropped in at night with his earphones, so we listened in. Tommy out collecting money for the Scouts.

Saturday, 15 November
All the Mossmans coming tonight, so Tommy went to Dennistoun in the afternoon to assist Hetty and her large family. Gordon came later on, himself, like a gentleman. We had a hectic evening, but the only casualty was a photo frame broken. I knocked it off the piano.

Sunday, 16 November
The Carmichaels all in at night. Jeanie MacKenzie also in with her boy. He fiddles, so we had some music. I accompanied on the piano.

Monday, 17 November

Our new gas meter of the large size fitted in today. So we should be able now to burn more gas. The large gold fish seems to be unwell.

Tuesday, 18 November

Tommy in the throes of his third quarterly examinations this week. I trust that he will bear well under the strain. The gold fish (major) seems to be all right now. He had evidently had a fin out of joint.

Wednesday, 19 November

Bought myself a new pipe. Agnes broke the gold fishes' habitation tonight (my fault). At night, we had an hour of music in the room.

Thursday, 20 November

We paid the people who supply gas. Agnes in town and got a new globe for the poissons. I worked late. Tommy came in for me at 8.45 to get some exercise.

Friday, 21 November

Working late. Jean MacKenzie in with wee Malcolm when I got home. Tommy at the Scouts. They had a picture show on tonight showing the 'jamboree'. I think that's the word. Agnes not keeping so well this week.

Monday, 24 November

Doctor up again this afternoon, thinks Agnes is still improving. He will be back in a month. Agnes gave herself a black eye on the press door.

Tuesday, 25 November

Tommy seemed off colour this morning. At dinner time, he had a sore head, so stayed off school. Agnes in washing house all day, and washed the floor at night. Did you ever? I worked late.

Wednesday, 26 November

Tommy off school, but seems to be a bit better. Worked late. When I got home, Nannie Gordon was in.

Thursday, 27 November

Got Tommy a jar of Virol to see if will help.[35] He is still off school.

Friday, 28 November

Tommy spent a restless night. In the wee sma' hours he suddenly appeared, non compos mentis. Agnes got a scare. I let Tommy into the kitchen bed, then I flitted to room. Very sad. Agnes started a new medicine tonight. Some tablets that the doctor recommended.

Saturday, 29 November

Tommy still in bed. The boy who always wears kilts up to see Tommy this afternoon. Rigged up a long

---

35   Virol was a vitamin preparation based on malt extract. It was marketed as 'the ideal food'.

wire so that Tommy can listen in, in bed. Amused him at night by playing various games, such as Ludo.

Sunday, 30 November
Tommy got up for half the day. Agnes in a very hysterical mood. She sat in room all night, and was in a terrible state of mind at night. It was pure misery. Went to bed in a wretched frame of mind.

Monday, 1 December
Spent a bad night, and in the morning was feeling extra bad. No appetite, sore head etc, so I did not rise all day.

Tuesday, 2 December
Still a sick man, so got in the doctor. He says I have the flu. Got sweating powders, which eased my head a little.

Wednesday, 3 December
Still feeling very bad, and at night extra bad. Have a bottle to take now.

Thursday, 4 December
Doctor up today. My temperature 102 degrees. Agnes asked him to examine Tommy. He did so, and found him somewhat strained after his illness. He is to keep off school for a while.

Friday, 5 December
Feeling a little easier today. Doctor up again. He gave me permission to shave myself at night. Josephine up to see me at night. Tommy is first in his school examinations. I am very proud of him.

Saturday, 6 December
Doctor up again. He allows me up for a little at night. Am wonderfully weak.

Monday, 8 December
Went round to see doctor in forenoon. In the afternoon, Tommy and I had a little walk. Felt as if I had been in bed for a year, but I'm coming on.

Tuesday, 9 December
Went to my work today at 10 a.m. Felt I had enough of it by 3.30 p.m., so home I came. Poor Agnes, she is not getting much of

a chance of benefiting by her treatment. Lily and John Martin
here at night. We gave them quite a nice time and made them
comfortable.

Wednesday, 10 December
Worked till my usual time tonight, and feeling not so bad. Agnes
made jam tonight out of a big can of fruit, apricots. It turns out a
brilliant success.

Thursday, 11 December
I'm beginning to feel more like myself. Agnes and Tommy at a
church concert tonight. We bought the tickets months ago. I should
have gone, but thought I had better not. Felt very worried all night
at not going.

Friday, 12 December
Feeling very tired today, but quite spry at night.

Saturday, 13 December
Much rain today. Don't feel so chirpy tonight.

Monday, 15 December
Agnes spent day in the wash house. I'm improving in health now,
but my throat a little affected at night.

Tuesday, 16 December
Got a letter from Duncan. He has now got a listening-in set, which
is the best one out. Agnes ironed all night.

Wednesday, 17 December
The cord of room blind broken, so I put a new one on at night.
Agnes took a run down to Ibrox after tea. Her aunt and Nannie not
in, but she saw the rest.

Thursday, 18 December
Agnes and Tommy washed the dinner set. Agnes thinks I'm a
semi-invalid, so she would not let me assist.

Saturday, 20 December
Feeling now like my old self. Tommy and I had a walk in the
afternoon. After tea, Agnes and Tommy went to town. They arrived
safely home. They had been at the boot shop, and brought home two
pairs of slippers for me. Of course, I only get keeping one pair.[36]

---

36   Agnes and Tommy have apparently bought two pairs of slippers to allow Thomas to
     choose the pair he wants, and they will return the other pair for a refund.

Monday, 22 December

Doctor up again to examine Agnes. Thinks she is getting on not bad, which eases me a little. Agnes at Greenlodge at night. Got a new pair of headphones today, 'Brandes', and they are magnificent.[37]

Tuesday, 23 December

Wild, stormy morning. Soot covering everything this morning. Heartbroken, I went to the slater and lodged a protest. I phoned the factor in same strain. The slater examined our lum during the day. The 'Ewbank Sweeper' we speculated in today brought joy and delight to Agnes.[38] Tommy got two books from Greenlodge for his Xmas. Turned out a nice day.

Wednesday, 24 December

Slater up mending the lum. We got a parcel from Greenlodge. Agnes got a jumper and my unworthy self some hankies. Got my hair cut.

Thursday, 25 December

Very nice day. This is Christmas Day, so I have a holiday. Got a letter from the long-lost Babinski. He is evidently having a thin time in Warsaw. We all went to Cinerama in afternoon. Ship ashore off Troon, so 5SC had to shut down at night as she was jamming the SOS signal.[39]

Friday, 26 December

Agnes in wash house all day. We got a Xmas parcel from Duncan.

Sunday, 28 December

Wild, wet ferocious day. We went out in the storm at night to see our Ibrox friends. Mr Gordon had his radio fixed up and I got a tune. It was not particularly strong.

---

37 C. Brandes of New York was a popular manufacturer of both telephone and radio headsets.

38 Ewbank carpet sweepers were made by Entwistle and Kenyon of Accrington, Lancashire.

39 5SC was the BBC radio station broadcasting from Glasgow.

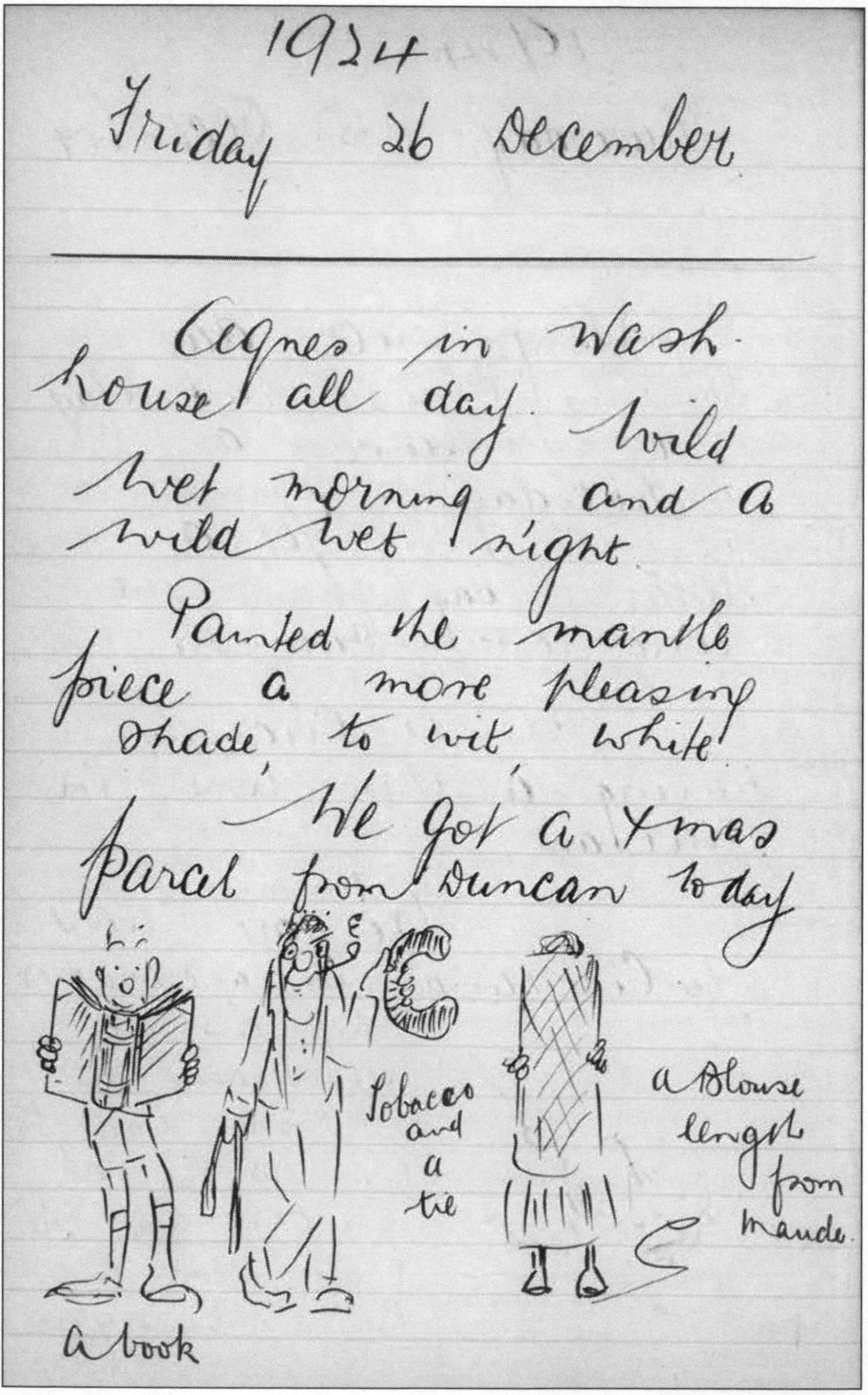

1924

Friday   26 December

Agnes in Wash-
house all day. Wild
wet morning and a
wild wet night.

Painted the mantle
piece a more pleasing
shade, to wit white.

We got a Xmas
Parcel from Duncan today

A book

Tobacco
and
a
tie

A Blouse
length
from
Maude.

Monday, 29 December

Weather the absolute limit. A perfect hurricane and, needless to say, it rained. Tommy and Jack Taylor at the Kelvin Hall Carnival. Tommy brought home a wonderful 'peary', the gyroscope.[40] Agnes spent the night making sash curtains for the room. I wrote Duncan and wished him a Happy New Year.

Tuesday, 30 December

Wrote to my good friend in Vienna. Agnes also wrote a letter to her good friend Hetty Mossman. We have been invited there next Saturday. Sorry we can't accept.

Wednesday, 31 December

Seeing that there will be no more days in this year, I got away at 12.45. I don't go back till next Monday morning. We are going to first fit the Carmichaels. The year is finished. Amen. 'God send every one their heart's desire.'[41]

---

40 A 'peary' or 'peerie' is a Scots word for a child's spinning top.
41 Thomas is quoting William Shakespeare's *Much Ado About Nothing*.

1925

Despite the potential for bad luck brought by an empty-handed first foot, Thomas and his family continued to thrive and prosper in 1925. They acquired a bicycle, Tommy won a school bursary and continued to do well in exams, and the family spent a month in a Milngavie mansion. Thomas and Agnes, now of a certain age, started wearing spectacles. And Thomas' employer moved premises, from 170 Ingram Street to 6 Frederick Lane, both in the centre of Glasgow. They also took over James Dean Bedding Limited, bedding and wire mattress manufacturers of 37 Cavendish Street, Laurieston, and Thomas worked there on occasion.

Thomas wrote less about the outside world, but still recorded some of the headlines of the day, such as the death of Queen Alexandra. He continued to correspond with fellow stamp collectors around the world, and 'listened in' to a number of far-flung radio stations. His world was expanding, but he recorded fewer of the incidents in his diary.

Thursday, 1 January
A Happy New Year to you all. At the appointed minute, we
trooped into the Carmichaels, and wished them all good things.
We got back again at 3.20 a.m., and so to bed. A hurricane raged
all day. Heavy snow in the morning. We did not go out at all.
Scrapped all the old calendars and put up the new.

Friday, 2 January
Another day of storm. Snow in the morning, then rain, and a
bitter cold day. We ventured to the Cinerama in the afternoon.
Jack Taylor up for his tea. He waited in with Tommy all evening.
He is our first foot and he came empty handed.[1] Ah-me.

Saturday, 3 January
Wild hurricane during the night. Agnes got alarmed and got up,
so up I got too. We sat in room for a little, had a cup of tea,
then to bed again. Wild showers of hail today, but not so stormy.
Tommy and I in the afternoon at Linn Park and Rouken Glen. We
admired the waterfalls.

Sunday, 4 January
Agnes pretty ill this morning, so I made breakfast for Tommy and
myself. Agnes off eating. Fine day. Agnes felt a little better at 3
p.m., so got up. Wrote to my Latvian friend.

Monday, 5 January
Back to work again, and Tommy back to school. Agnes seems a
little better. Wrote to my poor friend Babinski of Warsaw words of
comfort and cheer.

Tuesday, 6 January
I met Isa about 5 p.m. and went to Greenlodge with her. We met
Agnes and Tommy coming off the yellow car. We paid our respects
in a becoming manner and got home at 11.10 p.m.

Thursday, 8 January
Cleaned the kitchen window tonight. Agnes took a run out to see
Hetty Mossman. The baby has pneumonia.

---

1   Traditionally, a first foot brings a piece of coal (for warmth), salt (for wealth), black
     bun (for food) and whisky (for obvious reasons). Black bun is a rich, dark fruit cake.
     Gifts of the first three types were believed to ensure a supply of these commodities
     throughout the year, so an empty-handed first foot could be an omen of very bad
     times.

Friday, 9 January

Mr Gordon and small boy here in afternoon. Mrs Gordon, Nannie laid up, so they can't come tomorrow. Tommy at the Scouts at night. After tea, Agnes took a run up to Dennistoun. The poor wee baby had died at an early hour this morning. It was a sad blow to us all.

Saturday, 10 January

Agnes went to Dennistoun in forenoon to assist Hetty with the arrangements, Hetty being of no use at all, and then was buried one of the most innocent of God's creatures, wee Grace. Tommy and I went up after dinner. Gordon's two sisters were there. 'God gave and He took away.'[2]

Sunday, 11 January

I went to church myself in the morning. After dinner, I went for a run round the country. Agnes went down to Ibrox. Thankful that things seemed not so bad there.

Wednesday, 14 January

Agnes ironed collars all night.
Bathed my balmy toe at night.

Thursday, 15 January

Tommy out at night with Jack Taylor. I sat in, listened in, stuck stamps, and bathed my funny toe. Agnes went to Dennistoun to see all the Mossmans. Etta has the cough that whoops.

Friday, 16 January

A day that is very raw and cold. The wind it is that does it. Tommy went off to the Scouts at night. He came back shortly after. It appears that there was no meeting of that distinguished body tonight.

Saturday, 17 January

I stayed in and rested my foot.

Sunday, 18 January

We all went to church this morning. In the afternoon, Agnes and Tommy went out for a small walk. About 5 p.m., Josephine called.

---

2   Thomas is paraphrasing Job, chapter 1, verse 21.

Monday, 19 January
The doctor up tonight. He thinks Agnes is still improving. Tommy bought a flash lamp. Mrs Carmichael looked in and sat down for a few hours.

Tuesday, 20 January
Old Mrs Baxter buried today. She is the wife, or was the wife of the late Alexander Baxter.[3] We shut the place in the afternoon, but we were all inside. Took Agnes and Tommy to the Majestic tonight.

Wednesday, 21 January
Mr Cochrane's wife died very suddenly last night, just after Mr Cochrane got home from the funeral.[4] It was a terrible blow. Got word today that Tom Marks, the finest man in our kirk, is dead.

Thursday, 22 January
Agnes took a run out to Parkhead in the afternoon. Complains of a pain in the chest, so at night I rubbed it with holy oil. Made a new telephone extension board tonight, of ebonite.[5]

Friday, 23 January
Our place shut today 1 p.m. for Mrs Cochrane's funeral. Out of respect to Mr Cochrane, I attended. It was in the Western Necropolis. I felt very vexed indeed for Mr Cochrane. He looked what he must have felt, heartbroken.

Saturday, 24 January
A total eclipse of the sun between 3 and 4 p.m. Tommy went out and had a good view. It appears it is the 'most total' for 200 years. Tommy out with his ma at night for a new cap.

Sunday, 25 January
The sun apparently none the worse for its extinction yesterday. Tommy out a walk in the afternoon. Agnes went to church at night.

Monday, 26 January
Rung up Nannie Gordon and invited them all out on Saturday.[6] Agnes baked all night.

---

3   The Baxter family are the proprietors of Paterson, Baxter and Company, where Thomas is employed.

4   Mr Cochrane, who was probably one of the managers in Paterson, Baxter and Company, had been attending the funeral of Mrs Baxter.

5   Thomas has made a board that allows more than one set of headphones ('phones being short for telephones) to be connected to the wireless at once; ebonite is a very hard rubber.

6   Thomas has access to a telephone at work.

Tuesday, 27 January
Tommy wandered into kitchen this morning in his sleep at 2 a.m. Agnes got a kink thereby. Met my niece Isa about 5 p.m. and took her home with me. The rest of the family arrived at intervals. All present except Josephine, who is making holiday at Rothesay.

Thursday, 29 January
Got a fine collection of stamps from Italy.

Friday, 30 January
Ella rung me up to let me know they would be out on Saturday. Agnes baked accordingly. Tommy at the Scouts.

Saturday, 31 January
All Ibrox duly arrived. Charles Petrie (Nannie's boy), the wireless expert, examined my installation and thinks it quite decent. Nearly as good, in fact, as one he once had. Mine must be a good one indeed.

Friday, 6 February
Was speaking to Ella Gordon today in shop where she works. The factor called today, and got payment in full. Tommy at the Scouts at night.

Saturday, 7 February
After dinner, I took a walk through the Queen's Park, Shawlands, along the Cart to Cathcart and then the car home. Not bad for my bad toe. After tea, Agnes took Tommy to town and got him a new pair of boots.

Sunday, 8 February
We all at church this morning. Tommy at Sunday School. An eclipse of the moon occurred tonight. It was very unexciting.

Monday, 9 February
Got a letter from Latvia and one from Austria, with the usual donations.

Friday, 13 February
A vile day of snow in the forenoon and a most outrageous wind.

Monday, 16 February

Doctor up this afternoon, and still thinks Agnes is improving. Grace à Dieu.[7] Put a screw nail or two in the rocker to prolong its life another year or two.

Tuesday, 17 February

Agnes and Tommy at a pantomime tonight with Mrs Carmichael and Peggy. Pavilion.[8]

Thursday, 19 February

Agnes went to Dennistoun at night to see Hetty Mossman. I listened to a wonderful Russian pianist and wrote Mr Gaube of Vienna.

Friday, 20 February

Bought a new pair of 'breeks' today to keep me going till the summer time.[9] Heard the Prince of Wales tonight, and Baldwin.

Saturday, 21 February

Tommy sat his Sunday School Bible examinations today in the church. After tea we all went to a picture house in Shawlands. When we came out, we saw an open air meeting making a noise. Jack Archibald was one of them, so we had a word with him. The King is not well.

Sunday, 22 February

Agnes and I went to church. Business – Communion. Tommy and I had a walk through Ruglen and Burnside. I saw the war memorial for the first time.

Monday, 23 February

I got my hair cut. My hat now fits me easier. Agnes went round and had a word with Josephine at her shop this afternoon. Wrote my friend Schopp of Riga tonight.

---

7   'Thanks to God.'

8   The Pavilion Theatre, in Renfield Street.

9   'Breeks' is a Scots word for trousers.

Thursday, 26 February
Agnes very stiff and sore after her labours in the wash house yesterday. Tommy went to the library at night, and I stuck in a stamp or so.

Friday, 27 February
Tommy at another Bible examination tonight.

Saturday, 28 February
Paid my wireless licence today, 10/-. Agnes owes me for same 5/-. Took Tommy a walk round the country in afternoon. We went to Shawlands Picture House at night.

Monday, 2 March
When I got home at tea time, Mrs Gordon and Ronnie were in possession. Owing to Tommy having a cold, the school saw him not today.

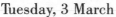

Tuesday, 3 March
Kept Tommy in bed all day. His fellow Scout Jack Taylor up and kept him company at night.

Wednesday, 4 March
Tommy still in bed. He has an alarming cough. My niece Lily came at night to see him.

Thursday, 5 March
Tommy up at tea time, but still coughs a lot. We got word that a pair of gentlemen would call tomorrow to sweep the lum.

Friday, 6 March
The men duly called this morning and swept the lum. Tommy up nearly all day, but still got bad cough.

Saturday, 7 March
Tommy still spluttering. We begin now to think of the whooping cough.[10]

Sunday, 8 March
We all have the cold now. Tommy, I think, is a little better. All the Mossman family here before 5, then Josephine came and then Jack. Hetty got huffed, over some fancied wrong to wee Billy.

---

10 Before vaccination was introduced in the 1950s, whooping cough killed a number of children every year. It is one of the most contagious bacterial infections, and there is no treatment for it.

1925

Friday 6 March.

Some showers today
The men
duly
called this
morning
and swept
the lum.

Tommy
up nearly all day
but still got bad cough

Agnes cut her finger
today, and it seemed
to annoy her at
times. I put it in
bandages at bed time
and hope for the best.

Monday, 9 March

In the afternoon, Agnes took Tommy to town, where he got measured for a new suit. He is now at the stage that nothing fits him ready made. A wee chap dropped in at tea time with a paper for the bursary Tommy is trying. The date is Saturday.

Tuesday, 10 March

Heard the great Tetrazzini tonight per wireless." Think I'll get her for the kirk choir. Tommy at school today.

Wednesday, 11 March

Agnes and Tommy went to the Cinerama tonight. His cough does not seem so bad.

Thursday, 12 March

Agnes spent an enjoyable day in the wash house.

Saturday, 14 March

Tommy and I went out together in the morning, as he is sitting for some bursary in a school situated in the Gorbals.[12] Agnes took Tommy round to the doctor at night. His cough is evidently to do with his adenoids. Got a bottle to drink and one to snuff and gargle with.

Sunday, 15 March

Fine warm, sunny day. Tommy and I out a walk in the afternoon. Agnes went to church at night. We heard Paderewski tonight.[13] He was magnificent.

Monday, 16 March

Doctor up his monthly visit, and thinks Agnes is still improving. We all went to Greenlodge. Being a nice night, we walked over.

---

11   Louisa Tetrazzini was an Italian coloratura soprano who had a successful operatic and concert career in Europe and America from the 1890s to the 1920s.

12   The school is most likely Hutchesons' Grammar School in Crown Street, and the bursary offered by Hutchesons' Educational Trust.

13   Ignacy Jan Paderewski was a Polish concert pianist and composer. He was also a diplomat and politician, and was Prime Minister of Poland from January to December 1919.

Tuesday, 17 March

Agnes at Ibrox in the afternoon. I dropped in on my way home and had a crack with my good friend Father Petrauskis. Got a letter from my friend in Riga.

Thursday, 19 March

Agnes at a kinderspiel. Tommy at Jack Taylor's. Fitted the wireless into a new box (larger and more commodious premises) and put an ebonite top on it. I got it to work all right when finished.

Friday, 20 March

Tommy had a holiday today, his school being used as a polling booth. He went as usual to the Scouts at night, where they are taught to do a good deed every day.

Saturday, 21 March

Agnes in town in afternoon and got a pair of gloves. Tommy's new suit seems to be a bit too tight.

Sunday, 22 March

We all at church this morning. Took Agnes a walk in the afternoon by Mount Florida and Hangingshaws. Tommy got a stiff leg with cricket.

Monday, 23 March

Agnes took Tommy into town and got his suit made more to his size.

Tuesday, 24 March

Got a letter from Duncan. Got measured for a new suit. Agnes at Cinerama tonight.

Thursday, 26 March

I cleaned kitchen window tonight. Agnes at Josephine's shop and paid her for Tommy's suit.

Friday, 27 March

Tommy got his Tenderfoot badge tonight.[14]

---

14   The Tenderfoot badge was the first rung on the ladder of Scouting progress.

Monday, 30 March
Agnes in wash house all day. After tea she took Tommy round to the doctor. He said he would better stay off school till after the Easter holidays. Tommy is quite agreeable.

Wednesday, 1 April
During the wee sma' hours my ear was most painful. Agnes doctored it in various ways. Agnes at the Cinerama with Mrs Carmichael at night.

Friday, 3 April
Doctor up to see about Tommy's cough. It may be a slight form of the cough that whoops. In any case, it does not seem to be anything serious.

Saturday, 4 April
Agnes not very well today. Gordon Mossman here before tea time. He admired the wireless and gave us good advice generally.

Sunday, 5 April
Agnes in bed till 2 p.m. Very ill indeed. She then got up, disgusted with everything and everybody. Very sad day.

Monday, 6 April
Agnes up this morning, but back to bed again, all out. Isa and her boy came up at night to comfort Agnes etc. Fed them well, and they left about 10.30. Tommy out for a little today.

Tuesday, 7 April
Agnes in bed all day. Mr Gordon here for a little this afternoon. Josephine here at night to comfort us. I'm getting worried.

Wednesday, 8 April
Agnes weak and all out this morning, but up for dinner and tea. The house was evidently like a pigsty and no food was being cooked etc etc etc etc etc. Agnes inclined to be hysterical. Very miserable day. Lily here at night, then Jack. So Tommy, Jack and I went into the place for the bicycle and wheeled it home.

Thursday, 9 April
Doctor up to see Agnes in the early evening. Stopped her pellets and gave her a bottle. Agnes now up. Miss Marks up to see Tommy, then Mrs Carmichael came in to see Agnes.[15] After all the

15   Miss Marks was Tommy's Sunday School teacher.

visitors were gone, and after we had examined the bike, I washed the floor.

Friday, 10 April
Agnes feeling much better now. I listened to the *Messiah* all night. We cleared out the pantry to find a corner for the bike.

Saturday, 11 April
Got a letter from Mr Gaube. Fine warm day, and a holiday. Had a number of priceless volumes left over after cleaning out the pantry. Took them up to the Arcade.[16] They changed hands for £20. No, I mean two shillings. After dinner we all had a walk in the Shawlands district.

Sunday, 12 April
Tommy and I went to church. At dinner time, Nannie Gordon dropped in. We fed her, showed her the new bicycle and let her go. In the afternoon, we took car to Rouken Glen and walked to Netherlee via Clarkston, and car home.

Monday, 13 April
Spring holiday. Vile day of wind and rain. After dinner we all went to the Shawlands Picture House. We spent the evening cleaning our bicycle. Wonder if I'll ever be able to have a spin on same.

Tuesday, 14 April
Got an Easter greeting from Babinski. Tommy at the Art Galleries in the afternoon. Borrowed an inflator at my work, and at night we pumped air into the bicycle. The air came out again. What is wanted is a little valve tubing. Wee Alex Carmichael in to see the bike.

Wednesday, 15 April
We tackled the bike again tonight and the results were very satisfactory.

Thursday, 16 April
Was working late at our new factory, teaching the lady clerk how to keep books.

---

16   The Queen Arcade, on the north side of Renfrew Street, was well known for its booksellers.

Saturday, 18 April

Tommy went into town in afternoon and bought a bicycle inflator
for 1/6. Knocked my variometer over, and burst its works a little.
Mended it, and it goes yet. Reservoir burst at Skelmorlie. Five
lives lost.[17]

Sunday, 19 April

Feeling fatigued, worn out, done etc, after all my worries etc, I had
my breakfast in bed. After tea, Agnes and I had a walk round the
Giffnock quarries.

Monday, 20 April

*Fine summer-like day. Tommy out on the bike
during the day. He says he can now manage
it. My turn next. Agnes and I had a walk
by Pollokshields at night.*

Tuesday, 21 April

Tommy back to school again, his holidays now over.
Agnes spent a short time in the wash house this forenoon. A wasp
went down her back and cheered her up somewhat. At night I
went out to my Ruglen tailor for a fit-on.

Wednesday, 22 April

Doctor up to see Agnes and seems to be quite well pleased. I
worked late at night in Ingram Street.

Thursday, 23 April

Working later at the bedding factory.

Monday, 27 April

Agnes down at Ibrox in afternoon to see her aunt. She likewise
dropped into Lily's office and had a crack with her. Lily tells
her that her ma is not very well, so Agnes took a turn over to
Greenlodge after tea.

Tuesday, 28 April

Agnes in wash house at night. Tommy out at night with his bike.
He sustained a few minor wounds on his leg. Cut, bleeding etc.

---

17 On Saturday, 18 April 1925, an embankment on the reservoir serving Skelmorlie
    gave way, releasing millions of gallons of water on the village. Five people, four of
    them children, were killed and a number of houses, gardens and other premises were
    damaged or destroyed.

Wednesday, 29 April
Agnes went round to the doctor in the forenoon. Tommy not out on his bike at night. I meandered out to Cathcart and visited the library at night.

Thursday, 30 April
I cleaned all the windows. Tommy gave his bike another airing at night. Ella Gordon here at night.

Friday, 1 May
Went out to Ruglen and got my new suit.

Saturday, 2 May
Paid the doctor his bill. Tommy at the Cinerama at night with Jack Taylor.

Sunday, 3 May
Tommy out in full uniform with the Scouts in the morning for church parade. I went out a little in the afternoon. Agnes and I at church at night. After that I took a run over to Greenlodge.

Tuesday, 5 May
Robert Baxter and I through at Grangemouth in the motor car in the forenoon.[18] Made some alterations to my telephone wires at night.[19]

Wednesday, 6 May
Letter from friend Schopp. Mr A. Baxter offered me his Milngavie house for the month of July.[20] I am thinking about it. Agnes went to the Cinerama herself. Heard by the wireless SOS that Mr Armstrong in the next street is missing.

Friday, 8 May
Tommy has done very well so far in his examination. Good lad. Told Mr A. Baxter that we would take his Milngavie house for the month of July.

---

18   Robert Baxter is one of the proprietors of Paterson, Baxter and Company.

19   The 'telephone wires' are the wires for the radio headphones.

20   Alexander Baxter is one of the proprietors of Paterson, Baxter and Company. His house is called Kildare. Milngavie is a middle-class suburb to the north-west of Glasgow.

Sunday, 10 May
We all at church this morning. In the afternoon I took a walk around the 100 Acre Dyke. After tea we all took car to Linn Park and home by Carmunnock Road. Agnes exhausted by the walk.

Tuesday, 12 May
Factor up for his rent and got it. Working late.

Wednesday, 13 May
Doctor up to see Agnes. Says she has had a surfeit of the pellets, so puts her on the bottle again. Working late.

Thursday, 14 May
Put up new wire in the kitchen, and bored a hole in the wall under the bed, and connected the room up with the telephone extension.[21] It was a hard job.

Saturday, 16 May
Dull and warm. Tommy out a cycle run with Jack Taylor.

Sunday, 17 May
My firm flits tomorrow, so I will not have a holiday.[22]

Monday, 18 May
My firm removes today to other premises. We last removed in 1901.

Wednesday, 20 May
Doctor paid us his usual visit. Working late. Tommy is first in his last school examination.

Sunday, 24 May
We all at church in morning. Josephine landed herself on us about 4 p.m. and landed out about 10 p.m. Sent Duncan a small note regretting that I could not produce a house in Largs for his holidays.

Tuesday, 26 May
Agnes did not feel well enough to rise this morning. Working late tonight.

Wednesday, 27 May
Doctor up on his weekly visit. Thinks Agnes is getting on. Worked late.

---

21   Thomas has extended the wiring for the radio headphones into the front room.

22   To 'flit' is to move house or premises.

Thursday, 28 May

Not working late. Linoleum being laid in the counting house, so the place is dismantled for the night.

Friday, 29 May

Gave my back a fearful wrench this morning when I stretched myself. Thought I was mortally wounded. Pained all day. Managed to work late.

Saturday, 30 May

My back still very sore. I rested on the couch all afternoon.

Sunday, 31 May

Agnes and Tommy at church this morning. Rested all day, but I am improving.

Tuesday, 2 June

Nice sunny night, so I meandered in Cathcart direction. Agnes at Ibrox in the afternoon. Tommy with the Scouts at night – a march out. I saw him among them at Mount Florida.

Wednesday, 3 June

Tommy got a very sore throat, so I went round to the doctor with Tommy. As the doctor was coming up to see Agnes, he examined Tommy when he came up. He said that it might be diphtheria, but will come back tomorrow.

Thursday, 4 June

This is my birthday, but I went to work with a very worried mind. Doctor had not been up by dinner time, but Tommy seems easier. I went back to my work not quite so worried. The doctor up shortly after, and says it is only a touch of tonsillitis. Peggy Carmichael phoned me the welcome news, which cheered me up. Tommy allowed up, but to keep the house for the rest of the week.

Monday, 8 June

Worked late at the bedding firm. Saw little Mary home. Home myself about 10.30. Agnes made rhubarb jam.

Tuesday, 9 June

Another scorching day. Tommy took bicycle to town and got the seat raised a little. Alex Carmichael borrowed said bicycle at night for a spin. We all out by Mount Florida and Hangingshaws at night. Wrote my friend in Vienna.

Wednesday, 10 June

Heat terrific today. Hottest so far. Doctor up this afternoon and thinks Agnes is still getting better. Tommy back at school now. We are going to spring clean, so we washed the dinner service. I polished up the kitchen clock. Tommy, wise in his generation, went to the Scouts.[23]

Thursday, 11 June

The kitchen got whitewashed tonight. We then got the paintwork washed. Being so busy I forgot to mention that on 10 June 1910, Agnes and I got married. We did.

Friday, 12 June

A brilliant night, so I walked to Ruglen up the Croftfoot Road, and back by the Linn Park. Not bad for my 'no weel' toe. Farewell to Bubbles and Babinski. Tommy gave them to a school mate. Babinski - farewell!

Saturday, 13 June

We all went to Linn Park at night. I showed Agnes and Tommy how to putt. I should mention that the child won.

Sunday, 14 June

We all at church this morning. Tommy got presented with various prizes. A Bible, two books and two certificates. We all at Queen's Park in the afternoon. Invaded by all the Mossmans about 5 p.m. After tea we took them a walk to Ruglen. They left us there.

Friday, 19 June

Working late. A woman called today, so Agnes let her wash the stair and clean the room windows.

Saturday, 20 June

A perfect summer day. Agnes and I at Ruglen tonight. We sat for a minute in the Overtoun Park.

Sunday, 21 June

Weather perfection. Agnes and I at church this morning: Mass. After dinner, Tommy and I went to Bellahouston Park. After tea we all went to Clarkston, and home by Giffnock and Thornliebank.

---

23 The phrase 'wise in his generation' is a well-worn Victorian literary phrase, possibly derived from the Gospel of St Luke, chapter 15, verse 24.

Monday, 22 June
Tommy wins the bursary he tried – £20. Well done, Tommy! Mrs
Gordon and Ronnie dropped in this afternoon. At night, Tommy
cycled to Paisley.

Wednesday, 24 June
Doctor up today. Agnes won't see him again, I hope, till August.
Agnes and I took a little walk at night.

Thursday, 25 June
Agnes very busy now, getting ready for Milngavie. She spent part
of the day in the wash house. Tommy out for his usual spin at
night.

Friday, 26 June
Tommy stopped school for the holidays, and got the class prize
for the year. Agnes and Tommy came to the firm at 4.30. We
motored to Milngavie, had tea and then looked around the house.
Mr Baxter then took us a fine spin in the motor round the country.
After supper we had some music, then he motored us to the car at
Hillfoot. We got home just before midnight.

Tuesday, 30 June
Got our packing done. Went to cab office
and ordered a taxi for tomorrow.

Wednesday, 1 July
Agnes and Tommy off by taxi to Queen
Street Station. I saw them off by 12.33
train to Milngavie. They got a taxi there,
which deposited them at Kildare,
our country residence for July. They dined in
state with the Baxter family, who then went
away and left Agnes in possession. I arrived
at tea time. Very warm day and a terrific
thunderstorm at night. It is a grand start.

Thursday, 2 July
This is our country seat. Fine sunny, warm day. Travelling now
by train to my work. To cheer me up, a man dropped dead this
morning in station. Isa phoned me today that my aunt in Belfast
offers her house to us for our holidays. Nothing doing. We meander
around the country at night.

1925

Thursday   2   July

This is our
Country Heat.
Fine sunny
warm
day.
Travelling now by
train to my work.
To cheer me up a
man dropped dead this morning
in station.   Isa phoned
me today that my aunt
in Belfast offers
her house to us for our
holidays.   Nothing doing.
We meander round
the Country at night.

Friday, 3 July
Fine warm, sunny day. In the afternoon, Tommy went to Govanhill
for his bicycle. He came into Paterson, Baxter and Co with it, and
we took it out by Milngavie train.

Saturday, 4 July

*Another rare day. Spent the afternoon chiefly
sitting on the lawn and getting sunburnt.
We went down to the village at night, as I
required tobacco. Being in Milngavie, the said
tobacco was nicely scented, which displeased
me greatly. We saw a stand-up (or lie-down)
fight between two natives.*

Sunday, 5 July
Very hot day. We sat about the lawn chiefly.

Tuesday, 7 July
We went round the waterworks at night.[24] Kelvin Hall burned
down.[25]

Saturday, 11 July
Brilliant day of sunshine. Very hot. I spent the afternoon basking
in the sunshine. Agnes went to Govanhill in the afternoon for
some stuff. About 9.15 I went out for a walk. Up the old road
behind the waterworks and back by the Strathblane Road.

Tuesday, 14 July
Great heat today. Mrs Carmichael out seeing us in the afternoon. I
met Peggy at Queen Street Station at night, and took her out with
me. We had some music.

Friday, 17 July
This is Fair Friday, so I got the 12.38 train home. Dull, wet day. At
night we went to Baldernock.

---

24 The waterworks, which include Mugdock and Craigmaddie reservoirs, were built as
    part of the scheme to bring fresh water from Loch Katrine to Glasgow, which was
    inaugurated in 1859 by Queen Victoria.

25 The Kelvin Hall had been built as the Industrial Hall for the 1901 Glasgow
    International Exhibition, then found a new use as the city's civic exhibition and
    entertainment space. The wooden structure was destroyed in a blaze in July 1925, and
    the present building opened in 1927.

Saturday, 18 July
On holiday today. Fine day. At night we went out the Craigton
Road and back by Mugdock Castle.[26]

Monday, 20 July
Still on holiday. Dull day. Around by the waterworks. My wee toe
blistered.

Tuesday, 21 July
Back to work again. Scorching sunny day. Tommy at Blanefield on
his bicycle.

Thursday, 23 July
Got a letter from A. Baxter saying that Wee Sandy was not well.
He thinks it is the measles. At night Tommy and I over the moor.

Friday, 24 July
Bright, sunny, warm day. Johnny and Lily here all day. We sat on
the lawn and got a few photos taken.

Sunday, 26 July
Got a telephone message from A. Baxter that Wee Sandy was very
ill, and they were motoring home. They all arrived at 7 p.m. in two
motors. Great excitement. The house was full. Alex, Tommy and I
out for a walk about 10 p.m.

Monday, 27 July
We go home today. Alex drove us in his motor to station at dinner
time. We had our tea in our own house. Hallelujah. The house is
full of Carmichaels' furniture. They duly shifted it to give us room.
And so ends our Milngavie holiday.

Tuesday, 28 July
*Agnes celebrated her return by a visit to
the wash house at night. The spring of my
eyeglasses broke today. Agnes got a sore leg.*

Wednesday, 29 July
Got my glasses mended. Tommy at Milngavie for his bike, and
drove it home. Tommy got a cyclometer for his bicycle. Agnes and
I went to the Majestic at night.

---

26 The fourteenth-century castle was in ruins by the twentieth century, but its tower had
    been incorporated into a mansion designed by the architect James Sellars for local
    historian James Guthrie Smith in 1875.

Friday, 31 July

Agnes went round and saw the doctor about her leg. The lump is caused by too much walking, but is not a serious matter.

Saturday, 1 August

After tea, we all went to Linn Park. We had a round in the putting green. We ran up against our respected 'sky pilot' and had a few words with him.[27]

Sunday, 2 August

In the morning, we all went to church, where all good people ought to go. In the evening we went to Greenlodge. Had a walk through the Green first, which is an unholy sort of place.

Tuesday, 4 August

Agnes and I at Queen's Park at night. Paid my house insurance today in case of accidents.

Wednesday, 5 August

Paid the rent today. Went up to Dickson and left my glasses to be converted into a pair with ear-legs. Tommy at Art Galleries in afternoon.

Thursday, 6 August

Agnes went to Ibrox in the afternoon. Got my specs today. It cost me 7/6, which I duly paid and which Agnes owes me.

Sunday, 9 August

This is Tommy's birthday.[28] The child is growing a big boy now. To celebrate the event, I took them to church this morning. After tea we all went to Rouken Glen.

Friday, 14 August

Tommy at Erskine Ferry in afternoon. At night I went to Thornliebank and back by Eastwood golf course and Cathcart. Agnes bought a new aluminium teapot.

Saturday, 15 August

At night we went to Shawlands Picture House.

Sunday, 16 August

Brilliant day. In the afternoon we all had a seat in Eastwood Golf Course.

---

27 The term 'sky pilot' refers to any member of the clergy. Here, Thomas means the minister of his church.

28 Tommy turned 13 that day.

Monday, 17 August
Agnes went to the doctor. Her mouth not much better. She is on a very light diet. Tommy at Dunlop on his bicycle. I went to library at night.

Tuesday, 18 August
Tommy at school again. All the folk from Ibrox here tonight. Mr Gordon brought his wireless set to test on my aerial.

Wednesday, 19 August
Agnes went to Calder Street to interview a party who had a house in Rothesay that might suit us. After the interview, she decided it would not suit us.

Thursday, 20 August
Saw Agnes off this morning by 8.55 train to Rothesay from Central Station. She goes to look for a house. She got home dead beat at 7 p.m. She was successful.

Friday, 21 August
Agnes went to see her doctor. He thinks she is improving, but she is still on a starvation diet. Think I need a holiday.

Saturday, 22 August
Sunny day. Tommy out cycling with Mr Gordon and Nannie.

Monday, 24 August
Agnes went over to Greenlodge at night. My niece Lily is getting married next month. Agnes got home at the scandalous hour of 11.35 p.m. I let her in.

Tuesday, 25 August
Agnes in the wash house. After tea, Tommy and I took car to Spiers Bridge, walked to Clarkston via Patterton, Newton Mearns and Old Mearns Road, and got car home.

Wednesday, 26 August
Wrote to my respected aunt in Belfast.

Thursday, 27 August
We are now thinking about holidays. Bought a new hat.

Friday, 28 August
Instructed the railway company to lift our hamper on Monday. I spent the night mending the aforesaid hamper.

Saturday, 29 August

I went over to the bank and lifted a wad of notes for our holiday. Of course, I had the teller's consent. Agnes did a little baking at night, and I did a large amount of not much. A letter from Gaube today.

Sunday, 30 August

Donned my new hat and took Tommy to church this morning. We saw two baptisms. Josephine arrived at our abode of love about 5 p.m. Agnes and I, but chiefly Agnes, packed the hamper.

Monday, 31 August

In order to get the full benefit of the ultra-violet rays (if any), I got my hair cut. I stopped tonight for my holidays.

Tuesday, 1 September

At last. We are off. We rose early and took car to Central Station. Got 9.50 train to Gourock, then boarded the good ship *Mercury*.[29] We arrived in Rothesay at 12.15. Was very pleased with our house. Think we will get on well with this landlady. After tea, we all out by Craigmore.[30] Very heavy rain. We came back by the Skipper Wood. Agnes pretty tired, and no wonder.

Wednesday, 2 September

Nice sunny morning, so after breakfast Tommy and I climbed the Barone Hill, and came back by the forbidden path that takes you by the waters of Loch Fad.[31] In the afternoon we all went to Port Bannatyne.[32] After tea all to the picture house.[33]

Thursday, 3 September

Brilliant sunny day. In the forenoon, Tommy and I walked to Kerrycroy.[34] I bought a cap today. In the afternoon we all went to Loch Fad. After tea, we all went to Port Bannatyne. I have a lump on my right cheek.

---

29 The paddle steamer *Mercury* was built by Napier, Shanks and Bell of Yoker in 1892, and was being operated by the London, Midland and Scottish railway company in 1925.

30 Craigmore is at the east side of Rothesay Bay.

31 Barone Hill and Loch Fad are to the south of Rothesay.

32 Port Bannatyne stands just beyond the west end of Rothesay Bay.

33 The Picture Palace in East Princes Street.

34 Kerrycroy is about 3.5 miles south of Rothesay.

Friday, 4 September
Another brilliant day. Took a walk through the Skipper Wood in
the forenoon. This is 'Rothesay Illuminations', so at night we all
went out and saw the fireworks, illuminations etc. It was not bad.

Saturday, 5 September
Weather like yesterday. In the morning Tommy and I cut through
the Skipper Wood and on to Kerrycroy. In the afternoon we all
at Port Bannatyne. At night we lost ourselves nearly in the golf
course up by Canada Hill.

Sunday, 6 September

Fine day and quite warm. Tommy and I
meandered a little before dinner. After tea
we all took the bus to Kerrycroy and walked
back. The swelling on my face looks like
suppurating. My-oh-my.

Monday, 7 September
In the forenoon, Tommy and I visited the castle, our
thirst for excitement still being unglutted. We then paid a visit to
the wee museum. After dinner, we all took the car to Ettrick Bay.[35]

Tuesday, 8 September
Nice sunny day. In the forenoon, Tommy and I walked to Port
Bannatyne and tried the putting green there. After tea, I went to
the doctor. He says my complaint is a wen.[36] I go to the hospital
tomorrow and he will operate. Nothing serious, he says.

Wednesday, 9 September
At 12 noon, I presented myself at the Victoria Cottage Hospital.
The sinful part of my cheek cut open, and the inside dug out,
then a stitch put in and plastered up again. I got home not worth
a button. Tommy met me after the little diversion in case I would
be 'non compos mentis'. At night we went to the Picture Palace.
I don't feel brilliant. My face is stiff and sore.

---

35   The car was a tramcar, operated by the Rothesay and Ettrick Bay Light Railway,
     which ran from Port Bannatyne to Rothesay and on to Ettrick Bay. Ettrick Bay, on
     the west coast of Bute, is well known for its sandy beach.

36   A 'wen' is a harmless cyst, especially on the face or neck.

Health and illness

Before the coming of the National Health Service in 1948, the provision of hospitals, family doctors, dentists and opticians was through a patchwork of private partnerships and individuals, charity and voluntary organisations and statutory bodies. In Glasgow in the first half of the twentieth century, there were three main types of hospitals. The first type was the voluntary hospital, run by a board of management and funded by voluntary subscriptions. These included the Glasgow Royal Infirmary in Castle Street (opened in 1787), the Western Infirmary in Dumbarton Road (1874) and the Glasgow Maternity Hospital in Rottenrow (1858). The second type was operated by Glasgow Corporation as the local public health authority, which, under the Police Act of 1866, had to provide permanent fever hospitals for treating people with all kinds of infectious diseases. These were Belvidere Hospital in London Road (1829, now demolished) and Ruchill Hospital in Bilsland Drive (1900, now derelict). The third type was the Parish Council hospital, operated by the organisation responsible for the relief of the sick poor. These included Stobhill General Hospital in Balornock Road (1904) and the Southern General Hospital in Govan Road (1872), which became the responsibility of Glasgow Parish Council in 1912, when Govan was integrated into the city. Both transferred to Glasgow Corporation in 1930.

The Victoria Infirmary in Langside Road, where Tommy was treated for appendicitis in 1929, opened in 1890 as a voluntary hospital with 84 beds. By 1906 it had 260 beds, and a new 120-bed wing was added in 1927. The Victoria opened a convalescent home called Brooksby in Largs in 1897, and built the first country auxiliary hospital in Scotland at Philipshill, near East Kilbride, in 1927. The inspiration for the Victoria Infirmary came from the Glasgow Southern Medical Society, which had been set up in 1844 by a small group of local general practitioners. The society, and Dr Ebenezer

Duncan and Dr Lawson Kelly in particular, lobbied for a new hospital for this growing part of the city. When fund-raising was complete, the architects Campbell Douglas and Sellars won the competition to design the new voluntary hospital in 1882, building work began in 1888 and the infirmary was formally opened by the Duke of Argyll on St Valentine's Day 1890. At that point, the hospital consisted of two pavilions set at right angles to a central administration block, and a nurses' home. The hospital was named after Queen Victoria and was given permission to display the Royal Arms above the entrance, beneath a carving of a puma, symbolising medical care.

The Livingstone family doctor was Dr William Gray of 63 Smith Street in Govanhill (telephone Queen's Park 222). Before the coming of the National Health Service in 1948, doctors provided their services free to working men under the National Insurance Act 1911, but this did not necessarily extend to their wives and children. Medicines were purchased at a pharmacy. Many poor people depended on the charity of doctors for health care, or put their trust in cheap and sometimes dangerous home remedies.

The Livingstone family dentist was R.H. Nathaniel Leiper of Westbourne, 631 Paisley Road West in Ibrox. Before the NHS, the only source of free dental care was in dental schools, where students provided fillings and extractions but were not qualified to administer anaesthetic, which made for interesting encounters. The National Insurance Act provided funds for dental care, but only when there were surplus funds; the first time this happened was in 1922. Insurance societies also offered policies that paid the basic costs of visits to dentists' surgeries. Dentists were expensive to visit, and dental health was very poor. In Glasgow, it is said, many young women had all their teeth extracted before marriage, to spare their new husbands the cost of dental care in the years to come. Since this was paid for by their fathers, it can be thought of as a rather unusual dowry.

The Livingstone family optician was R. Dickson of 116 New City Road, Cowcaddens. Before the NHS, there were no free or subsidised sight tests, lenses or frames, and every customer had to pay for the services they used. For diseases of the eye, people could visit the Glasgow Eye Infirmary for no cost. This facility, which was founded as a voluntary hospital in 1824, operated from two addresses: the in-patient department was at 174 Berkeley Street, near Charing Cross, where there were more than 100 beds, and the out-patient department was at 80 Charlotte Street, in the East End.

Thursday, 10 September
Feeling much easier, and not so bad generally. Nice sunny day. In
the forenoon, Tommy and I walked to Ettrick Bay by St Ninian Bay
Road. We paddled on the golden sands. After tea we took the car
to Port Bannatyne.

Saturday, 12 September
Warm, sunny day, the nicest day so far. Tommy and I did a little
putting, then we went up to the hospital, where I got a smaller
patch on my face. Agnes met us. After dinner we all walked up
the Moor Road through Knocknicoll Wood, and got the bus back
from Kerrycroy. After tea we putted, then took our landlady to the
pictures. Bought a new pipe.

Monday, 14 September
Tommy and I went up to hospital again. The doctor took the stitch
out of my face.

Tuesday, 15 September
This is a sad day, for me anyway. Our holidays are now over.
Tommy and I did our last putt. We then went to the pier, where
the landlady saw us off on the good ship *Kenilworth* at 2.15. We
got home about 5.15 p.m. Nice sail. A fine holiday, which I might
have enjoyed better.

Wednesday, 16 September
*Back to business as usual, also
Tommy to school. Ordered a new pair
of glasses today, so that I would
have one of each kind.*

Thursday, 17 September
Nannie Gordon here for a little at night.
Agnes and I then went to Greenlodge. Agnes
in the wash house today.

Friday, 18 September
Went round to the doctor and showed him the face. He, of course,
thought it was not quite better, and might have to be done over
again. Came away duly cheered. Tommy at a Scout social.

Saturday, 19 September
Took a walk over to Shawlands in the afternoon. A man in that
district owes my firm some money. Agnes and Tommy went into
town in afternoon. New shoes for Agnes and a new school case

for Tommy. Got my new glasses today. I am one guinea the poorer.[37]

Sunday, 20 September
We have not been at church for some time, so we all went this forenoon. In the afternoon, I took a run down to Ibrox and asked the girls to Morgan Street for their tea. They duly arrived.

Monday, 21 September
The back of the kitchen rocker not in a good way, so I put on a new bit of canvas. Agnes thinks she could have done it better.

Wednesday, 23 September
My niece Lily having a show of her wedding presents at Greenlodge, so Agnes went over in afternoon to give assistance. Tommy and I went over about 8.30.

Friday, 25 September
I away from my work at 4 p.m. We all went to the wedding in London Road. My niece Lily and John Martin were made one at 7.17 p.m.

Sunday, 27 September
I have got the cold. We got out all our postcard albums and took out the cards. Agnes is going to burn them in the wash house. Ah, me.

Monday, 28 September
This is the autumn holiday. I don't feel too well. My cold is pretty bad.

Tuesday, 29 September
Agnes went to the wash house at night. My cold not much better, and I feel sort of wobbly. Wrote to my friend in Latvia.

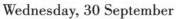

Wednesday, 30 September
Agnes went to the wash house in the forenoon. I think she is now finished. Wrote to Mr Gaube of Vienna.

Sunday, 4 October
Having some work to do, I went into the office after breakfast and broke the Sabbath day. To make up for it, I took Agnes to church at night. Tommy went to Sunday School.

---

37   A guinea was one pound and one shilling (£1.05).

Monday, 5 October

My cold going away very slow-like, so I got a bottle of oil of cod. Tommy filled up his lamp with water and a compound which makes a gas, and went out on his bicycle.[38]

Tuesday, 6 October

Dropped in on my way home and had a crack with Father Petrauskis. When I got home, Mrs Gordon and the wee fellow in.

Wednesday, 7 October

Agnes went to a Scout meeting in the afternoon. After tea we all went to the Cinerama.

Friday, 9 October

Working later at night. Agnes went and had a consultation with the doctor. He thinks she shows a little improvement.

Saturday, 10 October

Fine day. Tommy out on his bicycle and came back with it punctured. All the Mossmans invaded us at tea time, so we were not lonely.

Sunday, 11 October

Tommy went to church this morning. Then mended his punctured bicycle in the afternoon.

Tuesday, 13 October

Sunny, cold day. Got my hair cut.

Wednesday, 14 October

Agnes at the Scouts in the afternoon. The one and only 'Sandow' died today.[39]

Thursday, 15 October

Very cold day. Put on my overcoat today for the winter. Agnes at Parkhead in the afternoon.

---

38 Water dripping onto calcium carbide reacts to form acetylene gas, which is then ignited.

39 Eugen Sandow (born in Prussia as Friedrich Wilhelm Müller) was the first modern bodybuilder and physical-culture exponent. He promoted the first bodybuilding contest in 1901.

Friday, 16 October
Nice sunny day. Agnes and Tommy in town this afternoon. Tommy
getting a new coat and LONG trousers.

Sunday, 18 October
All of us to church today. In the afternoon we all went to Ibrox
and walked all the way. We listened in to Mr Gordon's wireless
and got devoured by their dog.

Monday, 19 October
Agnes went to Partick in the afternoon to see Lily. The elder up for
a little at night.

Wednesday, 21 October
Went into Bows on my way home and got blinds for the
room windows. Put them up at night, with many an oath.

Thursday, 22 October
Finished the job tonight of hanging blinds, with many a
sigh.

Friday, 23 October
*Tommy tried on his first pair of long trousers
tonight*

Thursday, 29 October
Wet day and extra wet night. Was working late tonight at
Cavendish Street.[40]

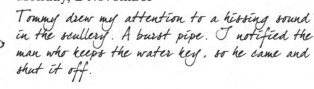

Sunday, 1 November
We all encouraged the church-going masses by
attending worship. In the afternoon we all took a walk through
the Queen's Park.

Monday, 2 November
*Tommy drew my attention to a hissing sound
in the scullery. A burst pipe. I notified the
man who keeps the water key, so he came and
shut it off.*

40   Number 37 Cavendish Street, near Eglinton Toll, was the address of James Deans
     Ltd, bedding and wire-mattress manufacturers. Thomas indicated earlier that his
     employer had recently taken over a bedding factory.

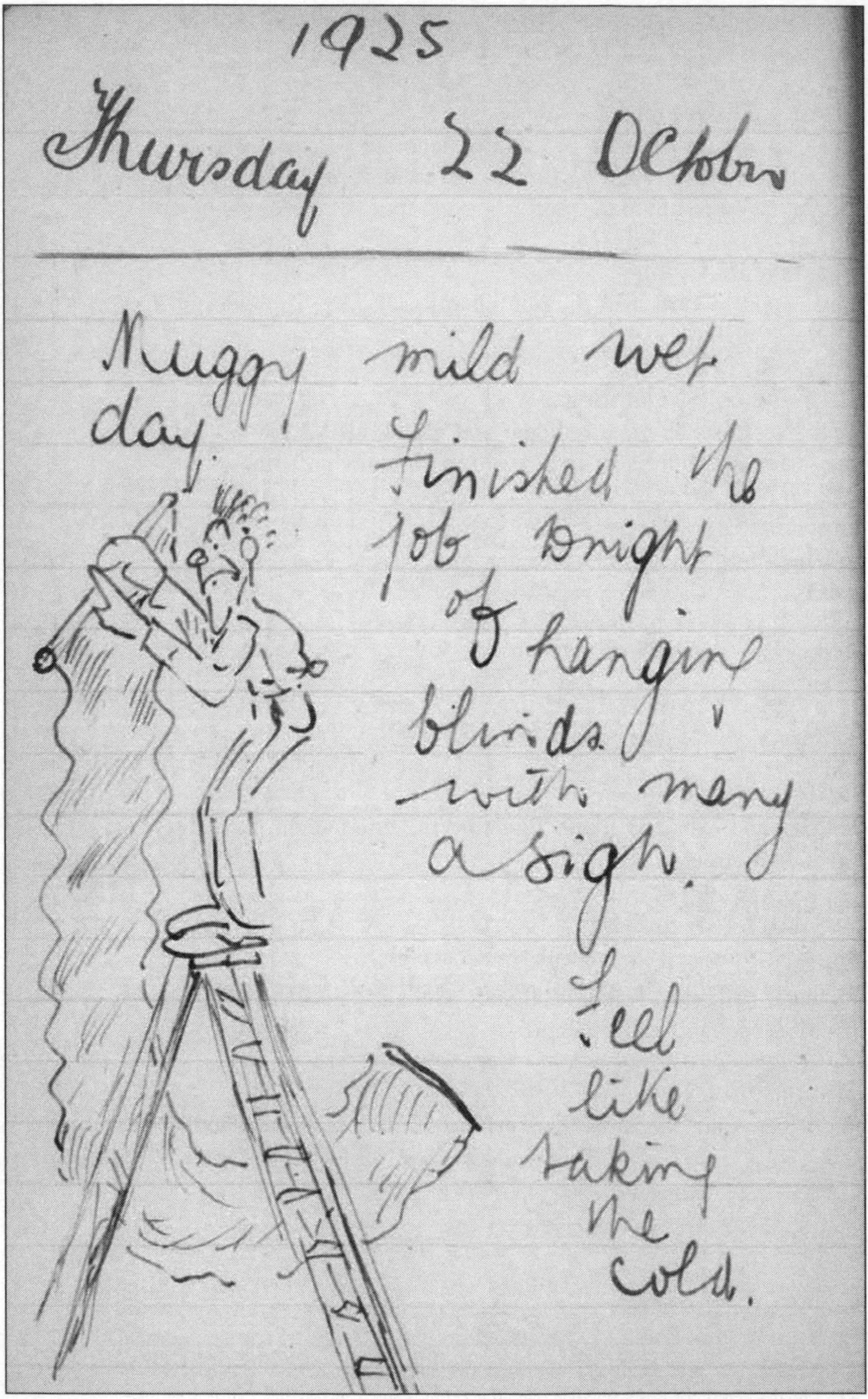

1925

Thursday   22 October

Muggy mild wet
day. Finished the
job bright
of
hanging
blinds
with many
a sigh.

I feel
like
taking
the
cold.

Tuesday, 3 November
The plumber up this morning and patched up the leak.

Thursday, 5 November
I mended the little shelf in scullery that the plumber destroyed.
Heard the great Chaliapin tonight.[41]

Friday, 6 November
The factor up today. and robbed us as usual.
Tommy at the Scouts.

Saturday, 7 November
In the afternoon, Tommy went to the 'picture show' in
the McLellan Galleries.[42]

Sunday, 8 November
In the morning we all went to church. In the afternoon, I took
Tommy out for a walk. Cathcart, Merrylee, Shawlands and
Queen's Park.

Monday, 9 November
Mr Gordon and Ronnie here at tea time.

Tuesday, 10 November
This is a red letter day. Agnes' birthday.

Thursday, 12 November
Working late. My neck got a crick in it, so Agnes rubbed it with
the juice 'Sloan'.[43]

Friday, 13 November
Listened tonight to France, Belgium, Holland and Germany. Not to
mention Scotland and England.

Monday, 16 November
Wild foggy day. Tommy's quarterly examination this week. Poor
lad.

---

41 Feodor Chaliapin was a celebrated Russian opera singer. He also sang Russian folk
    songs, and introduced the West to 'The Song of the Volga Boatmen'.

42 The McLellan Galleries, at 270 Sauchiehall Street, was built by coachbuilder
    Archibald McLellan to house his collection of paintings. After his death in 1854,
    Glasgow Corporation bought the gallery and his collections, and opened it to the
    public.

43 Sloan's Liniment was a popular over-the-counter medical product that was rubbed
    into painful muscles or joints. The main ingredient was derived from chilli peppers.

Tuesday, 17 November

The fog continues. Agnes ironed most all night.

Friday, 20 November

Fog bad as ever again. Tommy gets finished with his week's examination. Two sad events today. Queen Alexandra died today, and I burst up my variometer.[44] Sad, sad.

Saturday, 21 November

Another wild, foggy day. Bought a new variometer today. Agnes' uncle Jack in for a little at dinner time. Faked up the new variometer, but NBG. Took it back and got another. Left it to be wired up.

Sunday, 22 November

A much nicer day. Tommy and I out for a little in the afternoon. At night, Agnes and I went to church. Tommy attended his two Sunday Schools. No wireless.

Monday, 23 November

Agnes in town this afternoon to pick a coat. She took my niece Lily with her, so Lily dined with us. She got her coat, and got me a new 'hairy' waistcoat.

Tuesday, 24 November

Called in at the Clydesdale and got my new wireless set. With a flutter at my waistcoat, I hooked it on at tea time, put on the 'phones and listened. It worked. Quite as good as the old one, so couldn't wish for anything better.

Wednesday, 25 November

Agnes's new coat arrived tonight. It is the nicest coat she has had, since 1910 at least. Agnes, Tommy and Mrs Carmichael at a concert tonight. I rested at home.

Thursday, 26 November

Agnes and Tommy beat the room carpet in the back green.

---

44   Queen Alexandra was the wife of King Edward VII and mother of King George V. She died, aged 80, at Sandringham.

Friday, 27 November
Benny the painter up at night, and did his duty to the room.

Sunday, 29 November

Agnes got four big scratches on her back. Origin unknown.

Thursday, 3 December
Frost and fog. Have a pain in my side, to my great alarm. I blame spring cleaning. Agnes at Parkhead in afternoon.

Monday, 7 December
Got a letter this morning from the long-lost Babinski. Poland is evidently in a bad way. Frost away now. Feel as if I had eaten too much apple cake.

Tuesday, 8 December
Mrs Gordon here for a little in the afternoon. We all at Partick to see my niece Lily's new home.

Thursday, 10 December
We laid the room carpet this evening.

Friday, 11 December
Tommy's school card shows him as being first in examination.

Saturday, 12 December
Tommy out on his bicycle this forenoon. After tea, I took a run down to Ibrox to see the wonderful wireless that Mr Gordon has made. It is a wonderful set, in many a way.

Sunday, 13 December
Agnes and Tommy went to church. I had a lazy day and did not go out.

Monday, 14 December
Agnes keeping herself warm in the wash house afternoon and night.

Tuesday, 15 December
Govanhill's new electric lights turned on tonight.

Wednesday, 16 December
Agnes dropped a pot on her foot. What next?

Saturday, 19 December
My toe pretty sore. Bathed and painted it.

Monday, 21 December
Snowed and sleeted all day. Wrote to Duncan.

Tuesday, 22 December
Winter commenced yesterday. What we were getting was evidently summer. Agnes washed a few hundred collars, most of them mine I expect.

Wednesday, 23 December
Tommy stops for his holidays today. Tommy went to the Scouts. The draw is taking place there tonight, and we are interested in it. When Tommy came home, we ceased to be interested in said raffle.

Thursday, 24 December
Tommy in town buying a book for his Xmas. A box of hankies arrived today for Agnes from Nannie Gordon, and a fine book at night from Greenlodge for Tommy.

Friday, 25 December
Being Xmas day, I have a holiday. Thinking it was cold this morning, I hung the thermometer outside and it dropped to 27 degrees. This confirmed my supposition. We got a Xmas box from Duncan and Maud today. A large supply of tobacco for me, a wee fancy beady mat for Agnes and five shillings for Tommy. In the afternoon we went to the Cinerama.

Saturday, 26 December
Back to work again. We got a parcel from Greenlodge. A pair of boot trees for me and slippers for Agnes. Bought a new alarum clock at 4/9. Tommy out at Burnside in forenoon with Jack Ferguson. Agnes in wash house a part of the day and is dead beat by night.

Sunday, 27 December
We all at Ibrox for our dinner. They had a goose, so we dined on a large scale.

Monday, 28 December
Got a Christmas greeting from Warsaw. A man up in the afternoon from the BBC. He was looking for people causing noises etc. We pled not guilty. Agnes had a busy night washing tea sets, making ginger wine etc.

Wednesday, 30 December
Agnes tore a bit of her arm yesterday putting up curtains. Killing herself generally at night with hard work.

Thursday, 31 December
Stopped today at 12 noon for the New Year holidays. Alex Baxter gave me a calendar for Agnes with a view on it of Kildare. We spent a busy night getting ready for one minute past midnight.

1926

Thomas and his extended family faced many challenges in 1926, mostly relating to illnesses of various degrees of severity. Thomas' toe bothered him much of the year, Agnes' various ailments made her depressed and hypercritical, and Tommy fell off his bike. Tommy was the rising star of the family, winning a number of prizes and a place at a more academic school. With foresight and maturity, he left the Boy Scouts because they might have interfered with his studies in the future. And he moved from Sunday School to Bible-study class. He was growing up, and fast.

In the outside world, the General Strike in May, and the coal miners' strike that held on until November, were the last industrial struggles caused by the unravelling of emergency legislation passed during the Great War. For Thomas, they represented two extremes: potential revolution and personal inconvenience.

But whatever life and the world threw at him in 1926, Thomas managed to end December on an optimistic note, celebrating three of the positive highlights of the year.

Friday, 1 January
At the correct minute, Mr and Mrs Carmichael and Peggy came in to first foot us. Alex came in with two pals but went away. Peggy gave us some music. All away 3.40 a.m. Turned out a dirty, wet day so we did not go out. Played Agnes and Tommy various games.

Saturday, 2 January
Still on holiday. Got a card from Vienna. In the afternoon we went to the Cinerama. At night we played cards, draughts etc.

Sunday, 3 January
We all went to church this morning.

Monday, 4 January
Started work again. Agnes at Ibrox tonight. I bought a new hat.

Tuesday, 5 January
We all went to Majestic at night. Tommy went to Ibrox in afternoon to see how Nannie is keeping. Got a letter from Duncan and Maud.

Wednesday, 6 January
Agnes went to Dennistoun to see Hetty Mossman.

Thursday, 7 January
Tommy and Jack Taylor at the Art Galleries in the afternoon.

Saturday, 9 January
Tommy at a birthday party at Jack Taylor's.

Monday, 11 January
Agnes at Ibrox in the afternoon. Tommy back at school.

Tuesday, 12 January
My toe sore most wicked today. Changed my boots at dinner time, which seemed to ease it a little. All Greenlodge here tonight.

Wednesday, 13 January
Very cold and some fog. Bathed my daft toe at night with Reudels.[1]

---

1   Reudel Bath Saltrates was a crystalline mixture that was added to hot water and used to bathe the feet. Its advertising promised: 'Get rid of your foot troubles.'

Thursday, 14 January
Snow and sleet in the afternoon. My toe now easy.

Friday, 15 January
Snowed, rained and sleeted all day. We all went to the Hampden at night and saw *Charley's Aunt*.[2]

Sunday, 17 January
Heavy snow in the afternoon and evening. Tommy went to Ibrox in the afternoon and from there to Sunday School. Agnes went to church at night. Tommy has written a short story, which I read tonight.

Monday, 18 January
An absolute thaw this morning. Roads are in a fine old mess. Agnes in wash house most of the day.

Tuesday, 19 January
Hetty and her two cherubs here in the afternoon. Tommy Scouted at night.

Wednesday, 20 January
On my way home at night I called in at a Jewish shop in the Gorbals and got two chair springs for three pence. I sold a pair of blankets at the same time. Tommy wanted a game of draughts, so I gave him it and duly wiped him out.

Monday, 25 January
Put the new springs in kitchen chair, and sorted it up good as new.

Wednesday, 27 January
My stamp collection growing so much that I had to buy another album today.

Thursday, 28 January
Agnes and Tommy out for a little at night. Our old minister, Mr Tainsh, died today.

Friday, 29 January
My head sore all day. Tommy at the Scouts as usual. Heard the one and only Sapellnikoff.[3]

---

2   *Charley's Aunt* was a 1925 silent comedy, directed by Scott Sidney and starring Syd Chaplin (half-brother of Charlie), based on the very popular stage play of the same name.

3   Wassily Sapellnikoff was a Russian concert pianist, closely associated with the music of Pyotr Ilyich Tchaikovsky.

Sunday, 31 January
Tommy and I at church.

Tuesday, 2 February
Stayed in bed all day. Head sore and sort of sick. A party in the
house of Carmichaels tonight. I did not go, but persuaded Agnes
and Tommy to go. They made me comfortable before they left, with
headphones, tobacco and literature handy. I got on fine.

Wednesday, 3 February
Dull, cold sort of day. Went to my work at dinner time. Don't feel
so well as I thought I was. Felt sick at night. We played at Ludo.

Friday, 5 February
Terrible wet day. After dinner Agnes took Peggy Carmichael to a
Burns Concert. Tommy did not recite his piece owing to a cold. He
got a volume of Burns nevertheless, as he had been picked out of
the school (in his class). I rested at home.

Saturday, 6 February
*Rained all day. My cold not quite better and my
nose is very sore. We played at Ludo and Agnes
washed all the hankies.*

Monday, 8 February
Don't feel extra well today. Times are very exciting.[4] Mrs
Gordon and Nannie here tonight.

Wednesday, 10 February
Extra cold day. Agnes did some sewing machine work and broke
the needle. I put in a new one.

Thursday, 11 February
*Wrote to Gaube tonight. Had a
slight pain in my back.*

Friday, 12 February
*Got a new case for Tommy at
15/-. In my young days, a
school bag was easier got.*

---

4   Mine owners and the mineworkers' union were beginning to square up for the dispute
    that would cause the General Strike in May. The slogan of the Miners' Federation of
    Great Britain was: 'Not a penny off the pay, not a minute on the day.'

Monday, 15 February

Agnes in town in afternoon and finished up the night in the wash house. I stamped TCL on Tommy's new case with stencils I borrowed from my work.

Tuesday, 16 February

Very cold. Stormy, wet day, with snow and hail for variety. Tommy at the Scouts tonight and knocked some pieces out of his knee on way home.

Wednesday, 17 February

Agnes and Mrs Carmichael at the Hampden Picture House tonight.

Saturday, 20 February

Tommy sat a Bible examination in the afternoon. Out for an hour myself at night.

Monday, 22 February

My ear has a whistle in it.

Tuesday, 23 February

All Ibrox here for tea. Agnes squirted water into my fizzly ear to see what would happen.

Thursday, 25 February

We all went to the Majestic at night. *The Hunchback of Notre Dame* was the sermon.[5]

Friday, 26 February

Tommy sat another Bible examination tonight.

Sunday, 28 February

Nice forenoon. Before dinner, Tommy and I did the Tory Glen, Mill Wynd, Croftfoot, Carmunnock Road, Mount Florida walk. Nannie Gordon here at dinner time. We all went to the Camphill Museum, then car to Linn Park.[6]

---

5 The first of many film adaptations of the Victor Hugo novel, directed by Wallace Worsley and starring Lon Chaney (1923).

6 Camphill House was built in 1818 as a family home for Robert Thomson of the Adelphi Cotton Works in Hutchesontown. In 1894 the house and its grounds were added to the Queen's Park and converted to a museum of costume. It also had displays of relics connected to the Battle of Langside. The museum closed in the 1980s and the house is now flats.

1926

Tuesday 23 February

Some heavy rain
today very mild.
All above
here for tea and
away 11 pom

Agnes
squirted
water
into my
fizzly
ear
to see
what would
happen.

Thursday, 4 March
Snow and hail blizzards all day. Jack Taylor up with Tommy at night.

Saturday, 6 March
Cold day. Some rain. Lily and John Martin here for tea.

Monday, 8 March
Wet, stormy day. Paid to the government 10/-, being the amount of my wireless licence. Went round and saw the doctor about my ear. I have to soak them both in olive oil for a few days.

Wednesday, 10 March
Bought a new pipe at 3/6.

Thursday, 11 March
Agnes at Parkhead in afternoon. Mr Gordon here at night with his valve set.

Friday, 12 March
Went round and saw doctor regarding my ears. He syringed them and gave me a wee bottle of ear drops to put in said ears, at least for the deaf ear, which is inflamed.

Saturday, 13 March
Tommy sat a big bursary today. He out on his bike after noon. We played Ludo at night.

Sunday, 14 March
We all at church this morning. At night, I went out for about an hour.

Tuesday, 16 March
Was speaking to my niece in town today. Josephine has got her shop sold. She gives it up at the end of the month.

Friday, 19 March
Went round at night to the doctor. He says the inflammation in my ear is better.

Sunday, 21 March
This being Communion Sunday, Agnes and I went to church. After dinner, I took Agnes out a walk. Isa dropped in just as we got home. Josephine has a sore neck, which may be serious. I went home with Isa to see Josephine.

Friday, 26 March
Left my TMC 'phones at the Clydesdale to be overhauled.[7] Agnes got a bad cold at night. Bathed her feet etc.

Saturday, 27 March
Agnes had a terrible night. Seemed a little better in the morning, but got worse during the day. She kept in bed all day. Very fevered etc. Tommy sat an examination in Bellahouston Academy today. I washed floor.

Sunday, 28 March
Agnes had a very bad night and very ill this morning. So sent Tommy on his bicycle after breakfast for the doctor. He came. Agnes got flu. Temperature 102 degrees. Got powders. She felt a little easier.

Monday, 29 March
Doctor up again. Agnes' fever now abated, but can eat nothing. Agnes' throat and chest pretty sore at night. Got my 'phones back today, but they are no better.

Tuesday, 30 March
Agnes very husky yet, but not so sore. Mrs Gordon here in afternoon, Josephine in evening, and Mrs Carmichael sat for a brace of hours. Lost my pocket book today. Among other documents, it contained a 10/- note. Farewell!! Left my 'phones again to be repaired.

Wednesday, 31 March
Tommy broke a plate and cut his finger in an alarming manner. Doctor up and sees a big improvement in Agnes. Says she has got laryngitis, but that it will pass away. Got my 'phones tonight, much improved. Agnes got up tonight, weak of course, but we had a game of Ludo. I feel feverish. Sore throat, chest and up the pole generally.

Thursday, 1 April
I feel all out in the morning, so do not rise. Agnes did so. After a bit I got up and went round to the doctor. He gave me powders and said I could risk going about, so I went to work after dinner, feeling not quite too bad.

---

7   TMC was a London company that made headphones and other electrical items. The Clydesdale Supply Company was a Glasgow wholesaler and retailer of musical instruments, record players, radios, sheet music, records and associated merchandise.

Friday, 2 April

I forgot my flu powder at dinner time, so Agnes sent Tommy in to my work with it. Safety first. Mrs Gordon here in afternoon and Hetty Mossman at night. Stopped today for the Easter holidays.

Saturday, 3 April

On holiday, but did not go out. Washed the floor in afternoon with Agnes' assistance. I felt very tired after this little effort. Flu epidemic all over Glasgow.[8] Let Glasgow Flourish.[9]

Sunday, 4 April

Beautiful sunny, warm day. Went out for half an hour. My legs feel as if they were all hinges, and my head pretty sore.

Monday, 5 April

This is the spring holiday, so I am off the chain. Nice warm day. After dinner, we took car to Mount Florida and staggered about Cathcart a little. This is Agnes' first appearance out, so she is a bit wobbly.

Tuesday, 6 April

Back to work again. Felt shaky in forenoon. Got word from Babinski.

Thursday, 8 April

Tommy away all day, a cycle run to Stewarton with Jack Taylor. Feeling 100 per cent, I cleaned room windows at night. Miss Grant of our church came in at night and talked good-oh for a brace of hours.

Friday, 9 April

Agnes washed stairs at night, so she improves. Tommy burned his finger today. Did my usual hard night's work.

Saturday, 10 April

After tea, we all went to the Cinerama to see Charlie Chaplin in *The Gold Rush*.[10]

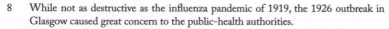

8   While not as destructive as the influenza pandemic of 1919, the 1926 outbreak in Glasgow caused great concern to the public-health authorities.

9   The motto on the Glasgow coat of arms.

10   Charlie Chaplin wrote, directed and starred in this 1925 silent film, in which his tramp character went to the Klondike in search of his fortune.

Monday, 12 April
Went out to Ruglen at night and told my tailor to proceed in the
construction of a new suit worthy of my handsome figure. I walked
both ways.

Tuesday, 13 April
Agnes out in the afternoon, but felt very ill. She is not picking up
very well. Tommy started school again after his holidays. Old Mr
Armstrong next door has died.

Wednesday, 14 April
Wrote Mr Gaube at night, and chucked in a few
stamps.

Thursday, 15 April
Agnes says I smoke too much. My toe very
sore. Agnes ironed handkerchiefs all night,
and for ever and ever.

Saturday, 17 April
Agnes and Tommy at French's regarding a new suit.

Monday, 19 April
Mrs Carmichael in the wash house on our account.

Tuesday, 20 April
Tommy at a Scout concert. Agnes and I went to the Majestic.

Wednesday, 21 April
Agnes and Tommy once more at French regarding new suit.

Saturday, 24 April
Tommy went to town in afternoon and got a new carrier for his
bicycle, and put same on at night.

Monday, 26 April
I ordered two bags of smokeless coal from the corporation. They
promise delivery in 10 days. Agnes started to clean out the
kitchen press. Wrote to my friend in Riga.

Tuesday, 27 April
Agnes whitewashed the bunker. Wrote Babinski.

Wednesday, 28 April
Agnes looking sad and worried at night. Ah, me.

Thursday, 29 April

I was in Paisley this afternoon on business. Agnes went round and saw her doctor. Gets a new bottle. The coal situation is getting serious. There may be a big strike.

Friday, 30 April

Tommy resigns from the Scouts as they might interfere with his studies later on. Agnes took Tommy into town for a fit-on. Is there going to be a coal strike at midnight?

Saturday, 1 May

Agnes and I went into Bow's in afternoon to see about a wash stand capable of accommodating the wringer. We did not get suited. The big coal strike is now a fact, and a general strike is threatened.

Monday, 3 May

Agnes had a bad night. Not well at all. The Trades Union Council calls a general strike to take place at midnight.[11] Made the kitchen table so that the wringer could stand on it, but it did not work very well.

Tuesday, 4 May

The great strike is now in operation, No trains, cars, papers, no nothing. A few cars running, but no papers at night. Have to get my news now by wireless. Isa rang me up to say that Josephine had been operated on.

Wednesday, 5 May

Very cold day. About 100 cars running today. The Glasgow press publish an emergency newspaper.[12] Business at a standstill. Some small riots in town at night. Serious times.

Thursday, 6 May

Cold day. Students drive the cars in Glasgow now. About 140 cars on today, but I have to walk morning and night. The minimum car fare is 2d. A few more riots in Glasgow and over the country generally.

---

11 The General Council of the Trades Union Congress called a general strike from 3 May in an attempt to force the British government to prevent worsening conditions and reduced wages for miners. Workers' reaction to the call was immediate and overwhelming, and caused even the TUC to be concerned about a potentially revolutionary situation. King George V, who dismissed suggestions that the strikers were revolutionaries, said: 'Try living on their wages before you judge them.'

12 The proprietors of the various Glasgow newspapers pooled their resources to produce this paper.

Friday, 7 May

Cold day. Interviewed corporation regarding my smokeless coal. It is going to be twinless also. Some more riots over the country. 190 cars on today. My toe is beginning to feel effects of the strike.

Saturday, 8 May

Extra cold day. 219 cars on today. Some more hooligan riots. Heard Baldwin, the prime minister, make a statement on the strike on my wireless.

Sunday, 9 May

Agnes at church herself in morning. Agnes in a very bad state today. Miserable, depressed and hysterical. 242 cars running today.

Monday, 10 May

A few train accidents today.[13] 300 cars out. Agnes spoke to a wife tonight who offered her a wringer stand for 5/-. The great strike is doomed to failure.

Tuesday, 11 May

400 cars now running. Tommy went to the woman's house at night who had the wringer stand and brought it home. It looks all right. Wrote Duncan.

Wednesday, 12 May

Collapse of the Great Strike. The TUC calls it off unconditionally and so the great plot fails.[14] In gratitude, we go to the Majestic at night. We are now preparing for spring cleaning.

Thursday, 13 May

Kitchen and lobby whitewashed for 5/6. Very confused position with the strike. The railway refuse to go back. Cars are now practically normal.

Friday, 14 May

The railway strike is now settled.

Saturday, 15 May

Dockers still out. Can get newspapers now.

---

13   The *Flying Scotsman* was derailed by strikers near Newcastle.

14   On 11 May two unions took the TUC to court, arguing that it had no right to compel them to strike. The court upheld the challenge, and the TUC, no longer protected by the Trade Disputes Act, called off the strike the following day.

Monday, 17 May

This is a holiday. Bright, but windy and cold. Tommy and I out
for a little in the forenoon. Turned out a nice sunny day. After
dinner we all took bus to Rouken Glen and walked from there to
Clarkston.

Wednesday, 19 May

Worked late. Tommy at the King's Theatre seeing *Macbeth*. Agnes
in wash house.

Saturday, 22 May

Warm, sunny day. Went out to Ruglen in afternoon and got my new
suit.

Sunday, 23 May

All at church. In the afternoon we all out for a walk. The dock
strike now settled, but the coal situation is unchanged.

Tuesday, 25 May

Paid 3/3 for a bag of coal today. Working late.

Wednesday, 26 May

Took Agnes with me at dinner time to Kyle Park and Co where
we ordered a new umbrella, latest pattern. Tommy got his bike
repaired for 8/-, which will leave him tight for a day or two.

Friday, 28 May

Called into Kyle Park and Co at dinner
time and got Agnes' new chubby umbrella.

Saturday, 29 May

Agnes took Tommy into town in forenoon,
where he got a nice new rainproof coat of
a blue colour for 35/6.

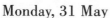

Monday, 31 May

We are going to Milngavie on Wednesday. Nannie rung
me up to see if Tommy would dine with them during the time
he attended school. After tea, Tommy went down to Ibrox on his
bicycle and let them know that he would not manage.

Tuesday, 1 June

Got word from A. Baxter that Wee Sandy was ill, so their departure was delayed. So we are not going to Milngavie on Wednesday. We may get away at the end of the week. Very sad.

Friday, 4 June

This is my birthday.[15] Alex Baxter told me we could go to Milngavie tomorrow. At night I ordered a taxi and then we had a busy night packing up. We are going away for a brace of months.

Saturday, 5 June

Brilliant day of sunshine. Tommy got word he had won a £20 bursary. Good lad. Alex Baxter told me today Mrs Baxter was not well. So we can't go to Milngavie today. I telephoned the taxi men I would not require their services, and sent Agnes a wire saying that it was off. We went to the picture house at Shawlands at night.

Monday, 7 June

Got a phone message this forenoon that we could now go to Milngavie. I ordered a taxi by phone, met Agnes and Tommy at Queen Street Station and we all went out by the 3.30 train. I did not go back to my work. Tommy and I out over the moor at night. And so we began our country residence.

Tuesday, 8 June

Took the bus to my work in morning. Train back at dinner time, and then went back again with Alex in the motor, and motor home at night. We all out for a little at night by the waterworks.

Wednesday, 9 June

Alex Baxter showed us how to get sounds out of his valve set.

Thursday, 10 June

Poured all day long. A. Baxter did not go to his work today, having the cold. I went over to Dunalastair in the morning to see him etc.[16] The lad who drives motors took me to my work in Alex's car, then took it back to Milngavie. I had to travel in the bus thereafter. Rung up Isa in afternoon to see how Josephine is keeping.

---

15 Thomas was 44.

16 The Baxter family appears to have two houses in Milngavie, as well as a holiday home in Crail.

Friday, 11 June
Tommy went home for his bicycle. Mr Baxter away to Crail for the weekend.

Saturday, 12 June
In the afternoon, Tommy and I took certain parts of the Kildare wireless to be charged.[17] Turned out a nice night, so we did the Baldernock walk.[18]

Sunday, 13 June
Hot, sunny day. We sat in the lawn all afternoon. After tea we went to Mugdock and back by Strathblane Road.[19]

Monday, 14 June
This is Tommy's first day at school again. He dropped into Miss Mark's house at dinner time and got his religious prizes. Two books, a Bible and two certificates.

Tuesday, 15 June
Tommy came with us in the motor this morning. A. Baxter off to Crail at night, so we had to take the bus. We had a walk at night.

Wednesday, 16 June
Rang Mr Gordon up at night and had a crack with him. Agnes' aunt was there about 10 o'clock, so I rang up again and Agnes cracked with her.

Monday, 21 June
Instead of going to school today, Tommy went into town and consulted the doctor about his cough. Doctor says it is a little irritation of the bronchial tubes, and gave him a bottle.

Tuesday, 22 June
We had a small walk round the village. Tommy got cold in the head.

Thursday, 24 June
Tommy got a postcard to lift £10 of his bursary money.

Friday, 25 June
Tommy came in the motor with us in the morning, and got his cheque for £10. We all out over the moor at night.

---

17 Alex Baxter's valve set is powered by a battery, which has to be recharged periodically by an electrician. Thomas' crystal set is powered by the signal received by the aerial.

18 Baldernock is a hamlet to the east of Milngavie.

19 Mugdock and Strathblane are to the north of Milngavie.

Saturday, 26 June
Fine day. I get my holidays today. We spend them in Milngavie.

Sunday, 27 June
Hot, sunny day. After dinner, Tommy and I over the golf course
and back by Mugdock.

Tuesday, 29 June
Hot, sunny day. At night, Mr Baxter took us a run in his motor to
Loch Katrine.[20]

Wednesday, 30 June
Very hot day. Tommy got his holidays today. He brought home two
volumes, prizes.

Saturday, 3 July
Blazing hot day. We all out at night. Bardowie Loch and back by
Baldernock, through the farm and down Strathblane Road.[21]

Monday, 5 July
Fine day. After dinner, Tommy and I went to Mugdock down
the 'Khyber Pass' and along a footpath which landed us at
Blanefield.[22]

Wednesday, 7 July
After breakfast, Tommy and I started out to climb Tambowie.[23] It
would have taken too long, so we did not go to the top. In jumping
off a wall, I twisted my ankle. Walked about five miles after that.
After dinner, got it bathed and bandaged. Turned sick, sore head,
and went to bed for the afternoon.

Thursday, 8 July
Being a cripple, I spent the day sitting on the lawn.

Tuesday, 13 July
Blazing hot sunshine. 85 degrees in the shade, 125 in sun. The
record for 10 years. Hosepiped the garden. A. Baxter had supper
with us.

---

20   Loch Katrine, in the Trossachs to the north of Glasgow, is the source of most of the
     city's water supply.

21   Bardowie Loch is to the east of Milngavie.

22   The 'Khyber Pass' is the local nickname for a steep path between Mugdock Wood and
     Craigallion Loch. It is now part of the route of the West Highland Way.

23   Tambowie is a hill to the north-west of Milngavie.

Wednesday, 14 July

Hotter than ever. A. Baxter in at night. We tried out the new piano rolls.

Friday, 16 July

This is Fair Friday, so got away at 12.30. Fine, warm, sunny day. About 9.30 p.m. I went out myself a walk by Strathblane Road and Mugdock.

Saturday, 17 July

Fair Saturday, so I am on holiday. A beautiful day of heat and sunshine. I took train in the morning to town, met Nan Gordon at the New Savoy and took her back to Milngavie by bus.[24] We all had a fine day, took photographs and had a walk by Mugdock village.

Monday, 19 July

Still on holiday. After dinner we all wandered to Bearsden.

Tuesday, 20 July

Rose early and got the 7.07 a.m. train to my work

Friday, 23 July

Fine sunny day. Tommy and I cleaned out garage.

Monday, 26 July

Fine weather. Tommy took his bicycle home today as it needs a new tyre etc. Went over the moor myself at night. Our time will soon be up.

Friday, 30 July

The Baxter crowd are due back tomorrow, so we all got our packing done. Ah, me.

Saturday, 31 July

At an early hour, Tommy and I carried the hamper down to the station and deposited it at Left Luggage. I then got a bus to my work. The Baxter tribe arrived about 5 p.m. We all escaped about 8 p.m. A. Baxter took us in his own car to Milngavie station, and we got a train, then a taxi, and home about 9 p.m. Amen.

---

24 The New Savoy was a cinema on the corner of Hope Street and Renfrew Street. It was later the Majestic Ballroom, and was demolished to make way for the Savoy Centre.

Monday, 2 August
Agnes, Tommy and I at the Majestic tonight.

Tuesday, 3 August
Paid my fire and burglary insurance today. Agnes spent afternoon and evening in the wash house.

Wednesday, 4 August
Hot, sunny day. After tea I took car to Mosspark then walked to Renfrew Ferry. Took car from there home, via Paisley, Barrhead and Thornliebank. A run of 80 minutes for 2d.

Thursday, 5 August
Heat wave continues. After tea we all took car from Gorbals to Renfrew via Barrhead and Paisley, then car back via Govan.

Saturday, 7 August
More good weather. We went to Linn Park at night and putted. I won.

Sunday, 8 August
We all went to church this morning. After tea we all walked down to Ibrox and spent the evening with the Gordons.

Monday, 9 August
Got a postcard from Paris from my good friend Gaube. This is Tommy's birthday, so we celebrated in the Majestic.

Tuesday, 17 August

Brilliant sunshine. Tommy at Fenwick in the afternoon on his bicycle. A wee chap called E. Peril, Pearl, Perle or Perl, put his head through a window at our corner and was taken away in an ambulance for repairs.

Saturday, 21 August
Went out with Agnes in afternoon to see a mirror that had tickled her fancy. We ordered same which, being duly delivered, I hung up at night. We went to Shawlands picture house with the odd change.

Saturday 31 July 1926

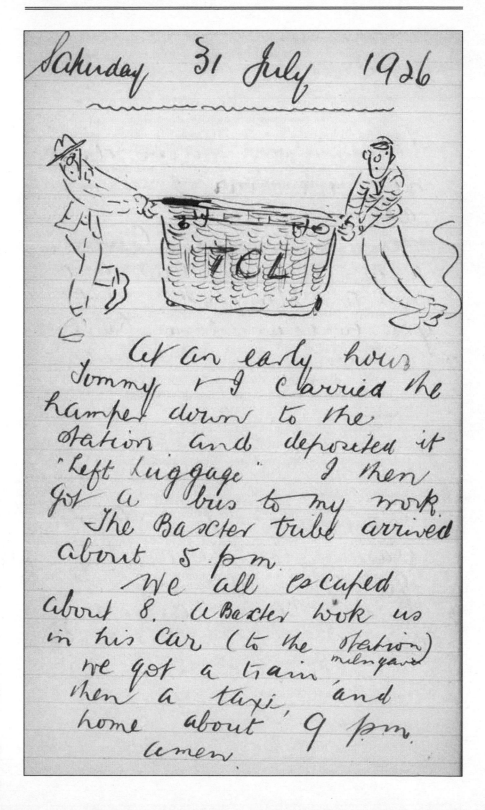

At an early hour
Tommy & I carried the
hamper down to the
station and deposited it
"Left Luggage." I then
got a bus to my work.
The Baxter tribe arrived
about 5. p.m.
We all escaped
about 8. A Baxter took us
in his car (to the station)
we got a train, milngavie
then a taxi, and
home about 9 p.m.
Amen.

Sunday, 22 August
Agnes made rhubarb jam. I ate a piece with jam and butter, and found it quite good.

Monday, 23 August
Our new mirror has certain defects in it, so Agnes went over to the dealer and lodged a complaint. He took it back, and gave us one the same, minus the defects. Tommy's holidays are now over. He is now a pupil in Albert Road Academy.[25] He went into town in the afternoon for a lot of new books.

Saturday, 28 August
Sunny, warm day. Agnes went into the town in afternoon. She was speaking to the Misses Henderson, her cousins, of Montrose Street. After tea we all took car to Hillfoot, then we walked to Anniesland via Bearsden, and car home.

Sunday, 29 August
All at church. Very warm day. Agnes and Tommy went to Sighthill Cemetery in afternoon.

Monday, 30 August
Heat wave on still. To keep cool we all went to the Majestic at night.

Thursday, 2 September
Tommy collapsed this morning. When I picked him up I thought the worst, but he was all right in a minute or so. We kept him off school. It gave me a shock.

Monday, 6 September
Hetty Mossman here in afternoon, but did not get in. Agnes went over to Greenlodge but did not get in. At night, Agnes went to Dennistoun and saw the Mossman family.

Wednesday, 8 September
Tommy got a new fountain pen today.

Saturday, 11 September
Nice sunny day. We went to the Shawlands place of entertainment at night.

---

25   Later known as Pollokshields Senior Secondary, and now a primary school.

Monday, 13 September

The nozzle blew off the gas tonight and left us in the dark, and covered the kitchen with red hot bits of materials.

Tuesday, 14 September
Bought a new gas burner for 1/9 and fitted it.

Thursday, 16 September
Dull day. Coal 3/9.

Saturday, 18 September
All the Mossman folk here this evening. Gordon showed us how to weave carpets.

Tuesday, 21 September
Coal 4/- a bag. Agnes in the wash house.

Wednesday, 22 September

After tea I went to Ruglen and brought home my trousers (an extra pair on order).

Thursday, 23 September
Coal 4/3. Tommy has a gum boil.

Friday, 24 September

Agnes washed the stairs at night. A man keeked round at her, said something, then ran. Agnes much alarmed thereby.

Monday, 27 September
This the autumn holiday. A beautiful, warm, sunny day. After dinner, we took the bus to Carmunnock, looked at the village, then walked to Clarkston via Busby and car home. We went to the Majestic after tea.

Tuesday, 28 September
Having been troubled for some time with a bad tooth, I went down to Ibrox at night to have it out. Was there at 6.45 and got out at 9. Of course, he was not all that time pulling the tooth. Mr Leiper, my usual dentist, laid up with pleurisy, so a substitute took his place. I survived.

Wednesday, 29 September
My jaw very sore. Coal now 4/6. Cut up a lot of black wool for the carpet.

Thursday, 30 September
Bought a new pipe at one shilling.

Monday, 4 October
Gave my neck a twist this morning when I was brushing my hair. It gave me much pain all day. Agnes rubbed my dislocated neck at bed time.

Tuesday, 5 October
My neck still painful. I spent an uneasy sleep with my neck last night. Felt sick-ish all this evening. Agnes rubbed the erring neck again tonight, and hope for the best.

Wednesday, 6 October
Neck very sore but well otherwise.

Thursday, 7 October
Agnes rubbed my broken neck tonight.

Sunday, 10 October
All at kirk. Tommy joined Bible class at 5 p.m.

Tuesday, 12 October
My neck seems better now. Did a few hours work on the rug. My thumb sore now.

Sunday, 17 October
We all at Mass, Tommy as a spectator. Nannie Gordon here in afternoon, so we all had a walk. Tommy got a book from his late Sunday School teacher. We spent the evening in melody.

Monday, 18 October
Did some work at the carpet. So did Agnes.

Tuesday, 19 October
Fog and frost. No coal to be got. Agnes in the wash house afternoon and night. Thumb sore.

Wednesday, 20 October
We got a bag of coal for 4/9. Thumb still sore.

Thursday, 21 October
Got another bag of coal for 5/-. Thumb getting better.

Friday, 22 October
Hard frost this morning. Our coal gives no heat. German stuff likely.

Saturday, 23 October
Bad gas, bad coal, and Tommy has got a cold.

Tuesday, 26 October
Finished a love letter to Duncan, to my great relief. Hetty Mossman and Etta here in the afternoon. Sawed some wooden blocks tonight to save the coal. The coal men are very coy.

Wednesday, 27 October
Tommy received 10/- from the gas company for an essay he wrote some time ago. Agnes went to Greenlodge in afternoon. Josephine is very ill indeed.

Friday, 29 October
Got a bag of coal at 5/3.

Tuesday, 2 November
Raw, cold, dismal day. Cut up a lot of wool for the carpet and then did a little weaving.

Thursday, 4 November
Worked a lot at the carpet tonight.

Friday, 5 November
So that I may be able to buy coal, I filled in the requisite form, and posted it to the Coal Controller.[26] We can get coal, so far, if we like to pay for it.

Sunday, 7 November
Tommy went to church himself this morning. I went over to Greenlodge at night to see Josephine.

Wednesday, 10 November
Agnes went to see Hetty Mossman in the afternoon. After tea she went to Greenlodge. This is Agnes' birthday.

---

26   The post of Coal Controller had been created in 1917 to oversee the nationalised coal industry.

Thursday, 11 November
Agnes went to Partick in afternoon to see Lily. I cut up wool at night for the carpet.

Friday, 12 November
Mild, dirty, wet day. Coal now 4/- a bag.

Monday, 15 November
Nan Gordon here for her tea, then went to a church concert with Agnes.

Thursday, 18 November
Dirty, wet, cold day. Coal now 3/6 a bag.

Saturday, 20 November
In the afternoon I went down to Govan and had a look round the works where Mr Gordon is installed.

Sunday, 21 November
Agnes not well at all. She got up at breakfast time in a wretched condition and went back to bed in a more wretched condition. I'm no blinking use, evidently.

Monday, 22 November
Coal 3/3 now. Agnes at Greenlodge in the afternoon.

Thursday, 25 November
Dirty wet cold day. Working late. Coal now 3/-.

Sunday, 28 November
Agnes and Tommy at church. I stayed in and mismanaged things as usual. Gave them cold pie for dinner. Agnes told me a few home truths as to my general character and disposition. I was not flattered. To regain my self respect I went a long walk to Barrhead.

Monday, 29 November
The coal strike is now over, as far as Scotland is concerned.[27]

Friday, 3 December
Coal down to 2/9.

---

27   The miners, who had been out since May, went back to work. They were forced to accept longer hours, reduced wages and local agreements.

Monday, 6 December

Had a pain all day under my waistcoat, lower section. It may not be appendicitis.

Tuesday, 7 December

Fine day. Feel very much off colour. Tommy has a
holiday today owing to the election. I duly recorded
my opinion as to the shutting of pubs, and Agnes voted at night.
Ella Gordon here at tea time, also Josephine.

Wednesday, 8 December

*Painted Agnes' mouth with nitrate of silver,
by doctor's orders.[28] Agnes cleaning out
pantry today. She thinks I'm lazy, so I
knitted the carpet all night to prove I'm
not. Agnes annoyed that I voted yesterday
during the day.*

Sunday, 12 December

Agnes and I went to church this morning. A new stained glass
window there blessed to the memory of the late Tom Marks. A
dull, cold day. Agnes very dumped and not extra friendly. A
miserable day. Don't feel well at night.

Monday, 13 December

Agnes and Mrs Carmichael at a church concert. Coal now 2/1.

Tuesday, 14 December

Our worthy elder up tonight with our cards for next Sunday Mass.
We discussed divers righteous subjects.

Thursday, 16 December

To make me proof against the cold, I got a bottle of cod oil. Cut up
a lot of wool, and did a little carpet knitting.

Saturday, 18 December

Tommy at a classical concert in the forenoon.

Sunday, 19 December

*We were awakened at 1 a.m. by the police, because
the door of the business premises was insecurely
fastened. So I had to walk into the town and*

---

28   Silver nitrate is still used in the treatment of mouth ulcers.

fasten the insecure door securely and walk home again. Got back to bed about 2.30 a.m. We all at church for Mass.

Monday, 20 December
Very cold day. Coal is now 2/1.

Wednesday, 22 December
Made up parcels at night to send to our various friends.

Friday, 24 December
Got away at 1 o'clock for the Xmas holidays. Duncan sent Tommy 5/- for his Xmas. Agnes gave me a new tie, and we gave Tommy an 'Eversharp' pencil.[29]

Saturday, 25 December
On holiday today. Agnes got hankies from Maud. Foggy day. We went to the Majestic at night. Agnes got the cold and is not well at night. A miserable holiday.

Sunday, 26 December
Lily here in afternoon, then Nannie came. She brought 5/- for Tommy, a pair of gloves for Agnes and hankies for me.

Monday, 27 December
Agnes met me in town at 5.15 and we got some wax cloth for the lobby. We put the old stuff on pantry floor, then laid the new lot. We got a religious calendar from Greenlodge and I got some tobacco from Duncan, about half a pound of black Irish.

Wednesday, 29 December
Stuck in stamps all night.

Friday, 31 December

Got away at 1 p.m. Took a run over to Greenlodge in afternoon. After tea, Agnes and I went to the Majestic. Great events of this year: the General Strike; the big coal strike; Tommy starts a new school, Albert Road Academy; we stay two months in Milngavie for the summer; I started to eat butter and jam on the one piece.

---

29   Eversharp pencils, the first propelling pencils, were made by Wahl-Eversharp of Chicago.

1927

Thomas and Agnes, illnesses aside, had a more settled year. However, young Tommy's tastes were changing. No more nights at the Majestic for him, now that he and his friends had discovered organ recitals and highbrow concerts. The family had a relatively happy holiday in Port Bannatyne, but no summer sojourn to Milngavie.

The diaries also indicate that the family was walking less, and the outside world intrudes into the diaries less and less. There were fewer mentions of the wireless and the stamp album, as the novelty of these simple pleasures perhaps faded, and there was more emphasis on Thomas and Tommy taking more of their share of domestic duties.

Saturday, 1 January

We all trooped into the Carmichaels' at the proper moment and wished them 'Mony o' them'. After a little music, etc, we left them at 3.40 a.m. Blustery, bleak sort of day. Tommy is going to keep a diary, poor lad. We all went to the Cinerama to finish the holiday.

Sunday, 2 January

We all went to church this morning. Wrote Duncan at night.

Tuesday, 4 January

At work again. Got a letter from Chile with a philatical donation.[1] Mrs Fraser (Maggie MacKenzie) has invited us out for tea at an early date. 'Twould be churlish to refuse.

Wednesday, 5 January

We got a letter from Nan Gordon intimating that they could not visit us as her ma was ill. Agnes took a run down herself at night to Ibrox.

Thursday, 6 January

Very cold day. Agnes spent the day in the wash house. Tommy complains of internal pains! New Year??

Friday, 7 January

Agnes done up, and says that the wash house is killing her. I don't know how to help. Tommy took castor oil, which helped him.

Saturday, 8 January

My niece Isa is to be married soon. Tommy went over to Greenlodge in the forenoon with our donation. Agnes not in very good form tonight.

Monday, 10 January

Agnes very sick all the night, and had to keep her bed all day. She can eat nothing.

Tuesday, 11 January

Agnes much better today, and up all day. She and Mrs Carmichael went to the Cinerama in afternoon.

Wednesday, 12 January

Very cold and very wet. We all went to the Frasers' party. Coal now 1/11½.

---

1   Thomas, ever the player with words, has invented 'philatical'. 'Philatelic' would be correct.

Saturday, 15 January
This is 'Students' Day'.[2] We all at the Mossmans' tonight.

Sunday, 16 January
Agnes and Tommy at church. The students collected for charity
£14,300.

Tuesday, 18 January
Agnes at Cinerama in the afternoon. My treatment of Agnes every
day is brutish. This is not my opinion.

Wednesday, 19 January
Fog and frost. Agnes in wash house all day.

Thursday, 20 January
Agnes went to Greenlodge this afternoon to see Isa's presents. Isa
gets married tomorrow.

Sunday, 23 January
Agnes disgusted with everything, so out I went for a walk in the
afternoon. She went to church at night. So did I.

Wednesday, 26 January
A terrific gale brought down a chimney head next to ours. We
thought we were sent for. We were about scared to death all night.
Men up at the chimney head at 10 o'clock and threw over a lot
more of the stonework. The noise was wicked.

Friday, 28 January
In the afternoon, the gale started again worse than ever. 102 miles
an hour registered. Many houses collapsed and hundreds injured
and many killed. In the afternoon, the ambulance was called
out 70 times in four hours. We spent the evening in fear and
trembling, so to speak.[3]

Saturday, 29 January
Agnes at a City Hall concert tonight with Hetty Mossman. Between
them, they mismanaged the place to meet and Agnes did not see
her as arranged. So she went to Dennistoun, but she was not there,
so she goes back to the City Hall and, after many adventures,
meets her in the hall. She went to hear Gordon Mossman's brother
sing but, being late, did not.

---

2   This was the day that students of Glasgow University dressed up and paraded through
     the streets for charity.

3   The phrase 'fear and trembling' appears three times in the King James version of the
     Bible.

Sunday, 30 January

In the afternoon, Tommy and I took a walk as far as Mount Florida. I was appalled at the damage done by the gale, even in that short distance. Chimney heads levelled in nearly every building. 11 persons killed in Glasgow by the gale, six of them in one tenement.

Monday, 31 January

To restore our shattered nerves, we go to Majestic at night. 22 persons killed in the great storm, of which 11 were killed in Glasgow.

Tuesday, 1 February

Tommy wore a bow tie to school today. Some schoolboy joke.

Wednesday, 2 February

Converted an old soft hat into insoles.

Saturday, 5 February

Mr and Mrs Mossman and family here for tea. Gordon has now got another wireless set, and brought his new 'phones. I let him hear a wireless set.

Sunday, 6 February

Tommy and I walked to Linn Park in afternoon. Felt very tired. After tea I went to Greenlodge to see how Josephine was keeping.

Monday, 7 February

Agnes in the wash house all day.

Thursday, 10 February

Agnes met me in town at 5.30, then we went to the boot shop. A pair of boots for me and a pair of gym shoes for Tommy was the result.

Sunday, 13 February

Agnes and I went to the kirk at night. The rain coming down in buckets. We were daft. Agnes feels like taking the cold now.

Monday, 14 February

Tommy's face a little swollen. Agnes' cold very bad at night. Wrote to New Zealand.

Saturday, 19 February
Dirty wet day. Mrs Gordon, Ella and Ronnie here in the forenoon.
We went to Majestic at night.

Sunday, 20 February
Fine day. Tommy at church in morning. Nobody else out all day.

Monday, 21 February
Agnes in wash house all day. Lily in for an hour or so in the
afternoon.

Wednesday, 23 February
Some rain. Agnes not well at all today. She says she has too much
to do.

Thursday, 24 February
Agnes at Greenlodge in the afternoon. Josephine's condition is
serious, I'm afraid.

Saturday, 26 February
Agnes sick this morning and did not get up for breakfast. She
feels a bit better in the afternoon, so we went to Majestic at night.
Fine day.

Sunday, 27 February
Tommy and I at church in the morning.

Tuesday, 1 March
Agnes made marmalade. I feel sick tonight.

Sunday, 6 March
Tommy at church in the morning. I went a walk in the afternoon.
Agnes not out at all.

Tuesday, 8 March
Fine sunny day. Agnes spent it all in the wash house.

Wednesday, 9 March
Agnes at Greenlodge in the afternoon. Josephine not well at all.

Saturday, 12 March
In the afternoon, we went over to Greenlodge, and found Josephine
much better than I expected. My nephew Tom Carlyle was there. I
did not wait for my tea. After tea in our own wigwam, Agnes and I
went to Majestic.

Expansion of Glasgow

Glasgow Corporation played an active part in returning the city to a peace footing after the First World War, and in developing the city to meet the new challenges of a greatly changed world. One substantial activity was the construction of new council-housing estates, which became possible after the passing of the Housing (Scotland) Act 1919 (also known as the Addison Act). Many of these estates were built on land purchased outside the city boundary, which added to the size of the city. The Act obliged local authorities to construct houses for all their working-class citizens and made funds available to subsidise them. The Act had two main effects: it cleared many slum areas and it made it unprofitable for any private-sector developer to build new working-class houses. Soon, Glasgow Corporation was the sole landlord for working-class citizens.

The first wave of council housing in Glasgow, built in the 1920s, offered low-density schemes of semi-detached houses with gardens, set in wide and tree-lined streets. They were built in a circle around the city: in Knightswood, Yoker and Scotstoun in the west; Mosspark, Craigton and Carnwadric in the south; and Carntyne, Riddrie and Shettleston in the east. These estates, which were termed 'ordinary', were occupied by upper working-class and lower middle-class families.

The second wave, which included Drumoyne in the south-west of the city, was intended for the lower and middle working classes. These 'intermediate' houses were built to slightly lower standards and rents were lower. The third wave was designed to accommodate lower working-class families who were being made homeless by slum-clearance projects in Anderston, Townhead, Cowcaddens and Calton. New houses were provided in Blackhill and other schemes. In total, the three waves of development created fifty thousand new houses by 1939. The council had a policy that there would be no public houses in its housing developments, and many of the schemes were built without an appropriate number of shops and other community facilities.

Many of these housing projects were built on farmland bought by the council, and the city boundary was extended to incorporate them. Between the passing of the Act in 1919 and 1931, the area of Glasgow grew by more than a half, from 19,183 acres to 30,044 acres. Some of this area was developed as public parks.

Private developers, such as Mactaggart and Mickel and the Western Heritable Investment Company, built homes for purchase or rental by the middle classes in areas such as Hyndland, King's Park, Broomhill, Kelvindale, Alexandra Park, Shawlands and Newton Mearns.

To complement its new housing estates, the corporation constructed public parks, which were intended to provide facilities for sport and exercise, attractive flower displays and quiet spaces away from the often crowded houses and workplaces of the city. Between the two world wars, Glasgow acquired and developed Auldhouse Park (19 acres, purchased 1918), Linn Park (212 acres, 1919), Cowlairs Park (35 acres, 1920), Hogganfield Park (124 acres, 1920), King's Park (98 acres, 1920), Dawsholm Park (72 acres, 1921), Maryhill Park (23 acres, 1922), Cardonald Park (7 acres, 1928) and Knightswood Park (142 acres, 1929).

Linn Park, which Thomas visited and enjoyed, was once part of the estate of Hagtonhill, the property of the Maxwells of Pollok. Colin Campbell, the owner of a West Indies shipping line, bought the property in 1820, built a mansion house there (which he used as his summer residence) and named the estate 'The Lynn', after the waterfall on the White Cart Water, which flows through the area. John Gordon of Aitkenhead bought the estate in 1840, extended the house and added to the trees, shrubs and plants that Campbell had laid out. Glasgow Corporation bought the 180 acres of The Lynn in 1919 for £10,000. The council added the lands of Cathcart Castle (more than 18 acres, at a cost of £2,300) in 1927 and Court Knowe (4 acres, £150) in 1933. The mansion house is now private housing.

Sunday, 13 March
In the afternoon, Agnes and I went round and admired all the new houses in the King's Park district.[4]

Wednesday, 16 March
Agnes went to town in afternoon and got new shoes. After tea she went to Ibrox.

Saturday, 19 March
Tommy sat for a big bursary today in Hutchesontown school.[5] We went to Majestic at night. Agnes has a sore finger. Her arm is now sore, and she does not feel well at night. I am scared to death.

Sunday, 20 March
Agnes and I at church this morning. Agnes' head sore all day, but the alarming symptoms mentioned last night have gone.

Monday, 21 March
Agnes went over to Greenlodge in afternoon, but nobody in. Found out afterwards that Josephine is away to Rothesay for a holiday. Elder here at night with the Communion cards. Agnes had to leave him with me, as she is going to a concert with Mrs Carmichael. Tommy spent evening cleaning his bicycle.

Tuesday, 22 March
Agnes and Mrs Carmichael at the pantomime. Tommy occupied the evening (some of it) oiling his bicycle.

Wednesday, 23 March
Agnes in wash house all day.

Friday, 25 March
Tommy out at night with some of the lads of the school at some organ recital.

Saturday, 26 March
We went to the Majestic as usual.

Sunday, 27 March
We all at church – Communion. In the afternoon, we all had a walk. Car to Cathcart and through to the Newlands park.

---

4   King's Park is a large owner-occupied residential housing estate on the south side of Glasgow, developed by Mactaggart and Mickel from 1925.

5   Possibly Hutchesons' Grammar School in Hutchesontown, a district in the Gorbals.

Monday, 28 March
Agnes out after breakfast arranging with factor to get our lum swept. She got fixed up, so we made the necessary arrangements at night. Tommy out at night with a lad with a name like 'Skragovitch'.

Tuesday, 29 March
We all rose very early to allow the sweep to perform his duties. Sweeper duly arrived, but the chimney head is evidently in a bad state, and as the sweep did not want his neck broken, no lum was swept. Very sad. Agnes went to interview factor anent same, but saw him not.

Wednesday, 30 March
Agnes at the factor in the morning, but the interview not very satisfactory.

Friday, 1 April
Man up today about the chimney.

Saturday, 2 April
Tommy got a flute today at 4/-. We went at night to Majestic.

Monday, 4 April
Tommy's flute exploded tonight. Agnes made candy for Tommy's school concert.

Tuesday, 5 April
Took the flute back to the music shop and got the money back. Mislaid my umbrella. Where? No answer!

Wednesday, 6 April
Tommy at practice tonight for the concert. Agnes in the wash house in afternoon, and out at night at a concert with Mrs Carmichael. Our lum was unexpectedly swept this morning, and a new can put on.

Thursday, 7 April
Agnes spent the day in the wash house. Tommy at school concert. Miss Grant, of the kirk, here at night. She told us that the minister's wife is no more. Very sad.

Sunday, 10 April
We all at church this morning. Agnes went to Ibrox at night.

Thursday, 14 April

Heavy rain afternoon and night. Agnes went into town this forenoon and bought me an umbrella. See and not lose it.

Friday, 15 April

Got away about 4.15, this being Easter.

Sunday, 17 April

Dull, windy, showery. After dinner, we took car to Burnside, had a look round and took car home again.

Monday, 18 April

After dinner we took the bus to Carmunnock and walked to Clarkston via Busby. We dropped into Miss Balfour's shop and had a word or two with Miss Hillcoat. After tea we went to the Govanhill Picture House.[6]

Tuesday, 19 April

Agnes and Mrs Gordon out in afternoon regarding a new dress for Agnes.

Thursday, 21 April

Agnes and Tommy in town in afternoon regarding new suit for Tommy. Jack Ferguson and Tom Carlyle here at night. Being an intelligent lad, Tom spent the evening looking at my stamps.

Friday, 22 April

Agnes at Ibrox at night seeing a wedding. I don't feel extra well.

Sunday, 24 April

Agnes and I went to church at night. Agnes washed a few hankies at night. 14 for Tommy, four for me and two for herself.

Monday, 25 April

Winter commences. Snowed all day. Nan Gordon here at night.

Wednesday, 27 April

Bright, sunny day, but cold wicked. Agnes and I went to the Majestic. Agnes got a sore eye.

Thursday, 28 April

Bright, sunny day. Cold the blinking limit. At night I went out to Cathcart Library. Some heavy rain then. Agnes' other eye feels sore.

---

6   The Govanhill Picture House, now derelict, stands at 49 Bankhall Street in Govanhill. It was designed in a flamboyant Egyptian style by the architect Eric A. Sutherland, and opened in 1926. It is a B-listed historic building.

Sunday, 1 May
Tommy and I at church this forenoon. In the afternoon, I had a
walk via Cathcart.

Monday, 2 May
Agnes at Ibrox re dress, and Charing Cross direction re big fire in
Lyons.[7]

Wednesday, 4 May
Got my hair cut. My hair is getting scarce on the top.

Saturday, 7 May
Hot, sunny day. Summer at last. Tommy out on his bicycle. Agnes
and I went to Majestic. Last time?

Sunday, 8 May
Heat terrific today. Sun temperature 113 degrees. Tommy at church
himself. After dinner I out to Ruglen, Overtoun Park, Calderwood
Road, Eastfield and back to Ruglen. Being boiled by this time, I
took car home.

Monday, 9 May
Cold, bleak day. Summer is now over. Agnes in wash house all
day.

Tuesday, 10 May
Colder than ever. Agnes down at Ibrox after tea re dress. Dress not
yet ready.

Wednesday, 11 May
After tea, a young female came with Agnes' new dress. Feeling the
want of exercise, I went to Linn Park at night. When I got back,
Ella Gordon was here.

Thursday, 12 May
Agnes at Ibrox tonight with her dress, to get some alterations.

Friday, 13 May
Agnes bought a new hat.

Saturday, 14 May
We all went to town. First call we made at the Polytechnic, where
we fitted Tommy with a new hat, of the bashed-in variety. Agnes
then left us, and went to Ibrox to see her dressmaker. Tommy and

---

7   The printing works owned by Lyons Ltd, at 474 Sauchiehall Street, near Charing
     Cross, was destroyed by fire on the night of Saturday, 30 April 1927.

I then went up to New City Road and consulted with Mr Dickson, the eye man. He measured Tommy for a pair of glasses.

Wednesday, 18 May
Went up to New City Road at dinner time and got Tommy's specs. We are out of pocket 24/2 on this transaction. Tommy playing hockey at school. The minister here at night.

Thursday, 19 May
Agnes washed blankets today. I went to the Majestic at night myself. Why, I don't know.

Monday, 23 May
Holiday. Dull day and not very warm. At night Agnes and I went to the Govanhill Picture House. Tommy swotted all day.

Friday, 27 May
Agnes at doctor tonight about her eyes, which have been giving her trouble. She got a bottle and a box of ointment.

Sunday, 29 May
Nice day. Tommy and Agnes at church. In the afternoon, we all at Clarkston, then on to Newton Mearns and got bus back to Eglinton Toll. It cost us 2/- our little trip, which is very sad.

Monday, 30 May
Agnes went to Partick in afternoon, then Lily whisked her off to Knightswood, where the Ferguson clan have got a sort of mansion. I worked late to further the firm's interests.

Tuesday, 31 May
At night I went my favourite Busby – Carmunnock walk. My feet very sore, as I have a blistered toe.

Saturday, 4 June
Heavy showers and hail. Cold like. Tommy at a picnic somewhere in Hamilton district. He got home 10.10 p.m. Agnes and I went to the Govanhill Picture House at night. My birthday.

Friday, 10 June
Tommy is first in his examination. On Friday 10 June 1910, Agnes and I got married. May she never regret it.

Saturday, 11 June
A warm sunny day at last. Agnes and I at the pictures, then a walk round the Hangingshaws.

Sunday, 12 June
Brilliant sunny day. We all at church this morning. In the
afternoon, Agnes and I had a look around Mosspark.

Monday, 13 June
As a precaution against lightning, I put a gadget on pipe outside
scullery window and so earthed my aerial thusly.

Wednesday, 15 June
Very warm day. Agnes and I out for a little and listened for a few
minutes to a band in the 'wee park'. Was speaking there to Mr
Carmichael.

Saturday, 18 June
Bought a new cap today of a purple hue.

Sunday, 19 June
Stormy, wet, cold day. We all at church. Mass. Agnes and I went
again at night. Agnes can't read with her eyes.

Monday, 20 June
An old neighbour who emigrated to Orkney was visiting us
at dinner time. Tommy visited the gas works today. Josephine
here when I got home at tea time. Agnes' eyes giving her much
trouble.

Wednesday, 22 June
Tommy takes a notion for shorthand, so I got him a volume dealing
with these matters.

Thursday, 23 June
We do not stay in Milngavie this year.

Friday, 24 June
Agnes at doctor, and got better news about her eyes.

Monday, 27 June
We are getting ready for spring cleaning, so we washed the dinner
service and I took down the wires of my wireless.

Tuesday, 28 June
Painter in at night and did the whitewash trick. He sized the walls
in readiness for paper. We gave him supper, and he departed at
11.30 p.m.

Wednesday, 29 June

Went to the paint shop and got 4lbs of paint for 2/8. I am going
to paint a picture, maybe. The professional here in due course,
and decorated the kitchen in a pleasing manner with paper.
We allowed him once more to sup with us, and he got away
12.30 a.m.

Thursday, 30 June

Dark, wet night. Tommy stopped school for the holidays. He was
first-prize man for the year, at least, he divided it with another lad.
So got a volume of deep literature, which I will never read. Agnes
went to her doctor re eyes. I made a start with the paintwork.
Visibility poor.

Friday, 1 July

Got my painting finished, and hung the clock. We got word from
East Kilbride that our friends, to wit Miss Balfour and Miss
Hillcoat, intend giving us a call.

Saturday, 2 July

The Misses Balfour and Hillcoat arrived in the late afternoon.

Monday, 4 July

Warm and sunny. Agnes took a trip to Port Bannatyne and looked
for a house. After much looking, she clicked, so we go there our
holidays.

Saturday, 9 July

Tommy and I to Knightswood at night. Duncan there for his
holidays.

Tuesday, 12 July

Dull day. The king and queen in Glasgow opening the new Kelvin
Hall, laying the memorial stone of the King George V Bridge and
opening the new headquarters of the Air Force at Coplaw Street.[8]
I saw them in town, and Agnes and Tommy had a squint at them
about Eglinton Toll. Duncan here at night.

Wednesday, 13 July

Agnes in town in the afternoon and got a new waterproof coat. I
went to the library for a little at night.

---

8   The Kelvin Hall reopened as an exhibition centre, and the headquarters of the
     Auxiliary Air Force 602 Squadron was at 46 Coplaw Street.

Friday, 15 July

This is Fair Friday so I stopped work at 1 p.m. Tommy and I at Rouken Glen in the afternoon. I took him out on the boating pond for an hour. We got a postcard from Partick – Lily is now a ma. It is a boy.

Monday, 18 July

Terrific heat and sunshine. I went a walk through Queen's Park in forenoon. We spent rest of day at Milngavie. We were chased twice for trespassing.

Friday, 22 July

Agnes at doctor. Duncan here at night.

Sunday, 24 July

Heard the King of Belgium this forenoon from Ypres, opening of the Menin Gate.[9]

Wednesday, 27 July

Agnes went to Partick in the afternoon to see the new baby. Mrs Gordon here in the forenoon to tell Agnes she had a house in Dunoon. Seeing we are going away our holidays soon, I paid the rent. I might spend it to a better purpose in Port Bannatyne.

Saturday, 30 July

Tommy went to town in forenoon and paid the insurance. I went out and engaged a taxi for Monday morning. I also got my hair cut.

Monday, 1 August

The holidays start. Our taxi arrived at 9.30. We sailed from the Broomielaw per the Lord of the Isles at 10.30.[10] Fine sunny day, so had a fine sail. We arrived at Port Bannatyne about 2.30 and then it rained. Tommy got 2/- from Mrs Carmichael this morning, so he will stand me motor drives. Turned out a nice night. Tommy and I putted, then we had a little walk round the shore.

---

9   The Menin Gate Memorial to the Missing was unveiled by Field Marshal Lord Plumer, in the presence of Albert, King of the Belgians, and General Ferdinand Foch of France. At the end of the service buglers from the Somerset Light Infantry sounded the last post and pipers of the Scots Guards played a lament.

10   The paddle steamer *Lord of the Isles* was built by D. and W. Henderson of Partick, and launched in 1891. In 1927 she was owned and operated by Turbine Steamers Ltd.

Tuesday, 2 August
Walked into Rothesay in forenoon. Met Agnes and Tommy there, and all got car back. After dinner we all putted, then went to Ettrick Bay.

Wednesday, 3 August

Tommy and I putted, then had a walk along to the 'One Man Cemetery'. Took a path there that brought us back to the old mill wheel. After dinner we all walked to Rothesay.

Thursday, 4 August
Lovely day of sunshine and great heat. In forenoon, Tommy and I putted, then walked to Ettrick Bay. After dinner, we took bus to Rothesay, and Agnes bought a walking stick. We took the moor road between Loch Fad and Loch Ascog, cut through the Knocknicoll Wood, and landed in Kerrycroy. Had a seat there, and got motor back.

Friday, 5 August
Took Tommy out in a boat and gave him a lesson in rowing. After tea, we all walked to Ettrick Bay. Got caught in a terrific downpour of rain, and had to shelter in the doorway of a cottage. When we got to Ettrick Bay, more thunder and lightning, so we took car back.

Saturday, 6 August
Fine sunny day, and a nice breeze. After dinner, we all went to Rothesay. Met Miss Henderson, our landlady of 1925. She came with us, so we did the Loch Fad walk. Brought Miss Henderson home to tea with us. We played Ludo.

Sunday, 7 August
A bright, sunny evening. After tea we all went to Rothesay, and along to the Mill Hole, past Bogany Point, turned inland at this point and arrived back to Rothesay by the Serpentine. We passed a house with a monkey making faces at us.

Monday, 8 August
In forenoon, I allowed Tommy to row me about the bay. Then we putted. In the afternoon we all went to Ettrick Bay, got chairs, and were then chased home by the rain. After tea we took car to Rothesay and went to the pictures. Agnes fed up.

Tuesday, 9 August

This is Tommy's birthday.[11] After breakfast, Tommy and I out for a couple of hours in a boat. After dinner, Agnes ventured out in a boat with us. She stuck it for an hour and a half. Then we had a game of putt.

Wednesday, 10 August

A perfect deluge in the morning, but cleared up. We all got 12.15 boat to Dunoon. We were met there by Mr Gordon, Nan and Ronnie. After dinner we all did the usual walk to the water works and then back to tea. We got our photos taken by Nan. Boat back to Rothesay about 6.30.

Thursday, 11 August

Tommy and I out in a boat for a brace of hours. Tommy went overboard for a 'dook'. He thought it a trifle cold. After dinner, we all in a boat for an hour, then to Ettrick Bay. We got chairs and made ourselves comfortable.

Friday, 12 August

The finest day we have had. Brilliant, hot, sunny day. Tommy and I walked to Rothesay and met Nan Gordon at pier about 10.30. Took her back per bus. Before dinner, Tommy and I showed her how to putt. After dinner, we went along the shore and basked for a few hours.

Saturday, 13 August

Very warm, sunny day. Tommy and I took car to Rothesay, through Skipper Wood and along to near Ascog. Afternoon, all to Rothesay, then climbed the Barone Hill, up one side and down the other. Coming near 'time up', so I arranged to have our hamper lifted on Monday.

Sunday, 14 August

Dull, bleak day. Took a small walk myself. Agnes went to Rothesay and visited Miss Henderson. Feeling very sad. We have spent 27/6 on bus and car fares, and three shillings and four pence on gas.

Monday, 15 August

Rained all day. We spent the forenoon getting ready to depart. Gave Tommy his last walloping at putting. We boarded the good

11 Tommy was 16.

ship *Eagle III*.[12] She weighed anchor at 4.15. After a dreary sail, we arrived at the Broomielaw about 8 p.m. We got a taxi and were home about 8.30. We were warmly welcomed home by the Carmichaels. They took us in and gave us a good tea. Amen.

Tuesday, 16 August
Dull day. Started work. Went to library at night.

Thursday, 18 August
Dull day. Pouring wet. Agnes in the wash house all day.

Monday, 22 August
Tommy started school again.

Tuesday, 23 August
Agnes went to the wash house at night. Broke a box for Agnes to assist the boiler fire. Tommy at the Cathedral organ recital.

Thursday, 25 August
I went to Carmunnock and Cathkin Braes at night.

Saturday, 27 August
Agnes and I went to the Majestic. The 'big picture' did not please Agnes, so we are not going back.[13]

Sunday, 28 August
After tea, Agnes and I out at Shawlands and into Mount Florida and Cathcart via Blue-Bell Woods.

Tuesday, 30 August
Warm, sunny day. Took a walk at night round by the Dumbreck Road. Tommy went to the Cathedral to hear organs and such-like things. Agnes went to Ibrox.

Thursday, 1 September
Awakened about 1 a.m. by the most terrific peal of thunder and lightning. Kept me awake for a couple of hours. Agnes did not enjoy it.

---

12   The paddle steamer *Eagle III* was built by Napier and Miller in 1910, and operated by Buchanan Steamers Ltd.

13   The 'big picture' was the main feature film. There would have been a number of shorts, and perhaps even a 'B' movie on the programme as well.

Friday, 2 September

Fine, sunny, warm day. Bought a new hat today. A nice night, so Agnes and I went to Linn Park and did a putt.

Sunday, 4 September
We all at church. Thought I would be none the worse of some medicine, so before dinner I took a fair supply. I did not venture out again.

Monday, 5 September
Agnes got her eyes tested for new glasses.

Thursday, 8 September
I went to the optologist at tea time and got Agnes' specs. She will read now in elegance and ease.

Saturday, 10 September
Mrs Gordon, Nan and Ronnie here tonight.

Tuesday, 13 September
Tommy at Cathedral tonight.

Monday, 19 September
We had a surprise visit about 8.45 p.m. from Isa and Jack Ferguson with Jean and Ella Carlyle.

Tuesday, 20 September
Tommy at the Cathedral, listening to high brow music.

Friday, 23 September
Agnes made apple jelly.

Saturday, 24 September
Agnes and I went to the Majestic at night.

Sunday, 25 September
Tommy went to a kirk in Kelvingrove at night.

Wednesday, 28 September
Agnes went to the eye place and got a prescription. Not any the wiser as to what's the matter with her eye. Mrs Carmichael went with her.

Thursday, 29 September
Agnes' eye making her very sad.

Friday, 30 September
Got some correspondence from New Zealand and Germany. The stamp season is now approaching.

Sunday, 2 October
All of us at church. Nan Gordon here in afternoon, then Josephine, Lily and the baby came in.

Wednesday, 5 October
Agnes at the ophthalmic place today. She has to continue the treatment and go back in a fortnight.

Saturday, 8 October
Tommy went to an organ recital in the university this afternoon. Agnes and I went to the Majestic at night.

Monday, 10 October
Mrs Gordon here in forenoon. She wanted me to get a table cloth, which I duly did. Ella called at night for same. I saw Ella and table cloth duly away at a decent hour.

Tuesday, 11 October
Got my new overcoat today.

Saturday, 15 October
Agnes and I at the Govanhill Picture House tonight. Agnes decides not to go back to the Ophthalmic Institute. They seem too busy to give her eye proper attention.

Sunday, 16 October
Agnes and I went to church, Communion. In the afternoon, I visited James Brown, one of the staff, who is ill.

Wednesday, 19 October
Went to see James at night.

Sunday, 23 October
Agnes not up this morning. She had to content herself with what scraps of food I could make for breakfast. She then got up. I went out to see James in the afternoon.

Thursday, 27 October
We were awakened this morning by an 82 mph gale. Great alarm. Tommy gave a Shakespeare lecture at school today, with lantern views.

Friday, 28 October
Agnes made two apple cakes and I made a turnip lantern.

Saturday, 29 October
All the Mossmans here at 5 p.m. We had a miniature Hallowe'en party, with dooking etc. All complete.

Sunday, 30 October
All at church. Took a run over to see James in afternoon. Agnes very tired, her eyes sore, and very dejected-like all day.

Monday, 31 October
Agnes at a church social at night with Mrs Carmichael. I got a speck in my eye, which caused me great pain. We called in Mr Carmichael at tea time, and he took it out with Agnes' assistance. My eye pretty sore all night.

Tuesday, 1 November
Agnes recorded her vote this forenoon, and I did the same at night, and may the best man win. Municipal elections are trump. In the afternoon, Agnes hied herself to Partick and saw Lily and the baby.

Wednesday, 2 November
Tommy went into Central Station after school to see the Royal Scot engine.[14]

Saturday, 5 November
Tommy went to an organ recital in university this afternoon. Agnes and I went to the pictures at night.

Monday, 7 November
Out in the Dennistoun district on business this forenoon. Having a little time to myself, I dropped in and saw Hetty Mossman.

Thursday, 10 November
This is Agnes' birthday. She is now x–x years old.[15]

---

14 The Royal Scot steam engine was built in 1927 by the North British Locomotive Company in the north of Glasgow for the London Midland and Scottish Railway. It is currently in the collection of Bressingham Steam Museum in Norfolk.

15 Agnes was 48.

Friday, 11 November
This is the day of two minutes' silence. I observed it at Jamaica Street corner.

Saturday, 12 November
Tommy at Dennistoun in the afternoon with some organ experts interviewing some kirk organ there. He came home about 5 p.m. to intimate that he was going out for tea with a lad called David MacPherson, who was with him. He evidently visited another lad after tea, and was home at 11.30. We lectured him on his late hours. I discover I have a sore tongue.

Sunday, 13 November

Bathed my tongue.

Thursday, 17 November
Met Miss Henderson (of Rothesay) in town today. Took her home with me for dinner.

Sunday, 20 November
Very cold day. Tommy off his bite in the morning, and not well, so we put him to bed in the kitchen. Agnes and I slept in the room.

Monday, 21 November
Tommy in bed all day.

Wednesday, 23 November
Tommy got up in the afternoon. Agnes and I slept in the kitchen tonight.

Saturday, 26 November
Agnes and I went to the Majestic.

Monday, 28 November
Tommy off to school again. Agnes at a church social tonight with Mrs Carmichael.

Tuesday, 29 November
Went into the coal bunker and did some necessary repairs. Agnes thinks she could have done it better.

Wednesday, 30 November
Agnes was going to Knightswood this afternoon. I got a telephone message this morning that things were a bit warm and exciting there, so Agnes was not to go. In the afternoon, I got another

message. A little girl has arrived. Isa is the ma. Put a new cord on the TMC 'phones.

Friday, 2 December

Being scared to death, I went round and saw my doctor at night re tongue. He says nothing wrong, quite normal. So that's that. Came home walking on air. He gave me a line to say that my teeth could do with a little overhaul by the dentist. Some day, I will give this to my society, and thus get the machinery started. [16]

Saturday, 3 December

Don't feel very well at bed time. My chest and throat feel bad, so I gargled.

Sunday, 4 December

Not well at all this morning, so I stayed in bed. I got up about 5 p.m., but don't feel right.

Monday, 5 December

In bed till 7 p.m. Hetty and Etta here for a little in the afternoon.

Tuesday, 6 December

In bed today till 12.30. Got up for dinner.

Wednesday, 7 December

Went to my work today. Feel better today, but not so well at night.

Friday, 9 December

Tommy finishes his week's school examination. Agnes broke a jug tonight.

Saturday, 10 December

Agnes bought a new jug.

Sunday, 11 December

Very cold day. We all went to church and got frozen.

---

16 Thomas was a member of the Scottish Clerks' Association, which provided health insurance.

Monday, 12 December
Agnes met me in town this afternoon, then we went and picked a new carpet square for the room.

Tuesday, 13 December
We all polished furniture at night.

Thursday, 15 December
We cleaned pictures and washed the dinner set.

Sunday, 18 December
Agnes at Ibrox tonight. I spent the evening sticking in stamps.

Monday, 19 December

Arctic conditions prevail. Bought 2¼ yards of 27 inch parquet on way home from my work. After tea, got an SOS from the Carmichaels re their new blind. I went in but it seemed a dud, so we gave it up instead of putting it up.

Tuesday, 20 December
We lifted the old carpet. It has had its day. There are many feet that walked over it that will never walk again.

Wednesday, 21 December
The carpet arrived today. Put up new blinds and generally got room ready for the new carpet.

Thursday, 22 December

We got the carpet laid tonight. Mr Carmichael came in for a little to admire it.

Saturday, 24 December
Cold wicked today. We all got Xmas presents from Belfast today. We went to the Mossmans' at night. A big fire in the Gallowgate.[17] So Gordon, Tommy, Billy and I went out and saw it.

---

17   The blaze destroyed a six-storey warehouse on the east side of Graham Square, off
      Gallowgate, next to the Corporation Cattle Market.

Sunday, 25 December
Very cold. Some snow. Four firemen killed in the big fire.

Monday, 26 December
Agnes in wash house all day. Tommy and I attended to the
household duties. Took down one of the room blinds and put it up
again in a more horizontal manner.

Wednesday, 28 December
Agnes and Tommy at Ibrox tonight with presents for Ella, who is
getting married on Saturday.

Thursday, 29 December
Put up a new blind in kitchen, and sent the kitchen mantle (gas)
to sleep in the process. So Tommy had to run down for a new one.
Agnes made ginger wine.

Friday, 30 December
We got a box from Josephine etc, with various gifts therein.

Saturday, 31 December
Ground white with snow. Snowed heavily till about dinner time.
We are now getting ready for Ne'erday. Ring out the old —

1928

The Livingstone family enjoyed another relatively peaceful and prosperous year. Tommy won another bursary and continued to shine at school, as well as developing his interest in the fine arts. Thomas got false teeth, and Agnes had continuing bouts of serious illness, leading to episodes of short temper, which Thomas found very distressing. In the wider world, the illness of King George V was one of the few news items that penetrated the walls of the Livingstone household.

Sunday, 1 January
– Ring in the new. A minute or so after midnight we were invaded by Mr Carmichael and his brother, Mrs Carmichael, Peggy and Alex, also Jean MacKenzie and her boy. We had supper then music. All away 3.15 a.m. At night, we all at Ibrox. Ella and her man there.

Monday, 2 January
After tea we all went to the Govanhill Picture House.

Tuesday, 3 January
Still on holiday. Shifted lobby clock to a more suitable position.

Thursday, 5 January
Tommy had two lads up tonight from the school. We had a musical evening.

Saturday, 7 January
Mrs Gordon, Nan and Ronnie here at night.

Monday, 9 January
Tommy back at school today. Agnes in wash house at night.

Saturday, 14 January
Agnes and I at Govanhill Picture House tonight.

Tuesday, 17 January
Agnes at Lily's in afternoon.

Saturday, 21 January
Tommy at concert in forenoon. Agnes and I at Govanhill Picture House tonight.

Sunday, 22 January
Tommy and I at church this forenoon. After dinner we all went out for a little stroll and got bus back from Mount Florida. Agnes collapsed at tea time.

Monday, 23 January
Agnes went and saw the doctor in the forenoon. He says it is nasal catarrh. Agnes and Mrs Carmichael at a concert tonight.

Tuesday, 24 January
Wet, cold day. Snow and sleet and all these nasty things.

Wednesday, 25 January
Agnes all out this morning. Throat very bad. Got in the doctor. Agnes kept in bed all day. The flu and tonsillitis. Cold wet day.

Thursday, 26 January
Agnes still in bed. Mrs Carmichael made the dinner. As I am no use at bed making, Agnes got up and made it herself.

Friday, 27 January
Doctor up today. Agnes to be allowed up, so she up for a good part of the day. She did a big ironing at night, and enlightened me as to my character in general and particular. Sad times.

Saturday, 28 January
Agnes up all day, and not too bad. Tommy washed the floor.

Sunday, 29 January
Agnes up all day, but not well at all. I went out for half an hour. Got a touch of neuralgia.

Monday, 30 January
Agnes extra bad this morning. Sent for doctor. Got a new bottle for her stomach, but she does not need to stay in bed. A little better at night. I've got neuralgia bad.

Tuesday, 31 January
Agnes not so bad today and up all day. Nan Gordon here at night.

Wednesday, 1 February
Agnes took her breakfast in bed. My tooth sore.

Thursday, 2 February
Doctor up today. I cleaned all the windows at night.

Saturday, 4 February
Mrs Carmichael not well, so Agnes spent the evening in her house.

Sunday, 5 February
Agnes and I went out for a little. Josephine and Jack here at night, as Jack wanted to take Tommy to one of his religious meetings. Tommy went, but don't think he'll be back.

Monday, 6 February
Agnes paid the doctor a visit. After tea I went round for her
bottle of 'dope'. My nose very sore.

Wednesday, 8 February
Agnes' back sore. I rubbed it.

Thursday, 9 February
Agnes' back not so sore, but I gave it another rub.

Saturday, 11 February
Agnes and Tommy in town in afternoon. Tommy needs new shoes.
Agnes does not feel well at all.

Sunday, 12 February
Tommy sampled Daisy Street Church at night.

Thursday, 16 February
After tea, Tommy and I went to La Scala, to see *Metropolis*, the
great German film.[1]

Sunday, 19 February
Tommy at new church this morning. Put on my new shoes and took
Tommy out a walk.

Tuesday, 21 February
Agnes made marmalade.

Thursday, 23 February
Went to the dentist straight from work, and got two teeth out. More
to follow.

Saturday, 25 February
Took old TMC 'phones to the Clydesdale to be repaired. Took
home a pair of Claritone, which did not please me.[2] After tea, I
took them back and said I would prefer my money back. Nothing
doing. I gave them the extra cash and got a pair of Brandes. Went
home cussing. The new 'phones, fortunately, are 100 per cent.

---

1   The La Scala picture house, at 147–163 Sauchiehall Street, opened in 1912 in a
     former warehouse, converted by the architects Neil Duff and James McKissack. It
     closed in 1984, and the basement became the Ultratheque disco with a clothes shop
     above. The whole building is now a Waterstone's bookshop. *Metropolis*, a German
     expressionist film directed by Fritz Lang, was released in 1927. It was the most
     expensive silent film ever made.

2   ATM Claritone headphones were manufactured in the UK under licence from the
     American Marconi Company.

Sunday, 26 February
Tommy at Candlish Church.[3]

Monday, 27 February
Got our lum swept today, and at night we washed the dinner set.
The King George V Bridge opened to the public today.[4]

Friday, 2 March
On my way home from work, I went over the new George V
Bridge, called in at the Clydesdale and got the old, renovated
'phones. This cost me 2/6.

Monday, 5 March
Put rubber soles on Agnes' shoes. My toe very sore.

Wednesday, 7 March
Went down to the dentist and got six teeth out. Spent remainder of
the night bleeding to death.

Thursday, 8 March
My face swollen somewhat. Am on a soft diet now. Lily and baby,
Isa and baby, all here in afternoon. A female up from the kirk.
Agnes told her we had left aforesaid kirk.

Friday, 9 March
Wrote Mr Braid for our 'lines' re the kirk.[5]

Sunday, 11 March
Heavy snow fell all day. Nan Gordon here at night. Ate a little
bread.

Monday, 12 March
The great snow blizzard continues.

Tuesday, 13 March
Some snow again, but thawed somewhat.

---

3   The Candlish Memorial Church stood at 283 Calder Street in Govanhill. It was
    designed by the Glasgow architect John Honeyman and opened in 1874. Tommy is
    evidently shopping for a suitable church.

4   The bridge links Oswald Street, on the north bank of the Clyde, with Commerce
    Street.

5   Thomas was asking the minister of their former church to send the documents
    confirming their membership of the United Free Church of Scotland to the church
    they were now worshipping in.

Monday, 19 March
Agnes at Co-op Exhibition with Mrs Carmichael. Tommy's big
examination starts today. The 'Highers', he calls it.[6]

Wednesday, 21 March
Thought I had some odd teeth to come out, so went down to my
dentist at night. He said they would come out themselves in a
week or so.

Thursday, 22 March
Fine day, but very cold. Stuck rubber soles on my boots.

Saturday, 24 March
Put a new burner on the kitchen gas pipe.

Wednesday, 28 March
This is the last day of Tommy's examination. Hope he has passed.

Saturday, 31 March
Tommy sat for a bursary in Bellahouston Academy. Tommy in town
with some pals. Agnes and I at the Majestic.

Monday, 2 April
At night I went down to my dentist and got my bottom jaw
measured for teeth and then got an overlooked stump extracted.
Very wet night.

Friday, 6 April
*Got a letter from my friend Señor Hector
Gatica Díaz, Chile. At a ridiculous and late
hour, minister came up to see why we left the
church.[7] We wiped the floor with him, and he
departed a sadder and wiser man.*

Monday, 9 April
Spring holiday. Some rain, dull and mild. In the afternoon we all
went to Paisley. After tea, Agnes and I at Majestic.

Tuesday, 10 April
Agnes at Paisley this afternoon to see Ella. I went to my dentist at
night and got another impression of my lower jaw.

---

6   Only more academic pupils were allowed to sit the Higher exams, for the Higher
     Education School Leaving Certificate.

7   Presumably Mr Braid.

Friday, 13 April

Mrs Carmichael shut herself out, and Tommy had to go to town
and get key from Peggy. The Atlantic crossed by aeroplane east to
west for the first time by a German, with an Irishman.[8]

Tuesday, 17 April

Mrs Carmichael and Agnes at a moral picture in the St Andrew's
Halls this afternoon.

Sunday, 22 April

Fine sunny day. Tommy out in forenoon, I in the afternoon.

Tuesday, 24 April

Tommy at dentist in forenoon getting a tooth out. I went at night
and saw same gentleman to get some teeth in, but he was not
ready. Mild and breezy.

Thursday, 26 April

Agnes having a big day in the wash house. I went down at night
to my dentist, and got my lower jaw filled with teeth. Got home
10.15 p.m. feeling very uncomfortable. I may get used to them,
and I may not.

Friday, 27 April

Took out my teeth at tea time and felt more comfortable thereby. I
may get used to them.

Saturday, 28 April

Fine day. Agnes and I at Clarkston and Eastwood Toll after tea. I
left off my teeth today. It is evident I am not getting used to them.

Monday, 30 April

Went down to dentist at night and got him to ease the teeth a
little. Got home 10.30 hoping for the best.

Tuesday, 1 May

Enter the merry month of May. Nice warm day. Agnes and Tommy
in town this afternoon re a suit for the lad.

Wednesday, 2 May

Eating better now with my new demi-set of teeth.

---

8   Captain Hermann Köhl and his navigator, Major James Fitzmaurice, flew from
     Baldonnel Aerodrome to Greenly Island in Canada between 12 and 14 April in a
     Bremen aircraft.

Sunday, 6 May
To get the real country air, we took car to Airdrie in the afternoon.
It was a long haul, and the air was of doubtful quality. After tea I
took a walk Queen's Park way, and saw some real country.

Monday, 7 May
Very warm day. Took a walk round the Linn Park at night. The
walking season has started.

Friday, 11 May
Dull and cold. Tommy got word that he had won a £20 bursary.
Good lad.

Sunday, 13 May
Tommy at a church in Langside Road this morning. After dinner,
Tommy and I went for a large walk to Gorbals Waterworks and
back by Barrhead.

Tuesday, 15 May
Got a letter from our relations of Knightswood. They are having a
holiday at Ardbeg, Rothesay.

Thursday, 17 May
Tommy's new suit arrived.

Saturday, 19 May
I went to library at night for a space.

Monday, 21 May
This is a holiday, so out we go. We took car to Hillfoot and walked
through Bearsden and on to Anniesland. Got bus home from there.

Tuesday, 22 May
Met Agnes in town today, where we arranged with French to make
me a suit. I assisted Agnes with the dinner set, giving it a bath.
Looks as if spring cleaning was about to start.

Wednesday, 23 May
Agnes got a sore back, so at night I applied a little gentle friction.

Thursday, 24 May
When I got home, rubbed the windows to clean them, and rubbed
Agnes to relieve her pain.

Friday, 25 May
Had a fit on, so my suit should fit me, but will it? Gave Agnes a little gentle massage at night. It seems to be helping her.

Sunday, 27 May
Rained heavily most of the time. During a dry blink, I went to the Queen's Park and watched the vegetation sprouting.

Wednesday, 30 May
Sunny and warm. Feeling the call of the country, Tommy and I walked out via Newton Mearns to Patterton.

Sunday, 3 June
Agnes and Tommy at a church this morning. Blazing hot sunshine all day. Agnes and I went to Pollok Estate.

Monday, 4 June
This is my birthday.[9] Agnes gave me a new shaving stick.

Wednesday, 6 June
Agnes went to Ibrox at night. I was out for a little, and Tommy tinkered with his velocipede.

Thursday, 7 June
I went down to my tooth expert and got my top jaw measured for teeth. Have to go back in about a fortnight.

Saturday, 9 June
Went to the library after dinner, and took Agnes after tea to the Majestic.

Sunday, 10 June
Tried on my new suit. The jacket could be better. To freshen me up, I took two large spoonfuls of castor oil. It certainly made me lively.

Monday, 11 June
Agnes met me in town at 5 p.m. and we left the mis-fit jacket. Tommy broke his watch.

Wednesday, 13 June
Rained in solid chunks all day long. Left Tommy's watch to be mended with a man up New City Road way.

---

9   Thomas was 46.

Friday, 15 June

After tea, I took a walk to Paisley, via Kennishead and Nitshill.
It was a longer walk than I anticipated. After 10 p.m., when I
got home, Agnes cleaning windows and working very hard, which
caused me remorse of conscience.

Saturday, 16 June

Tommy at a school picnic out by Cadzow Estate.[10]

Sunday, 17 June

Very cold day. Did not go out. Agnes thinks life very sad.

Monday, 18 June

Agnes took a run up to the Mossmans'. After tea we both had a
walk round the new houses in King's Park.

Wednesday, 20 June

Went at night to the tooth expert and got a final overhaul. I have
to get my teeth in three weeks.

Thursday, 21 June

Rained all the day. Tommy at the swimming pond today. Swimming
is a very useful art this wet weather.

Friday, 22 June

Got my new suit today.

Saturday, 23 June

All the Mossmans here 5.30. After tea, we all round King's Park
admiring the new houses.

Sunday, 24 June

Put on my new suit today, and after tea took Agnes and Tommy out
for an airing.

Wednesday, 27 June

Tommy lifted £10 today, proceeds of a bursary. At night, Tommy and
I did the Kennishead – Nitshill – Paisley walk. Quite a good walk.

Thursday, 28 June

Tommy got presented with the first prize at school today, a volume
re the Duke of Wellington. Good lad. Big railway smash at
Darlington.[11] 24 lives lost.

---

10   Cadzow Estate was in Hamilton.

11   Two steam trains collided head-on at Darlington Bank Top railway station, in County
     Durham, killing twenty-five people.

Friday, 29 June
Tommy got his summer holidays today.

Tuesday, 3 July
Josephine, Lily and the baby here.

Tuesday, 10 July

Went down to Ibrox at night and got my new teeth. Paid the good man 5/- for extra trimmings on them.

Thursday, 12 July
Went down to Ibrox at night and got my new teeth improved a bit. Was in the Jamiesons' house next door and tried my hands (and feet) at their organ.

Friday, 13 July
Fair Friday. Got away at 1.45. Dull, bleak, miserable day, and rained at night.

Monday, 16 July
Still on holiday. Fine day. After dinner we all visited our relations who have a castle in Knightswood. We got a nice drive in the bus back.

Saturday, 21 July
Brilliant, warm, sunny day. After tea, we all out Kilmarnock Road and back by the Mearns Road.

Saturday, 28 July
Tommy into town at night with Agnes. He got a new cap, 'hooker doon'.[12]

Sunday, 29 July
Tommy started shaving today. He has the razor I bought 20 years ago.

Monday, 30 July
Agnes at the factors in the morning with the rent, also a few words re the damn hooligans. I confirmed said complaint in writing. Went down to see my dentist before tea. He is still on holiday, so I did not see him. Fine sunny night, but we are all too busy to go out.

---

12   A 'hooker doon' is a cloth cap with a peak.

Tuesday, 31 July

Stopped work tonight for the holidays. After tea I went down to Leiper and got my teeth eased a little. Spent a busy night packing up.

Wednesday, 1 August

At last, the first day of our holidays. Rose up early and washed the kitchen floor. Our taxi called at 10.15 a.m. We departed from Broomielaw at 11 a.m. per the good ship Eagle III. We had tea on boat. After a nice sail, we arrived Port Bannatyne 3.15 p.m. Nice warm, sunny day. After an early tea, we all walked into Rothesay, had a seat on the esplanade and watched the aboriginals from Paisley. We took the car home.

Thursday, 2 August

Great heat and sunshine in forenoon. Tommy and I walked to Ettrick Bay and then to St Ninian's by the shore. We saw a seal there. We walked on to Rothesay via Barone Road. We were devoured by flies. After tea, we all putted.

Friday, 3 August

Another hot, sunny day. In the morning, Tommy and I putted, then out for an hour in a boat. Agnes went to Rothesay herself in forenoon. After dinner we all had a walk round Ardmaleish Point. We saw an owl. My toe is blistered.

Saturday, 4 August

Warm, sunny day. In the forenoon, Tommy and I took car to Ettrick Bay. Paddled my miserable toe. After tea, Agnes went up for Miss Henderson. We all then walked out Bogany way, and back by the Skippers Wood. Had a seat there till 10.30 then watched all the bonfires being lit.

Sunday, 5 August

Brilliant day, best so far. Tommy and Agnes went to church in morning. After dinner we took car to Ettrick Bay, hired chairs, and basked in the sunshine for a brace of hours.

Tuesday, 7 August
Poured all forenoon. After dinner, Tommy and I took bus to
Rothesay, went up the Minister's Brae, on to Loch Ascog and back
to Rothesay by the shore. We had Miss Henderson up for tea.

Wednesday, 8 August
Some showers in forenoon, but turned out a nice day. After dinner
we all to Rothesay by car, up High Street, looked through the
cemetery and on to Loch Fad. Bus home. After tea, we went out for
a little and watched a football match.

Thursday, 9 August
Rained all afternoon. After tea we went to the pictures 'De Luxe'.[13]
Nice night when we got out, so walked home. We got devoured by
midges all the way. Tommy's birthday.

Friday, 10 August
Tommy and I started out in the morning to do the big walk round
the island. Weather conditions turned out very bad, so we went no
further than Ardmaleish. After tea, not so wet, so we all at Mill
Wheel and up the hill at Hillton Farm.

Saturday, 11 August
Poured all day long. At night we went to the Palace. Not so bad.
Agnes fed up.

Sunday, 12 August
At last. Hot, sunny day. In the morning I walked to Greenwood
Crossing, then jumped on a bus making for Ettrick Bay. Met
Tommy there. After tea, all at Rothesay and a walk through the
golf course and down the Serpentine Road.

Monday, 13 August
Fine forenoon. Tommy and I putted twice. After dinner, dull and
windy. We all out in a small boat, but it was too rough for my
liking. After tea, took car to Rothesay.

Tuesday, 14 August
Dull at times, bright at times, wet at times and breezy all the
time. In the morning, Tommy and I walked to Ettrick Bay. In the
afternoon, Agnes went to Rothesay and visited Miss Henderson.
After tea, we got some packing done. Arranged with the necessary
party to have our hamper lifted tomorrow.

---

13 The De Luxe Picture House stood in Store Lane, Rothesay. It was designed by
    the architect Albert Victor Gardner – who also designed the Majestic cinema in
    Govanhill – and opened in 1912. It was demolished in the 1960s.

Wednesday, 15 August
Fine day, but very stormy. Agnes wanted some of the famous
Rothesay kippers, so Tommy and I went into that village for a
supply. After dinner, Tommy and I did a final putt. Our hamper
lifted about 10 a.m. Our steamer left 4.15, arrived Glasgow 8.10.
Our sail home was very comfortable, and not too many aboard. We
got a taxi home. We all got our tea in the Carmichaels.

Thursday, 16 August
Back to work again.

Sunday, 19 August
At 11 a.m. Mrs Gordon dropped in to see us, which was
a very inconvenient hour. Agnes had not yet got up.
Having a rest after her hard working holiday.

Monday, 20 August
Tommy started school again.

Tuesday, 21 August
Dull, warm and thundery. When I got home for tea, Agnes
was off to Ibrox. Tommy went to an organ recital at Cathedral.
While I was mourning their absence, Josephine arrived about
7.35 to cheer me up. I made her a bit of supper.

Friday, 24 August
Agnes made plum jam at night. Got a funeral invitation for old
Mrs Cairns. She was the mother-in-law of the sister of my late
brother-in-law. Agnes thought I should not go, so I did
not.

Monday, 27 August
At night, Tommy and I went to Rouken Glen. We tried
our hand at putting on the very third-rate greens there.

Tuesday, 28 August
*Left my mis-fit trousers with the mis-fitters
to be rectified.*

Tuesday, 4 September
Old and young Mrs Cowie up in afternoon. Tommy at
Cathedral organ recital.

Wednesday, 5 September

Agnes met me in town at 6.20, then we went to the boot shop and I got a pair of square toed shoes.

Sunday, 9 September

Tommy up early and went to some church some miles away. In his absence, Agnes and I cut up rhubarb to replenish our stock of jam.

Thursday, 13 September

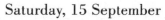

A man up called today and sold Agnes a gas iron. One shilling a week for 20 weeks. Agnes did an ironing at night with it.

Saturday, 15 September

I went to Linn Park and had a seat in the new portion. I was greatly appreciated by the midges.

Tuesday, 18 September

Agnes went to Knightswood after dinner. Tommy at Cathedral organ recital. My toe misbehaving, so soaked it in Reudels.

Thursday, 20 September

Nice sunny day. Getting cooler. Agnes not in at tea time as she was out seeing a wedding. Cleaned kitchen windows.

Saturday, 22 September

Agnes in town in afternoon, and came back with a new cardigan for herself and a new cushion for the chair. I went to a library after tea.

Tuesday, 25 September

Sunny, but cold, and I've got it. My nose running like a blinking hose pipe all day. Went to bed after tea.

Friday, 28 September

Bitter cold day. Don't feel so well at night. Took two Yeast-Vite tablets.[14]

---

14   Yeast-Vite, which promised 'a lightning pick-me-up', was introduced in the 1920s. It
     is based on yeast, and contains caffeine and B vitamins.

1928

Monday 24 September

Autumn holiday Some rain
in forenoon. after dinner
we had a walk Shawlands
and Cathcart. after tea
Agnes + I at majestic.
Would not be surprised
if I had the Cold.

Tuesday 25 Sept

Sunny but Cold. and I've
got it
my nose
running
like   a
              blinking
              hose pipe
              all day
              went to
bed after tea.
Tommy at Cathedral
to-night and was
home at 10 30 pm

Saturday, 29 September

We all at Dennistoun for tea. New piano in the Mossman household. After tea, we all round the new houses at Riddrie.[15] Gordon gave me a big hone for sharpening knives.

Sunday, 30 September

Agnes went to Ibrox after tea. Ronnie is not well.

Wednesday, 3 October

Nan Gordon rung up to let us know that Ronnie was in hospital with double pneumonia. Agnes went down to Ibrox at night.

Sunday, 7 October

Agnes in a jumpy sort of mood.

Wednesday, 10 October

Ronnie is improving.

Thursday, 11 October

Got a phone message from Isa that my sister Mary and her man would visit us at night. Josephine, of course, would come also. They duly arrived at 7 p.m. I saw Tom Carlyle away by 9.35 train from Central, and about 10.45 saw the two ladies off per bus to Knightswood.

Saturday, 13 October

Agnes and I went to Majestic at night. Train smash in Queen Street tunnel last night. Two dead and 50 injured.[16]

Thursday, 18 October

Poured solid all day. The wireless ceased to function at 9.30 p.m. Something wrong with 5SC evidently. On again after 10 p.m.

Friday, 19 October

Nan Gordon here at night. We taught her to play the game of Ludo.

---

15 Riddrie is a large housing estate built by Glasgow Corporation, to the east of Dennistoun.

16 A signalling error caused two trains to collide on one track in the tunnel leading north from Queen Street Station. The crash killed both drivers and one passenger, and caused at least fifty injuries.

Saturday, 20 October

Agnes went to town, met Nan Gordon there, and introduced her to our family optologist. Nan is after a pair of specs.

Tuesday, 23 October

Cold, wet day. Bought a hard black hat. Agnes got sore throat.

Sunday, 28 October

After dinner I went to Queen's Park for some fresh air.
Agnes in a sad way. Her cold seems worse than ever. I went out at night for a Sunday paper to cheer her up.

Monday, 29 October

Got my hair cut. Rained from early morning till bed time. Agnes not up for her breakfast, but seems a little improved at night. This is Agnes' day in wash house. On inquiry, she did not go.

Saturday, 3 November

Agnes and I at Majestic.

Sunday, 4 November

Agnes fed up and went to Ibrox for some more cheerful company. I got a sore eye.

Monday, 5 November

Eye still bad. Agnes at some affair with Mrs Carmichael tonight. Tommy and some of his class at some opera at the Theatre Royal.[17]

Tuesday, 6 November

Eye not so bad now. We recorded our vote today in the municipal election.

Sunday, 11 November

This is Armistice Day. Listened in at 11 a.m. for the broadcast, but nothing came through. Why, I know not. Agnes made a dumpling today for her birthday of yesterday. Dull, wet day. Ten years ago today, Jenny Roxburgh died.

---

17   The Theatre Royal stands at the north end of Hope Street.

Thursday, 15 November
We lifted room carpet and folded it up. Carried room chairs down to back green, where we gave them a cleaning.

Saturday, 17 November
Agnes and I went into town in the afternoon and got wallpaper of a pale purple shade for the room. We were out of pocket 10/6 for this.

Wednesday, 21 November
Working late. Benny up at night and gave the room its first spasm.

Thursday, 22 November
Wet, stormy day. My old gamp gave up the ghost, so I left it to be repaired and bought a new one.[18] Benny finished the room tonight.

Saturday, 24 November
We re-laid the carpet in the afternoon. The King is not well.[19] God save the King.

Sunday, 25 November
Got into trouble with Agnes re some tobacco ash, so out to Queen's Park to soothe me. Spent forenoon rubbing white spots off, which Benny had splashed about.

Tuesday, 27 November
Tommy started to learn Greek today.

Friday, 30 November
King seriously ill.

Sunday, 2 December
Bad news about King.

Monday, 3 December
King easier but heart weak.

Tuesday, 4 December
The temperature of the King rising. Looks serious for George.

---

18 'Gamp' is an antiquated word for umbrella.

19 King George V was suffering from pneumonia and other respiratory illnesses.

Thursday, 6 December
King improves.

Friday, 7 December
We took the couch down to the back green and Agnes beat it. My back is out in an eruption, caused by a jaggy semmit.[20] The King also is not comfortable.

Monday, 10 December
Agnes got top boots.

Tuesday, 11 December
Very cold and dull. Put on my heavier coat. Anxiety must continue yet re the King.

Wednesday, 12 December
Agnes in wash house at night. Operation on King.

Monday, 17 December
Agnes in wash house in afternoon and a concert at night. Bolivia and Paraguay at war.[21] Where are the police? King not so well again.

Tuesday, 18 December
King a little better.

Thursday, 20 December
I don't feel extra well at night. I have a pain.

Friday, 21 December
Feel all right again. The King also improves.

Saturday, 22 December
Agnes and Tommy in town re Christmas presents.

Sunday, 23 December
Agnes in bed till about noon. A vile day of misery and horror. Everything wrong. Awful.

Monday, 24 December
Got our Xmas from Duncan, but nothing for Tommy, so Agnes and I put 5/- in his stocking at night between us.

20   A 'jaggy semmit' is an irritating vest.
21   Oil had been discovered in Gran Chaco, an area of disputed ownership between the two countries, and Bolivia began to act aggressively towards its smaller neighbour.

Tuesday, 25 December
I had a holiday today. At 4 p.m., the MacPherson and Geddes up
for Tommy and took him away. At 6 p.m. Peggy Carmichael in to
let us know that Alex was in the Royal Infirmary. He fell off a
building and broke his arm, and some minor injuries. Agnes spent
a bit of the evening in the Carmichaels'. Tommy home at midnight.

Thursday, 27 December
The King not so well again.

Saturday, 29 December
Agnes working hard. Her temper getting frayed and I get it in the
neck. Ah, us.

Monday, 31 December
I am now on holiday. I took a walk to the People's Palace. We
spent night getting ready to first foot the Carmichaels.

1929

For Thomas and his family, this was Tommy's year. Their son lifted
all the glittering prizes – school Dux, first place in the Glasgow
University entrance exams and two bursaries – and began his
academic career. He also spends a worrying period in the Victoria
Infirmary. The rest of the family fade slightly from the picture, as
nieces and nephews marry and have families of their own. Again,
few events from the wider world make an impact on the diary, and
the impression is of a very close-knit family caught up in its own
dramas. The outside world comes crashing in on the last day of the
year, with horrifying news from Paisley.

Tuesday, 1 January
We all in Carmichaels' and heard their new gramophone. We came into our own house again 2.45 a.m., and so to bed. Rose up to a New Year Day of intense fog and frost. I took a walk to Queen's Park and got some sunshine at the flagpole. Tommy's pals up for him in the afternoon. Agnes and I went to the Majestic at night.

Wednesday, 2 January
Back to work again, but left at 11.45 a.m. Fog and frost worse than ever. The temperature is 25 degrees. The Geddes and MacPherson up for tea. We had various music.

Thursday, 3 January
Agnes over seeing Mrs Cowie in the afternoon.

Friday, 4 January
Fog and frost unholy. We had a little party tonight. Mr and Mrs Carmichael. Mr Carmichael's brother, Peggy and Mrs MacKenzie. The gramophone was brought in and it ground out tunes for a solid couple of hours. It left me in a dazed condition. All away 12.30 a.m.

Saturday, 5 January
Fog and frost almost gone, but very cold. At night we played our usual peaceful game of Ludo. Agnes inclined to be sad at night.

Wednesday, 9 January
Vile day. Sleet, snow and rain. Flu epidemic in Glasgow.

Sunday, 13 January
Frost and fog. Tommy and I in Linn Park before dinner.

Monday, 14 January
Better day, but very cold. Agnes at the Royal Infirmary to see Alex Carmichael. Flu very bad in town.

Thursday, 17 January

Dull and extra cold. Tommy gave a lecture today at school on R.L.S.[1] I feel as if I might be taking the cold. Agnes says she has taken the cold. Ladies first.

Monday, 21 January

Fog and frost. We had Mr and Mrs Gordon's company at dinner time. Mr Gordon is off his work with a game leg or something.[2] He is attending the Victoria Infirmary, hence this visit.[3] Bought my third pair of Brandes 'phones today. The entire family is now supplied.

Wednesday, 23 January

Agnes and Mrs Carmichael at the Royal Infirmary.

Saturday, 26 January

Flu still sweeping the country.

Monday, 28 January

Vile foggy and frosty day. Heavy snow at night. Alex Carmichael comes out of hospital after a stay of over a month.

Tuesday, 29 January

My delicate toe giving me pain.

Wednesday, 30 January

Wet but mild. Flu dying out Agnes at the Coliseum in afternoon. seeing and hearing The Singing Fool.[4] The new 'talkies'.

---

1 Robert Louis Stevenson, Scottish poet and author.

2 'Game', pronounced 'gammy', means twisted or lame.

3 The Victoria Infirmary is in the south of Glasgow, near the Livingstones'.

4 The Coliseum, at 79–97 Eglinton Street, opened in 1905 as a music hall, became a cinema around 1925 and was the first Glasgow cinema to show a talking picture, in January 1929. It was demolished in 2009 after a fire. *The Singing Fool* was a 1928 musical drama starring Al Jolson, directed by Lloyd Bacon and one of the first Hollywood films to feature music and talking.

Friday, 1 February
Got a hair cut and singe today.

Monday, 4 February
Agnes and Tommy have got the cold, so they bathed their respective feet at bed time, and think they will get better.[5]

Tuesday, 5 February
Agnes and Tommy a little better.

Friday, 8 February
Agnes baked two cakes and I oiled Tommy's ear. He says the wax is hard.

Sunday, 10 February
All Ibrox here at night. Mr and Mrs Gordon, Nan and Ronnie, and Jim, Ella and baby. All away about 10.30. Agnes collapsed and nearly died then. Sick headache, the bile etc. Terrible.

Monday, 11 February
Snow blizzard and extra cold. Agnes not so bad now. She went to the guild at night with Mrs Carmichael. I syringed Tommy's ear to restore his hearing.

Wednesday, 13 February
Sunny day. Cold terrific. In the morning the temperature in the city was 20½ degrees.

Thursday, 14 February
Sunny day, but colder than ever. Temperature now at 19 degrees. Spent night trying to keep warm. Wrote gas office re our room fire.

Friday, 15 February
Light snow fell today. Cold still most awful. The coldest week for 35 years. The gas man here and sorted the gas fire. He also looked at the kitchen fittings.

Saturday, 16 February
Got a postcard from Hetty Mossman. They have removed to King's Park. Glasgow is the coldest spot in Britain today. The thermometer at 17 degrees this morning. Tommy's ear seems all

---

5   Bathing or 'steeping' the feet was a folk remedy for the cold. As Thomas hints, it has
     no scientific basis.

right now. Tried to snow this afternoon. Feel glad to be home this weekend. Agnes seems a wee bit frigid tonight.

Sunday, 17 February
Temperature much higher today. Fine sunny day. Took a walk after dinner through Queen's Park and Maxwell Park. Talking to George Anderson in Queen's Park. Felt very sorry for him. He has only one eye, and the sight is gradually leaving it. He can't even read anything. I have a lot to be thankful for. Agnes and Tommy out a walk themselves.

Wednesday, 20 February
Thawed a little today. Agnes in town this afternoon for a pair of gloves. She was much pleased with them, which thereby pleases me.

Thursday, 21 February
Thaw more pronounced. Hallelujah. Some more rain. Let it rain.

Friday, 22 February
Not so cold. Agnes and Mrs Carmichael at a propaganda concert of the Co-op tonight. Agnes thinks she will join.

Saturday, 23 February
We all at Ibrox for tea. We were delayed by football lunatics, for which I am to blame. Otherwise we spent a pleasant evening.

Tuesday, 26 February
Hard frost. Cold wicked. Agnes at a concert with Mrs Carmichael in the Couper Institute.[6] Home 10.40. She seems peeved at something.

Thursday, 28 February
Thermometer this morning 20 degrees. Sunny day but fiendishly cold. This is the coldest month since 1895 (when I was a wee boy). Agnes froze herself to death in the wash house all day, but thawed a little at night.

Friday, 1 March
Above freezing point today. Agnes at the Mid-Argyll Concert tonight with the Carmichaels. She waited after the concert to see the grand march or something.

---

6   The Couper Institute is a public hall in Cathcart.

Sunday, 3 March
Frost this morning, but very mild day. Agnes in a wild sort of mood. I went to the Mossmans' in the afternoon and saw their new house in King's Park. Came home frozen stiff at 10.15. Agnes already in bed. Miserable day.

Wednesday, 6 March
Agnes in town in afternoon and got herself a pair of shoes. She and I at Majestic tonight.

Sunday, 10 March
My head sore.

Monday, 11 March
My head still sore so I gargled my nose.

Tuesday, 12 March
Head still sore, so sucked up impregnated water with my nose.

Wednesday, 13 March
My head not so bad. My nose sore.

Saturday, 16 March
We all at Paisley seeing Ella and her man. Had a pleasant time.

Friday, 22 March
All in Carmichaels' tonight. Got a little gramophone music.

Sunday, 24 March
I went to Knightswood in afternoon. Knocked myself down in running for the bus, and knocked a few chips off myself.

Wednesday, 27 March
Warm sunny day. Heat wave. Tommy got his Easter holidays today.

Friday, 29 March
Heat wave continues. Tommy and a pal went a big walk today round about Milngavie. Agnes baked at night.

Saturday, 30 March
I am on holiday. Warm and sunny. Tommy and I at Queen's Park in forenoon. John, Lily and small Ian here in afternoon.

Monday, 1 April
Spring holiday. After dinner we went to Eglinton Toll and examined all the cars. The only possibility being the one marked Hillfoot,

we boarded it. We came off about Canniesburn and walked down to Anniesland. We got the King's Park bus, and took it right to the terminus, as Agnes thought she had not walked far enough (which is extraordinary). We walked home from King's Park.

Thursday, 4 April

Tommy with a certain youth called McLennan at the swimming baths. Question – Can he swim yet?

Friday, 5 April

Tommy complained of a pain inside when he got up. It got worse and he was in agony all day. Sick and vomiting. Got the doctor. He not quite certain. Temperature and pulse normal. Gave him a solid dose of castor oil. I am feeling very uneasy at night.

Saturday, 6 April

Doctor up again. Tommy still in pain and his temperature up. Says it is appendicitis. Alex Carmichael came to my work for me, as I had to go with Tommy to the Victoria Infirmary in the ambulance. Got home feeling pretty dazed. The ambulance came at 3 o'clock. An immediate operation decided on there, so I left him feeling utterly desolate. Tommy seemed cheerier. Went to infirmary again about 6 p.m. Did not see him, of course, but nurse told me he had been through his operation. Went home and gave Agnes the news. We could not settle. We miss him terribly. Phoned infirmary about 10 p.m., was told he had come through the operation and was as well as could be expected. Fine, sunny day.

Sunday, 7 April

Agnes and I at Victoria Infirmary this morning. Being early, we walked. Felt dead beat when I got there. We saw Tommy, looking not so bad, but I turned faint. Tommy not very comfortable. Some pain and no sleep, but he had not been sick. Mrs Gordon and Nannie came in shortly after we got home. They went away shortly after, but Nannie came back later on, with Peggy Paterson. I went to Knightswood at night and let them know. Got home about 8.45. Felt very uneasy at night, and turned shaky. Dull day.

Monday, 8 April

Wet forenoon, but brightened up. Phoned the Victoria. Report got was 'improving, comfortable night'. Agnes not too well at night, and feel very uneasy myself. We miss him terribly.

Tuesday, 9 April

Warm and sunny day. Today's phone message: 'Very comfortable
night and getting on very well.' Agnes at Ibrox in afternoon. J.
Geddes up for a little at night. Feel as if I could settle down to
nothing at all.

Wednesday, 10 April

Bright cold day. Visiting day. Mrs Carmichael went with Agnes to
see Tommy. McLennan and Geddes also there. I rushed there after
tea and managed in for a little. Felt wonderfully cheered when I
saw him. He is now lying flat and the tube is out.

Thursday, 11 April

Bright cold day. Phoned Ward 3. The message I got: 'He is very
well.'

Friday, 12 April

Agnes not very well at all during the night, and no wonder. All the
news I got from the infirmary: 'Very comfortable', but I treasured
same. A. Baxter gave me 5/- to cheer Tommy up. Agnes out at
night, seeing Carmichaels' new house. Bright day, but very cold
wind.

Saturday, 13 April

We went to the Victoria in afternoon. Mr Carmichael came with
us. Lily met me at the gate. Tommy's two pals, Geddes and
MacPherson, also turned up. The Sister told Agnes that Tommy
was worrying about the big examination, which was keeping him
back. Agnes very much dumped.

Sunday, 14 April

Nan Gordon here early in the morning. She came to the Victoria
with us and came back for dinner. The Sister told me he was
getting on quite well. Agnes thought he was not looking so
cheery, and came away very miserable. After Nan Gordon went
away, we went to the Mossmans'. Saw the Carmichaels' new
house en route. Home about 10.30 p.m. Felt very depressed at
night and utterly miserable. Felt as if Tommy would never be
back again. Bitter cold day.

Monday, 15 April

Today's phone message: 'Very well, improving.' Mrs Baxter sent
Tommy a pound note, via Alex, via me.

Tuesday, 16 April
Bright, sunny day. I went to infirmary at night, feeling terribly worried. To my great joy, Tommy seemed very cheery and comfortable and feeling fine. Left him with feelings of relief and gratitude to give Agnes the good news. Was speaking to J. Geddes on way home. We both feel much cheerier tonight.

Wednesday, 17 April
Today's report: 'Much better, getting on nicely.'

Thursday, 18 April
Agnes at the Victoria today with Isa and wee Helen. Tommy quite cheery.

Saturday, 20 April
We all at Victoria. MacPherson and Geddes there. Tommy getting on fine.

Sunday, 21 April
Agnes and I at Victoria this morning. Tommy fine and cheery, talks of getting out now. The wound is now clean.

Tuesday, 23 April
Went and saw Tommy tonight. He told me the stitches were taken out six days ago and he is feeling fine.

Wednesday, 24 April
Agnes and Hetty Mossman seeing Tommy today. Tommy fine and eager to get out.

Friday, 26 April
Getting anxious again, so phoned Victoria. 'He is very well.' Which eased me greatly. Went to the library tonight to get a volume for Tommy.

Saturday, 27 April
Wild snow storm in the forenoon and again in the afternoon. We went to see Tommy in afternoon. Jack Ferguson also there. Tommy getting on fine, but not up yet. Called in at the Geddes' for a volume for Tommy. I feel a bit depressed at night.

Sunday, 28 April
Dull, cold, bleak day. We all at the Victoria this morning. James Geddes there, too. Tommy fine, but had been sick, which made us a bit uneasy.

Monday, 29 April

Phoned infirmary and got word: 'Very well, will be up soon.'
Feel greatly relieved. Agnes in wash house all day. We feel much
cheerier again.

Wednesday, 1 May

Fine day but cold. Saw Mrs Carmichael in town. She told me she
would go with Agnes to the Victoria. They duly went. McLennan
and Geddes also there. Tommy getting on, but not up yet. James
Geddes here at night re the university papers. Agnes went to
Ibrox. Nannie is not well. I still feel a little uneasy because
Tommy is not up yet.

Friday, 3 May

Phoned infirmary today and got the great
news: 'Very well and up yesterday'. Went
home walking on air and gave Agnes the glad
tidings. We got a postcard from Tommy to
bring his clothes on Saturday, as he gets out
then. We were glad. I went out at night and
told Geddes. Phoned Mr Gordon re Nannie.

Saturday, 4 May

This is a great day. Agnes and I went to the Victoria at 2.15 p.m.
and brought Tommy home in a taxi. He is looking fine and not so
bad at all. We spent rest of day looking at him. He is eating well
and went to bed between 8 and 9 p.m.

Sunday, 5 May

Spent the day watching Tommy to see that he did not bend too
much. I'll get over it, I suppose. Tommy feeling fine, good appetite
and up most of the day. MacPherson and Geddes came up in the
afternoon to see him. I went out about 9 p.m., phoned Mr Gordon
re Nannie.

Monday, 6 May

Tommy eating well and feeling fine.

Tuesday, 7 May

Tommy went out and got his hair cut. The rector up in afternoon to
see Tommy.[7] Tommy still keeps fine.

---

7   Because Tommy's school was an academy, its head teacher was called a rector.

Wednesday, 8 May

The doctor up to see Tommy and thinks he is fine. Says he can go to school on Monday. Agnes and Tommy out for a little in afternoon.

Thursday, 9 May

Tommy went out in afternoon and saw James Geddes. Mrs Carmichael here in afternoon. Alex has to go back to Royal Infirmary to get his arm done over again.

Friday, 10 May

Tommy went round to the school to see how they were getting on there. New postage stamps out today.[8]

Saturday, 11 May

Nice day. Tommy and I at Queen's Park in afternoon.

Sunday, 12 May

Fine day and warmer. Tommy and I walked to King's Park via Mount Florida and took the bus home.

Monday, 13 May

Tommy at school today and feels none the worse. Agnes at factor re lum. Lily and Ian here in the afternoon. An old friend of Tommy's, a John McKendrick, here at night.

Wednesday, 15 May

The man what sweeps lums up, and operated on said lum.

Friday, 17 May

Tommy has a holiday today. As Tommy needs a new coat, Agnes and he went into town and got same. A chaste shade of grey. His last coat was a dark blue.

Saturday, 18 May

Tommy needs new hat, so Agnes took him into town once more and got said chapeau for the lad. Like his coat, it is a chaste shade of grey.

Monday, 20 May

Kitchen whitewashed. This is a holiday. Spent it cleaning paint work of kitchen. At night, Tommy and I went out the Newton Mearns Road, sat on a dyke and watched all the motor cars. Very warm day.

---

8   The stamps commemorated the Universal Postal Union Congress being held in London.

Wednesday, 22 May
Tommy reported at the Victoria today and at school in the afternoon.

Saturday, 25 May
Tommy and I at the Cinerama in the afternoon, hearing the new organ.[9] After tea, we all at Queen's Park.

Tuesday, 28 May
Tommy's class had a medical examination today. Tommy passed.

Wednesday, 29 May
At night, Tommy and I had our favourite seat in the Newton Mearns Road.

Thursday, 30 May
This election day, so Tommy has a holiday. Agnes and I duly recorded our vote.[10]

Friday, 31 May
Tommy sat a bursary exam in the Faculty Hall.[11] The Bethia Stewart Bursary, I think you call it. At night, Tommy and I putted in Linn Park. Brilliant sunny day.

Sunday, 2 June
Kitchen covered with soot this morning when we got up. Agnes was distinctly peeved.

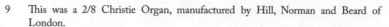

SOOT

Monday, 3 June
Tommy sat the first day (English) of the great university bursaries examination.

Tuesday, 4 June
The Labour government is now in.[12]

---

9   This was a 2/8 Christie Organ, manufactured by Hill, Norman and Beard of London.

10 The General Election returned a hung parliament, with the Liberals holding the balance of power.

11 The Faculty Hall is the headquarters of the Royal Faculty of Procurators in Glasgow, and stands at 12 Nelson Mandela Place (formerly St George's Place).

12 Ramsay MacDonald, MP for Seaham, was the new Prime Minister.

1929
Wed. 29 May

At night Tommy
& I had
our favorite
seat in the
Newton Mearns
Road. When
we got home
the young Mrs Cowie was
in. After supper I
saw her away
Nice sunny day

Thursday 30 May

Agnes at Wash
house all day
We dropped
the wringer on
the stair, to
the detriment of said

Wednesday, 5 June

Tommy at university again. Latin exam this time. Got bad news about James Geddes' father. He is lying in Victoria Infirmary with broken leg. His coal lorry got smashed with a tramcar. The horse also badly hurt. This is Derby Day, so I lost my usual shilling.

Thursday, 6 June

Tommy sat his French examination at university.

Friday, 7 June

Tommy on holiday. He went round to the Geddes stable to see the horse.

Saturday, 8 June

Dull sort of day. After tea we at King's Park via Mount Florida. Got the funny bus back. It has a fancy top.

Monday, 10 June

Tommy sat the last of his university examinations.

Wednesday, 12 June

Tommy at Victoria today seeing Mr Geddes.

Thursday, 13 June

Tommy at school today for the last time.

Friday, 14 June

Tommy sat oral exam for French in Faculty Hall this forenoon. Very busy packing for our holidays.

Saturday, 15 June

Our holidays now begin. Our taxi came at 9.25 a.m. We sailed per *Isle of Arran* at 10 a.m.[13] We had a cup of tea on board and after a nice sail arrived at Rothesay 1.20 p.m. Our landlady had the table set, so we lost no time in having our tea. Agnes then went out for a few messages. Tommy and I went out to explore. Discovered a battleship in the bay, viz the *Rodney*.[14] So we boarded it and overhauled it.

---

13   The paddle steamer *Isle of Arran* was built by T.B. Seath and Co. of Rutherglen in 1892, and was operated by Williamson-Buchanan Steamers Ltd.

14   HMS *Rodney* was a Nelson-class battleship built by Cammell-Laird at Birkenhead and launched in 1925.

Sunday, 16 June
In the afternoon, Tommy and I out by Bogany Point. After tea we all walked to Port Bannatyne. Showery day and not very warm.

Monday, 17 June
After breakfast, Tommy and I putted, then looked through the new museum. After tea, all to the Palace, with Miss Henderson, who had supper with us.

Tuesday, 18 June
After dinner, we all at Loch Fad. Pouring wet night.

Wednesday, 19 June
Rained all day. At night, we went to the De Luxe.

Thursday, 20 June
In forenoon, Tommy and I out by Kerrycroy and back by Loch Ascog. After dinner, all at Port Bannatyne and putted. Bright, sunny day but too windy.

Friday, 21 June
In forenoon, Tommy and I out the Barone Road to Ettrick Bay via St Ninian's Bay. Windy and cold.

Saturday, 22 June

Tommy brought in the Herald this morning to see results of the bursary examination.[15] To our joy and pride, he is first out of 438 competitors. Spent the day saying: 'Is it possible?' Bought a new paper on the strength of it. After tea we went to the Palace with Miss Henderson.

Sunday, 23 June
In the forenoon, Tommy and I out near Port Bannatyne and back by Skeoch Wood. After dinner I feel sick and tired and have to lie down for a while. After tea, we all to Skippers Wood and Craigmore way. Sunny day, but blew a gale and pretty cold.

Tuesday, 25 June
At Palace at night. Warm, sunny day.

---

15 The newspaper was the *Glasgow Herald* (currently called *The Herald*).

Education in Glasgow

Glasgow greatly expanded in the decades before the First World War, adding burghs such as Govanhill, Pollokshields, Hillhead and Maryhill in 1891 and Govan, Partick and Pollokshaws in 1912, taking the population from around 500,000 in 1891 to more than a million in 1921. At this time, education was provided by school boards, which were organised on the same boundaries as parishes. Because of its expansion, and the parish boundaries, the educational system in Glasgow by the time of the First World War was being administered by five different school boards. The reach of Govan Parish School Board across the River Clyde and into the West End can still be seen prominently on a number of school buildings in the area, such as Dowanhill Primary School and Church Street Public School, where the name of the school board is a permanent part of the stonework.

The Education (Scotland) Act of 1918 resolved this anomalous boundary issue – which was not confined to Glasgow – by disbanding almost 1,000 school boards and setting up 20 local education authorities. The 1918 Act also made the city's Roman Catholic schools the responsibility of the Glasgow Education Authority; they had previously been administered and funded by the Roman Catholic Church. Between 1918 and 1929, the Glasgow Education Authority – the largest in Britain – was the sole provider of state-funded education in the city. In 1929, the education authority was taken over by the local authority to become the Glasgow Corporation Education Department. During the time of Tommy's education, the city also had fee-paying schools. The education authority directly operated Allan Glen's (founded 1853), the High School (1824), the High School for Girls (1894) and Notre Dame High School (1897; for Roman Catholic girls). In addition, it grant-funded Hutchesons' Boys Grammar (1650), Hutchesons' Girls Grammar (1876) and St Aloysius College

(1859; for Roman Catholic boys). There were also five independent schools, four of which received contributions from the education authority. These were Kelvinside Academy (1878), Laurel Bank (1903; for girls), Park School (1880; for girls) and Westbourne (1877; for girls). There was also Glasgow Academy (1845), which was completely independent of the state system.

The Post Office Glasgow Directory for 1927–8 gives a snapshot of the Glasgow Education Authority (of 129 and 151–155 Bath Street, Glasgow G2) at the time Tommy was successfully working his way to the top of the education system. The directory lists the forty-five members of the authority, all drawn from the great and the good of the city (and beyond); these include fifteen reverends and two very reverends, two knights of the realm and four women. There is also a listing of all the authority's schools in the city, divided into 15 districts. The schools listed for district 11, Cathcart, where the Livingstone family lived, were: Annette Street School (in Annette Street), Batson Street Special School (Calder Street; annexe of Hollybrook Street Special School), Battlefield School (Carmichael Place), Calder Street School (Calder Street), Cathcart School (Craig Road), Hollybrook Street Special School (Hollybrook Street), Holmlea School (Holmlea Road), Holy Cross Roman Catholic School (Daisy Street), Mount Florida School (Cathcart Road), Polmadie School (Polmadie Street), Queen's Park School (Grange Road) and Victoria School (Batson Street).

Tommy began his education at Victoria Primary School in Batson Street, Govanhill, just around the corner from his home in Morgan Street. In August 1923, he left primary school and moved on to Strathbungo School in Craigie Street (in the education authority's district 14, Pollok). In December that year, he scored 89 per cent in his exams, and in April 1924, he scored 92 per cent. That May, the school magazine published Tommy's 'first literary efforts', as Thomas describes them in his diary, and one of his paintings was displayed in an exhibition in the Kelvin Hall. In his second year of secondary schooling, Tommy came first in the school exams in both December and April and sat a bursary exam, which netted him £20. In the school year 1925–6, he was again first in the exams and landed a second £20 bursary. In August 1926, Tommy moved to Albert Road Academy (also known as Pollokshields Secondary, in the Pollok school district), where he had similar success. In the following academic year, he sat his Higher exams, came first in his school exams and once more won a £20 bursary. His sixth year at school was interrupted by an operation to remove his appendix, but he again covered himself in glory in the exams, various bursary exams (including the Bethia Stewart bursary, which paid £130) and the Glasgow University bursary exam, in which he came first out of 438. He topped all this off with being awarded the Dux medal at school. 'The boy is a marvel,' wrote his proud father.

Tommy started his university career in October 1929, and soon began winning more bursaries (including a Carnegie bursary of £9 a year) and passing History, Latin, Moral Philosophy and other exams with flying colours. At the time Thomas stopped writing his diaries, in April 1933, Tommy had almost finished his fourth year at university and was facing his final honours exams.

Thursday, 27 June

Blazing hot day. Tommy and I meandered to Craigmore and putted
in the quaint green there. Too warm to walk back, so we took the
bus. Went to the esplanade and sailed round the *Nelson* three
times in the *May Queen*, and three times round went we.[16] After
dinner, we find that the *Nelson* is open, so we all went on board
and inspected he, she or it.[17] Beautiful night. We are all going
up to Glasgow tomorrow for the day. Tommy receiving letters of
congratulation every day, and he is to be presented at the school
with the Dux medal.

Friday, 28 June

I did not go to bed last night in case we would sleep in.
Wakened Agnes at 3 a.m., then went to bed myself. All up by
about 6 a.m., Agnes, of course, being already up. Left Rothesay
at 7.50 a.m. and travelled to Glasgow via Wemyss Bay. Tommy
left us there and went straight to the school. Agnes and I went
to Mrs Carmichael.[18] Not in, but met her in Morgan Street, so
we went up and had a cup of tea in our own house. Got a letter
there for Tommy. Found out after that it was advising him he had
won a Bethia Stewart Bursary for £130. The boy is a marvel.
Agnes and I then went to the church hall and had a seat on the
platform, in a blaze of reflected glory. Tommy got a great ovation,
and he ought to be very proud of it. He got presented with the
Dux medal, and a gold wristlet watch from the scholars. Agnes
and I went home, as Tommy had to wait to be photographed for
The Bulletin.[19] He followed later on. We all went to town and had
our dinner there. We got the 4.30 train back to Wemyss Bay, and
arrived Rothesay 6 p.m.

Saturday, 29 June

Blazing sunshine all day. Tommy and I spent the forenoon and
afternoon putting. We go home today. Got *Columba* at 5.15
p.m.[20] Had tea on board, not very many on board so had an
exceptionally fine sail. Arrived Broomielaw about 8.20 and home
by 8.30 per taxi. Amen.

---

16 Thomas is paraphrasing the traditional Scottish ballad 'The Mermaid'. The final verse
    is: 'Then three times around went our gallant ship / And three times around went she
    / Three times around went our gallant ship / And she sank to the bottom of the sea.'

17 Traditionally, ships are referred to as 'she'.

18 Mrs Carmichael had the keys to the Livingstones' house while they were on holiday.

19 *The Bulletin* was an illustrated newspaper published daily in Glasgow.

20 The paddle steamer *Columba* was built in 1878 by J. and G. Thomson of Clydebank,
    and operated by David MacBrayne.

Sunday, 30 June
Fine warm day. Agnes slaving all day and not very cheery.

Wednesday, 3 July
Tommy gets his heart's desire: *The Oxford Book of English Verse*.[21]
Agnes in the wash house all day.

Monday, 8 July
Ibrox (Mrs Gordon, Nan and Ronnie) here after tea. Tommy and I
took Nan out. We went to Linn Park and putted.

Tuesday, 9 July
Tommy at Cardonald in the afternoon, coaching a fair female. He
got paid in advance, to wit 50/-. Geddes up at night.

Thursday, 11 July
Tommy got a tie and socks from Josephine, perhaps in appreciation
of the honour he has done to the family.

Friday, 12 July
This is Fair Friday, so I quit work at 2 p.m. Fine sunny day.
Tommy had brought back a book of his pupil's by mistake, so we
both meandered down that way, and Tommy returned book to that
young lady.

Saturday, 13 July
After tea we all did the Patterton – Newton Mearns walk. Fine
sunny day.

Sunday, 14 July
Tommy at the Victoria today seeing Mr Geddes. Duncan and Maud
here. They are on holiday (at Helensburgh). After dinner we took
them to Pollok Estate. We got our photos taken. Blazing hot day.

Monday, 15 July
Still on holiday. Another scorcher of a day. After
dinner, we took bus to Milngavie and wandered round
by Mugdock and the waterworks.

Tuesday, 16 July
*Started work again. Went to my work minus
keys, so Tommy brought them in.*

---

21   Edited by Arthur Quiller-Couch and first published in 1900 by the Oxford University
     Press.

Thursday, 18 July
Tommy and Geddes out for a joy ride in the coal lorry.

Monday, 22 July
Got the photos from Duncan, which I will duly acknowledge some day.

Wednesday, 24 July
Geddes' horse shot today, as it was a hopeless case.

Sunday, 28 July
Rained all day. I went to Victoria Infirmary to see Mr Geddes. He is in Tommy's old ward. I saw Nurse Allan, the fair lady who used to let me in at night to see Tommy. My heart was a bit lighter than the days I used to go.

Tuesday, 30 July
Tommy got official word from the university that he has been given a bursary of £40 a year for four years. Think I'll retire.

Friday, 2 August
A Mrs Spence came in this evening to engage Tommy to tutor her girl in Latin. We cut rhubarb tonight.

Sunday, 4 August
Tommy at Bolton Drive in afternoon, arranging for a new pupil. He clicked. After tea all the Mossmans dropped in (except Billy). We took them to the Queen's Park and then gave them supper.

Monday, 5 August
Tommy started with his new pupil today, one hour per diem.

Wednesday, 7 August
Tommy went to see Dr Sewell today at the Victoria. He passed. Sighthill Cemetery in liquidation.[22] Agnes attended a meeting of plot holders in the Merchants' Hall to see how things were.[23]

Thursday, 8 August
Tommy at Arkieson with Agnes in the afternoon for a new suit. After tea, Tommy and I at the Cinerama.

---

22   The Sighthill Cemetery Company Limited continued in existence until 1953. The cemetery was taken over by Glasgow Corporation in 1954.

23   The Merchants' Hall, the headquarters of the Merchants' House of Glasgow, is at 7 West George Street.

Friday, 9 August
Fine day, and Tommy's birthday.[24]

Friday, 16 August
James Geddes up at night. He had to go away about 10 o'clock to
feed the nag. Tommy went with him.

Tuesday, 20 August
Did some repair work on the rocker chair at night, and bashed my
thumb.

Wednesday, 21 August
At night I played some more with the rocker. Tommy's new suit
arrived.

Thursday, 22 August

Tommy's new jacket too long in the sleeves, so
he took it back and got them shortened. You
can now see the wristlet watch. I observe that
he wears watch on his right wrist. While I
was enjoying myself mending the rocking chair,
Josephine, Isa and wee Helen arrived, so I
struck work.

Saturday, 24 August

Bought a quaint looking object
called the Yankee Pipe, said to
be as dry as the States.[25]

Sunday, 25 August
Tommy out with his new suit at night. Agnes thought him very
late, and went out to look for him. As she was very nervous
etc etc, I went with her. She had to turn back as she could not
walk, and I thought I would never get her home again. A nerve
or something in her foot very painful. I got scared to death and
thought various wild things. Tommy appeared a little after 10
p.m. He had dropped in on Geddes. Sunday boating started today
on Hogganfield Loch.

---

24   Tommy was 18.

25   America was 'dry' between 1920 and 1933, thanks to the National Prohibition Act of
     1919.

Monday, 26 August
Mr Geddes gets out today. He has been in the Victoria for three months. Agnes' foot not much better. A man up tonight to see if Tommy would like the job of coaching his girl in mathematics. Nothing doing. Tommy not a specialist in that branch of science, but recommended his pal Geddes.

Tuesday, 27 August
Agnes' foot seems a little easier today. She managed out for the messages. I dropped in and paid Mr Arkieson for Tommy's suit. It cost £5 5/- net. However, Tommy made enough to pay for it with his teaching, which eases things a little.

Sunday, 1 September
My gum is so sore I can't wear my bottom teeth, so out they go.

Monday, 2 September
Still keeping out my bottom wallies.[26] Tommy at Mount Vernon tonight visiting MacPherson. Stuck in one or two stamps at night.

Tuesday, 3 September
At night, Nan Gordon here. All the Ibrox folk seem to be much below par, as usual.

Thursday, 5 September
Tommy's photo in The Bulletin today with his classmates as an example of the brains of the country today. We visited Jeanie MacKenzie (Mrs Brash) at Knightswood. We went with Mr and Mrs Carmichael, also Mrs MacKenzie.

Friday, 6 September
Nice sunny, warm day. Agnes and Tommy at Rothesay today looking at a house for some more holidays. They got home in the afternoon after a successful visit. Tommy out seeing Geddes at night and invited K. MacPherson up, who came about 10 p.m. The wireless is not giving me satisfaction, so I gave it an overhauling.

---

26   'Wallies' are false teeth.

Monday, 9 September
Brilliant day of sunshine. Tommy got a letter of congratulation today from Sir John Gilmour.[27] It had come to his notice etc etc. He is the bloke who keeps Pollokshields School up in gold medals. I went out for a little to Pollokshields Library, where the gentry get reading the papers for nothing. Took half a hundredweight of school books up to the ABC for sale.

Tuesday, 10 September
We lit a fire at night. It is likely on now for good. Tommy at the ABC shop and got nine shillings for the books I left. They will make pounds on them, most likely. Got my silver locks cut tonight.

Wednesday, 11 September
A wonderful fine day, and very warm. Tommy and I wandered over to Maxwell Park and putted. I lost.

Friday, 13 September
Arranged with the railway company to lift the hamper. Mr Baxter has given me a week's holiday, so I'll be with Agnes and Tommy at Rothesay part of the time.

Sunday, 15 September
Agnes very busy getting ready for the holidays.

Tuesday, 17 September
Agnes and Tommy depart today for Rothesay. They left in the forenoon. I took my dinner in town, which I did not enjoy. Got a phone message from my niece Lily inviting me to Riddrie tomorrow. Felt lost when I got home at night. Worked for a few hours making a new cat's whisker stand for my wireless. Gave a beggar two pence.

Wednesday, 18 September
Got a postcard from Agnes. All well. Went to Riddrie straight from my work. Had a pleasant evening there, and a crack with an old friend, John Ferguson, on holiday from Peru.

---

27   Sir John Gilmour, Bt, was a Conservative and Unionist politician and a leading Orangeman. He was MP for Glasgow Pollok from 1919 to 1940, and Secretary of State for Scotland between 1926 and 1929.

Thursday, 19 September
At night, listened in, played with stamps and mourned the absence
of my loved ones. Sent Agnes a love letter. Wrote Duncan a letter.
Not so long now to Saturday.

Friday, 20 September
Got a letter from my well-beloved and a postcard from Tommy.
They say they will be glad when I come down. Ha ha. Got tired
of dining in town, so came home today and boiled an egg. A little
ceremony took place tonight in my place of business. We gave
James Brown a fountain pen. He leaves next week.

Saturday, 21 September
Got the 1.10 train to Wemyss Bay and boarded the Rothesay boat.
Very stormy. Arrived there about 2.45. Agnes and Tommy met me.
Very nice place they have, and a fine view. After some dinner, we
meandered about and had a cup of tea in a Rothesay tearoom.

Sunday, 22 September
Heavy rain in the forenoon, dull, gloomy day. The girl who sets
the table and attends us generally is an awful nice girl. So also is
Miss Irvine, the landlady.

Monday, 23 September
Fine day. After tea, we all walked to Port Bannatyne.

Tuesday, 24 September
Nice warm day. Tommy and I putted. After tea, we all at the De
Luxe.

Wednesday, 25 September
Warm, sunny day. I climbed the Barone Hill. Nancy (our maid) at
Skelmorlie today, so we all went down at night to pier and met her
coming home.

Thursday, 26 September
Fine sunny, warm day. Tommy and I boarded Kilchattan Bay
bus, got off at Kingarth Church and then struck along a road two
or three miles till we came to the ruins of St Blane's Chapel.[28]
We then climbed over hill and dale and valley etc for a few
miles and landed on the coast about the south end of Bute, then
walked back to Kilchattan Bay. Tommy lost his cap somewhere
on this walk.

---

28   The twelfth-century St Blane's Chapel stands on the site of a monastery founded by
     Blane in 575. It is near the southern tip of the island of Bute.

Friday, 27 September
Tommy bought a new cap. After tea, we were at Craigmore, then home to see the illuminations and fireworks.

Sunday, 29 September
Bright, sunny day but some very heavy showers. Agnes and Tommy at church in forenoon. After dinner, Agnes took a run up and saw Miss Henderson. Tommy and I wandered out by Craigmore, then went on the pier and saw all the steamers.

Monday, 30 September
Up at 5.30 a.m. Gave Agnes and Tommy an affectionate farewell, fell down the stairs and departed for home. Got the 6.45 a.m. boat for Wemyss Bay. Got to my work about 9 a.m. At dinner time I went over to Central Station and met Agnes and Tommy.

Tuesday, 1 October
Tommy at Art Galleries with Aby Bloch and at night he was up seeing Nicolson. The alarum clock has struck work. Wishing I was back at Rothesay.

Wednesday, 2 October
Tomorrow is Nancy's birthday, so I sent her a card.

Thursday, 3 October
Listened to the Ninth Symphony at night.[29]

Saturday, 5 October
Tommy at university organ recital in the afternoon. Agnes and I, having lower tastes, went to the Majestic at night.

Wednesday, 9 October
My leg with the varicose veins giving me concern, so I went over and saw the doctor. He says he will cure them. Good man.

Friday, 11 October
Tommy had Nicolson up at night. This lad knows a little about postage stamps, so I let him see a volume containing a few specimens. Will reserve the other volume for another night.

Saturday, 12 October
Got word today that Tommy will get the Carnegie Bursary, which will help things a bit. It comes to £9 a year. In preparation for tomorrow, I washed my leg well and put a bandage on to keep it clean.

29　Ludwig van Beethoven's Symphony No. 9 in D minor, Op. 125 'Choral'.

1929

Friday 11 October

Tommy had Nicolson up at night. This lad knows a little about postage stamps so I let him see a volume containing a few specimens. Will reserve the other volume for another night. Poor lad!

He away about 11 pm

Bright sunny & breezy day.

Sunday, 13 October

In much perturbation of spirit, waited for the doctor. He arrived at about 2 or 3 p.m. He duly put a puncture in a vein and squirted juice in (quinine-urethane). Tied my leg up and departed. This is the first dose and I survived.

Monday, 14 October

Tommy enters a new life today. His first day at the university.[30] He goes in the forenoon only, 9 to 12, which is very convenient. My leg pretty sore today, but not enough to prevent me walking.

Friday, 18 October

Agnes and I at the Housing Exhibition.

Saturday, 19 October

Bathed and bandaged my leg in readiness for tomorrow. Feeling very uneasy about the blinking thing.

Sunday, 20 October

Doctor up today, put more juice into my leg and said it was doing fine. This put my mind at ease. I was getting a bit uneasy.

Monday, 21 October

Got measured today for a new suit by Mr Thomas Arkieson. Leg sore.

Tuesday, 22 October

Got a first fit-on by the tailor. Tommy gave his lecture tonight on Edgar Allan Poe in some church.

Wednesday, 23 October

Tommy was at the university Dialectic Society.

Thursday, 24 October

Got a second fit-on today. Bought a new alarum clock in the Poly for 3/11.

---

30   The University of Glasgow was the only university in the city until 1964, when the University of Strathclyde received its Royal Charter. They were joined in 1993 by Glasgow Caledonian University.

Saturday, 26 October
My new suit arrived.

Sunday, 27 October
Doctor up about 7.30 and gave my leg another jag and says it is
doing fine.

Monday, 28 October

Wet morning. On goes my big coat. My leg pretty sore.

Wednesday, 30 October
Left my suit for a few alterations. Agnes got a sore throat
and not well generally. However, she managed out at night
with Mrs Carmichael. Tommy at the Dialectic. Both home
by 11 p.m.

Friday, 1 November

Paid my tailor.

Sunday, 3 November

Doctor up about noon. Gave me two injections. Had to stand on a chair. Felt sick etc. He is now finished. I go and see him in three months. Agnes and I at Ibrox at night.

Monday, 4 November
Leg feels sore once more. Wrote the Scottish Clerks'
Association to see if the treatment I got comes under the
'panel'. Bought a new house pipe for 18 pence.

Wednesday, 6 November
Just after tea time, my niece Ella Carlyle came to see us. She
is learning to be a nurse. I saw her home all the way to Stobhill
Hospital.

Friday, 8 November
Dropped into the Glasgow Corporation housing scheme office in
the Trongate this forenoon to tell them I would like a nice house
in the Govanhill district. The place was so busy, I went away with
my message undelivered.

Tuesday, 12 November
Agnes in town in the afternoon. She got a form for the house that we want.

Sunday, 17 November
Agnes at church with Mrs Carmichael in the morning. In the afternoon, I went to Linn Park.

Monday, 18 November
Posted the application for a new house, so should get one about 1940.

Wednesday, 20 November
Agnes and I at the Cinerama. First time I have heard the 'talkies' and I thought it great. Tommy at the Dialectic.

Sunday, 24 November
Agnes at the Candlish Church tonight. She complains of a pain in her back which hurts her when she breathes. Feel greatly alarmed at this intelligence.

Monday, 25 November
We gave Tommy a new fountain pen for his birthday or Christmas, I forget which.

Wednesday, 27 November
Agnes at church concert with Mrs Carmichael. Tommy at his Dialectic. I sat in and enjoyed myself.

Tuesday, 3 December
Had a night in the house. Listened to the glorious 'Fifth'.[31]

Wednesday, 4 December
Met Agnes in town at 5.30, then to Partick. An affair at Lily's house. Mary from Edinburgh there, also Wee Jean. Then came Wee Ella, Tommy, John Martin and Josephine. Jean is going to Australia.

Monday, 9 December
Wakened about 4 a.m. Terrific storm, thunder and lightning, wind and rain, altogether most unholy. Agnes felt quite nervous about it all, and got no sleep. The spire of Gorbals parish church demolished by the lightning. Saw an armchair I liked, so told Agnes. So into town she went with Tommy and ordered it. £2. 5. 0. She paid.

---

31   Ludwig van Beethoven's Symphony No. 5 in C minor, Op. 67.

Tuesday, 10 December
The new chair arrived. So off with the old.

Friday, 13 December
Agnes gave the old chair to the coal man. Farewell.
1910–1929.

Wednesday, 18 December
Tommy got first instalment of his bursary, to wit £20. Mild day.

Thursday, 19 December
Tommy booked seats at City Hall. So at night off we go like
gentlemen and heard the Scottish Orchestra, among other things,
play the Fifth Symphony. Gave the kitchen mantelpiece a touch of
varnish when I got home.

Friday, 20 December
Tommy now on holiday. He was at some affair at the university,
Daft Friday.[32]

Tuesday, 24 December
Got a nice Xmas greeting from Athens of a philatelic nature. I'm
not well at all. Josephine, Isa and the two wee Archibalds here
about 4 p.m. Got from Ireland today, tobacco for me, a tie for
Tommy and an overall for Agnes. Josephine brought two cakes of
shortbread. I took toddy at night.

Wednesday, 25 December
A Merry Christmas to You All. Felt all out this morning, throat
bad, nose and head stuffy. Being a holiday, I took the chance and
stayed in bed all day.

Thursday, 26 December
At work again. Got in at 10.30, but don't feel well.

Friday, 27 December
Agnes and Tommy at Paisley Road looking at a bookcase. They
clicked. It cost 50/-.

Monday, 30 December
Bookcase came to hand today, so Tommy spent the night filling it
up.

---

32   Daft Friday, the Christmas ball held every year since 1909 in the Glasgow University
     Union, is a black-tie affair. The 100th anniversary event was held on Friday, 18
     December 2009.

Tuesday, 31 December

Frosty but some rain. Got away from work at 3 p.m. Mrs
Carmichael from Furnace dropped in to see us at dinner time.
Appalling disaster at Glen Cinema, Paisley, today. Panic – 70
children lose their lives.[33]

33   On the afternoon of 31 December, during a children's matinee performance, a reel of
     film began to give off thick black smoke. As the auditorium filled with smoke, panic
     set in, and children stampeded towards the fire escape, which was padlocked. Seventy
     children died in Britain's worst cinema disaster.

1930

For Thomas and the world, the year rolled by with few great upheavals. Various infirmities, inclement weather and soot presented obstacles to domestic bliss, but the Livingstones battled on, sustained by the church, the countryside and the cinema. Tommy continued to shine at university, and diversified into boating. Agnes doggedly completed her weekly punishing stint in the wash house, with no help from the men of the house. The outside world intruded only when disaster struck at home or abroad.

Wednesday, 1 January
Happy New Year? Got first-fitted in due course by all the
Carmichaels. Mrs MacKenzie and Willie also here. All clear by
3.50 a.m. Rained all day, so not out. This is a holiday, so not at
my work.

Thursday, 2 January
Broke my specs, so took them to be mended by my optologist.
Tommy had Geddes and Nicolson up for tea. Nicolson spent the
evening admiring my stamp collection.

Friday, 3 January
At my work again. We all at the Carmichaels' tonight and had a
good time. Nannie Gordon tried to get in when we were out. Us
being out, she did not get in. Very sad.

Saturday, 4 January
Went up and saw Dickson and lifted my renovated specs, Agnes
being the poorer by this little transaction.

Monday, 6 January
Tommy starts his intellectual labours once more at the university.

Tuesday, 7 January
Got some stamps from a new man in Warsaw.

Wednesday, 8 January
Agnes over at Cowies' tonight. Wrote New Zealand.

Saturday, 11 January
Mrs MacKenzie up in afternoon re Agnes' new frock. It not ready
yet, to Agnes' great displeasure. We all at the Mossmans' for tea.
Terrific snow blizzard now on.

Wednesday, 15 January
Tommy out in the afternoon selling *Ygorra* magazines.[1]

Friday, 17 January
Tommy had a dress rehearsal tonight. He goes out tomorrow as an
old lady, in the sacred cause of charity.

---

1   *Ygorra* magazine was a staple of the annual university charity drive. It contained
    jokes, cartoons and adverts. The name derives from the cry 'Ygorra buy one' ('You have
    got to buy one').

Saturday, 18 January
Fine day, sunny and mild. Tommy out all day with the students, and filled two boxes with gold, silver, copper and notes.[2] He called in at my place of business and got a donation there. I was out at the time.

Sunday, 19 January
Tommy collected yesterday £17,250.[3] At least he helped.

Monday, 20 January
Agnes has very sore back, but spent the day nevertheless in the wash house. To save her life, I brought home a bottle of Angier's Emulsion.[4] Tommy at some affair in the university today. Mr Baldwin mixed up with it in some way.[5] Rained today with great freedom.

Friday, 24 January
Agnes has now got her new frock. Agnes says Angier's Emulsion does not agree with her. Solemn thought.

Saturday, 25 January
Received another letter from Warsaw.

Thursday, 30 January
Mrs Thomson of Garthland, Cardonald, here at night to engage Tommy as a tutor to her girl, for an hour or so on Saturdays. Tommy clicked.

Friday, 31 January
Frosty morning. Bitter cold day. Got my hair cut, and now hope for a heat wave.

Saturday, 1 February
Tommy at Cardonald to give lesson the one.

Sunday, 2 February
Josephine not so well.

---

2 The student fancy-dress parade, with rattling cans, boxes and buckets, was the highlight of the charity event.

3 This was the total collected by the students that day.

4 Angier's Emulsion was a cough mixture made from petroleum and hypophosphates. It was made by the Angier Chemical Company of London, and advertised using the slogan 'it has no equal as a lung healer'.

5 Stanley Baldwin, former Prime Minister, was Rector of Glasgow University between 1928 and 1931.

Tuesday, 4 February
Cut my finger this morning on my safety razor, which is absurd.

Thursday, 6 February
Bitter cold day. Put on my cotton pants (made in Japan, number 39) as woollen pants. Made my legs too itchy.

Saturday, 8 February
Very cold. Lily, her man John and the wee man Ian here.

Monday, 10 February
The alarum clock ceases work. Agnes at a Co-op concert in Dixon Hall.

Wednesday, 12 February
Fog and frost. Agnes bought me a cardigan to keep me warm in the house. We sent 10/- to Albert Road school fund.

Friday, 14 February
Agnes and Mrs Carmichael at St Mungo Hall. Some Co-op propaganda stunt.

Sunday, 16 February
Fine sunny, frosty day. After dinner, I went to Linn Park via old Cathcart and back by the Carmunnock Road and King's Park.

Monday, 17 February
Fog and frost. Tommy went to St Andrew's Hall at night with MacPherson to hear the great pianist Schnabel.[6] Agnes and I enjoyed ourselves in our own simple little way by visiting the Govanhill Picture House.

Tuesday, 18 February
Ella Carlyle here at tea time. Big train smash at Rutherglen last night in the fog.[7] 50 injured. I just missed being in it by 20 years.

Thursday, 20 February
Bought a new house pipe. Paid the gas department for their rotten gas.

---

6   Artur Schnabel was an Austrian classical pianist, especially known for his interpretations of Beethoven and Schubert.

7   A signalling error caused two trains to collide. The final toll was 98 people injured.

Saturday, 22 February

Went round and showed doctor the leg he had treated. He thinks it is all right now.

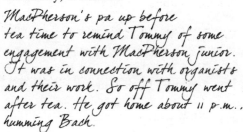

Wednesday, 26 February
Put up the kitchen blind.

Saturday, 1 March

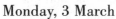

MacPherson's pa up before tea time to remind Tommy of some engagement with MacPherson junior. It was in connection with organists and their work. So off Tommy went after tea. He got home about 11 p.m., humming Bach.

Monday, 3 March
Paid the postmaster 10/- so that we may all be allowed to listen in another year.

Thursday, 6 March

Tommy visits MacPherson, who has the flu.

Tuesday, 11 March
Agnes and Mrs Carmichael at an exhibition in Kelvin Hall this afternoon. She bought a wonderful bread knife there.

Wednesday, 12 March
Bitter cold. Ordered Kincole today.[8]

Friday, 14 March
Sunny, but still very cold. The bag of Kincole arrived this morning. And by night is condemned utterly.

Saturday, 15 March
Cold something wicked. Tommy and I at an organ recital in the university and heard the great Dupré.[9]

---

8   Kincole was a smokeless fuel, derived from coal, made and sold by Glasgow Corporation.

9   Marcel Dupré was a French organist, a former child prodigy and best known for performing the complete works of Johann Sebastian Bach from memory in a series of ten concerts in Paris in 1920 and again in 1921.

Monday, 17 March
Got a letter and two newspapers from New Zealand. Mrs Cowie up at night.

Tuesday, 18 March
Stopped work today about noon as Mr S.P. Cochrane (partner in my firm) is being buried. He died on Sunday morning. I did not go to the funeral as my knee is very sore. McLennan and Bloch up for Tommy in afternoon and took him a walk to Carmunnock.

Wednesday, 19 March
We got in real coal today. Earl of Balfour dead.[10] Bought a new watch today. Paid 35 belgas for it.[11] Being a man of refinement, I bought it in Edwards, Buchanan Street.

Thursday, 20 March
Broke mainspring of my new watch last night. Took it back today, and got another one.

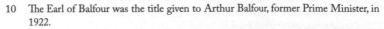

Friday, 21 March
My new watch is keeping well.

Saturday, 22 March
Ella Carlyle arrived here about tea time. As she is not due back at Stobhill till 2 p.m. on Sunday, we kept her here all night.

Sunday, 23 March
Ella got her breakfast in bed. Tommy and I saw her to Stobhill after dinner. After that, Tommy and I walked through Springburn Park and into the wee museum.[12]

Tuesday, 25 March
Tommy and his pals walking in Milngavie direction. Have got a pain in my side. Pleurisy? Strained? Or what?

---

10   The Earl of Balfour was the title given to Arthur Balfour, former Prime Minister, in 1922.

11   Thomas paid £1. Between 1926 and 1935, Belgium conducted its foreign exchange in the belga (rather than the domestic franc), at a fixed rate of 35 belgas to £1 sterling.

12   The museum was in the lower part of Mosesfield House.

Wednesday, 26 March
Tommy at St Andrew's Hall tonight, listening to the Orpheus Choir.[13]
Agnes and I went to the Majestic and saw *The Manxman*.[14]

Thursday, 27 March
Agnes at Knightswood in the afternoon. Brought home word that
my uncle, Joe Webb, is no more.

Tuesday, 1 April
Agnes very vigorous tonight. Sort of spring cleaning the room and
washing the stairs.

Wednesday, 2 April
Agnes at the Waverley Picture House in the afternoon with Mrs
Carmichael. Tommy and McLennan walking out Milngavie way this
afternoon. My leg very sore and looking inflamed, so I'm concerned.

Thursday, 3 April
Leg still very sore, so went to the doctor at night. He thinks it is
some skin irritation and gives me a prescription for some juice to
rub on the afflicted member. By this time, the chemists were all
shut, so Tommy went into town, to the ever-open Boots. As it was
to be made up, he came home and then went back for it. Rubbed
my naughty leg with same and hope for the best.

Friday, 4 April
Leg feels easier. Agnes not pleased generally with me. Very sad.

Saturday, 5 April
Got letter from Poland.

Sunday, 6 April

---

13   The Orpheus Choir, conducted by Hugh Roberton, operated from 1906 until his
retirement in 1951. It gained a worldwide reputation for the quality of its singing and
the inventiveness of its repertoire.

14   *The Manxman* (1929) was the last silent film directed by Alfred Hitchcock. It was
based on a romantic novel by Hall Caine, and starred Carl Brisson and Malcolm
Keen.

Monday, 7 April

Tommy at Leiper to see about some doubtful teeth, and arranged to get a pair stopped.[15] Tommy went to Theatre Royal and saw some opera stuff – *Tannhäuser*.[16]

Wednesday, 9 April

I went round and saw doctor re leg. It seems all right now.
Tommy's pal Geddes here at night.

Thursday, 10 April

Tommy at the dentist forenoon, and got tooth number one stopped.

Friday, 11 April

Got word from Partick that Lily is a ma again.

Saturday, 12 April

Mrs Jameson wakened us this morning to tell us about some tram smash in Partick.[17] Foolish woman. I wrote to Warsaw.

Monday, 14 April

Agnes saw factor this morning re sweeping of lum. He offered her a house in Bolton Drive, which our financial circumstances do not permit us to accept.

Tuesday, 15 April

Tommy down at Leiper and got another tooth stopped, and last one polished.

Wednesday, 16 April

Tommy starts university today. He is cycling there now.

Thursday, 17 April

The sweep here this forenoon and swept the lum.

Friday, 18 April

Agnes smashed a big pot which contained an aspidistra. This is Good Friday.

---

15   Tommy is to have fillings in two of his teeth.

16   *Tannhäuser* is an opera in three acts by Richard Wagner. It was first performed in Dresden in 1845.

17   One person died and fifty-nine were injured when a tramcar filled with passengers jumped the rails at Dumbarton Road and Primrose Street, Whiteinch, ran across the street and fell into a shop.

Saturday, 19 April

I am on holiday today. Spent it in the scullery. Painted the roof white and the sides light brown.

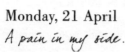

Sunday, 20 April

Feeling stiff and sore.

Monday, 21 April

A pain in my side.

Tuesday, 22 April

My side or back not any better.

Wednesday, 23 April

Side very sore this morning. Evidently I have dislocated my entire spinal column.

Thursday, 24 April

Side very sore yet.

Friday, 25 April

Side very sore. Old Mrs Hepburn across the road is dead.

Saturday, 26 April

My side seemed sorer than ever this morning. I went to the doctor at night. He says it is a strain, and will take its time.

Sunday, 27 April

Feel much better. Agnes' back is sore.

Wednesday, 30 April

Agnes seeing Hetty Mossman in the afternoon. At night I went to Queen's Park and watched football.

Monday, 5 May

Agnes spent the evening in the wash house and I watched football at Queen's Park.

Tuesday, 6 May
Agnes in the wash house all day. I wasted the evening watching football. It was a little cold.

Thursday, 8 May
Kenneth MacPherson up in the afternoon.

Monday, 12 May
Invested in a sand glass to enable Agnes to boil eggs. Agnes getting ready for spring cleaning. My gum is sore.

Wednesday, 14 May
Tommy got his English certificate, First Class, and passed with distinction.

Thursday, 15 May
Prize day at the university. Tommy brought home eight volumes. Third prize for English (five volumes), fourth prize for Latin (two volumes), special prize for Latin (one volume), also Latin Certificate passed with distinction etc. He has done wonderfully well. Agnes and I go to the pictures at night.

Friday, 16 May
Got bill from Dr Gray for 25/-, this for doing away with my varicose veins.

Saturday, 17 May
Rained in a solid, painstaking way from dinnertime.

Friday, 23 May
Tommy sat his first degree examination today (History).

Tuesday, 27 May
Tommy sat his English examination today. Mrs Carmichael here in afternoon. Agnes went to Ibrox tonight.

Wednesday, 28 May
At Paisley today on business, so dropped in and saw Etta for a little.

Sunday, 1 June
Tommy and I out after dinner by old Cathcart. Did not feel well coming home. Think my best days are over. Agnes not in very good form, which depresses me greatly.

1930

Wed. Thur. 15 May

Some heavy showers
Prize day at the university.

Tommy bought home 8 volumes.
3rd Prize for English (5 volumes)
4 " " Latin 2 "
special " " 1 "
also latin certificate passed
with distinction etc.
He has done wonderfully
well. Agnes & I go
to the Pictures at
night. Got the clock
to go once more.

Tuesday, 3 June

Great heat today, and brilliant sunshine. After tea, I walked out to
Overtoun Park via King's Park, and climbed on to the railway at
Croftfoot, then along the line into King's Park. My foot very sore.

Wednesday, 4 June

This is my birthday, so Agnes and Tommy into town this afternoon,
where Tommy got a new hat.

Saturday, 7 June

After tea, we all at Overtoun Park, via bus to King's Park. Walked
a bit of Croftfoot Road, then cut into Castlemilk Road. Saw Jean
MacKenzie's new house there, so we went and inspected it. Of
course, we were asked in.

Monday, 9 June

Rained all day. Agnes in wash house all day. The usual
combination.

Tuesday, 10 June

On this day, exactly 20 years ago, Agnes and I got married. When
I got home at tea time, Josephine, Lily, Ian and the new baby had
arrived. John (Lily's man) arrived later on. I played some of the
old tunes on the piano, which pleased Josephine.

Saturday, 14 June

See by the *Herald* that Tommy has passed his History examination.

Monday, 16 June

I wrote to Rothesay and fixed for the house, 65/- per week.

Tuesday, 17 June

Kenneth MacPherson up tonight. Tommy has passed his Latin
examination.

Wednesday, 18 June

Agnes and I went and saw all the fun of the fair at Myrtle Park. A
show on there.

Thursday, 19 June

Tommy has passed his English exam, so that's the lot. Good lad.

Friday, 20 June

Ella Carlyle here at night. Kenneth MacP dropped in about
9 o'clock to see Tommy about Ben Lomond. They intend climbing
it tomorrow. He took supper with us.

Saturday, 21 June
Fine day up till tea time, then rain in buckets. Tommy left here before me in the morning. He got to Ben Lomond all right. Home 10.15 p.m., very wet indeed but very sunburnt.

Tuesday, 24 June
It being a nice night, I took a walk to Rutherglen. Met an old school mate, James Murray. He is church officer in the parish kirk. We went in, looked it all over, and I tried my hand at the organ.

Wednesday, 25 June
At night, Tommy and I to Ruglen, dropped into the library and had a crack with my old friend James Mackie.

Friday, 27 June
After tea, Tommy and I putted in Maxwell Park. I won. Agnes ill and depressed at night.

Tuesday, 1 July
Agnes went and got her eyes tested for new glasses.

Thursday, 3 July
Agnes got her specs tonight. 12/6.

Wednesday, 9 July
Tommy at Theatre Royal tonight seeing a Shaw play.[18] I cleaned room windows. Got a snap brim hat today.

Saturday, 12 July
Brilliant day of sunshine. Tommy and I at Queen's Park in afternoon and had a great view. We all at Linn Park after tea. Jamieson house, next door to us, was burgled in our absence. Great excitement.

Sunday, 13 July
Two gentlemen from the CID interviewed me this morning re the burglary. I was not arrested. Maud and Duncan arrived before dinner. After that function, we took car to Killermont. Tommy stayed in. Ella Carlyle in when we got home.

Friday, 18 July
This is Fair Friday, so I was away at 12.30. Nice sunny afternoon. Tommy and I at the Art Galleries.

---

18   George Bernard Shaw was an Irish playwright.

Sunday, 20 July
Big fall of soot all over the floor this morning, which made Agnes weep. What a mess. After tea, Agnes and I took the bus to Botanic Gardens.

Monday, 21 July
Dull, cool day. Holiday. We all took bus to Mugdock and had a nice walk.

Tuesday, 22 July
Lizzie Campbell up in forenoon telling Agnes of death of one of Nin's sisters. After tea, Agnes went to Ibrox. No one in, so she went to Mrs Cowie.

Friday, 25 July
Dull, cloudy day. Tommy got spill on his bike. Bandaged him up in several places.

Saturday, 26 July
Better day. A shower or two. Went to the Art Galleries in the afternoon. Nicolson up for a minute or two at night to see how Tommy was after his accident.

Wednesday, 30 July
Nice night. Tommy and I out to Mount Florida. His hands are very sore-looking.

Thursday, 31 July
Agnes at the Majestic. Now a talkie.

Tuesday, 5 August
Nice sunny night. Tommy and I at Carmunnock Road, Croftfoot and King's Park.

Thursday, 7 August
Agnes met me at 5 p.m. and then we went and got waterproofs. Agnes' has to be made, and will be ready in time for the holidays. Mine has to be altered slightly, and will be ready tomorrow. Very nice night, so I went to the Queen's Park and watched various football matches.

Friday, 8 August
Weather cool and unsettled. Some rain. Tommy and I out at Cathcart. We had a crack with Mrs King (Florrie Peden) and her man. Got a couple of cigars and a rose from her. My waterproof delivered today.

Saturday, 9 August
Isa and her two wee girls here. The smallest is the nicest
baby I've ever seen.

Sunday, 10 August
*Showery day. After tea I put on my new coat
and took Tommy to Ruglen via Tory Glen and
home by King's Park. Met John Steel and had
a crack with him. Have not seen him for over 30
years. He was in my class at school.*

Tuesday, 12 August
Agnes getting a fevered rush now.[19] Nin Henderson's wife
dropped in at night and wasted a few hours of Agnes' valuable
time. She was duly cursed.

Wednesday, 13 August
Arranged with railway company to lift hamper.

Thursday, 14 August
Hamper lifted at dinner time. Agnes' coat not yet arrived. We are
annoyed.

Saturday, 16 August
Nice sunny day. Hurrah! We are off. Agnes and Tommy off to
Rothesay by 10.30 train. I managed by the 1.10 train, via Wemyss
Bay. Beautiful sunny day. Had our tea in a tearoom there, then
had a general look round.

Sunday, 17 August
Fine sunny day. After dinner, we all at Craigmore. After tea, all at
Port Bannatyne.

Monday, 18 August
Rainy day. Tommy and I visited the wee museum. After dinner, we
took bus to Kerrycroy then walked back to Bogany then bus.

Tuesday, 19 August
Rained all day mostly. Tommy and I walked to Ettrick Bay. In
afternoon we all walked to Kerrycroy via Loch Ascog. At night we
went to the Palace to get dry.

---

19   Agnes was packing for the family holiday.

Wednesday, 20 August

Nice day. Tommy and I walked to the end of Loch Fad and across the moor to Kerrycroy. In the afternoon we all at Port Bannatyne, putted then went out in a boat. Agnes did not enjoy the boat. It made her giddy.

Thursday, 21 August

Discovered plate of my teeth cracked. Phoned dentist. Rained all day.

Friday, 22 August

We took a sail to the Kyles. A lovely sail. We got off for an hour, left the boat at Tighnabruich and rejoined it at Auchenlochan. After tea, we took a turn round Rothesay and were speaking to Frank Ruth and Nell. We got 'chips' for our supper from Miss Irvine.

Saturday, 23 August

Fine, sunny forenoon. Tommy and I meandered over to Port Bannatyne, went out in a boat, then putted. We played cards with landlady at night.

Sunday, 24 August

We all at church. After dinner, I over the Chapel Hill direction.

Monday, 25 August

Fine forenoon. Tommy and I climbed the Barone Hill. We all at Kilchattan Bay after dinner. Pouring wet night. We played Ludo with Nancy.

Tuesday, 26 August

Dull and warm. Tommy and I boated in Rothesay Bay. Turned out a great day of sunshine. We did the Knocknicoll Wood walk. After tea, we took Nancy to the Palace.

Thursday, 28 August

Very hot day. Tommy and I for a brace of hours in a boat at Port Bannatyne. Tommy did a bathe. After dinner, we did the 2.30 p.m. sail to Loch Long. We got an hour ashore at Largs. Some very heavy rain on sail back.

Friday, 29 August

After tea, we went out and saw the procession. When it got dark, we watched the illuminations and fireworks. Such excitement. Arranged with a porter to call and lift our hamper tomorrow.

Saturday, 30 August
Dull, gloomy day. So are our spirits. We all departed by 10.35
Wemyss Bay boat. When we got to Central, found our hamper not
on same train. Not in next train either, so home we went. After
some dinner, Tommy and I got our hamper in the Left Luggage
Department. Took it home in a taxi. The pirate charged us 4/6.
Mrs Carmichael dropped in at a late hour and had supper with us.
I saw her home.

Monday, 1 September
At work again. Paid the gas bill. Went down to Leiper at night with
my disabled teeth.

Tuesday, 2 September
Went down to Leiper and got my teeth. Renovated and in full
working order.

Thursday, 4 September
Got some very bad news from Knightswood. Josephine very ill.
Agnes and I went at night, but she was practically unconscious.

Friday, 5 September
Agnes went to Knightswood afternoon. I went after tea. Josephine
unconscious, and the end very near. Duncan wired for Mary
through from Edinburgh.

Saturday, 6 September
Worked in the afternoon. Duncan dropped in and gave me the
sad news. Josephine died at noon. I soon quit work. After tea,
Agnes, Duncan and I went to Knightswood. Tommy already there. I
phoned a telegraph to Tom Carlyle about the funeral. We got home
about 11.30. Duncan is staying with us till it is all over.

Monday, 8 September
Warm, sunny day. Stopped work about 12. Home for dinner, then
Agnes, Tommy and I to Knightswood. Duncan had gone earlier
in the day. The funeral left 3 p.m. and proceeded to Riddrie
Cemetery. Donald was buried there in 1916. This ends a tragic
married and widowed life.

Tuesday, 9 September
Duncan and Tommy took a run out to Knightswood before dinner.
Duncan left for Belfast in the afternoon. He gave Tommy a ten
shilling note. I don't feel very well.

Monday, 15 September

Fine sunny day. Agnes enjoyed it in the wash house. The
Shamrock getting licked.[20]

Friday, 19 September

The man next door showed me his valve set.

Tuesday, 23 September

*Agnes in town and got a new fur affair to
go round her neck. Mrs Carmichael and Peggy
up about 6 o'clock to see a wedding from
our window. Wrote Mary re our forthcoming
Edinburgh visit. The skin is peeling off my big
toe. Very peculiar.*

Friday, 26 September

*Feel as if my recently mended dentures
were bust again.*

Saturday, 27 September

Met Agnes and Tommy in Central Station and got the 1 p.m. train
to Edinburgh. Tom Carlyle met us there, then we got the car to
Mary's house. Tommy Carlyle home for a short visit, so we saw
him. Met Dorothy. Last time I saw her she was in her crib, 18
years ago. She is a nice little girl. Tom Carlyle, Dorothy and I
went to the Astoria Picture House.[21]

Sunday, 28 September

Nice sunny day. After breakfast, Tommy and I walked into
Edinburgh. Went up to the War Memorial (too early). We then
went to Holyrood (too early), then to the Scott Monument (shut).
After dinner, we all had a fine walk through Corstorphine Park,
which is a great place.

Monday, 29 September

Another fine day. Tommy and I rushed out after breakfast, went to
the War Memorial and Castle, then the art galleries, then climbed
the Scott Monument. It was so packed, we could not get out on the
top balcony. After dinner, Tommy and I sallied out again. We went
to Calton Hill and climbed to the top of the Nelson Monument.

---

20   Sir Thomas Lipton's fifth and final attempt to win the America's Cup, in *Shamrock
     V*, was not going well.

21   The Astoria, in Manse Road, Corstorphine, opened in 1930. It closed in 1974 and was
     replaced by a supermarket.

We then had a look round the Old Calton Burying Ground. We had a great view from the Nelson Monument. We next went into the National Portrait Gallery and Museum. After tea, we amused ourselves with music and cards. Got a lot of stamps from Tommy Carlyle.

Tuesday, 30 September
Agnes and Tommy not coming home till tea time, so I left myself by 8.50 train. Tom Carlyle saw me off. And so ends our Edinburgh weekend, and I enjoyed it fine.

Friday, 3 October
Went down to Leiper LDS and arranged to send my teeth down on Monday for repairs. Have got a sore throat. Agnes got me a bottle of cod liver oil to put the breath of life into me again. Agnes got a lump in her neck, which gives us both some worry.

Saturday, 4 October
Agnes at doctor about her neck. He says the gland is swollen, which was evident. He thinks it will go away. Wait and see.

Sunday, 5 October
We all at the Candlish Memorial Church this morning. British airship R101 wrecked in France. 47 lives lost.[22]

Monday, 6 October
Tommy took my teeth down to Leiper this morning, and I went in at night and brought them home.

Wednesday, 8 October
Another death in the R101 disaster, making the total death toll 48.

Saturday, 11 October
After tea, Agnes and I went to the Candlish Memorial Church and booked three seats for the month for 5/6 each.

Sunday, 12 October
We all at church and filled up our new seat. After the service, Agnes and I interviewed the minister, gave him our lines, and told him to carry on.

Monday, 13 October
Tommy resumes his studies at the university.

---

22 The R101, a British rigid airship, crashed near Beauvais in France on its maiden overseas voyage, killing 48 people.

1930

Sunday   5 Oct.

Heavy rain at times
           We all at the
           Candlish memorial
           church this
              morning.
           after dinner
              agnes took
           a run out
           to see Hetty
           mossman.
              one of the
           small Dunns
Came to the door to buy
Candy apples   no sale.
         British airship R101
wrecked in france
47 lives lost.
my throat not yet better.

L⁰
WORTH
OF
CANDY
APPLES,
PLEASE

Tuesday, 21 October
My mended teeth not feeling very comfortable. I went down to Leiper and got him to alter the jaggy portion. Came home feeling more comfortable.

Wednesday, 22 October
Isa here when I got home, with wee Kathleen and Helen. Gordon and Hetty Mossman dropped in about 8 p.m.

Thursday, 23 October
Put some artistic work in Ella Carlyle's album.[23]

Friday, 24 October

Tommy got some suitable garb for the boating club he has joined, in connection with the university.[24] He is going to row boats up and down the Clyde. Nancy Irvine (from Rothesay) dropped in to see us at dinner time.

Saturday, 25 October
Tommy at his first boat practice in forenoon.

Sunday, 26 October
We all at church.

Thursday, 30 October
Soot very much in evidence this morning. Agnes moaned and I wrote the factor. Minister up this afternoon with the Communion cards.

Friday, 31 October
Got an affair from Mrs Dunn, made by her man, evidently called a buzzer. You fit it over the fire at night, and no soot comes out. Perhaps you can also use it as a fire tickler. A very ingenious affair.

Saturday, 1 November
Tommy at his boating and Agnes and I at the Majestic.

Sunday, 2 November
Agnes and I at Communion this morning.

---

23   Ella has evidently loaned Thomas her album – probably a book of her family and friends' signatures and comments – for him to add some of his cartoons.

24   Glasgow University Boat Club, which was founded in 1867, has its own boathouse on the River Clyde at Glasgow Green.

Tuesday, 4 November
Agnes and I voted in the municipal elections. Mrs Dunn stopped in at night with another gadget for the fire. An affair to balance pots etc on the fire. Very good indeed.

Wednesday, 5 November
Man up examining the lum.

Friday, 7 November
My specs have a broken leg, so I left them with Ferguson for surgical treatment.

Saturday, 8 November
Agnes and I went to Majestic at night. Called in at Ferguson on our way home and got my specs. The little job cost 1/9.

Monday, 10 November
Agnes celebrates her birthday in the wash house.

Tuesday, 11 November
I did my two minutes' silence at Jamaica Street corner at 11 a.m.

Wednesday, 12 November
Our new chimney can put on this afternoon. It was a sooty job. Agnes at an affair at St Andrew's Hall at night. She came home fed up and disgusted. The lum to blame.

Thursday, 13 November
Very stormy day. The new lum drawing very well indeed, and burning huge amounts of coal.

Saturday, 15 November
Great excitement next door about 10 p.m. The wee chap Stevenson bleeding at nose all day. I rushing about looking for a doctor. Got Dr Gray by phone. He arrived about 11.30 p.m. We then settled down.

Sunday, 23 November
None of us at church in the morning, but Agnes went at night. In the afternoon I walked King's Park, Croftfoot Road, Burnside and bus home.

Monday, 24 November
The generous Glasgow Corporation (Gas Department) offer to sell us our gas fire for 8/-.

Wednesday, 26 November
Tommy boating in afternoon and dialecting at night.

Saturday, 29 November
Tommy boated as usual. Agnes and I at Majestic as usual.

Monday, 1 December

General Coal Strike begins in Scotland today.
Started to wear garters. 'Honi soit qui mal etc
etc'.[25] Agnes in at gas company and gave them
8/-. The gas fire is now our own. I can now
spit in it if I want to.

Saturday, 6 December

Agnes dropped an egg and the sand
glass on the hearth this morning. They
broke. Coal strike over.

Sunday, 7 December
Tommy went to the University Chapel with
Nicolson. Agnes and I did not go to church. Death
fog in Belgium causes death of 60–70 people.[26]

Friday, 12 December
My garters scarring me, so I left them off forever. Tommy got a
holiday, but went to the 'Union', as Baldwin was doing something
to it.[27]

Saturday, 13 December
Agnes and I at the Majestic at night and saw *Rio Rita*.[28]

Sunday, 14 December
Went to church all by myself. After dinner, I took a walk out old
Cathcart way. Went in and saw Mrs King and had a cup of tea
there.

---

25   The motto of the Most Noble Order of the Garter is 'honi soit qui mal y pense'
     ('shame on him who thinks evil').

26   Smog lying in the narrow industrial valley of the Meuse killed 60 people. A
     commission of enquiry established that sulphur dioxide and sulphuric acid in the
     smog were to blame.

27   Stanley Baldwin, the Rector of Glasgow University, was officially opening the new
     Glasgow University Union building in University Avenue.

28   *Rio Rita* (1929) was an RKO Pictures musical comedy directed by Luther Reed and
     starring Bebe Daniels and John Boles.

Tuesday, 16 December

As we are going to put spring blinds up in the room, I dropped into a certain joiner and got a certain necessary piece of wood for three pence. Took down the old blind fixtures at night.

Wednesday, 17 December

Listened at night to Beethoven's great Mass in D.[29]

Thursday, 18 December

Put up the new blind fixtures in room. Man up today to overhaul gas fire.

Friday, 19 December

Man up today and finished overhauling the gas fire. Put certain improvements thereon. He also (for 2/6) put a gadget in kitchen to connect up the gas iron. Listened to the *Messiah* tonight.[30]

Saturday, 20 December

Got letter from New Zealand. Tommy composed a poem which is in today's *News*.[31]

Monday, 22 December

Addressed Christmas cards at night.

Wednesday, 24 December

Parcel from Duncan. Tobacco for me and 5/- for Tommy.

Thursday, 25 December

This being Christmas, I have got a holiday. Parcel arrived from Maud for Agnes. Looks like a big tea cosy, but it isn't. At night we went to the Majestic and Tommy came with us. The large picture was *Blackmail*.[32]

Friday, 26 December

Tommy at Partick in forenoon with gifts for the wee Martins. In the afternoon he went to Knightswood with likewise for the wee Archibalds. I got my hair cut so that I will be tidy for the New Year.

---

29   Op. 123, *Missa Solemnis*.

30   George Frideric Handel, *Messiah* (HWV 56).

31   The *Glasgow Evening News*.

32   *Blackmail* (1929) was a thriller directed by Alfred Hitchcock and starring Anny Ondra and John Longden.

Saturday, 27 December

Mrs Carmichael up in afternoon and gave Agnes a woollen sort of jacket. Agnes made the New Year wine (ginger).

Monday, 29 December

Got two ties today, one from Agnes and one from Tommy. Isa dropped in. She gave Agnes a pair of stockings and a religious calendar from Lily.

Wednesday, 31 December

Got away from business at 2 p.m. Agnes over at the Cowies' for a brace of hours at night.

1931

For the Livingstone household, the year seemed much like any other recent one, but there were persistent clues that the economy was stagnating and that a great depression was beginning. From the nine liners parked off Rothesay and Port Bannatyne to the unemployment riots, and from work being suspended on Hull No. 534 in John Brown's to Tommy's observation that 'business is at a standstill', the clues were all there. Britain leaving the Gold Standard and the split in the Labour Party over how to respond to declining economic conditions all pointed in the same direction. However, Tommy and his family still had their annual holiday, and continued to spend money on new furniture and clothes. Illness dogged their progress, as ever, and Tommy continued to claim the glittering prizes.

Thursday, 1 January

A Happy New Year to ye all. We first footed the Carmichaels at
the correct moment this morning. We arrived back 4 a.m. A day of
frost and fog. Big Welsh coal strike starts today, and it so cold. We
all went to the Majestic at night and saw *The Love Parade*.[1] Agnes
'wabbed oot' at night.[2]

Friday, 2 January

Still on holiday. Fine cold, dry day. Took a walk out to Ruglen
in the afternoon. Went into library and thought to go into the
museum, but it was shut, so home I came. After tea, Agnes and I
went to King's Park. We thought to visit the Mossmans, but they
were out, so home we came again.

Saturday, 3 January

Started my work again, as my holidays are finished. Marshal Joffre
dead.[3] Smash on the Edinburgh to London (LMS) line: three
killed.[4]

Wednesday, 7 January

Ella Carlyle here when I came home at tea time.

Friday, 9 January

Agnes did some washing at night, and I assisted by 'cawing' the
wringer.[5]

Sunday, 11 January

At night, Agnes and I went to King's Park. We got in this time.
Gordon has a new valve set, so we heard 50 stations or so. Feel
my neck sore, coming out in an eruption.

Monday, 12 January

My neck very sore, and a fearsome rash has developed. Wrote to
Duncan.

Tuesday, 13 January

All busy at night fashioning Tommy's KKK garb.[6] My neck very sore.

1   *The Love Parade* (1929) was a Paramount Pictures musical comedy directed by
     Ernst Lubitsch and starring Maurice Chevalier and Jeanette MacDonald.

2   Agnes was exhausted.

3   Joseph Jacques Césaire Joffre commanded the French forces between 1914 and 1916,
     and was then appointed Marshal of France.

4   An express passenger train was derailed just north of Carlisle, killing three people and
     injuring thirty-five.

5   Thomas was turning the handle of the wringer.

6   The Ku Klux Klan is an American white supremacist group, founded in 1865.

Wednesday, 14 January
Neck seems a wee bit easier now. All busy at night with the KKK.

Thursday, 15 January
The KKK garb now finished, except for the pictures on it. My neck improving.

Friday, 16 January
Tommy finished the pictures on his KKK.

Saturday, 17 January

Bright, cold day. Tommy out collecting coins for charity? He came home at tea time a tired wee boy.

Sunday, 18 January
Agnes and I at church. This is Communion. Agnes and Tommy at church tonight, hearing the *Messiah*. I, being bad, did not go.

Monday, 19 January
Tommy helped to collect £15,000 on Saturday last.

Tuesday, 20 January
Tommy got a cheque for 5/- from the *Evening News* for his poem. They do not overpay. I took a turn out to Knightswood at night, and brought home Father's box with most of his diaries. Isa half-dead with the cold.

Wednesday, 21 January
Am just a wee suspicious I may have the cold.

Thursday, 22 January
Am almost sure I have the cold. My nose ran and ran all day in a most distressing manner. I forgive you, Isa. Tommy seems to have a touch of the same disease. Agnes in the wash house, being strong and healthy.

Friday, 23 January
Stayed in bed till tea time. Tommy did not go to the university. I feel not so bad at night. Rain today.

---

7   Tommy has chosen to dress in a fancy-dress version of a Ku Klux Klan uniform. At the time, this would not have seemed as inappropriate and offensive as it does in the present.

Saturday, 24 January
Wet cold day. Kept my bed till dinner time. Tommy did not go to see his boat. Wee female Cowie up in the afternoon with some literature for Agnes. Agnes says: 'I'm taking the cold.'

Sunday, 25 January
Cold, windy and wet. I went out in the afternoon to see if I was sort of well. I managed all right.

Monday, 26 January
I have got a very sore nose and lip with the cold. Went to my work. Cold day, sleet in morning and frost at night. Agnes seems to be taking the cold very badly at night.

Wednesday, 28 January
Got a letter from Duncan. Also from Isa, with a photograph. My cold bad in forenoon, but improved at night.

Friday, 30 January
Tommy's books threaten to over-run the entire house, so Agnes got two boxes from the grocer, which I have to make into a bookcase (some day). Saw a golden wedding in the paper of an old Sunday School teacher of mine (Mr Delaney), so I wrote him a nice wee letter. Agnes still spluttering with the cold.

Saturday, 31 January
We all went to see Lily and family at Partick about 5.30 p.m. They have or had the flu.

Monday, 2 February
At night Bessy Percy up for Agnes and they went to the Guild. Tommy went to Newlands, and I sat in myself in comfortable misery. Paid rent today.

Tuesday, 3 February
Big earthquake disaster in New Zealand. Napier destroyed.[8]

Wednesday, 4 February
Agnes annoyed with my evil pipe and my neglect of duty with the ash pan.

---

8   The 1931 Hawke's Bay earthquake, also known as the Napier earthquake, killed 256 people and devastated the Hawke's Bay region on the east coast of North Island.

Friday, 6 February

Agnes awoke at this morning about 3 o'clock shaking and
shivering, hot and cold, and in a bad way generally. Gave her a
wee drop of whisky and a hot water bottle. She seemed very ill.
I phoned for the doctor when I went to my work. He duly came
– bad case of the flu and gave her powders. Tommy stayed in
and washed the floor etc. Mrs MacKenzie made the dinner. Isa
here at night.

Saturday, 7 February

Doctor up in afternoon. Agnes' temperature normal now, and much
better. She may get up a little tomorrow. Mrs Carmichael made the
dinner today. After tea, I went round to the doctor and got a bottle
for Agnes, and a collar (not from the doctor) for Tommy. Bought
myself a new pipe today. Lily here at night. Agnes quite cheery
tonight.

Sunday, 8 February

Agnes woke up about 5 a.m. with an awful headache and fits of
sweating etc. I did what I could, and gave her castor oil. It left
her sick all forenoon. Tommy and I, after much travail, produced
a poached egg, but she vomited like unto the bile, so she ate
nowt. Mrs Carmichael in for a little, likewise Mrs Jameson. Agnes
seemed a little easier at night.

Monday, 9 February

Agnes seems a little bit easier today. Got up at night to get her
bed made. Mrs Carmichael, Jameson and MacKenzie all here in
forenoon. Mrs Carmichael made the dinner and Agnes ate a tiny
wee portion. Nan Gordon came here at night. Agnes turned very
bad at night with her head, and in a helpless condition generally.

Wednesday, 11 February

Agnes had another very bad night with her head, so I phoned the
doctor in the morning. He duly came, gave her more powders,
and said it was flu and neuritis.[9] Mrs Carmichael again made the
dinner. Agnes feels a wee bit better again.

Thursday, 12 February

Agnes got a sleep during the night. Mrs Carmichael made the
dinner. She up at tea time and retired about 10 p.m. Ella Carlyle
here tonight.

---

9   'Neuritis' is a general term for the inflammation of a nerve or of the peripheral nervous
     system.

Friday, 13 February
Mrs Carmichael made the dinner. Nan Gordon here. At night,
she made Tommy's bed. I cleaned room windows and washed
32 collars. Tommy washed the floor and took the mats down and
shook them. Agnes up tonight on or about 7.15 p.m.

Saturday, 14 February
Doctor up today and is quite pleased with Agnes' progress.
Have to give her Epsom salts.[10] Agnes in a very depressed and
miserable state, but got up at night and took a good whack of
Epsom salts. Mrs Carmichael, Mrs Cowie and Mrs Jameson all
here in the afternoon. Mrs Cowie left Agnes some grapes. Tommy
and I, after Agnes had done a specimen, ironed the 32 collars, so
that will do us for a week or two.

Sunday, 15 February
Tommy went to church this morning. I tidied up generally in my
inefficient way. Agnes does not feel well and is scared to death.
Gave her another large dose of salts. Agnes made the tea. The
salts took effect. Feeling somewhat relieved, I went down to Ibrox
to see Agnes' uncle, who is not very well.

Monday, 16 February
Agnes very drowsy all day, and did not rise till after tea. Mrs Jameson
and Mrs Stevenson both here in the forenoon, and Mrs Cowie and
Mrs Carmichael in the afternoon. Got a letter from Warsaw.

Thursday, 19 February
I went out at night and left the order with the grocer, and brought
in oranges and lemons.

Friday, 20 February
Agnes made the dinner, and feels a wee bit better. I went round to
the doctor and got her bottle renewed. Mrs Jameson in for an hour
in the afternoon. Mrs Carmichael dropped in after tea time.

Saturday, 21 February
Went to my work this morning in a snow blizzard. Washed the kitchen
floor in the afternoon, then went for a bath. Agnes up and about.

Sunday, 22 February
Went to church myself this morning. Agnes up before dinner and
not so bad. Feeling fed up with the kitchen, she sat in the room
for a while. Ella Carlyle here at night.

---

10   Epsom salts (magnesium sulphate) are commonly used as a saline laxative.

Monday, 23 February

Agnes up all day. She did some washing, such as dishes and hankies. Mrs Jameson in for an hour or so in forenoon, Mrs Carmichael also. Mrs Cowie here in the afternoon. We discussed the possibilities of getting a new bookcase. The two boxes for this job may not do. Dame Melba dead.[11]

Tuesday, 24 February

Agnes got up after breakfast, and washed the dishes etc. Took a run down at night to my dentist. Paid him all I owed him, which came to 10/-, which was not much for the work done.

Wednesday, 25 February

Agnes out for the first time this afternoon. Mrs Carmichael went with her. The lady from the church here at night. Told Agnes that the minister is leaving, which I was very sorry to hear, as I rather liked the good man. A man cleaned our windows today.

Thursday, 26 February

Agnes went into town and looked at a cabinet, priced 26/9. She thought it would do all right as a bookcase, so ordered it to be delivered to our address at once, if not sooner.

Friday, 27 February

The cabinet or press or bookcase arrived this afternoon.. We wonder now where to put the blinking thing. Agnes got a wife to wash the stairs at night.

Saturday, 28 February

Agnes went into town in the afternoon. She got half a dozen stainless knives to give to Mrs Carmichael as a little mark of appreciation. Agnes still pretty weak, and sickish. Lily here at night.

Monday, 2 March

Agnes up all day and a wee better. She went out in the afternoon, had a cup of tea with Mrs Carmichael and gave her the 'little minding'. Paid my wireless licence today, AD 995889, to conform with Wireless Telegraphy Acts, 1904–1926.

Wednesday, 4 March

Wrote Buenos Aires.

---

11   Dame Nellie Melba was an Australian opera soprano.

Saturday, 7 March

Agnes washed the floor herself today. We spent the afternoon putting the new bookcase into the lobby, and the big clock in the kitchen.

Tuesday, 10 March

Had a cut on my finger. Put iodine on it. It turned out to be corn cure and it made me jump.

Wednesday, 11 March

Agnes and I at Majestic. *High Society Blues*.[12] Agnes cleaned the kitchen windows. She is getting on. Tommy lifted £20 bursary money due to him today.

Saturday, 14 March

Heard the Prince of Wales from Buenos Aires.[13]

Sunday, 15 March

We all at morning church. Agnes at Ibrox tonight. Ella very ill. Nannie's gentleman friend was there. Finished reading Pa's diaries. Made me melancholy.

Tuesday, 17 March

At night, Agnes and I went to the Majestic. *Common Clay*.[14]

Thursday, 19 March

Bought an enormous pipe.

Saturday, 21 March

International – Scotland 28, England 19. Rugby, of course.[15] I listened in to it. Wrote Mary. CPR liner ashore on Wee Cumbrae.[16]

---

12 *High Society Blues* (1930) was a 20th Century Fox musical romance directed by David Butler and starring Janet Gaynor and Charles Farrell.

13 Edward, Prince of Wales, was the son of King George V. He was later King Edward VIII and then Duke of Windsor. Prince Edward and his brother Prince George opened the British Empire Trade Exhibition during their visit to Buenos Aires.

14 *Common Clay* (1930) was a drama directed by Victor Fleming and starring Constance Bennett and Lew Ayres.

15 Scotland were playing England in the 1931 Five Nations Championship at Murrayfield.

16 The Canadian Pacific liner *Montclaire* ran ashore on the south of Little Cumbrae in the Clyde in fog and bad weather. The passengers were taken by the ship's boats to Largs, and the liner, which had been built at John Brown's in Clydebank in 1921, was refloated at high tide the next day.

Sunday, 22 March

All at church today. Agnes baked an apple cake, then she and I had a walk. Nice spring-like day and quite mild. Railway smash in England. LMS Railway. The Royal Scot express wrecked. Six killed.[17]

Thursday, 26 March

Agnes at a church social at night. Our minister's farewell.

Saturday, 28 March

This is the great international, so I put on the 'phones and listened in. Scotland 2, England 0. The official attendance was a record, a world record, in fact. 129,810.[18] Got a letter from Buenos Aires. Arnold Bennett, the man who writes, dead.[19]

Sunday, 29 March

Agnes and I went to church. This is Communion. In the afternoon I walked Queen's Park, Thornliebank, Giffnock and Cathcart. Total cost of walk two pence and a sore toe. Agnes not singing the 'Chum Song' with me.[20]

Monday, 30 March

Tommy went to the Athenaeum and heard a programme of very modern music. I did not go with him.

Tuesday, 31 March

Agnes in town today and bought 40 tiles to decorate the kitchen fireplace. Wrote Mary.

Wednesday, 1 April

Agnes went over to see Mrs Cowie. 1,000 killed in an earthquake in Nicaragua.[21]

---

17   The *Grenadier Guardsman*, a locomotive of the Royal Scot class, fouled the points south of Leighton station, left the line and rolled over. Six people were killed and five injured.

18   Scotland were playing England in the 1931 British Home Championship. The match was held at Hampden, a mile or so south of Thomas' house.

19   Arnold Bennett was an English novelist, best known for the Clayhanger trilogy.

20   'The Chum Song' was recorded by Jack Hylton and His Orchestra for the members of the *Daily Record* Chum Club, which children could join for sixpence. The chorus was: 'Laugh away your worries, / Don't be sad or glum; / And everyone will know / That you're a chum, chum, chum!'

21   The 1931 Nicaragua earthquake devastated Managua and killed 2,000 people.

Thursday, 2 April
I broke up the two boxes which were meant for a bookcase for firewood. A total eclipse of the moon tonight. Forgot about it, so can't give you a description of it.

Friday, 3 April
This is Good Friday, so I got away at 4 p.m.

Sunday, 5 April
This being Easter Sunday, I ate my egg in duplicate this morning. The King has got the cold and my toe is sore.

Tuesday, 7 April
Agnes went to see the factor to bite his ear in order to get our lum swept. She did not see the requisite Mr Couts, so nothing done.

Wednesday, 8 April

His Majesty King George has sub-acute bronchitis. His Royal Highness TCL has very acute toe-itis. Agnes at factor in morning and managed her point. Agnes made a bag to collect soot for the garden of Gordon Mossman.[22]

Thursday, 9 April
Got the doctor's bill this morning.

Friday, 10 April
Got the gas bill today. Let them all come.

Saturday, 11 April
The Celtic playing The Motherwell at Hampden, so the village of Govanhill did not look like a village Sunday School trip.[23] Tommy got his poem back from *Chambers'*.[24] Too good for them. So he sent it to the *News*.

Monday, 13 April
Sweep up in the morning. Agnes collected some soot for the Mossmans' garden.

---

22   Soot adds nitrogen to soil and is also an insecticide.

23   Celtic were playing Motherwell in the final of the 1930–31 Scottish Cup. The score was 2–2, and Celtic won the replay on 15 April by four goals to two.

24   *Chambers' Journal* was a popular literary magazine that specialised in serial fiction. It was founded in Edinburgh in 1832 and was published in London from 1850.

Tuesday, 14 April

Agnes and I went to the Majestic and saw *Dancing Feet* (not mine).[25] King Alfonso kicked out of Spain, and that country, where the bullfights come from, is now a republic.[26]

Thursday, 16 April

Laid the tiles in the kitchen hearth place, but don't feel very hopeful. They may stick and again they may not. My big toe feels as if it has the toothache.

Friday, 17 April

The tiles don't seem a success, some of them loose, and some others standing crooked. No, they are not nice at all. A small burglary took place at my respected place of business.

Saturday, 18 April

Got ¾ of a stone of cement, but could get no sand, so the tile job is held up in the meantime. Went to church after tea and booked three seats for six months. Fee 16/6 the lot. Agnes paid the doctor his fee.

Monday, 20 April

I went to Grangemouth today on business with the firm's motor car. I went to put the fear of death into a debtor. The debtor was not afraid. Paid gas bill today. Agnes went down Cathcart Road way and got a huge poke of sand for three pence. I can now proceed with the tile laying. After tea, I spent three hours of anguish with cement, sand and tiles. I bought a trowel in Woolworths for the job. Census paper left tonight.

Tuesday, 21 April

The tiles seem to be sticking as they were meant to do. At night, Agnes went to Mossmans' with the soot.

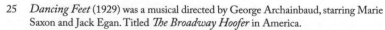

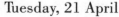

---

25 *Dancing Feet* (1929) was a musical directed by George Archainbaud, starring Marie Saxon and Jack Egan. Titled *The Broadway Hoofer* in America.

26 After republican candidates won the majority of seats in the local and municipal elections, the Second Spanish Republic was proclaimed on this date, and King Alfonso VIII fled the country but did not abdicate.

Sunday, 26 April
Filled in the census paper.

Monday, 27 April
The man lifted the census paper today.

Thursday, 30 April
Paid rent today, and at night I climbed aloft and did some whitewashing in the bathless bathroom.

Sunday, 3 May
Nice morning. Tommy and I at church. Broke my pipe on way home. Wrote to our New Zealand relation.

Monday, 4 May
A small sort of earthquake in Lancashire yesterday.[27] Took a walk to Linn Park, then helped Agnes to clean the kitchen wall paper.

Tuesday, 5 May
Got a letter from Mary re Irish Sweepstake.[28] Answered it.

Wednesday, 6 May
Bought a new pipe for 2/6. Got a letter from Duncan.

Thursday, 7 May
Got the illegal tickets from Mary, with one for myself.

Tuesday, 19 May
Tommy got his certificate for English. Passed with distinction.

Wednesday, 20 May
Tommy got first class certificates for Latin and Moral Philosophy. He got a large volume, being third prize for Latin. He is a lad of brains.

Saturday, 23 May
Johnny. Lily and the two small editions here about 4 p.m. I got into trouble with Agnes re 'grace'.

---

27   This minor event damaged hundreds of chimneys in the Pendlebury area of Manchester, and the shock was felt as far away as Bolton and Altrincham.

28   The Irish Free State Hospitals' Sweepstake was set up in 1930 to finance hospitals and medical services. The winner was determined by the results of a number of horse races. At this time, lotteries were not legal in the United Kingdom, but many people of Irish descent took part in the Irish sweepstake.

1931
Sunday 3 May

Nice morning
Tommy and
I at
church.
Agnes got a
sore head
so did not
go. Broke
my pipe
on way
home Turned out
a bleak day and
some rain.
Wrote
to our New Zealand
relation.

Sunday, 24 May

Agnes at a church at 2 p.m. with old Mrs Cowie to hear the lady minister.[29] Tommy and I cut up rhubarb in her absence. Agnes is still feeling popped about 'grace', or lack of it.

Wednesday, 27 May

Agnes in the new King's Park with Mrs Carmichael.[30]

Friday, 29 May

Warm, sunny day. Glasgow 'Civic and Empire Week' opened. The square decorated and bands every day next week.

Wednesday, 3 June

This is Derby Day, so I lost all my money, as usual. Agnes and Tommy in town. Tommy got measured for a suit, then they admired the square.

Thursday, 4 June

My birthday. Bleak, cold day. Bought a pair of shoes at 16/5.

Sunday, 7 June

We all at church and saw three christenings. After dinner, I tottered in my new shoes to the new King's Park and admired it greatly. Heard via the wireless that an earthquake had visited Britain at an early hour.[31] Earth tremors all over. My, oh my.

Wednesday, 10 June

This is the great anniversary.[32] Agnes celebrated it in the wash house. Man up at night giving an estimate for papering the drawing room, likewise putting whitewash etc on it. This depresses me.

Thursday, 11 June

Agnes in town. She bought home wallpaper for the room. Cleaned the kitchen and scullery windows. We lifted the room carpet and

---

29   This was likely to have been a United Free Church of Scotland (Continuing) congregation. The UF Church ordained women ministers in 1929, the same year that it merged with the Church of Scotland (which did not appoint a woman minister until 1969). The UF (Continuing) congregations were composed of people who opposed that union.

30   The 40 acres of land now known as King's Park (in the district of King's Park) were gifted to the people of Glasgow by Sir John Mactaggart, of the house-building firm of Mactaggart and Mickel, in 1930. It opened as a park, under the control of Glasgow Corporation, in 1931.

31   The Dogger Bank earthquake of 1931 began around 1.30 a.m. beneath the North Sea. Its effects were felt throughout Great Britain, as well as in France and Belgium.

32   Thomas and Agnes were married on this date 21 years previously.

rolled it up. We are sending it to the cleaners. Feeling thorough, I took out the frosted glass in the scullery window and cleaned it. I wounded my hand in several places thereby.

Friday, 12 June
Tommy's new suit arrived.

Sunday, 14 June
I went to church alone. Wrote to Argentina.

Monday, 15 June
Mrs Carmichael up in the afternoon. Miss McIntosh of the kirk up at night. Then Isa dropped in about 9 p.m. The carpet lifted by the cleaners today.

Wednesday, 17 June
The carpet arrived all right from the cleaners. The two painters came at night and did the paper hanging etc. We were let off with 20/-, and the paper cost about 9/- over and above this.

Friday, 19 June
The good elder up in the afternoon with our 'Mass tickets'. We got the carpet laid tonight and the room finished generally.

Tuesday, 23 June
Tommy paid his suit, which amounted to five guineas. Got a hot bath tonight.

Friday, 26 June
Tommy and I at the Cinerama seeing *Dracula*.[33] Prize day at Tommy's old school (Pollokshields), so he graced it with his presence.

Tuesday, 30 June
Agnes and Mrs Carmichael out in the afternoon at Thornliebank, looking at new houses.

Wednesday, 1 July
Lost half of my pipe on way home from work, which is very strange.

33 *Dracula* (1931) was directed by Tod Browning and starred Béla Lugosi and Helen Chandler. This was the first authorised film of the Bram Stoker book, and set the pattern for many subsequent interpretations.

Saturday, 4 July

Ella Carlyle here. After tea we all out for a walk to the Linn Park and back by Carmunnock Road, and bus from King's Park. Nice night, but a shower or two. Ella stayed with us overnight.

Sunday, 5 July

Warm, sunny day. After breakfast, Tommy and I took Ella a walk to Rutherglen, and let her see for her first time the land of her uncles etc. After dinner, Tommy saw Ella home to Stobhill.

Friday, 10 July

Tommy speculated in a pair of flannel trousers. King and Queen in Glasgow today, but I saw them not. Put domes of silence on big easy chair.[34]

Tuesday, 14 July

Agnes went away by 9.30 train this morning to look for our holiday house in Rothesay. She 'clicked'.

Wednesday, 15 July

Tommy met Duncan and Maud at Queen Street Station about 9.30. They went through to Edinburgh, and had a good day. Tommy bought a new hat.

Friday, 17 July

This is Fair Friday, so I got away at 1.45 p.m. Some heavy rain in morning, dull afternoon and very wet night.

Thursday, 23 July

Tommy ordered tonight his new Mattamac waterproof at 19/6 net, carriage paid.[35]

Friday, 24 July

Tommy took his bicycle away to be repaired. He is going to use it again. This gives Agnes and me an uneasy feeling. Foolish, no doubt, but there you are. He is going to golf now, and he has not got a motor car.

---

34 Domes of silence are rounded metal pads that are fixed to the undersides of furniture to make them easier to move around.

35 The Mattamac, sold by mail order by Pearson Brothers of London, was a 'featherweight waterproof' that could be folded and carried in a pocket.

Saturday, 25 July

Tommy got his bike. The repairs cost 2/-. We all went to the Majestic at night and saw Whoopee.[36] A pretty vulgar sort of picture.

Sunday, 26 July

Nice sunny forenoon, so after breakfast I hied me forth and had a seat in the King's Park. After tea, Tommy and I had a walk through the Queen's Park. Agnes did not go out, not being in the mood, but in a mood. A very uncomfortable sort of day at home.

Monday, 27 July

Tommy golfing in the forenoon with Nicolson. Tommy did the 18 holes in a couple of hundred or so.

Tuesday, 28 July

Tommy got his Mattamac.

Friday, 31 July

Agnes and Tommy spent the evening picking and getting ready currants for making jam (black currant jam). Paid the rent today. Paid the insurance likewise.

Tuesday, 4 August

Tommy golfing today. His score was 144. Went to Knightswood at night. Got one of my father's poem books from Isa.

Wednesday, 5 August

Heat wave continues. At night, Tommy and I had a walk over Cathkin.

Saturday, 8 August

After tea, listened in. Fine symphony concert, including the lovely 'Air on the G String'.[37]

Sunday, 9 August

Very warm, sunny day. Tommy and I went to Pollok Estate for a walk. Had a seat on the grassy path and admired the girls with their wee bowler hats. Only saw one. Tommy's birthday.

---

36   *Whoopee!* (1930) was an 'all-talking, all-colour' musical directed by Thornton Freeland and starring Eddie Cantor and Ethel Shutta. 'My Baby Just Cares for Me' was one of the hit songs from this film.

37   'Air on the G String' is a musical piece for string and piano, arranged by August Wilhemj from the Air of Johann Sebastian Bach's Orchestral Suite No. 3 in D major (BWV 1068).

Monday, 10 August
Tommy met McLennan in town in forenoon. They went to
Dumgoyne and climbed to the top.

Tuesday, 11 August
Agnes at Rouken Glen in the afternoon with Mrs Carmichael. She
left her good swish umbrella in the car, and said farewell to it. She
came home very sad. No nice umbrella for the holidays.

Wednesday, 12 August
After dinner, Agnes went to the tramway office and was overjoyed
to get back her lost umbrella. She was fined six pence. Gave the
railway company orders to lift our hamper tomorrow. We spent a
busy night packing up.

Thursday, 13 August
Isa and the two wee Archibalds here when I came home at tea
time, and us so busy getting ready for our holidays. The hamper
duly lifted.

Saturday, 15 August
This is the great day. Stopped for my holidays. So it is a double
cold, wet day. We boarded the 4.03 train for Princes Pier and got
down in great comfort.[38] Arrived at Rothesay 6.20 p.m. The house
promises to be very comfortable, and has a fine view of the pier,
and looks into the Skipper Woods from the kitchen.

Sunday, 16 August
Tommy and I went out to Bogany and back by the Skipper Woods.
We were speaking to Frank Ruth and Little Nell. Six big liners
lying idle in the bay.[39]

Monday, 17 August
Tommy and I walked to the Port and rowed round the three big
liners laid up there.[40]

Tuesday, 18 August
Fine, sunny day. In the forenoon Tommy and I went up the Barone
Hill. Afternoon, we all took the 2.15 LNE boat for the Kyles sail,
got off at Tighnabruich and walked to Auchenlochan, and got the
boat back to Rothesay. After tea we went to the pictures.

---

38   Princes Pier was in Greenock.

39   The presence of the liners – which included the Cunard transatlantic liner the
      Megantic – was an early sign of the coming world economic depression.

40   The 'Port' is Port Bannatyne.

Friday, 21 August
Dull, windy forenoon. Tommy and I walked to Port Bannatyne,
went out in a wee boat, putted and bus home. We were speaking
to George Anderson and his niece.

Saturday, 22 August
Fine, sunny day. Tommy and I hired a wee boat and went round
the six liners. We then putted. We met Nell Ruth and her man,
and had a pow-wow.

Monday, 24 August
Another beautiful day. Agnes and I putted and Tommy went out
all by himself in a wee boat. After Agnes and I had done our
putt, we toddled along to see if we could spot Tommy and the wee
boat. We spotted him. Tommy there, wee boat there, his oars not
there. Agnes in a fever, and rushed down to a wee steam boat and
implored them to save her child. The child was saved, sadder and
wiser, I hope.

Tuesday, 25 August
Fine sunny day. We all went to Largs by the 12 noon boat, had
our lunch in MacKay's and then a walk to the Pencil. Got the boat
back about 4.30. Glad to be back in Rothesay again: Largs no use.
After tea we all putted.

Wednesday, 26 August
At last. The big walk. Tommy and I set out in a day of glorious
sunshine. Left 10.30, took bus to Port Bannatyne, then we started
to walk round the north end of Bute to Ettrick Bay. The road
stopped opposite Colintraive, then we were into the wilds. Struck
the path again at Kilmichael. Then Tommy and I had a small sort
of dook. On again, I near dead with thirst. We got a jug at a house
and were directed to the pump. We drank a gallon or two. Then
we got into Ettrick Bay and bus back. Arrived Rothesay 7.45 p.m.
We enjoyed our supper. I took three large cups of tea, and other
articles in proportion.

Thursday, 27 August
Dull and warm. Tommy and I putted, then spent an hour and a
half in a wee boat. After tea, we all at the De Luxe.

Friday, 28 August
Nice warm, sunny day. We all climbed the Barone Hill. At night
we went out to admire the illuminations. We were speaking to
Nancy Irvine. We then went home and watched the fireworks from
our window. They did not surpass our expectations.

Saturday, 29 August
Fine sunny day, and our last. We got 2.50 boat to Wemyss Bay. Were home about 5 p.m., and got home quite comfortably. After tea, Tommy and I went to library for some literature.

Wednesday, 2 September
Agnes and I went to Govanhill Picture House at night. We saw and heard Janet Gaynor.[41]

Sunday, 6 September
After dinner, Tommy and I went to the King's Park. We were speaking to Mr T. Arkieson and and his good lady. Mr Arkieson is the man who got the last contract for suits for Tommy and me.

Wednesday, 9 September
Nice day. Agnes and I at the Majestic. Wrote to Mary.

Thursday, 17 September
Agnes and Tommy at church tonight. The induction of our new minister.

Friday, 18 September
Nice day and pretty warm. Tommy away to golf in the forenoon.

Sunday, 20 September
Nice, sunny day. We all at church. Afternoon, Agnes and I at Queen's Park. All off again to church at night. Wee Cowie and Mrs Cowie in our seats when we entered.

Monday, 21 September
Nice sunny day. Britain suspends the Gold Standard.[42] Got my hair cut.

Tuesday, 22 September
The pound sterling is falling abroad.

Wednesday, 23 September
Wee Betty MacKay came up at 10.30 p.m. with some flowers for Agnes. 'Say it with flowers.'[43]

---

41 Janet Gaynor was one of the few Hollywood actresses to make the transition from silent films to talking ones. Her 1931 films include *Daddy Long Legs* and *Delicious*.

42 The Gold Standard valued the pound sterling at a fixed amount of gold. By suspending the standard, the British government allowed the pound to find its own value in foreign exchange markets. It immediately fell by 20 per cent. This had the effect of making Britain's exports cheaper in international markets.

43 This slogan was devised for the American Society of Florists in 1917.

Thursday, 24 September
Nice sunny afternoon. The pound still falling. My, oh my.

Friday, 25 September
£1 is worth 14/6 abroad.

Tuesday, 29 September
The nice wee girl Miss McIntosh from the kirk landed here at
7.30 p.m. We were listening to Jeanette MacDonald singing
when she came in, so I clapped a pair of earphones on her.[44] We
then discussed the kirk and other appropriate subjects. She had
supper with us. I escorted the damsel home at 11.30 p.m.

Thursday, 1 October
We are going, or rather, Agnes is going in for horticulture. Mrs
Carmichael up at night with a bowl and bulbs. You put it under
the bed for a few months then take it out and you have the
flowers.

Friday, 2 October
Tommy Lipton dead.[45] Riot in Glasgow last night with the
unemployed.[46]

Saturday, 3 October
Another riot last night.

Sunday, 4 October
We all went to church. Tommy went at night to the YMCA in our
church.

Wednesday, 7 October
Sir Thomas Lipton buried today in the Southern Necropolis,
Caledonia Road. Parliament dissolved today.[47]

Saturday, 10 October
Tommy and MacPherson went to a City Hall concert. Agnes and I
went out a wee walk.

---

44 Jeanette MacDonald was an American singer and actress.

45 Sir Thomas Lipton made his name as the founder of a chain of grocery shops that
    used American-style marketing methods to boost custom and sales. He was a keen
    yachtsman and competed five times (and lost five times) in the America's Cup.

46 A Council of Action had been formed to defend freedom of speech on Glasgow
    Green. On 1 October, a mass meeting on the green – estimates range from 40,000 to
    100,000 people – turned into a riot when the police charged the crowd. Disturbances
    continued over the weekend.

47 The 1931 General Election was called because the Labour government was split on
    how to respond to the Great Depression.

Tuesday, 13 October
Listened to Baldwin.[48] I'm a Tory.

Wednesday, 14 October
I listened in to Clynes tonight.[49] I'm now a Socialist.

Thursday, 15 October
Nice day. Filled in my Income Tax paper for the optimistic
government. Agnes got a new hat and I got a new coat. Listened in
to Lloyd George.[50] I'm now a Liberal.

Friday, 16 October
Listened in to Sir J. Simon tonight.[51] I'm a National Liberal.

Saturday, 17 October
Got a letter from Poland. My stamp collecting friend there is now
dead. His widow sent the sad news.

Sunday, 18 October
Agnes and I at Communion. Edison, who invented everything in
America, is dead.[52]

Tuesday, 20 October
Mrs Cowie here tonight. Then Lily, my niece, arrived. Graham, the
big Labour man, took his turn at the broadcast tonight.[53] Seeing we
had visitors, I did not hear him, so I am not a Labour man.

Wednesday, 21 October
Listened in to H. Samuel.[54]

Thursday, 22 October
Mr Baldwin spoke tonight. The Tory man.

---

48   Stanley Baldwin was leader of the Conservative Party and MP for Bewdley.

49   John Robert Clynes was Labour MP for Manchester Platting, and had been Home
     Secretary until Parliament had been dissolved a week previously.

50   David Lloyd George was leader of the Liberal Party and MP for Caernarvon
     Boroughs.

51   Sir John Simon was leader of the Liberal Nationals (later known as the National
     Liberals) and MP for Spen Valley.

52   Thomas Alva Edison, who developed the phonograph, the motion-picture camera,
     the long-lasting electric lightbulb and other modern items, died on 18 October at the
     age of 84.

53   William Graham, President of the Board of Trade in the outgoing government, was
     Labour MP for Edinburgh Central.

54   Herbert Samuel was deputy leader of the Liberal Party, and MP for Darwen.

Friday, 23 October

Listened to Henderson tonight.[55] He is 'agin' the government. Bad man.

Saturday, 24 October

Got my new coat. I paid cash, three guineas. Listened in to Ramsay MacDonald, who said the final word.[56]

Sunday, 25 October

All at church, also the new overcoat.

Monday, 26 October

Went at night and gave the kirk 16/6. This allows us free access for another six months. Left my coat with tailor. Sleeves a trifle short.

Tuesday, 27 October

We voted at night. Listened in at night to some of the election results. Labour gets wiped out in England. Very sad for Labour. The Glasgow results will not be known until tomorrow.

Wednesday, 28 October

Paid the thief of a landlord his rent. Got my coat from the tailor. Labour loses some seats in Glasgow.

Friday, 30 October

The National Government has a 500 majority.[57]

Saturday, 31 October

The wee Dunns in for their Hallowe'en. We made them happy.

Tuesday, 3 November

We voted today, municipal elections.

Wednesday, 4 November

Agnes went to Leiper and got the length, breadth and depth of her mouth taken for new teeth. Labour loses heavily in England, Scotland much the same, in municipal elections.

---

55   Arthur Henderson was leader of the Labour Party, and MP for Burnley.

56   James Ramsay MacDonald was Prime Minister, and had been elected as Labour MP for Leicester. Ejected from that party in September 1931, he then formed and was leader of National Labour.

57   The National Government, while nominally cross-party and with Ramsay MacDonald as Prime Minister, occupied 554 seats. The Conservatives held 470 of these, National Labour 13, Liberals (Liberal National and Liberal) 68, and others 3.

Tuesday, 10 November
Agnes in the wash house. So it rained and poured all day, and this is her birthday. Ah, me.

Wednesday, 11 November
This is the day of two minutes' silence. I observed it at Jamaica Street corner. Agnes went to her dentist and got some more measurements taken.

Wednesday, 18 November
Agnes went down to Leiper and got her teeth.

Thursday, 19 November
Agnes went down to Leiper and gave the good man £3 10/- for her dentures. I paid gas bill.

Friday, 20 November
The clock stopped and will not go. Agnes' new teeth seem to be very comfortable.

Sunday, 22 November
Agnes cleaned the clock and got it to go.

Friday, 27 November
Business at a standstill.

Saturday, 28 November
Tommy had Kenneth MacPherson up for tea and supper. We played ping-pong.

Sunday, 29 November
After tea, feeling pain under the waistcoat, I thought a walk would do me good, so out I went.

Monday, 30 November
The pain here not so bad.

Tuesday, 1 December
The pain not quite better.

Wednesday, 2 December
Agnes had a very bad night with a pain. See previous page for locality. She went to bed a little earlier than usual after a wee half of castor oil. Tommy at St Andrew's Hall to hear the Orpheus Choir.

Sunday, 6 December
Tommy gave a lecture at MacPherson's kirk in the afternoon to the YMCA.

Monday, 7 December
Got a letter from Mary. She has moved to a new house and wants us through at the New Year.

Wednesday, 9 December
After tea, when Agnes was out for a few messages, my niece Ella arrived. After a bit Miss McIntosh dropped in. She sang a few warbles and stung me for two tickets for her choir concert in our kirk. In due course, Tommy saw Ella away and I escorted the kirk damsel home.

Thursday, 10 December
Got word today from Isa that Nellie, the widow of my brother Sam, was dead. Haven't seen her for 10 years. Work on the giant Cunarder at Clydebank (534) stopped.[58] No money. No trade.

Sunday, 13 December
Tommy and I at church. I'm afraid I'm taking the cold.

Monday, 14 December
Quite sure I've got the cold.

Tuesday, 15 December
Stayed in bed all day. Head sore, nose stuffy and juicy etc. Did not feel well at all.

Wednesday, 16 December
Feel a little worse now, so stayed in bed all day. Agnes took a run in the morning to my business address and let them know my sad condition. A family consultation decided on getting me medical skill. So Agnes left word with my doctor to call at his convenience.

Thursday, 17 December
In bed all day. The doctor thinks I have got the worst over. Prescribed a bottle for my chest and ½ dozen powders for my head.

---

58   Work resumed on the ship in question, then known as Hull No. 534, on 3 April 1934. She was launched from John Brown's yard, as the luxury liner RMS *Queen Mary*, on 26 September 1934.

Friday, 18 December

Feel easier today. Tommy went to the firm and let them know how I was. Tommy also called into my society today with a necessary document re my illness. I rose about 8.30 p.m., and feel not so bad.

Saturday, 19 December

Stayed in bed till about 4.30. Chest all right now.

Sunday, 20 December

Got up for dinner. Seeing I'm not well, I got soup with chickens in it. Am feeling weak but eating better.

Monday, 21 December

Staggered round to the doctor in the afternoon. He certified me as being fit for work. I have my own opinion on this. Spent rest of day in the house. Feeling depressed, scared and nervous. Agnes out shopping at night for Xmas cards. I have evidently been a cussed nuisance.

Tuesday, 22 December

Went to my work at 10 a.m. Not very well and feel worse at night. Got our Irish Xmas parcel sent off.

Wednesday, 23 December

Feel that I might, with great care, survive. Started my new tonic bottle. My niece Lily here. She gave Agnes a religious calendar and some mince pies.

Thursday, 24 December

Don't feel well. Got our Xmas parcel from Belfast. Tommy got a tie, I got tobacco and Agnes got something in the wearing (quite useless) line from Maud. All happy except Agnes. I got stamps from Athens, and won a box of biscuits at a raffle. So I have done well today. I will now hang up my stockings.

Friday, 25 December

Wish You All a Merry Xmas. Seeing this is a holiday, I stayed in bed all day.

Saturday, 26 December
At work again, feeling no so bad.

Sunday, 27 December
Stayed in bed till dinner time.

Monday, 28 December

Bought a funny wee black hat today. 8/6. Agnes does not like it. Wrote Ella re our Edinburgh visit. and got a letter from Mary re same. Tommy goes tomorrow.

Tuesday, 29 December
Agnes saw Tommy off to Edinburgh by 11 a.m. train.

Wednesday, 30 December
Agnes got a letter from her wee son, which cheered her up.

Thursday, 31 December
Left my work for the year at 1 p.m. Agnes and I met Ella at Queen
Street Station, got a train about 6 p.m. and arrived in Edinburgh
after a very comfortable journey. Tommy met us at the Waverley
Steps and showed us the way home. We then spent a very enjoyable
evening, and made merry with Tom, Mary and Dorothy.

1932

Thomas and his family continued to develop their own, more separate, routines this year. Tommy spent more time with his friends from university, Agnes devoted her afternoons and evenings to church socials and visiting friends and neighbours, and Thomas lost himself in classical music and his stamp collection.

Britain and the rest of the world were in the grip of the Great Depression, but Thomas seemed immured to its social and political effects. He was obviously aware of demonstrators and hunger marchers, but seemed to record their activities only when they slowed his journeys to work or pleasure. He was, however, acutely aware of the economic effects of the slump in world trade, especially as his employer's travelling salesman left and Thomas became his replacement.

Friday, 1 January
Tommy and I had a walk down town and had a look-in at the museum.[1] Saw a stamp collection there which made my tongue stick out a yard. Tom, Mary and Dorothy went to a wedding. Ella and Agnes went and viewed it from outside.

Saturday, 2 January
Tommy and I went out and admired the Dean Bridge.

Sunday, 3 January
Rained all day. Nobody out. We amused ourselves with the wireless, the piano, the gramophone and telling ghost stories. As a fitting climax a wire burst in the room and left that part in darkness. Tom Carlyle gave Tommy and I a nice new tie each. Good man!

Monday, 4 January
Alas and alack. Ella and I left by 8.50 a.m. train for Glasgow. Agnes and Tommy home at dinner time. I enjoyed my visit 100 per cent, Agnes about 10 per cent.

Tuesday, 5 January
Tommy off to his house of learning again. Old Mrs Cowie very ill, and taken to Victoria Infirmary in an ambulance. Agnes went up to the Cowies' at night.

Friday, 8 January
Agnes' mouth inflamed last night, so she left out her teeth today. Bought a new razor at 1/-, which is to beat all others. My first razor cost 21/-.

Saturday, 9 January
Agnes went to the Victoria Infirmary to see Mrs Cowie (the old one). Mrs Cowie (the young one) here at night.

Wednesday, 13 January
Mr and Mrs Carmichael, Peggy and Alex here at night. Music, etc. Tommy accompanied Peggy's song. I have got the sack.

Thursday, 14 January
The elder came up. Tommy and I gave him a cake and a dram. He left the Communion cards and departed. Good man. The dram, I might say, was of an innocent character.

---

1   Presumably the Royal Museum in Chambers Street.

Friday, 15 January
Tommy sold a few *Ygorra*s. Agnes put the final touches to Tommy's charity day rig-out.

Saturday, 16 January
Some heavy showers, and a high wind. Tommy out till tea time with the students, robbing the citizens in order to give to the hospitals.

Sunday, 17 January
Tommy collected for the hospitals over £11,000. He was assisted by a lot more students.

Monday, 18 January

A few mild riots in town. I was not killed. Agnes went to a Burns lecture at night with Mr and Mrs Carmichael. She came home about 9.30 p.m. The lecture was in a church, so she was quite sober.

Thursday, 21 January
I went out at night to see a certain Mr Main in Crow Road. He collects stamps (so do I). I duly admired his collection, and was home 11.50 p.m.

Friday, 22 January
Got measured for a new suit.

Saturday, 23 January
Agnes went to Victoria Infirmary to see old Mrs Cowie.

Sunday, 24 January
Tommy and I went to church. After dinner we went a walk – Mount Florida and back by King's Park. Wrote to New Zealand. Big mutiny at Dartmoor.[2]

Wednesday, 27 January
Agnes got a very green jumper from Edinburgh.

---

2 Around 250 prisoners rioted in Dartmoor, and were faced down by 21 warders with truncheons. No one was killed, but much of the prison was destroyed by fire. The ostensible cause was poor food. A trial of the rioters handed down an extra 100 years of sentences.

Stamp-collecting networks

Stamp collecting is as old as stamps themselves. When the penny black, the world's first postage stamp, was issued in the United Kingdom on 6 May 1840, John Edward Gray (1800–75), the Keeper of Zoology at the British Museum, bought some that day as a memento of the event. By the 1860s, the hobby of stamp collecting was established, and there were specialised albums, catalogues and equipment available for both children and adults. As other countries followed Britain's lead in selling prepaid stamps, the hobby spread across the globe and commentators devised the new word 'timbromania' (stamp madness) to describe this new phenomenon ('philately' was not coined until 1864). As more and more people began collecting, businesses specialising in buying and selling stamps and stamp collections became more common. Postal authorities, too, realised that there was a market for stamps beyond simply paying for postage and began to issue commemorative stamps, custom franking designs and first-day covers. As rich collectors began snapping up rare stamps, or complete collections, as investments, others entered the market with different motives to those who were happy to amass a few albums with common stamps of familiar countries.

The most famous name in stamp collecting, Stanley Gibbons, was born – most appropriately – in 1840, the year in which the penny black made its first appearance. He began collecting stamps while at school, and his early collection is said to have contained some rare and valuable stamps. He turned his hobby into a fledgling business at the age of 16 when he began selling stamps from a counter in his father's pharmacy in Plymouth, where he was employed as an assistant. In 1863, young Stanley bought a sackful of rare Cape of Good Hope triangular stamps from two sailors for just £5. In 1865, he issued his first price list in the form of a magazine, and the famous Stanley Gibbons catalogue was born.

Stanley moved his expanding enterprise to London in 1874, and when he retired in 1890 sold the business that still bears his name for £25,000 to Charles Phillips.

Stamp collecting may not have been the most obvious hobby for Thomas, but it did fit into a pattern. Here was a man who made a scrapbook of newspaper cuttings relating to the First World War, a man who kept a daily diary from 1913 and a man of great enthusiasms, who persisted in his hobbies for far longer than most people. For example, he was a compulsive long-distance walker, an early adopter of radio, a keen putter and – overall – a man with a clerk's mind for regularity and neatness. Stamp collecting appealed to all these sides of Thomas and fitted well with his gregarious nature. He was not simply happy to buy stamps from catalogues or rely on the mail arriving in his office. He sought out correspondents in the most unlikely places, in many cases in countries against which Britain had been at war less than a decade previously, and shared in their concerns and interests. Through his stamp-collecting circle, Thomas heard at first hand how the economies of Austria and Russia were slowly recovering after the First World War and how rampant inflation in Germany was driving people into poverty and starvation. Thomas also made friends with fellow philatelists nearer home, notably Father Joseph Petrauskis, a Lithuanian priest in Mossend, who was able to translate some of Thomas' letters from his correspondents in central Europe.

Thursday, 28 January
My philatelic friend, Mr Main, up tonight to see my stamps. We got up to the letter F, inclusive.

Friday, 29 January
Old Mrs Cowie got out of the infirmary today, so Agnes went round after tea to see her. My niece Ella here. Paid the factor his rent, £6. 1. 9. 'doon the stank'.[3]

Saturday, 30 January
Mrs Marson here at dinner time for a religious donation. China and Japan scrapping over Shanghai.[4]

Wednesday, 3 February
Went to my tailor and got a final fit-on.

Thursday, 4 February
The submarine *M2* located. Sunk over a week ago with a loss of about 50 lives.[5] Agnes and I went to the Govanhill Picture House.

Friday, 5 February
Dull, dark day. Feel very worried with the state of business. Nothing doing.

Saturday, 6 February
Called at my tailor and got my new suit.

Sunday, 7 February
We all at church. Agnes and Tommy went to the YMCA and heard a lecture about Tibet. My new trousers are too short.

Monday, 8 February
Left my too-short trousers to be lengthened. Went to Knightswood at night. Isa is not keeping too well.

---

3   A 'stank', in Scots, is a drain.

4   The Shanghai Incident began on 18 January, when a Chinese mob attacked and burned a Japanese warehouse in the port of Shanghai. In retaliation, the Japanese bombed the city on 28 January, and a battle broke out between the Chinese 19th Route Army and Japanese forces.

5   HMS *M2* was a Royal Navy aircraft-carrying submarine that sank off Dorset on 26 January. All 60 of its crew died.

Wednesday, 10 February

Called in at my tailor. Gave him £5 sterling and brought home my lengthened trousers. Agnes not very well pleased with them. Edgar Wallace, the man who wrote detective stories, dead.[6]

Thursday, 11 February

Loudens downstairs flitted to Ayr. We got our Apostle Spoons (in duplicate) today from the *Daily Express*.[7] The Pope and Mussolini now pals.[8]

Saturday, 13 February

Tommy had Kenneth MacPherson up for tea, ping-pong and supper. I'm not very good at ping-pong.

Sunday, 14 February

Agnes filleted, stoned or boned oranges. She is going to make marmalade.

Wednesday, 17 February

Agnes went to the church meeting at night. I don't go to many of these affairs.

Thursday, 18 February

Fog and frost. Mrs Cordon here in the forenoon to tell Agnes of Uncle Peter's wife's death. Got a box of toffee from Mrs Baxter. I had given young Sandy some foreign stamps.

Friday, 19 February

Norman Guy leaves our employment today, so I have to take up his duties as traveller. And my toe is so sore.

Saturday, 20 February

Paid the gas bill. Yesterday was pay day.

---

6 Edgar Wallace was an English writer who wrote 175 novels, most of them thrillers and detective stories. He is probably best known for writing the short story 'King Kong'.

7 At that time, many newspapers ran promotions that offered gifts in return for subscriptions or collecting coupons over the course of days or weeks.

8 The public reconciliation of Benito Mussolini, the Italian Fascist leader, and Pope Pius XI temporarily stopped the dictator's attacks on the Roman Catholic Church.

Monday, 22 February

Agnes bought a new and wonderful copper kettle. It is going to save pounds in the gas bill. She paid 1/- down and 1/- a week for 11 weeks. She and I went to the Majestic. 1/2 down.

Wednesday, 24 February

Started today to get orders. What a game!

Saturday, 27 February

Tommy spent the evening with the MacPherson (organist) and Geddes (fiddler).

Tuesday, 1 March

Paid wireless licence A1 470253, Wireless Telegraphy Acts 1904–1926.

Friday, 4 March

At night I went to my philatelic friend's house, Mr Main. We looked at stamps and had some music.

Saturday, 5 March

We all at Partick, where my niece Lily dwells. We visited her, in other words. Tommy walked, and studied all the libraries en route.

Monday, 7 March

Agnes at the Guild with Mrs Carmichael. In her absence, Mrs Cowie, the younger, came up to see her. I regretted Agnes' absence, but wished her better luck next time.

Wednesday, 9 March

We were wakened about 12.30 this morning by a policeman. He said the big gate at my work was open. I said it could stay open, then I went back to bed.

Sunday, 13 March

Nice spring like day. We all at church. Took a walk in afternoon to Pollokshaws and studied all the works I might sell canvas to.

Monday, 14 March

Very tired with my wanderings, and looked at my dinner with but little joy.

Thursday, 17 March

My work is wearing my delicate toe away.

Friday, 18 March

Dull day. Toe not so sore, but feel very tired at night.

Sunday, 20 March

Tommy and I papered the bathroom (no bath) today. Our first attempt and it was no' bad.

Wednesday, 23 March

At night, Agnes went to see Mrs Cowie. Tommy at Orpheus Choir concert. TCL, the gaffer, stayed at home.

Thursday, 24 March

The Merry Widow here at night for various religious donations.[9]

Saturday, 26 March

I usually have a holiday this Saturday, but owing to the 'hopeless dawn' sort of trade, we did not shut in case we would lose an order.[10]

Monday, 28 March

Spring holiday. Nice sunny day. In the afternoon, Tommy and I out a walk. Queen's Park.

Thursday, 31 March

Agnes got a sore mouth again, so out comes her teeth. Mrs Louden here in afternoon. Merry Widow here at night.

Monday, 4 April

Tommy got a new hat today, 10/6.

Saturday, 9 April

Rained all day. To make up for it, the water was turned off at night owing to a burst pipe. Tommy out with the lads. I listened in to the International: England 3, Scotland 0.[11]

---

9   This is Thomas' less than polite nickname for Mrs Marson. *The Merry Widow* is the title of the English translation (1907) of the operetta *Die lustige Witwe* (1905) by Franz Lehár.

10 Frank Bramley painted *A Hopeless Dawn* in 1888, taking his title from a passage in *The Harbours of England* (1855) by John Ruskin.

11 This match, in the British Home International Championship, was played at the Empire Stadium, Wembley, London.

Tuesday, 12 April
A wife up from the kirk today. Mr Gordon dropped in for the
afternoon, then the Merry Widow blew in at tea time. Isa dropped
in at night. What a day!

Friday, 15 April
Heavy rain and hail. I went to Paisley and Renfrew to get large
orders. I got one wee one. Had a cup of tea with Ella Gordon.

Thursday, 21 April
Nice day. Agnes in town re new wallpaper.

Friday, 22 April
*Called in at shop for the wallpaper, but
got it not. It was duly delivered by tea
time, how-some-ever.*

Saturday, 23 April
*For the sum of 1/ - I got the spring of
my stick-on specs mended.*

Sunday, 24 April
Fine day. We all went to church. Ella Carlyle here in the
afternoon. Mrs Cowie and Wee Helen here after tea. We all had
supper together.

Tuesday, 26 April
Fine sunny day. Agnes and Tommy washed the priceless
dinner service and packed it away. I shifted 'Big Ben' out of
the road. Tommy emptied the bookcase and packed the books
away. Tommy and I took the rocking chair to the back green
and Agnes gave it a dust-up. We are not removing, only spring
cleaning has started.

Sunday, 1 May
In the afternoon, I had a look round the People's Palace. Came
home after a most depressing walk through most depressing
localities. At night, Tommy went with MacPherson to Stevenson
Memorial Church.[12] Some special music on.

---

12   This church, which was originally named the Nathaniel Stevenson Memorial Free
     Church, stands in Belmont Street, Glasgow. It is currently called Kelvin Stevenson
     Memorial Church.

Friday, 6 May

Cold day. French President assassinated.[13]

Sunday, 8 May

After tea, Agnes and I went to the King's Park. We met and had a word or two with Frank Ruth and wife.

Monday, 9 May

Agnes went to the Mossmans' with a bag of soot (saved from our lum) for their bit garden.

Wednesday, 11 May

Agnes went to Tantallon Road to see our coast landlady re our coast house. Got fixed up. Gave her £1 as a guarantee of good faith etc. We go on holiday to Rothesay on 1 August.

Thursday, 12 May

Went out at night to see a sick member of the firm, to wit Charley. Did not see him, as he was at the pictures. I have no doubt he will be at his work tomorrow.

Friday, 13 May

Wet, mild day. Agnes spring cleaning the room. Tommy polished the piano. Got my hair cut. Lindbergh's kidnapped baby found murdered.[14]

Saturday, 14 May

Tommy at church in morning. Dull, dark, wet day. Japanese Prime Minister assassinated.[15]

Monday, 16 May

I spent the day getting orders, the first big round. Took train to Dalry, then bus to Ardrossan, then bus to Irvine, then bus to Troon, then train home. Arrived St Enoch about 6.30 p.m.

---

13   Paul Gorguloff, a Russian émigré, killed the French President Paul Doumer.

14   The Lindbergh Baby – Charles Lindbergh Junior – was kidnapped from his home in New Jersey on 1 March 1832. A ransom note was left in his place. His father, the first aviator to fly the Atlantic solo, paid a ransom, but the baby was not returned. He was found two miles from the family home on 12 May by a truck driver.

15   Inukai Tsuyoshi was assassinated by 11 young naval officers during an attempted military coup.

Friday, 20 May

Bought a new pipe, back to my old original shape.

Saturday, 21 May

Agnes and I at the Calder picture house.[16] Our first visit, and no doubt it won't be the last.

Wednesday, 25 May

Agnes and Tommy in town and got a sports jacket for Tommy and two mirrors. One for above the kitchen mantelpiece and the other goes above the piano. Ain't we swell.

Sunday, 29 May

After tea I went to the Linn Park. Bang went 2d.[17]

Thursday, 2 June

Another summer day. Walked out to Ruglen at night as far as Burnside. My toe sore, so I took the train home. The London, Midland and Scottish Railway Company (Caledonian Section) charged me 4d. Not worth it.

Friday, 3 June

I took a walk out Cathcart way and had a look in at the Couper Institute. My blasted toe is blistered. Don't like walking.

Saturday, 4 June

This is my birthday. I am an ancient old man now. I am 50. No public holiday declared, so at my work as usual.

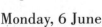

Monday, 6 June

At bed time I did not feel very well so took a wee nip of whisky and a brace of aspirins. And so to bed.

Tuesday, 7 June

My chest sore and choked up, so I stayed in bed.

Wednesday, 8 June

Stayed in bed till 3 p.m.

Thursday, 9 June

Went to my work today.

---

16 The Calder, at 302 Calder Street, was opened at the back of the Govanhill Picture House in April 1932 by Harry Winocur. The building was demolished in 1981.

17 Thomas is paraphrasing the Harry Lauder song 'Bang went Saxpence'.

Friday, 10 June
On 10 June 1910, I was at a wedding, and so was Agnes. We came home together, and are still there.

Saturday, 11 June
Agnes and I went to the Calder at night. When we got home, I boiled the new patent kettle. It had no water in it, so the patent dropped off. Very sad. It is now of no use till it is mended, if that is possible.

Thursday, 16 June
Agnes took the copper kettle (patent) to be mended. At night I had a walk to the parks of King's and Linn.

Friday, 17 June
The elder here at night and left the Communion passports for next Sunday.

Sunday, 19 June
Weather bright and glorious. Agnes and I went to church. Mass. She sad and gloomy.

Monday, 20 June
Miss McIntosh, she what sings in our choir, up at night for some donation pertaining to the church. I donated. (Don't mind if Agnes has refunded me or not.)

Tuesday, 21 June
Agnes and I went to the Majestic and saw Greta Garbo.[18]

Wednesday, 22 June
When Agnes was out messages, the Merry Widow came in. I gave her 1/- for some fund, then she departed. (Did you give me that bob, Agnes?)

Monday, 27 June
The MacPherson here for tea. Then he and Tommy went to hear organs. Agnes doing a recital in wash house at night.

Wednesday, 29 June
Tommy went to see Mr Leiper, the dentist, re some teeth.

Saturday, 2 July
Got our patent kettle back.

---

18 Greta Garbo's two most recent films were *Grand Hotel* and *As You Desire Me*.

Wednesday, 6 July
The MacPherson up for tea. Tommy went out and a wee female Geddes came up to let us know Tommy was at the Cinerama with James, the budding 'hoss' doctor.

Thursday, 7 July
My small toe still got a big blister, so Tommy let it out with a sharp instrument. Spent the day in Dalry, Ardrossan, Irvine and Troon, and walked about in great comfort. Home before 7 p.m.

Monday, 11 July
Agnes in the wash house at night. I went out for a walk. Dropped into the King at Cathcart and had a cup of tea. Home 11.30, then xx ?? !!!

Tuesday, 12 July
Was speaking to Agnes' Aunt Bella in town this forenoon. I was on my way to Renfrew. At night, I went as far as Queen's Park. Was home at a reasonable hour, so got into no trouble.

Friday, 15 July
Fine warm, sunny day. Mrs Cameron next door shut herself out, so Tommy opened the door for her in a burglar-like manner. This is Fair Friday, so I quit work at 1 o'clock. In the afternoon, Tommy and I went to Linn Park and putted. It was a draw. After tea, Tommy went to the Mitchell Library, and Agnes and I went to Rouken Glen and admired the old gardens. Got a letter from Duncan. He is not doing well.

Saturday, 16 July
On holiday, this being the Fair. In the forenoon I went to the Queen's Park. After dinner, Tommy and I went to the Art Galleries, and after tea Agnes and I went to the Calder. Nice day, but some rain at night. Sarah Paterson upstairs shut herself out, so I loaned her various house-breaking tools. This is getting too common here.

Monday, 18 July
Fair Monday. On holiday. Very warm day. After dinner, we all went to Nitshill by bus, and walked back to the 'roon toll'.[19] We all went to the Calder at night.

---

19   The round toll house is in Pollokshaws.

Thursday, 21 July
Tommy bought a new swim suit.

Friday, 22 July
Tommy at the baths today and got his new swim suit wet.

Tuesday, 26 July
We all at the Calder tonight and saw Greta Garbo. Her text was
The Rise of Helga.[20]

Thursday, 28 July
Left word with railway company to lift our hamper tomorrow.
Got said hamper packed at night. Agnes at the Calder with Mrs
Cameron.

Friday, 29 July
Paid the insurance and bought a new snap brim hat for 7/11. The
hamper duly lifted.

Sunday, 31 July
Too busy getting ready for Rothesay to go to church. Mrs
Carmichael up for a little re the key. She is going to look in
occasionally when we are away.

Monday, 1 August
Hurrah, hurrah, we're off. Got the 10.30 to Wemyss Bay and
arrived Rothesay about 12.30. After some dinner, Tommy and I
walked to Port Bannatyne and did some putting. Agnes got in a
few messages and tidied up. Nice sunny day.

Tuesday, 2 August
Rained all day. Agnes looked at the shops. I listened to a gospel
meeting. After tea, we all at the Palace.

Wednesday, 3 August
After noon we all at St Ninian's Bay. This is a new bus run. Fare
sixpence. Fine day on the whole.

Thursday, 4 August
Tommy and I went a walk up by the golf course and the camps.
A shower on the way back, so we went to the library. After
dinner, we went the Kyles sail. We sat on the boat all the time.

---

20   *The Rise of Helga* (1932) was an adventure-romance directed by Robert Z. Leonard
and starring Garbo and Clark Gable. In America, the film's tile was *Susan Lenox:
Her Fall and Rise.*

I was speaking to A. Baxter's cousin A. Baxter and his sister on the boat. Nice sunny sail.

Friday, 5 August
Rained all day. We all went to the De Luxe.

Saturday, 6 August
Tommy and I went to Port Bannatyne, got a wee boat and Tommy got a swim. After dinner it blew a hurricane and rained in buckets.

Sunday, 7 August
Warm, sunny day. Went out all by myself and had a seat in the Skeoch Wood and back by Chapel Hill. After dinner, Agnes and I sat on the esplanade.

Monday, 8 August
Warm, sunny day. In the morning, Tommy and I did the moor walk. In the afternoon we all took the bus to Scalpsie Bay. Return fare 1/-. Tommy got a dook there and a bee went up my sleeve and chewed my arm.

Tuesday, 9 August
Tommy and I out in a boat at Port Bannatyne. Tommy got a wee swim. After dinner we all did our favourite walk to Knocknicoll Wood and bus back from Kerrycroy. This is Tommy's birthday and he is now 21.

Wednesday, 10 August
Tommy and I at Port Bannatyne. I called in at the local yacht builder and told him where to buy canvas. After tea, we all went to the De Luxe.

Thursday, 11 August
Terrific heat and sunshine. Took the 'New Scenic Circular Tour', 1/6. After dinner, Tommy and I out in a small boat for a couple of hours and examined all the idle liners in the bay. At midnight a terrific thunderstorm started. I watched the most appalling display of lightning I ever saw till 3 a.m.

Saturday, 13 August
I went out in the morning and arranged re hamper. Met Frank and Nell Ruth just arriving. Tommy and I went to Scalpsie and Tommy got his dook. After dinner, Tommy and I went out in a wee boat and Agnes and I had a seat not far away.

Sunday, 14 August

Very wet morning and a stormy day. After dinner, Tommy and I went to Bogany Point and had a seat. I'm beginning to feel sad. I'm going home. Got the *Jeanie Deans* at 5.40 and was in Morgan Street about 8 p.m.

Monday, 15 August

Back to work again. Robert Baxter gave me two grouse he had shot. Was not too sure of them, but took them home at dinner time and hung them up in the kitchen. Boiled myself an egg or so and had some tea (Agnes not being home yet). As I was going away, I met Agnes and Tommy on the stair. Agnes gave Mrs Cowie the two birds, one for keeps and one to be returned ready for cooking.

Tuesday, 16 August

We dined on the bird and it might have been worse. Being a nice night, I meandered out to Ruglen, and back by the new bus route.

Wednesday, 17 August

Tommy got a cheque for 5/- for a poem he sent to the *News*.

Thursday, 18 August

Feel a pain in my internal parts. The bird has likely poisoned me.

Sunday, 21 August

Agnes and Tommy attended divine service in the Candlish and I attended profane service in Frederick Lane. My inside tender yet, a punishment, no doubt.

Tuesday, 23 August

Tommy at the Cathedral at night to hear divine music. I went to the Majestic all by myself to see *Frankenstein*.[21] Heard it was an horrible picture, but it did not come up to my expectations, so I was not so thrilled.

Wednesday, 24 August

Agnes and I went to the Calder. When we got home, Mrs Marson (the Merry Widow) dropped in. We gave her supper and put her out about 11.30 p.m.

---

21 *Frankenstein* (1931) was directed by James Whale and starred Boris Karloff and Colin Clive.

Thursday, 25 August
Agnes out at Ruglen this afternoon with the ancient Mrs Cowie.
They went to the cemetery. At night, I went to the Queen's Park
and watched bowlers and football.

Sunday, 28 August
Went to my work in the forenoon. I'm overworked. Feel I've got the
cold pretty bad. Took Yeast-Vite, aspirins and a wee half.

Friday, 2 September
I went to Kinning Park Library tonight. It is a most depressing
locality.

Tuesday, 6 September
Tommy at his usual Cathedral organ recital with Geddes and
MacPherson. He spoke to Nan Gordon and her gentleman friend
there.

Sunday, 11 September
Tommy went to church and I went to my work for a brace of hours
or so. I'm working at high pressure.

Monday, 12 September
As the lobby has to be papered, I took its various measurements
tonight.

Thursday, 15 September
Tommy and Agnes spent the entire day putting the paper on lobby.
They made quite a good job of it.

Monday, 19 September
At night I did the Busby – Carmunnock walk. Saw the electric
lights of Carmunnock doing their duty. First time I ever saw them
lit.

Monday, 26 September
This is the autumn holiday. Pouring wet morning, but turned into
a nice sunny day. We all went to Paisley in the car via Barrhead.
Held up for a while by the 'hunger marchers'.[22] I made a business
call, then we went into Paisley Abbey. Agnes then admired the

---

22   Thomas encountered the Scottish contingent of the Great National Hunger March
     against the Means Test, organised by the National Unemployed Workers' Movement.
     Groups from 18 areas of Britain worst hit by the Great Depression and unemployment
     marched to London, where they congregated in Hyde Park on 27 October. The 3,000
     marchers were met by a crowd of 100,000 people. The Metropolitan Police, fearing
     revolution, mounted a force of 70,000 police officers.

shops. Tommy and I went to the museum.

Thursday, 29 September
Fine sunny day. Agnes spent it in the wash house. I spent it in
Dalry, Ardrossan, Irvine and Troon.

Saturday, 1 October
Went to my work in the afternoon. I work more than I used to.

Sunday, 2 October
After dinner, walked out to Rutherglen and went into the cemetery.
Had a look at Sam's and Lily's graves. Felt melancholy.

Wednesday, 5 October
Agnes got new curtains for the room bed. The present ones have
been up 22 years.

Friday, 7 October
Patersons, downstairs, have got a 'hoss' in the Irish Sweepstakes.
This means about £140.

Tuesday, 11 October
Went to Whifflet today on business, likewise Airdrie and
Coatbridge. Called in and had a cup of tea with Hetty and Daisy
Crozier. It is exactly nine years since I did this. Agnes chilly on
receipt of this news.

Wednesday, 12 October
Mrs Marson up this afternoon with *Other Lands*.[23] Agnes away
with Mrs Carmichael to the Ideal Home Exhibition. Home 11
p.m. Then the heavens opened and the flood gates of her wrath
burst forth re my Coatbridge visit. She is now finished with me.

Thursday, 13 October
Called in at Ibrox in forenoon and had a crack with Mr Gordon
(bad man). Went out at night to King's Park and home by the
Carmunnock Road to cool my fevered blood.

Sunday, 16 October
Agnes went herself to church (Communion) and after dinner she
went to Sighthill Cemetery. Two places not calculated to make you
cheery, and it did not.

---

23   *Other Lands* was a magazine published by the United Free Church of Scotland
     between 1923 and 1959. It published articles about overseas missionary work.

Monday, 17 October

Pouring wet day which got worse and worser. Hoping to click for a good order, I went out to Whifflet this afternoon, but nothing settled yet. Also went to Coatbridge and Airdrie, but did not call on any lady friends this time.

Friday, 21 October

Getting cold, so I have started wearing my light Sunday coat.

Sunday, 23 October

Agnes not keeping too well, and went to bed at night disgusted with all and sundry.

Wednesday, 26 October

I was at Coatbridge and Whifflet this afternoon. Confined myself strictly to business. At night Agnes and I went to the Cinerama.

Friday, 28 October

Mrs Marson up before tea for some fund or another. Am thinking seriously of a valve set.

Saturday, 29 October

After tea, Agnes and I went to the Majestic. Tommy was at the Cinerama with the budding horse-doctor, to wit James Geddes.[24]

Sunday, 30 October

Agnes and Tommy went to church. Being a profane sort of fellow, I went to my work for a brace of hours. We decide to have a three-valve set.

Tuesday, 1 November

Went to Coatbridge etc today, strictly on business. Agnes at a 'magic lantern' show with the wee Cowie.

Saturday, 5 November

Agnes and I at the Majestic and saw the *Passionate Plumber*.[25] The Merry Widow up before dinner and sold a ticket.

---

24   James Geddes was evidently a student of veterinary science.

25   *The Passionate Plumber* (1932) was a slapstick comedy, directed by Edward Sedgwick and starring Buster Keaton and Jimmy Durante.

Monday, 7 November
At night Agnes went to the Guild and Tommy went to some
musical affair. I sat in and amused myself. Burned my diaries for
1907, 1908, 1909 and 1910.[26]

Tuesday, 8 November
David (my late office boy) up tonight to discuss a valve set. He is
going to make me one.

Thursday, 10 November
Agnes' birthday. I went to the library tonight.

Friday, 11 November
This is the day of two minutes' silence. I observed it at Jamaica
Street. Agnes went to Carmichaels' and heard it on their wireless
set.

Sunday, 13 November
Nice sunny day, so Agnes and I took a bus drive to the ancient old
Burgh of Rutherglen.[27] Tommy at the YMCA at night. They want
him to be president, but he refused to wear a crown.

Monday, 14 November
Agnes at Guild tonight with Mrs Cowie. Tommy at the university
same time. I sat in and enjoyed myself. Put some pictures in
Dorothy's book.

Wednesday, 16 November
David arrived at night with the new valve set and fitted it up.
Results not very good. My aerial too long. He is going to put
another loudspeaker in the set.

Thursday, 17 November
Put another outside aerial up tonight, 50 feet long. Think I'll need
to make it still shorter.

Friday, 18 November
Thought the valve set functioned not too badly tonight. I'll have it
good some day.

---

26 Thomas may have been worried that some entries in the diaries for the four years
    before he married Agnes would have upset her in her then very sensitive state of
    mind.

27 Rutherglen, now part of South Lanarkshire, was once an independent burgh. It was
    the oldest Royal Burgh in Scotland.

Saturday, 19 November
Bought an extra Exide battery, cost 4/6.[28] My niece Ella here today.

Sunday, 20 November
Went to my work in the forenoon, and may I be forgiven.

Monday, 21 November
Mrs Carmichael came up with Agnes after the Guild to hear the new wireless. I didn't bounce about it. Tommy spent the evening at MacPherson's and I stayed at home and tinkered with wires and stamps.

Wednesday, 23 November
David up at night and put in a 'Blue Spot' speaker.[29] Results very gratifying.

Friday, 25 November
The man Cameron, who lives next door to us, hurt in a bus smash. He is in the Victoria. Agnes went at night to the Western to see Isa, who is undergoing treatment there.[30]

Saturday, 26 November
Tommy at the Regal, studying the innards of the organ.[31]

Tuesday, 29 November
Mr Stevenson, who used to stay next door to us, up at night for some calculations he wished Tommy to do. He says our wireless needs a 'baffle plate'. Where will I get a 'baffle plate'?[32]

Thursday, 1 December
Put up a new earth wire for the new loud speaker.

Sunday, 4 December
Dull and cold. We all went to church.

---

28   Exide (which takes its name from 'excellent oxide') was founded as a battery maker in America in 1888.

29   The British Blue Spot Co. Ltd, of London, was a manufacturer of loudspeakers.

30   The Western Infirmary.

31   The Regal cinema stood in Sauchiehall Street. It was later known as the ABC cinema and is now a music venue with the same name. A Compton 3/12 cinema organ was installed in 1929.

32   A 'baffle plate', also called a 'baffle board', is a partition that stops the sound waves from the rear of a speaker interfering with the sound waves from the front.

Wednesday, 14 December

Feel very done out and ill at night. Listened to the *Messiah*, which cheered me up.

Thursday, 15 December

Got a bottle of cod oil to pull me through.

Tuesday, 20 December

We got a new gas meter today. I got a new hairy waistcoat.

Thursday, 22 December

Got all our Xmas cards and parcels sent off. Don't feel too well yet.

Saturday, 24 December

We got from Belfast today tobacco, a tie and a sort of jacket for Agnes. Mrs Carmichael in, and gave Agnes an affair for covering butter. Mrs Cowie also in, to let Agnes know that Wee Helen has pneumonia. My niece Lily in, leaving the good and moral calendar, and mince cakes.

Sunday, 25 December

Heard the King giving us a Xmas greeting per the wireless.[33] None of us at church. Tommy out a walk and Agnes went over to Cowies' to hear how Wee Helen was. Not out myself. Glad to sit and do nothing, and feel not so bad now.

Tuesday, 27 December

Agnes went round to the Cowies' at night. Wee Helen pretty bad. Nan Gordon here when Agnes was out, but Agnes back in good time. Nan was clothed in a new engagement ring.

Wednesday, 28 December

Very cold. Agnes saw Tommy off to Edinburgh by 11 a.m. train. I was passing station near the time, so dropped in. In the afternoon, Agnes went to Knightswood.

Friday, 30 December

Put a patent bolt on the door to keep burglars and such like vermin on the right side of it, which is the outside.

---

33 King George V gave the first annual royal Christmas broadcast this year. The idea came from John Reith, the founder of the BBC, who saw it as a way of launching the Empire Service (now known as the World Service). The king's speech was written by Rudyard Kipling.

Saturday, 31 December
Agnes and I off to Edinburgh by 4 p.m. from Central. Tommy met us at Princes Street station. Dull, cold day.

1933 and 1950

The Great Depression finally became more than a newspaper headline or an unruly mob to the Livingstone family, as the worldwide downturn affected them directly. The uncertainties and insecurities of the era became part of Thomas' daily life, and he wearied of writing his diary. He was tired to his bones of recording the frequent deaths of loved ones, the almost continuous illnesses of his wife and the evils of the weather that seemed to dog his days off. The sunny days and cheerful songs came along less frequently, and Thomas, after more than 20 years as chronicler and sketcher of the family fortunes, decided to lay down his pen. But there was one last, sad diary entry he felt compelled to make, seventeen years later.

Sunday, 1 January
Bright, sunny and windy. Tommy and I down town in the forenoon.
Not out again.

Monday, 2 January
Storm and rain. Not out at all.

Tuesday, 3 January
Bright and sunny. I went out by myself in the forenoon. Went into
the museum etc. We went home by 8.40 from Waverley.

Wednesday, 4 January
At work again. Our wireless seems balmy.

Tuesday, 10 January
David up at night and tinkered with the wireless, then rushed
away.

Wednesday, 11 January
We entertained all the Carmichaels tonight, also Mrs MacKenzie.
The wireless very weak.

Saturday, 14 January
David up in the afternoon, and played with the wireless for a few
hours, had his tea with us, then rushed away.

Sunday, 15 January
Agnes and I at church. Communion. Wireless up the pole again.

Monday, 16 January
Got a skilled man to sort the wireless. Wrote to Mary.

Wednesday, 18 January
Fog and frost solemn and grand, especially at night. Agnes and I
groped our way to the Majestic.

Saturday, 21 January
Very cold day. Tommy out today with the students in their charity
parade.

Monday, 23 January
Frost and fog. Don't feel very well. Tried a Yeast-Vite tablet at
night and felt better.

Tuesday, 24 January
Frost and fog. Don't feel so well again. Took Yeast-Vite again and
feel better. After I went to bed, very sleepless and shaky, so got
whisky. Agnes very upset with all this nonsense.

Wednesday, 25 January
Frost and fog. In bed all day.

Thursday, 26 January
Stayed in bed till after dinner. Tommy left word at my work in the
morning. Feel not so bad at night. Mr Carmichael's brother has
just died in the Victoria Infirmary, so Agnes went over later to the
Carmichaels'.

Friday, 27 January
Went to my work again. Feel not so bad, but at night not so good.
Went to the library for some literature.

Tuesday, 31 January
I feel all right now. Ulster railway strike started.[1]

Saturday, 4 February
Tommy at MacPherson's. Agnes and I went to the Majestic.

Thursday, 9 February
Was at Grangemouth today.

Sunday, 12 February
Agnes and Tommy at church.

Friday, 17 February
My toe very sore with looking for orders.

Sunday, 19 February
Mrs Cowie up about 8.30 this morning to tell us that Wee Helen
had died early in the morning. We got quite a shock. Poor Wee
Helen. I was at church myself in the morning. Agnes went to the
Cowies' for a little in the afternoon. Tommy gave a lecture at the
YMCA tonight.

---

1 The strike was called by the railway unions in opposition to the railway companies'
   demands for a 10 per cent wage cut for all employees, even those earning less than £2
   a week.

Monday, 20 February
Paid the gas bill. Agnes over at the Cowies' in the afternoon. Wee
Helen is to be buried in Arbroath on Wednesday. After tea, Agnes
went to Ibrox. Ella has a new baby boy.

Wednesday, 22 February
Agnes over at Cowies' at the funeral service. Then she went down
to the hospital at Paisley and saw Ella and her small boy. Got a new
HT battery today for 2/6.[2] It made a big improvement in our set.

Saturday, 25 February
Put up a nice new inside aerial, also a nice new earth wire. The
results are quite good. A result not so good was a grievously
wounded thumb, caused by the blinking pliers giving me a
severe nip.

Monday, 27 February
After tea, Agnes went over to Cowies' for a little. I went to the
library for a 'blood'.[3] Tommy went into town for some musical
affair.

Wednesday, 1 March
Paid wireless licence 10/-. AP 22126, Wireless Telegraphy Acts
1904–1926.

Thursday, 2 March
Cold and dull. Spent the afternoon looking for orders in Whifflet,
Coatbridge and Airdrie. Got none. Went straight for my tea to
Mosspark to see a stamp collection owned by a Mr Ferrie. Would not
mind adding it to my own. I've been in some quaint villages today.

Saturday, 4 March
Called in at my work for half an hour or so and investigated the
financial affairs of the office boy.

Sunday, 5 March
After dinner I went out to Ruglen and looked at the building that
had a fire a week or so ago. They had to jump out of the windows.
I stayed in that same building 23 years ago. So my life was saved.

Monday, 6 March
Did my Ayrshire journey today. Dalry, Ardrossan, Irvine and Troon.
Agnes in the wash house all day.

---

2   HT stands for high tension, which means high voltage.
3   A 'blood' was a thriller.

Wednesday, 8 March

Business is so bad and my firm is in such a bad way that I had to bring home the cheery news that my salary in future would be less by a pound a week. How nice! I have to concentrate more on outside work. 'Half a loaf' etc.

Thursday, 9 March

Very wet day. Spent it mostly outside looking for orders, and pretty well done out by 5 o'clock.

Friday, 10 March

Had the young and earnest Mr Main up at night to see my stamp collection. We have now got as far as 'N'.

Saturday, 18 March

Got my salary today. My next one will be much smaller. If my place was secure, I would be content.

Tuesday, 21 March

Dull and wet. Agnes in wash house all day. Tommy at MacPherson's at night and I at the library for a book or two.

Friday, 24 March

Nice sunny day. I feel most peculiarly tired. Tired in mind and body. Don't know how things will end.

Saturday, 25 March

Warm, sunny day. Took a stagger over to the library for a novel. Got my diminished salary today. Taking it weekly, to see where it goes. May I never be worse.

Sunday, 26 March

Another nice day. Don't feel very well at all.

Tuesday, 28 March

Spent the day at Hamilton, Wishaw, Motherwell and Larkhall on business. Warm, sunny day. I got home in time to go to the Calder with Agnes.

Monday, 3 April

Spring holiday. Blew a hurricane all day.

Wednesday, 5 April

Dull sort of day. Feel very tired.

Friday, 7 April

Nice sunny, warm day. Elder up with the Mass tickets. Nicolson also dropped in for the loan of Tommy's KKK costume. Irish rail strike over.

Saturday, 8 April

Dull day and not so warm. Saw by the papers that J.A. Herbert died this morning. I first knew him in February 1896, when I started work.[4]

Wednesday, 12 April

Hetty and Gordon Mossman here at night, and took away the parcel of soot Agnes had kept for them. Gordon managed some unholy tricks with my wireless set, and mucked up the re-action.[5] The Moscow trial started. Six British subjects involved.[6]

Thursday, 13 April

Was speaking to my nephew Tommy this morning. He was off to India again. Cleaned the clock at night.

Tuesday, 18 April

The great Moscow trial over. One of the British prisoners got three years, another five years and the rest expelled from Russia.

Friday, 21 April

At night, Agnes and I went to the Calder and forgot the cares of this world for a brace of hours.

Saturday, 22 April

Went to the library in the afternoon for some light literature. Agnes went to the kirk at night and booked three sittings for the next six months. We have moved over to a cheaper seat. We are no longer wealthy. My throat is sore and I don't feel my usual bright and cheery self. Think I'll stop keeping a diary.

Sunday, 23 April

Looked a nice day, but I did not go out. Sat in and read and read, and had an occasional smoke, and generally made myself a nuisance.

---

4   James A. Herbert was a draper and clothier, with a shop at 86 South Portland Street. Thomas evidently began work in the same or a related trade.

5   The 'reaction control' adjusted the sensitivity and selectivity of the tuning circuits.

6   Six engineers working for the Metropolitan-Vickers Company were accused of espionage and put on trial in Moscow. Their show trial led to a breakdown in British–Russian diplomatic relations.

1933

Sunday   23 April

Looked a nice day but
I did not go out. Sat
in and read and read
+ had an occasional smoke
and generally made myself
a nuisance.
    Agnes and Tommy went
to Church in the forenoon
my throat not quite
right yet

Monday   24 April

Nice warm sunny day,
but a dull wet night,
my throat a wee
bit tight but otherwise

I'm well. Agnes spent a busy night whitewashing etc. the "loft"

Tommy took our "wireless" to the shop that does our radio-wants, to get it all wired over again.

With these few remarks I will now close this diary and never write in it again. I have kept it faithfully for 20 odd years. It has seen many changes and dire events, and as for the future, I hesitate.

So, Amen

see over

Monday, 24 April

Nice warm, sunny day, but a dull, wet night. My throat a wee bit tight, but otherwise I'm well. Tommy took our wireless to the shop that does our radio wants, to get it wired over again. With these few remarks, I will now close this diary, and never write in it again. I have kept it faithfully for 20 odd years. It has seen many changes and dire events, and as for the future, I hesitate. So, amen.

* * *

Monday, 27 February 1950

Agnes, my darling wife and sweetheart, died early this morning. 'At the going down of the sun and in the morning, I will remember her.'

Mon. 27 Feb. 1950.

Agnes, my darling
wife & sweetheart,
died early this
morning.

"At the going down of
the sun and in the
morning, I will
remember her."